City&
Guilds

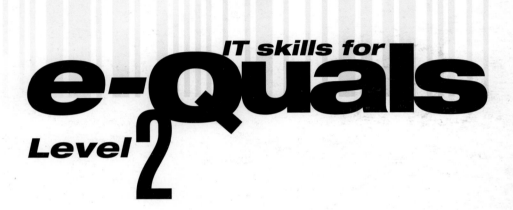

IT skills for
e-Quals
Level 2

Protocol Learning
Resources

Hodder & Stoughton
A MEMBER OF THE HODDER HEADLINE GROUP

Orders: please contact Bookpoint Ltd, 130 Milton Park, Abingdon, Oxon OX14 4SB. Telephone: (44) 01235 827720. Fax: (44) 01235 400454. Lines are open from 9.00–6.00, Monday to Saturday, with a 24 hour message answering service. You can also order through our website www.hodderheadline.co.uk.

British Library Cataloguing in Publication Data
A catalogue record for this title is available from the British Library

ISBN 0 340 84630 5

First Published 2003
Impression number   10 9 8 7 6 5 4 3 2 1
Year   2007 2006 2005 2004 2003 2002 2001

Typeset by Pantek Arts Ltd, Maidstone, Kent.

Printed in Italy for Hodder & Stoughton Educational, a division of Hodder Headline Plc, 338 Euston Road, London NW1 3BH.

e-Quals
Contents

e-Quals
Acknowledgements

Screen shots reprinted by permission from Microsoft Corporation.

This Product has been developed by Hodder & Stoughton Limited, is intended as a method of studying for the e-Quals qualifications and the content and the accuracy are the sole responsibility of Hodder & Stoughton Limited. Therefore the City and Guilds of London Institute accepts no liability howsoever in respect of any breach of the intellectual property rights of any third party howsoever occasioned or damage to the third party's property or person as a result of the use of the products.

e-Quals
Introduction

Welcome to e-Quals

This reference book is for existing computer users at Level 2 who wish to widen their knowledge and develop further skills. It is designed to provide easy to understand and comprehensive information for all the modules covered within City and Guilds e-Quals Level 2 – Diploma for IT Users. The book has been produced in co-operation with, and is fully endorsed by, City and Guilds.

The e-Quals suite of qualifications has been developed in consultation with IT and training professionals, combining the use of common IT applications with a range of study levels, this book covers Level 2 for the computer user. This multi-layered approach ensures its relevance to business and to future IT users. The programme offers achievable goals, progression, and the confidence that your achievements will be recognised.

Developed with flexibility in mind, the programme allows you to study and learn within the work or home environment. It also allows you to complete the programme at your own pace.

This reference book has been developed to provide you with the knowledge to assist you in achieving the e-Quals Level 2 diploma. There are tasks throughout that will test what you have learnt as you progress through the units. The book can be used as a quick reference point that allows you to consult and search for information in a format you are already familiar with, whenever you require reminders or hints regarding the e-Quals applications.

Keep your e-Quals reference book by your computer and further develop the skills required for tomorrow's IT Professional.

Course requirements

The e-Quals Level 2 qualification is divided into 11 units. To be awarded a full diploma, candidates must successfully complete the assessments for the core unit plus two optional units. Candidates will also receive a diploma for each individual unit achieved.

The 11 units offered, and covered in this book, are:

Core Unit

021 IT Principles

Optional Units

022 Word processing
023 Spreadsheets
024 Databases
025 Using the internet
026 Presentation graphics

UNIT 021 IT PRINCIPLES

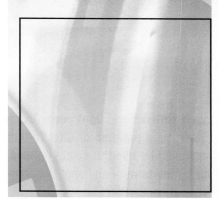

CORE

Note: Where general references are made to computer hardware, software, techniques and features, they apply to PCs, that is, the world of Microsoft, as opposed to computers made by Apple. Where a difference between the two might illustrate a point or be of interest, the manufacturer is specifically mentioned in the text.

Unless otherwise specified, 'clicking on' means clicking with the left mouse button.

PREPARE PERIPHERAL DEVICES AND HARDWARE FOR USE

Technically speaking, the processor, with its immediately surrounding circuitry and components, is the computer. Anything else connected to it is a **peripheral**. As explained in the Level 1 book, peripherals can be divided into input and output devices, the former sending information to the computer, the latter receiving information from it. All peripherals have a lead terminating in some sort of plug that connects into a socket on the computer casing, usually at the back. The sockets are labelled with little icons representing the peripheral. Plug and socket are designed so that there is (usually) only one way for them to connect. Rather than 'sockets' and 'plugging', computing jargon refers to 'ports' and 'docking'. Developments have produced a cordless mouse and keyboard, which work by the same technology as infrared remote controls for TV and hi-fi systems. These peripherals do not have cables or wires of any kind.

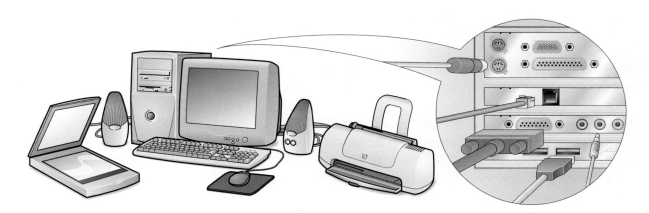

Peripherals – Input Devices

Of the various **input** devices, the keyboard is fundamental to the computer's operation and, historically, preceded all others, being essential for the user to 'talk to' the computer. From the earliest days, a flashing or blinking cursor on screen has indicated to the user where text and other characters will be placed or instructions executed. As alternative, quicker and more flexible ways of moving the cursor on screen (some with additional

1

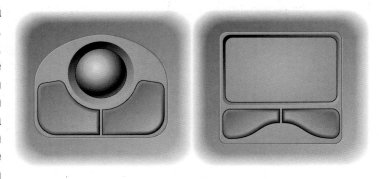

functionality built in) later developments produced a **mouse** (held in the palm of the hand on a flat surface, its movements are followed on screen by the cursor), **tracker-ball** (a ball, with one hemisphere proud of the panel, that is rolled by the fingers to move the cursor on screen), **touch pad** (a small flat panel sensitive to touch – the cursor moves according to the movements of a finger touching the pad) and a **joystick** (a small version of an aircraft's vertical lever of the same name, the movements of which cause the cursor to move on screen. Nowadays there are many other designs, however, they are still referred to as joysticks).

Bypassing all of these and allowing direct interaction with the screen are **touch screens** and **light pens**. Touch screens respond to a person touching icons displayed on screen, which either run a program or offer further options. A light pen, a small plastic stylus, can be held in the hand and may also be used to select options. Alternatively, the pen can 'write' on the screen, providing the user's hand traces the form of alphabet the computer can recognise. At the present time, computers cannot recognise every style of handwriting.

A **scanner** may be hand held or a fixed 'flat bed' scanner. It copies text and images and sends them to the computer where, displayed on screen, they can be edited according to the user's wishes. Images may also be directly imported to the computer from **cameras** that take digital photographs or video images. **Video** usually includes sound recordings but these may also be input by a **microphone**.

Peripherals – Output Devices

Of the various **output** devices, the screen is fundamental to the computer's operation and, historically, preceded all the others, being essential for the computer to 'talk to' the user. The screen is usually part of a **VDU** (Visual Display Unit), the casing that holds the technology to make the screen function. There are a variety of names for this piece of equipment but **monitor** is probably the most commonly used.

Monochrome (a single colour against a contrasting background) and Greyscale (black, white and shades of grey) monitors are unusual these days since most computers have colour monitors.

A **video adapter** (or 'display adapter card', 'video card', 'video hardware') is a printed circuit on a small rigid board or card that connects to an appropriate slot in the computer. The video card translates the computer's instructions into a form the monitor can use. The monitor and video card determine the screen display of any image and use software called a 'video driver' that allows communication between the video card and the operating system and/or applications program. The operating system and/or applications program also governs the types of display mode the computer is capable of using. Despite its name, this hardware and software is a functional part of the computer independently of *whether or not the user wishes to use or display images from a video camera*.

Characters and images can be displayed in either **text mode** or **graphics mode**. Text mode uses a character set provided by the manufacturer and displayed on a preset grid of rows and columns, usually 25 rows by 80 columns. The user cannot see the grid but will see a maximum of 25 characters down and 80 characters across the screen. Graphics mode uses many (sometimes hundreds) of 'dots' to compose each character or image on screen, which allows just about anything to be drawn on screen.

The physical size of a monitor is indicated by a measurement diagonally across the corners of the screen (remember that a small border will be obscured by the casing) and expressed in inches or centimetres. However, the size of the image displayed is governed by the resolution of the screen. Some monitors can only display at one resolution while others, called multisync monitors, can display images at different resolutions.

Resolution is measured in terms of pixels. 'Pixel' is an abbreviation for 'picture element' and describes a single 'dot', many of which make up an image on screen. An Apple Mac usually describes resolution in terms of dpi (dots per inch) e.g. 72 dpi means 72 dots horizontally and 72 dots vertically. With a PC, resolution is usually described by the number of horizontal pixels followed by the number of vertical pixels e.g. 640x480 means 640 pixels horizontally and 480 vertically, across the screen. This resolution is usually the 'default' resolution for PCs i.e. the resolution automatically used unless altered by the user. A higher resolution allows more data to be displayed on screen and hence the images and characters shrink in size. A lower resolution expands the image but displays less on screen.

Monitors use the same technology as television sets to produce an image i.e. a beam of electrons from an electron 'gun' at the back of the unit shoots forward to the back of the screen and traces back and forth horizontally across it, zigzagging from top to bottom, causing phosphor particles on the screen to glow, thus producing the picture we see. The glow fades rapidly and the phosphor must be bombarded by another beam of electrons, dozens of times a second, to glow again and so maintain the picture. The **refresh rate** is the time it takes for the electron beam to scan across and down the whole screen i.e. the time between each refresh of any one phosphor particle. The term is not applicable to modern flat screen monitors that do not use CRT (Cathode Ray Tube) technology but use LCD (Liquid Crystal Display) technology.

If the video card allows graphics or has a graphics adapter the screen can display graphics in one of several video standards and resolutions. The most commonly known is **VGA** (Video Graphics Array). VGA usually displays images at 640x480 and 16 colours or, with some video drivers, 256 colours. **Super VGA** provides higher resolutions (sometimes up to 1280x1024) and more colours. Further enhancements, such as **XGA**, are used in high-precision design work by engineers, architects and scientists, often using CAD (Computer Aided Design) systems.

Images on screen might be required as 'hard copy', which means they would be printed, usually to paper but possibly to card, transparency, label sheets or envelopes. The various types of printer and how they work are described in the Level 1 book. A special type of printer known as a plotter uses pens to produce very detailed and high-precision work such as designs, graphs, blueprints and engineering drawings as might be produced by the CAD work and XGA graphics referred to in the preceding paragraph.

When a particular image is left on screen for a long time that image can become 'burned in' and is faintly visible thereafter, superimposed on any image the screen is displaying, like a ghostly image. This problem is more common with monochrome than with colour monitors. However, to avoid it, a 'screen saver' program can be run (Windows comes with a number of them but many more are available and can be installed) after a time set by the user; it cuts in and displays some sort of moving image such as cartoons, deep space travel, fish swimming etc. Any movement of the mouse or touch of the keyboard will restore the original screen.

Just as a video card is required in order to produce an image on screen, a **sound card** or 'sound board' is required for the computer to produce sound beyond a few beeps, clicks and whirring sounds. With a sound card fitted to an expansion slot inside the computer, music, film soundtracks, any sounds accompanying multimedia software and voice messages can be played. This type of information is usually stored on CD-ROMs or DVDs (explained in the Level 1 book) and the sound card interprets the information and turns it into sound – provided there are some speakers available to hear it through. If speakers are not connected, it is possible to hear a CD through headphones that plug into a miniature 'jack' socket on the front of the CD or DVD drive. However, speakers which plug into another miniature 'jack' socket at the back of the computer and stand on desk or floor are available from about £10.00 upwards; some sets come with a 'sub-woofer' for good bass response and produce hi-fi sound but cost more, sometimes hundreds of pounds. Whichever speakers are purchased, the wires will fit the same miniature 'jack' socket and work with whatever sound card is installed. A range of sound cards are available. 'SoundBlaster' and 'Pro Audio Spectrum' boards are well-known commercial names from different manufacturers. They are good quality, setting the standard for most others.

Most speakers have their own volume (and some have treble and bass) controls. However, appropriate but standard software also provides volume controls. Click on Start, point at Programs, point at Accessories, point at Entertainment, click on Volume Control.

While sound cards can translate programs into sounds, very sophisticated ones working in conjunction with sophisticated software can translate written text into sounds. These can be used for a variety of purposes including composition of music and speech synthesisers for people who are unable to speak. Perhaps the most famous example of the latter application is the physicist Stephen Hawking who has lost his voice and mobility due to motor neurone disease but whose synthesised voice has been heard on television many times.

Storage Devices

Various storage devices are available but due to the increasing size of many software applications, those with smaller capacities are becoming more rare and those with larger capacities ever more common. It is usually the amount of data to be stored that will determine which storage medium is used – provided the type of drives available do not restrict choice. Capacities are measured in bytes according to the following groupings:

● 1 Kb (**kilobyte**) stands for about 1000 bytes (exactly 1024)

● 1 Mb (**megabyte**) stands for about 1 000 000 bytes (exactly 1024Kb)

● 1 Gb (**gigabyte**) stands for about 1 000 000 000 bytes (exactly 1024Mb)

Storage media can be 'write protected' which means that the data they hold cannot be added to or altered in any way – it can only be read and/or viewed by the user, hence the term 'read only'.

A **floppy disk** is a small (3.5in square), thin, hard plastic casing protecting a very thin and 'floppy' plastic disk coated with a magnetic film. Floppy disks slot into a 'disk drive' on the computer casing and can be used to store files and/or directories of data. The files stored can usually be both 'read' and 'written to'. However, sliding a small plastic lug to open a small square aperture in the lower left corner (label side up) will write protect the contents. Sliding it back, to obscure the aperture, will allow data to be edited. These 'floppies' and the data they hold can then be taken away for use on other computers not connected by a 'network' to the original computer or held

4

as 'backup' i.e. a copy, in case some irreparable damage occurs to the computer. Floppies cannot, by modern standards, store much data (a maximum of 1.44 megabytes) but are relatively inexpensive, some retail stores selling ten or so (or a few dozen at sale times) for a few pounds.

Magnetic Tape (sometimes known as 'tape streamers') can perform the same functions but store much more information than floppy disks (usually between 10–2100 Mb). Tapes can also be 'written to' or 'read from'. A small circle flush with the casing has a slot in it, enabling it to be turned back and forth (but not all the way round). One position will 'write protect' the contents, the other will permit the tape to be 'written to'. In order to utilise tape, computers need 'tape drive' slots where tape cartridges can be inserted. Although more expensive than floppies, tapes are also relatively cheap.

To prevent corruption or deletion of the data they hold, all magnetic media must be handled and stored carefully – preferably in rigid containers and not subject to temperatures below freezing or above 60°C or humidity below 8% or above 90%. Magnetic and electric fields from TVs and other electrical appliances, and spillages of food and/or drink can corrupt or destroy data stored magnetically, as can physical damage such as surface abrasion.

CD-ROMs (Compact Disk – Read Only Memory) and their drives (a different and slightly larger slot on the computer casing, which extends a tray to hold the CD when the fascia button is pressed and withdraws it into the body of the computer casing when the button is pressed again) are equivalent technologically to CD music disks and players. The data is not stored magnetically but optically and read by a laser beam. This allows the data to be stored much closer together and hence CDs can store much data – usually around 700–800MB (greater capacities will be available very soon). Whilst CDs should still be protected from physical damage – such as surface abrasion or bending since, although sturdy, they are brittle – they are not susceptible to the other risks magnetic media are prone to, as mentioned above. 'Read Only Memory' means just that: the data stored can only be 'read' by the computer. It cannot be 'written to' i.e. added to or altered in any way. Some modern computers have an additional facility called a CD re-writer, which does allow data to be 'written to' a blank or empty CD that can, at time of writing, be purchased for around 50p each.

Following the same trend as home entertainment, **DVD**s (Digital Video Disks) store even more data than CDs and commonly hold films and television programmes. Computer DVD drives (physically the same as CD drives) also read these disks and, although not yet common, DVD writers are available.

File compression enables a file to be translated into a coded format that occupies less space than the original – often about half the space. This can be desirable for two main reasons: to save space on disk(s) and to reduce the cost of transfer when sending files over the Internet – the smaller the file the quicker the transmission time. This technique has become known as **zipping** a file and a software program is required to do it. Similarly, a software program is required to **unzip** (decompress) a file so that it may be read. There are several versions or formats for doing this and a popular program for zipping and unzipping a variety of file formats is 'WinZip', used, as the name implies, with the Windows operating system.

Any storage medium that can be 'written to' will, without precautions by the user as indicated above, allow its files to be 'overwritten' i.e. changed or deleted by having other data stored. This can happen when a file is saved

with the same name as a previous file, even though the software will prompt the user with an on-screen warning asking if the user wants to replace the existing file with this new one. Alternatively, if a file is deleted, the information actually stays on disk but its 'address' becomes vacant as far as the operating system is concerned. The information will be overwritten when the operating system needs to use the space.

There are two main factors governing a computer's speed of operation:

1   The processor – governing how many instructions and processes can be executed in a given time that is measured by the 'clock speed'.

2   Hard disk access – the time it takes for the heads to move back and forth across the rotating disks to retrieve required data.

Since processors are electronic and disk drives are mechanical, even modest processors operate at speeds far in excess of disk access speeds – depending on circumstances, between 10 and 100 times faster. So, if the CPU had to wait for the hard disk to receive each instruction, the speed of the processor would be wasted and the computer very inefficient. To work more efficiently the computer needs something to hold information and instructions but which can also work at the same speed as the CPU. This is what RAM (Random Access Memory – see Level 1 book) does. To use a comparison with traditional work practices, it is far more efficient to get all the required information and files from their respective filing cabinets and storage areas, put them within easy reach and then sit down to 'process' the job, rather than get up and go to remote filing cabinets each time you need a particular file.

When a program and/or data is loaded from any storage media, some or all of it might be loaded onto the computer's hard disk and when the user wants to access it, some or all of it will be loaded into RAM allowing rapid access to the information. You can try a simple experiment for yourself: When you first boot your computer and just the desktop is displayed, select, say, the word processing application. Note how long it takes to appear, ready for use, on screen. It has just been loaded from the hard disk. Now close the application. In case the user wishes to use it again, it stays in RAM. Select it again and time how long it takes to load. You should see a dramatic decrease in time since on this occasion it has loaded from RAM.

You can see that insufficient RAM would bring back the same inefficiency – if RAM is quickly filled, we need to wait for disk access to provide the next piece of information. Hence RAM will be one of the considerations determining how 'fast' a computer is to use, which becomes an important factor when connecting to the Internet – see below.

Installation

The installation of the various input and output devices has become increasingly easy over the years and falls into two broad categories: internal and external.

Of the devices we have looked at, the video and sound cards are for internal installation, and then usually only for PCs; Mac computers have been more advanced for some years and had video and sound boards installed on the computer's motherboard (the board holding the CPU) by the manufacturers. The PC world is gradually catching up. However, if installation is necessary, electrical power to the computer should always be switched off. The side panel(s) of the computer casing should be removed (usually by undoing a couple of small screws and sliding the panel away from locating slots in the metal framework). If any 'expansion slots' are available, the long edge of the card can be inserted into the groove provided, standing the card at a right angle to the motherboard. This might be sufficient to make all necessary electrical connections but if not, instructions and the necessary wire or ribbon cable (a broad grey 'ribbon' made up of a dozen or so thin, parallel wires) will be supplied with the unit or card. If the card is to serve as an interconnection between the motherboard and a peripheral, it will have a 'port' or 'ports' on one end, which sits flush with or protruding from the rear surface of the computer casing, allowing a peripheral connection to 'dock'.

When booted, the computer will 'see' the new cards, which will become fully functional after any necessary software is loaded.

All the other devices we have referred to are external. These days, merely plugging keyboard, mouse and monitor into the appropriate sockets at the back of the computer casing is sufficient to 'install' them since the computer will 'see' them on booting. Since they are so fundamental to the operation of the computer and work in standardised ways, the relevant software is already on the hard disk. Sometimes it is even possible to plug them in after booting and be able to use them immediately. As mentioned, any speakers can be plugged into the correct miniature jack socket and will work with any sound card. Some require their own electrical supply through a standard household plug and socket.

Any device that requires software for it to function is sold with that software, usually nowadays on a CD-ROM. For example, a printer or scanner will come with a power cable, a connecting lead to the computer (often a USB, if not a parallel or serial connection) and CD-ROM(s), plus any other items necessary (e.g. ink cartridges for a printer). Usually there is an illustrated, step-by-step guide to installation in a manual. Better still, if the CD-ROM is loaded first, it will take the user through the installation step by step, using animated diagrams and procedures. At a suitable stage it will also load any and all necessary software, completing installation in minutes.

Once installed, various options are usually available with most peripherals. Perhaps one of the most commonly used and versatile peripherals is the printer. Whilst there are some manual adjustments to be made to the printer physically (usually adjusting paper guides to accommodate the particular medium being printed to), most options are available through the software. To locate these options open the file you wish to print, click on File, Print, Properties in the Print Dialogue box. Many combinations of options may be selected relating to the print medium (card, envelopes, transparencies) and how it is to be printed (e.g. collated, two-sided printing (which halves your paper bill and helps conserve natural resources)).

If we assume that a keyboard, mouse and monitor are taken as standard equipment, the particular software application you want to run will determine what hardware is required e.g. most games software will require a joystick, a good video graphics adapter and, for the best 'effects', speakers as well. Due to the enormous and rapid growth of multimedia applications (software that uses more than one medium e.g. text, pictures, sound and video), a standard was introduced in the early 1990s to bring some consistency into the commercial world of multimedia computing. If a computer shows an MPC logo, the prospective purchaser knows that it would be able to cope with multimedia PC software and has a CD-ROM drive, sound card, set of speakers or headphones, sufficiently powerful processor, enough RAM and an appropriate operating system. To cope with increasingly sophisticated multimedia, MPC 2 was introduced with appropriately increased capabilities, followed by MPC 3. Hence MPC standards have removed the need for users to ensure all necessary hardware and software is present for the applications they want to run.

Networks

So far, all the information given above can apply to a single computer, whether at home or in the office. In the office it has become increasingly useful to allow different computers:

● To share the same peripherals such as scanners, special printers or fax equipment and/or

● To exchange of messages (electronic mail or 'email') and/or

● To share data and/or applications

The same considerations might apply to some home computing needs but rarely so. Whatever the environment, computers that are connected together to allow interchange of information form a **network**. A network without access to the public telephone system is called a **LAN** (Local Area Network). The computers in a LAN may number two or three or many hundreds and are usually connected by wire cables.

When a LAN is connected to the public telephone system it becomes a **WAN** (Wide Area Network) and can thereby connect with other LANs of, say, the same company but located in another country. The connections might still be wire cables but can also be fibre-optic cables or radio waves.

As explained in the Level 1 book, computers communicate digitally, so for a LAN to function it only requires some special network cards, network software (to control the flow of information across the network) and the connecting wire cables.

As also explained in the Level 1 book, the telephone network uses analogue signals and therefore modems are required to turn a LAN into a WAN. The modem converts the digital signals of the computer sending the information to analogue and the modem at the receiving end converts the signals back to digital, for the receiving computer. The telephone network is gradually becoming a digital network but until this work is complete, modems will be required and until then, a modem is the only device which is truly both an input and output device.

When each computer has access to the information on the hard disk of any other computer connected to the network and no computer has the responsibility of delivering data to any other, all the computers could be said to be of equal status. Hence these networks are called '**peer-to-peer** networks'.

Most modern networks have a computer, the hard disk(s) of which is/are dedicated to holding data and/or program files for all the other computers to access and/or use. Its sole job is to 'serve' files to others and it is known as a 'file server'. The other computers are known as nodes or **workstations** and they are 'clients' of the server. Hence this type of network is known as a **client/server** network.

The **Internet** is perhaps the widest Wide Area Network although no one organisation or group is in control of it or responsible for it. Obviously the telephone service providers are crucial to its operation and, from the individual user's point of view, so are the **ISP**s (Internet Service Providers) through which most people gain access to the Internet. With access to the Internet, global email becomes available and access to innumerable sites set up by institutions, businesses, organisations and individuals to offer their services, products, information and/or interactive communication opportunities. One site can link with another either directly or indirectly via shared interests/information. Hence the whole system is known as the World Wide Web and individual sites as websites, with addresses that usually begin 'www'.

If a company has its computers connected by a LAN it is possible to give those computers access to a 'website' in the same style as websites on the Internet, with email facilities and other functionality. However, with access restricted to staff members only, this system is called an **Intranet** ('intra' = within, 'inter' = between). The system would not be available to 'surfers' or anyone else using the Internet, hence the inverted commas qualifying the 'website' as private.

A network opens greater possibilities for breaches of security and this will be considered a disadvantage. However, provided a system's security measures are adequate, this risk can be reduced to an acceptable level if not eliminated. A network also requires some additional hardware and software and, as a consequence, additional cost and maintenance. If the network is sufficiently large and/or complex it may also require one or more staff to manage and maintain it. If the cost of these additional elements is considered a disadvantage, it is outweighed by the benefits deriving from the network.

To ensure effective communication between many diverse applications and systems various standards have to be agreed and some of the most important are called **protocols**. We have seen that, at the present time, modems are required for WANs and the Internet, so the first protocol to consider is the communications protocol required for modems to be able to communicate. The type and speed of data communication needs to be set for each modem so that each can receive and transmit data and correct any errors. Once this has been established, the main purpose of the connection will be to transfer files ('downloading' if receiving files from a remote computer, 'uploading' if sending files to a remote computer). To do this a file transfer protocol (FTP) has to be established which governs the flow of data and checks for and corrects errors. In fact, addresses for Web documents on the Internet begin with 'http://www.' and this stands for 'HyperText Transfer Protocol' (Hypertext is the ability to move or 'jump' around from one part of the text to another by selecting icons or underlined text in documents or displays), followed by the abbreviation for 'world wide web'.

The beginning of any Internet address such as http:// or ftp://…, new://…, is called a Uniform Resource Locator or **URL** indicating a particular type or group of information resources.

USING SOFTWARE APPLICATIONS

Connecting to the Internet requires hardware, a modem and telephone connection being essential. A processor and RAM of sufficient power and size are also required to prevent the connection being tediously or prohibitively slow e.g. if using Windows 98 (see below for an explanation of Windows releases), 128 Mb of RAM and a 1 GHz (gigahertz) processor is a minimum recommendation; if using Windows XP, 256 Mb of RAM and a 1.3 GHz processor is a minimum recommendation.

Once connected to the Internet, its email facilities and vast resources of information are available to you. The ISP provides software according to your requirements – almost certainly email facilities, a 'home' or 'start' page with various options including, probably, a 'browser' (a program which allows the computer to download and display documents and images from websites – in fact, the 'home page' is usually the ISP's own website) or access to an established browser such as Internet Explorer or Netscape. Browsing web pages or actually searching for an item uses the same program but the latter use has led to browsers sometimes being referred to as 'search engines', a well known and efficient one being 'Google'.

One or more email addresses unique to you will be available from the ISP. The addresses are in two parts, separated by an @ symbol. The first half is your own unique identifier, chosen by yourself (if the name is already in use by someone else a message to this effect will appear). The second half is set by the service provider e.g. 'hotmail.com', 'yahoo.co', 'btinternet', but may end in a suffix denoting the owner's country e.g. 'uk' for United Kingdom, 'de' for Germany, 'au' for Australia etc. To keep your emails private you will also be able to choose a password that is never displayed on screen – asterisks appear to represent each character entered.

Obviously, messages can be sent and received. Clicking on the icon for 'new mail' provides a mask for your message with spaces for the address of the recipient and any who should receive copies, the subject and the message itself. Clicking on 'send' will despatch the message to the recipient's ISP's server. New emails showing sender and subject are found in the 'Inbox' with an adjacent little envelope symbol indicating they are unread. Clicking on an email will open it so that you can read it (some show the text of a message in a small preview screen without the email being opened but attachments are not available for viewing in preview). Closing the email by clicking on 'close' will return to your Inbox where the email will appear but without the envelope symbol. Since the messages are stored initially on the ISP's server, you can access your emails from any computer in the world, provided it has Internet access and appropriate hardware and software. Once accessed, the emails or their attachments (other files such as Word documents or photographs sent with the email) can, if you wish, be stored on your computer's hard disk. Alternatively, they can be stored in folders provided by the email service provider.

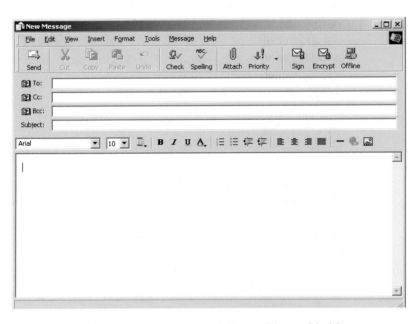

For example, rather than let all your emails remain in one stack in your Inbox, you can create and label folders to group them into sensible and relevant collections e.g. Work, Friends, Tax etc. Some email programs (such as the popular Outlook Express) can automatically file your emails into folders as they are delivered. There is usually already a folder called 'Drafts' for storing provisional mail that needs editing or expanding before sending. Obviously, as time passes more and more emails will collect so they must either be archived in folders or deleted. Otherwise they will fill the space allocated to you by the service provider, which means you must either purchase more space or lose new emails that cannot be delivered.

Browsing the Web or going directly to a website using its address might show information of interest to you. Web pages can be printed directly or stored on your computer's hard disk (as long as you comply with UK copyright law), after which they can be edited or used according to your own requirements. A document or image can be saved just as you would save any other file, giving it a title and selecting which folder to store it in. Although increasingly rare, there are sometimes formatting problems (e.g. if you try to view a spreadsheet in a word processing document (or even another spreadsheet program), it could just display meaningless characters. See also 'integrated software' below. Clicking on File will produce the menu from which 'Save' can be selected. However, selecting the option to **Import** will take into account any formatting differences and usually be able to translate between them.

The first computers would present a blank screen with a flashing cursor (a short vertical line) waiting instructions to be typed using the keyboard. Once work had begun on some application, it was necessary to use the arrow keys on the keyboard to move the cursor around the screen and locate it where editing or action was required. However, users found this a somewhat awkward and unfriendly 'operating environment'. Most office workers, prior to computers, had a variety of folders or ledgers etc. on or around their desks ready for use. Therefore later computers, pursuing a 'user-friendly' operating environment, showed the equivalent software on a screen 'desktop' as little pictures or images – **icons** – to represent familiar items such as wastebaskets, files and filing cabinets. An arrow replaced the cursor and could be moved around the screen by a hand held 'mouse'. Pointing and clicking with the mouse selected a particular option, some of which would make a rectangular box appear on screen (a **window**) displaying further options. These operating environments are known as WIMP (Window, Icon, Mouse, Pointer) or Graphical User Interface (GUI – pronounced 'gooey'). Users prefer this easy-to-use and friendly operating environment, which has been developed by Apple, IBM and Microsoft. Microsoft called its product **Windows**. GUIs and in particular MS Windows is the most common operating environment for PCs in use today, the successive years of issue (e.g. Windows 98) now being dropped from the name, the latest issue (as of September 2002) being Windows XP.

GUIs make the operation of computers much more user-friendly, whether downloading files from the web or using standard software and application suites. Nowadays, these two types of computer functionality are usually combined, since in order to edit or use downloaded files of any origin, applications software would almost certainly be needed – software which would probably have been on the computer's hard disk long before connection to the Internet gave it additional material to work with.

Three of the most popular applications packages are a **word processor** program (to enter text for letters, documents, listings etc.), a **spreadsheet** (for entering numerical data and performing calculations with that data) and a **database** (for collecting similar types of information together and creating, finding and displaying relationships between the data). Microsoft has the vast majority of business and personal users using their products, and market the three packages just referred to as 'Word', 'Excel' and 'Access' respectively.

Clicking on the appropriate icons will open the packages. Opening Word will present the user with a blank sheet with menu and tool bars top and bottom as described in the Level 1 book. Touching a key on the keyboard will enter that character on the 'sheet' on screen. Having written whatever text is required, the user can select from many options to determine the way in which that text is presented either on screen or paper. Perhaps the most commonly used options appear in the Page Setup dialogue box found by clicking on File in the menu bar, then clicking on Page Setup. Margins, page size and orientation can be altered and adjusted here, saving the changes by clicking on 'OK'. Text enhancements include a selection of fonts (styles of 'typeface' or characters) and sizes, as well as *italicising*, <u>underlining</u> or **emboldening** text. All these text options are available on the toolbar. A spelling and grammar checker is available as another tool. It will examine the text and indicate errors of grammar and/or spelling and make suggestions for corrections.

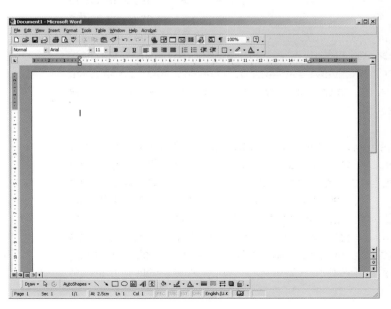

> **Tip**
>
> There are keyboard shortcuts to effect the text enhancements described in the main text (two keys with + in between means pressing them at the same time). **Ctrl** refers to the Control key, usually at bottom left and bottom right of the main keyboard.
>
> **Ctrl + B** emboldens text, **Ctrl + I** makes text italic, **Ctrl + U** underlines text

Word processors offer many features which are covered in the Word Processing chapter within this book. One feature of great benefit to any business or organisation that has to send the same letter to many different recipients is **mail merge**. This allows a set of different names and addresses and/or any other personal information specified, to be 'merged' with a standard letter, announcement or advertising leaflet so that each is personalised. The software that allows a user to combine data from different places within one application and/or combine data from different applications altogether e.g. import a picture from the Internet or a presentation package such as Powerpoint (see below) into a Word document, is known as **integrated software**. The advantages include ease of use, efficiency, power and flexibility. In the early days, trying to get one application to 'talk' to another could consume hours and cause great frustration – and still not work in the end!

When, for the time being, the user has finished working with the file, it can be saved under a name chosen by the user. Whenever a Word file is saved the software attaches '.doc' after the name chosen by the user, so that the software will always recognise it as a Word file. This '.doc' is known as a **filename extension**. Sometimes it is necessary for a word-processed document to be read by another word processing application made by a different manufacturer. This can be difficult and not always completely successful. If the file is saved as a text file, just the text is stored without the formatting information (styles and layout of the original) and this can be read and displayed by any word processing application. The filename extension for text files is '.txt'. Sometimes it is possible to save some of the formatting (paragraphs and/or layout) and still be able to use it on other applications. This option is known as a 'rich text' file and uses a filename extension of '.rtf'.

Opening Excel will present a new, blank spreadsheet, which is a grid of horizontal and vertical lines dividing the screen into 'cells'. Rows are numbered and columns are lettered, so the top left cell's 'address' is A1, the one below A2, and the one to the right B1 and so on. Cells may hold data as entered by the user or a 'formula'. The user can enter formulae and the formulae instructs the software to combine other cell contents and display the result in the box holding that formula. For example, if A2 holds 'cost price' and B2 holds 'VAT rate', C2 might hold the formula =A2+B2 and will always show the sum of the contents of cells A2 and B2. The top row (row 1) may hold the text entries 'Cost Price', 'VAT Rate' and 'Total Price' in cells A1, B1 and C1 respectively. Spreadsheets can be displayed showing only data or both data and formulae.

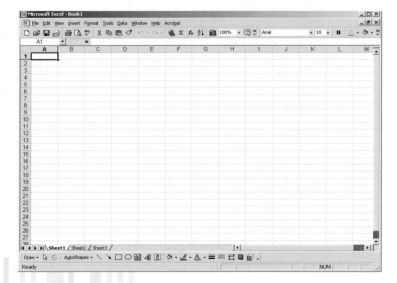

When, for the time being, the user has finished working with the file, it can be saved under a name chosen by the user. Whenever an Excel file is saved the software attaches '.xls' after the name chosen by the user, so that the software will always recognise it as an Excel file. This '.xls' is the filename extension.

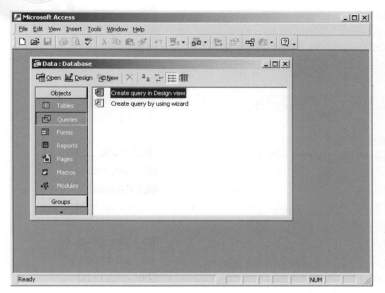

Opening Access will offer the option of opening an existing database or creating a new one. The database is made up of tables, designed by the user according to their requirements i.e. what the table will hold e.g. for a database of personal contacts the following would be useful: Name, address, telephone, facsimile, email, children's names etc. into which relevant data is entered. The examples of name, address etc. represent 'fields' and are called 'field names'. 'Field types' define the type of data to be entered to them e.g. text, number, date/time, yes/no, currency. Once tables have been created they can be interrogated in many different ways by 'Queries' and the results displayed by 'Reports' in many different arrangements and/or selections.

When, for the time being, the user has finished working with the file, it can be saved under a name chosen by the user. Whenever an Access file is saved the software attaches '.mdb' after the name chosen by the user, so that the software will always recognise it as a Microsoft Access database file. This '.mdb' is known as a filename extension (other database files can have '.dbf' as a file extension).

In addition there are other applications such as 'PowerPoint', a Microsoft presentation package providing 'slides' for presentation to an audience by hard copy or on screen, which will display text and/or images from any digital source and arranged according to the wishes of the presenter. The filename extension for PowerPoint files is '.ppt'.

CAD packages have already been referred to and assist designers and engineers to see their designs in three dimensions and rotate, stretch, sheer, reflect, or magnify them, or focus on one part, alter it and see the result on the whole. Graphics applications that provide facilities for such technical drawings and schematics are called **vector graphics**, in contrast to **bitmap graphics** that are used to store photographic images, creative artwork and editing of these images. Bitmap files (filename extension '.bmp') offer high resolution and can display millions of colours. Hence they consume much disk space. A more conservative use of disk space is achieved by storing the images as 'JPEG' files (Joint Photographic Experts Group; filename extension '.jpg'). JPEG is good quality but displays fewer colours than bitmap and the resolution is not quite so high.

Spreadsheets have been referred to above but there are also sophisticated financial packages available that will allow all sorts of data manipulation and modelling to allow businesses to predict profit, loss, overheads etc according to differing possible scenarios.

These and other applications usually have quite comprehensive 'Help' menus and/or 'guided tours' and/or 'read me' files to help first-time users. Moreover, provided one starts with 'dummy' data, there is no harm in entering data, exploring and playing with the applications in order to learn. Alternatively, many colleges offer very reasonably priced tuition for any age or status of person, studying at their own pace during daytime, evening or weekends and gaining qualifications.

These and other packages come with a license permitting use of the software according to conditions specified by the manufacturer. Most are copyrighted, forbidding copies to be used or sold by others. For businesses, which require many staff to be able to use an application, multi-licensing is available. An inspector from FAST

(Federation Against Software Theft) could inspect a company premises without notice and check the legality of the software on its computers. If they are in breach of legislation, the inspector can remove both the software and the hardware from the premises.

MANAGE AND MAINTAIN DIRECTORY STRUCTURES

Folders for storing associated files have been mentioned above with regard to email. The same types of grouping can be applied to any collection of files and we now look at the principles involved with using a directory structure for any software application(s).

The principle applied in both the Apple and PC worlds is that of a hierarchy. If you can understand the pattern and principle of your family tree you can understand a directory structure i.e. an ever-dividing tree with each branch connected to a common stem.

A group of files can be collected in a folder. A group of folders can be collected in a directory. With an ever-growing amount of information available, some of which might be closely related yet still distinct, the directory structure can be sub-divided further to produce sub folders and sub directories. Sometimes the names 'folder' and 'directory' are used interchangeably: it seems the defining factor is size, directories tending to be the larger collections.

The important thing to remember is that the structure is not provided as another rule to comply with or learn about, it is there to assist you, to be your servant. The measure of a directory structure's use is only how useful it is to you, the user, who will create it. In the Microsoft world there is a major directory called 'My Documents' (which can be renamed by the user, however, bear in mind that 'My Documents' is often specifically targeted in automatic backup programs). If you want, every file you ever write, download or import can be stored here in one great list. Although it would be listed alphabetically, finding it could become tedious and, more importantly, finding associated files would be even more tedious and time consuming. So, grouping files together and grouping folders together would soon become a necessity for efficiency and you would want to invent the directory structure if it was not already provided!

As with all systems that change with time, it would be best to manage and maintain your directories to ensure they are up-to-date and old files disposed of. To do this a number of commands are available. For our current purposes we are going to use them in a program called Windows Explorer, which you will find by clicking on 'Start' in the bottom left corner of the PC screen, clicking on Programs and then clicking on Windows Explorer.

The screen displayed will be divided vertically into left and right windows. The left pane shows the hierarchical tree (and is called the 'tree pane'), arranged vertically down the screen but with the branches

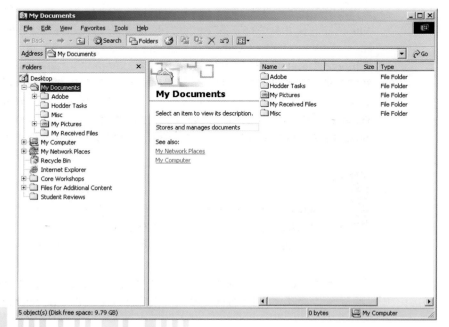

showing. On the right (called the 'details pane') are the contents of whichever directory or folder is highlighted on the left. Move the mouse around clicking on and highlighting different folders and directories and watching what happens. When you explore 'My Documents' you will recognise folders and files you have created. Clicking on a file, folder or drive (e.g. the floppy drive) and then clicking on Properties will display a dialogue box with various tabs each displaying different attributes and properties of the item selected.

If you right-click on a file, folder or directory commands will appear in a menu. The commands we will look at are: **delete**, **cut** and **copy**. If you select **delete** by left-clicking, a little window will appear asking if you are sure you want to delete the file (or, if it's a folder or directory, it and all the files within it). Clicking on 'Yes' will delete the file. If you change your mind after deleting a file but before you apply any of the commands to another file, right-click on a blank spot in the window or on the desktop. From the menu that appears, select 'Undo Delete'. If it's too late for this method there is an alternative.

When the user deletes files or folders, Windows does not delete them immediately. The Recycle Bin icon on the desktop is a folder icon and this folder holds all the files deleted from the hard disk (usually the C drive) but not files deleted from floppies or network servers. You can retrieve items you did not really want to delete from this folder – which will restore highlighted icons to their original location if you click on the icon and the restore option, all displayed in the same window. The Wastebasket icon on Apple computers serves the same function. At some point, in order to conserve disk space, it will make sense to empty the Recycle Bin or Wastebasket. For most practical purposes any deleted files would then be irrecoverable. However, as mentioned below with regard to 'defrag' programs, when a file is deleted, its 'address' becomes vacant allowing the processor to store new data at that address and, until this happens, the actual data representing the deleted file is still physically on disk. Hence, on occasion, for important reasons, 'disk doctors' can recover some or all data from deleted files remaining on disk.

Selecting cut will cause the icon representing that file or folder to disappear. In computing terminology it is held on a 'clipboard', out of sight of the user, awaiting a new destination. By right-clicking on the new folder a menu will appear from which paste can be selected. The file will now appear in the new location. Instead of selecting 'cut' in the first menu, 'copy' can be selected and the same relocation procedure followed. This time, the file will appear in the new location but the original will remain where it was.

Alternatively, by right-clicking on a file and keeping the button held down, the file may be **dragged** i.e. it will follow the movements of the mouse to a new location. As the icon moves over, or next to, a folder or directory, that folder or directory will be highlighted. Having selected the required folder, the right mouse button should be released. The familiar menu will now appear giving the options to move or copy the file to its new location. Selecting the appropriate option, by clicking the left mouse button, will **drop** the file into its new location.

Tip

It is possible to drag using the left mouse button. However, it is better to drag by using the right mouse button which gives the options as described in the main text. Otherwise Windows will decide whether to copy or move, according to which folders and disks are involved in the process.

To make backup copies of files or folders it is possible to use the copy and paste facility just described – one of the options in the 'right click' menu is to 'rename', allowing some reference to copy or backup to be included in

the filename. Another and rather neat option, is to right-click on the file, say 'xyz', to be backed up and select 'copy'. Right-clicking in an empty space in the same or a new location, will provide the same menu, from which 'paste' may be selected. A copy named 'copy of xyz' appears.

Remember that, in addition to these individual copies, it is wise to be backing up the entire contents of 'My Documents' and any other directories holding new (or difficult, costly or time consuming to replace) data or programs at regular intervals to a suitable medium (usually CDs currently, due to the size of the directories).

Tip

If it is more convenient to use the keyboard rather than the mouse, the following commands may be executed by pressing the following keys (two keys with + in between means pressing them at the same time). 'Ctrl' refers to the Control key, usually at bottom left and bottom right of the main keyboard.

Copy = **Ctrl+C**   Cut = **Ctrl+X**
Paste = **Ctrl+V**

If you accidentally misplace a file by any of the means just described, it can be found using the following **search** functions. Clicking on Start reveals a menu offering **Search** as an option. Search allows you to locate folders, files and programs anywhere on the computer you are using and, if it is connected to a network, on any disk or CD-ROM drives on the network. You can search by name, content, size, date last modified or date created or any combination of these features. Enter the details that you know about the files or folders that you are trying to find. If you have no idea where to look for it, entering C:\ will not extend the search in scope and time but will search the whole disk to locate the missing file. However, you may have to search all the available drives for the files or folders. If you cannot remember or do not know the whole filename, it is possible to enter part of the name. To 'tell' the computer that this abbreviation is not the whole name, a 'wildcard' character is entered. **Wildcards** are either an asterisk, which represents any number of characters, or a question mark, which represents a single character. The search function is not case-sensitive i.e. either capital or lower-case letters may be used. So, for example, entering Le*.doc in the 'Named:' field and 'C:\' in the 'Look in:' field and clicking on 'Search Now' will

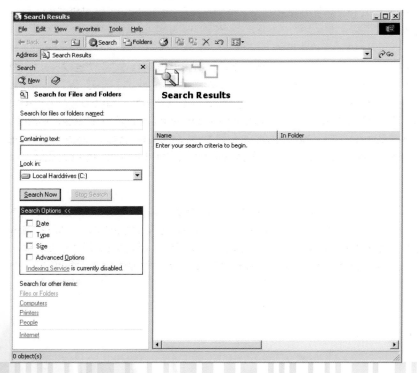

find all the files beginning 'Le' with a filename extension of .doc anywhere on the hard disk. Searching for 'Letter?' will find any file named 'Letter' and followed by a single character. Searching for *tax* will find any file with 'tax' anywhere in its name. If 'Letter to Tax Office' is entered, Windows will ignore everything after the first space. It will find the file sought, along with, probably, many others. To avoid this, enter the filename in quotes i.e. "Letter to Tax Office".

Clicking on the **Date** check box in Search Options allows searching on that basis and clicking on **Advanced** Options allows limits on the **size** of the file to be set.

The easy ability to find, copy and move files around and over networks, provides great benefits but, at the same time, great security risks. However, with much personal information including financial, medical and simply private data, sitting on computer disks, data protection has become important legislation in today's computer-dominated world. The Data Protection Act of 1998 contains eight enforceable principles of good practice. The principles stipulate that data must be:

- Fairly and lawfully processed

- Processed for limited purposes

- Adequate, relevant and not excessive

- Accurate

- Not kept longer than necessary

- Processed in accordance with the data subject's rights

- Secure

- Not transferred to countries without adequate protection

Another risk to files, the data they hold and, possibly the computer itself comes from viruses. Computer viruses are programs that reproduce themselves in any computer system they gain access to. The programs are varied and numerous and can cause irritating problems, such as causing text to gradually or suddenly disappear or become jumbled…to problems like unexpected shut downs, deletion of files and directories or major problems such as wiping the hard disk of crucial (or all!) data. Viruses can only gain access to a clean or healthy system by email or arriving on disk and being loaded by an unsuspecting user. A **virus checker** is software that examines new emails or newly loaded data for viruses and warns the user if any are detected. The virus checker will also disable the virus. As new viruses are being written all the time, virus scanners have to be up-to-date to ensure maximum protection. To date, viruses have not been written to be beneficial to the host system.

Whilst there are numerous reasons for good security and data protection, at the other end of the spectrum there are websites that are completely open to any visitor and some which offer free products, services and software. As described in the Level 1 book, many companies, institutions, organisations and individuals have websites which can be visited by anyone 'surfing' the net or going directly to the website by entering the website address in to their 'browser'. Where available, **Freeware** can be downloaded from a website by anyone who visits and stays connected long enough for the file(s) to be downloaded to their own computer. As the name implies, this software is free of charge.

Shareware is software which is available from a website but for a restricted time and/or with restricted functionality e.g. some software will be available for, say, 30 days continuous use before its functionality automatically ceases. The idea is that after using the software the user will want to purchase it. Alternatively, restricted functionality should be sufficient to impress the user and encourage them to purchase the full software application.

USING THE OPERATING ENVIRONMENT

If your computer is connected to a network it might be sensible to consider who might be able to access your files. Similarly, you might need to think about your own rights of access to files on other disks. As part of a network your computer will require you to 'login' (see Level 1 book) in order to use it. The 'login name' can be configured, by the system administrator, to only allow access to particular files and/or directories. Usually, the principle is that those personnel with limited responsibilities only have access to the limited range of files appropriate to their work, while more senior personnel with wider responsibilities can access a wider range. However, sometimes it is useful for personnel to view files yet not be able to alter them. In this case, the system administrator can configure individual files as 'read only' and therefore they can not be 'written to'. Normally the user who creates the file is the 'owner' and has all permissions (to read, write and execute the file). Other users can be given all rights or have restricted permissions (one or two of the three) according to their needs.

Whilst the system administrator is usually responsible for all the shared features of the computer system, it might be your responsibility to manage and maintain the computer you use. Here are some basic configuration aspects.

Clicking on Start, pointing at Settings and clicking on **Control Panel** will display a window with numerous icons. Double clicking on **Regional Settings** will produce a dialogue box with various tabs allowing the format and display of **currency** values, **numbers** and their decimal places, **language**, **date** and **time** to be altered. Note that to adjust the computer's current date and time, the icon labelled Date/Time, also in the Control Panel window, needs to be selected by double-clicking and the relevant values adjusted. Nearly all peripherals and internal settings can be adjusted by selecting the appropriate icons from the Control Panel window. This includes the printer and double-clicking on the printer icon will display a window showing all the printers the computer 'knows about' (usually those that have been previously installed. Even if the physical printer has long since disappeared, the driver software remains on disk until deleted). The **default printer** is the printer that will automatically be selected for any print job unless the user actively selects another. This printer is identified as such by a small tick against its icon. To change the default printer right-click on the relevant icon and select 'Set as Default'.

Many of these settings usually remain valid for long periods, if not the life of the computer. However, as will have been obvious from the preceding sections, other files will be in regular use and might be accessed many times during a working day. To save the time and tedium of 'digging down' through various menus, sub menus and options, it is possible to create a **shortcut** which is an icon that provides immediate direct access to a file, folder or program, usually from the desktop. Right-click and drag an icon from a folder or Explorer window to the desktop (or wherever you want to put it) and release the right mouse button. From the menu that appears, select 'Create Shortcut Here'. So, for example, if you regularly print a copy of your CV, rather than repeatedly opening the file and selecting Print, it might be useful to create a shortcut to your printer by dragging the printer icon from 'My Computer' folder to the desktop. Then each time you want a copy of your CV, drag the CV file icon (from, say, Explorer or even create a shortcut to it) to the printer icon and release.

The shortcut is simply a set of directions to the program or file you want. If a shortcut is deleted, the directions are deleted; the file or program actually stays intact in its original position. For a program especially, this is best practice since the program is usually with other files that have an associated functional significance and it ensures a straightforward upgrade path when new issues are released.

Tip

Always use a shortcut to put programs on your desktop. Do not left or right drag any program onto your desktop.

Similar to, or in some cases identical to, shortcuts are the icons on a 'toolbar'; a collection of buttons each of which may be clicked to perform a particular task. Windows users will be familiar with the toolbar in Microsoft Office, situated horizontally below the menu bar (showing File Edit View etc.), which is below the title bar (showing filename and application in use). This toolbar offers buttons that might execute a function (e.g. printer icon) or offer choices (of files or commands). The toolbar also offers icons to Cut, Copy or Paste, which add a third method to the mouse and keyboard options covered in the previous section. Other toolbars may also be displayed or all hidden. The choice is available from the menu bar. Click on View, point at toolbars and select accordingly – each option has a toggle action of 'off' or 'on', 'on' being indicated by an adjacent tick.

Once you have arranged the operating environment as required you will, no doubt, want to use various applications. Many applications have common features to allow you to navigate around them. Whenever a display exceeds the boundaries of its window, **scroll bars** allow you to move the image according to your needs. If the window is not high enough a vertical scroll bar will appear with arrowheads top and bottom. Clicking on them will move the window in the direction indicated at a steady pace. As it moves a length of bar, between the arrowheads, will slide up or down accordingly. It is possible to click above or below this bar for rapid movement or click on it and slide it to the position you want. If the window is not wide enough, a scroll bar will appear horizontally with all the features just described except that the movements will be left or right. Alternatively, the toolbar might also have a **zoom** facility in a little window showing a percentage and a down arrowhead to the right (if not, it can be found under View on the menu bar and clicking on 'zoom'). Clicking on the arrowhead will display other percentages (**reducing** or **magnifying** the image or document) or 'whole page' amongst other options. Clicking on them will display different views accordingly.

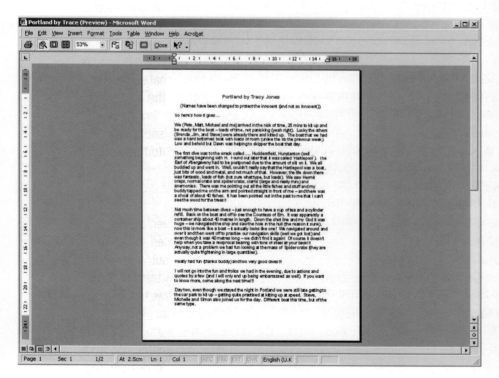

The image on screen is not necessarily exactly the same as the image that would print, if that option were selected. To check how the image would print without actually doing so and possibly wasting paper and printer ink, click on File in the menu bar and then click on Print Preview. The exact print image will then be seen on screen and if necessary, after closing the preview, adjustments can be made back in the application screen.

The power and features of modern computers combined with the flexibility of applications and peripherals provides the capacity for doing more than one job at a time e.g. it might be that you are writing and printing a document, while downloading some images from the Internet, keeping an eye on incoming emails and listening to a music CD. **Multi-tasking** allows this combination of activities to occur. It does so because the processor

19

spends a few milliseconds on one job, a few milliseconds on the next and so on, until it is back with the first. Due to the time interval spent on and between each job being so small, the 'gaps' are imperceptible to the user. However, although the processor will only allow a certain maximum load, a noticeable degradation of speed will be seen if a great many tasks are given at any one time. As mentioned above in connection with Internet connections, to avoid a tediously slow computer, sufficient thought (and money!) must be spent to ensure adequate processor power, RAM and modem speed. There are ways to keep your computer performing at optimum efficiency, whatever its hardware configuration, as the next paragraph reveals.

One single file is not always stored in one single location on the hard disk. The processor manages the disk space according to its changing contents. For example, imagine three files stored physically adjacent to each other and that the middle one is deleted. The processor remembers that this space is vacant and when it stores a new file allocates it to this space. If this space is insufficient to store the new file, the portion that will fit is stored there and the remainder stored in a new location or locations, not necessarily adjacent to each other, while the 'addresses' of all the different places are remembered by the processor. After a time many of these fragmented files accumulate on the disk. One of the limiting factors of computer speed is the disk access speed – the time it takes for the heads to travel back and forth over the rotating hard disks. Each time a fragmented file is loaded to memory, the heads have to travel over many places to find the complete file, reducing the efficiency of the computer. Hence, every so often, it is a good idea to run a program called 'defrag', which will rearrange all the parts of fragmented files so that they occupy adjacent areas on the disk, allowing the computer to operate more efficiently.

To run defrag, double click the 'My Computer' icon on the desktop. Then right click on the symbol for the hard disk and select 'Properties' from the menu displayed. Click on the 'Tools' tab in the dialog box displayed and then click on the button 'Defragment now'.

Occasionally errors occur in files or programs (due for example, to switching off the power while applications are running and/or without shutting the computer down properly). Another useful program that will correct logical and physical errors on the hard disk is **Scandisk**. To run Scandisk, click on Start, point at Programs, then Accessories, then System Tools and, finally Scandisk. If the computer has previously been shut down improperly, Scandisk will usually run automatically on rebooting or booting.

> **Tip**
> For trouble-free defragmenting, ensure that no other application is running whilst defrag runs i.e. close all other applications and processes and then run defrag.

Responding to automatic error messages and prompts generated by the computer in the event of faults, misuse (or simple mistakes such as failing to load a disk in the disk drive or paper in the printer) will prevent more costly or time-consuming problems. Similarly, observing recommendations in the following section will minimise any problems for your computer or yourself.

HEALTH AND SAFETY REQUIREMENTS

Ergonomics is the study of biology and engineering in relation to people in their working environment. You might see 'biotechnology' in American texts but it means the same. Obviously, depending on the capabilities of any machine and its operator, some ways of using the machine are more efficient than others. However, modern working practices have to accommodate a much broader range of issues. The EEC introduced the 'Council Directive on the Minimum Safety and Health Requirements for Work with Display Screen Equipment' (the VDU Directive) and employers had to comply with this legislation by 1996. A more detailed Directive concerning seating followed from the British Health and Safety Executive. The main objective of all this legislation is to ensure that the whole operator/computer work area is considered as a single unit rather than an ad-hoc arrangement where key factors important to the user's well being are ignored. Modern ergonomic studies enable ideal working practices to be defined for maximum efficiency and optimum performance levels for staff, taking into account productivity, health and safety in conjunction with the operation and capabilities of the equipment available. The application of ergonomic solutions involves not only employers and staff but also designers and manufacturers of office equipment and furniture.

Some of the more important health and safety considerations follow.

Firstly ensure that the working environment is safe both for yourself and others e.g. fire doors/exits and the paths to them must be kept clear and well marked. Electrical supplies should not be via innumerable trailing gang sockets holding so many plugs as to exceed the safety limit of their electrical current capacity.

Operate the equipment to prevent injury or discomfort to yourself e.g. bad posture maintained for hours will cause pain or discomfort later and aggravate any existing problems such as back problems. RSI is Repetitive Strain Injury and results from repeating movements, such as mouse movements or typing, over many hours. Eyestrain can result from looking at screens for hours and the radiation from screens can have adverse effects on users. Take frequent breaks away from the screens and work in well-ventilated and naturally lit rooms. Position chairs, screens and keyboards to allow good posture (neck and back straight).

VDU Check List

● Adjust seat height until the forearms are horizontal – with the elbow, wrist and fingertips in a straight line to the middle row of the keyboard.

● Use the seat tilting forwards if possible so the spine is in its natural balanced position.

● Adjust backrest height and angle to support the lower back. Sit back in the chair to maintain full lumbar support.

- For prolonged VDU work the chair should have short 'L' shaped arms, ideally height adjusting to prevent strain on the neck and upper limbs.

- Use a footrest if seat position is correct and feet do not reach the floor.

- Raise the desk or keyboard if the working surface is too low to maintain an upright posture.

- Adjust screen height and angle so that head remains upright with the top of the screen on eye-level (neck flex less than 15 degrees with a visual angle 0 – 21 degrees).

- Use a copyholder to raise input data up to eye-level.

- Avoid screen and keyboard glare. Position machine to give even illumination.

- Move whilst working. Alternate feet positions. Rock regularly if the chair has this facility.

- Break up VDU work with other job functions.

Operate the equipment according to the supplier's, manufacturer's and/or workplace requirements and recommendations. Observe and respond to any error messages displayed by the equipment (error messages on screen may indicate any of a variety of usually simple problems needing attention – no disk in disk drive, connections not made, printer out of paper etc). Where you are unable to safely rectify problems, report them according to established procedures.

It is a good idea to monitor and maintain simple physical aspects of the hardware such as broken or frayed cables, loose connections or trapped wires.

Prevention is better than cure; so keeping the apparatus clean can prevent problems. However, it can also cause problems if not conducted sensibly: with an electrical feed to most computer parts it is obviously dangerous to the computer and possibly yourself to use water or any liquid near or on a computer. If it is necessary to clean away marks and dirt, make sure you are using appropriate cleaning agents on a damp cloth or other applicator and that the power to the computer is switched off. Allow time for it to dry before switching on again.

Regular cleaning need only ensure the removal of dust from surfaces (be aware of the electromagnetic field of your vacuum cleaner if bringing it close to magnetic storage media).

Maintain safe working practices at all times and you will ensure a rewarding and productive use of computers both professionally and personally, for yourself and others.

e-Quals
UNIT 022 WORD PROCESSING

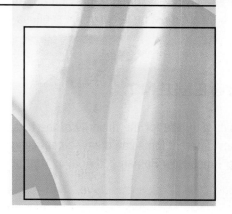

Word processing software is used to create many different types of documents. Indeed modern word processors are so good that they can produce not just letters, envelopes and reports, but professional looking posters, flyers, leaflets, newsletters, labels, business cards, etc. They have many features to allow you easily to control the look of your documents, from text effects and layout through to handling inserted objects such as graphics.

PLANNING

When creating a new document, spend some time on planning the design before you begin. Even simple documents containing only text will need to have font styles and sizes considered for best impact on the reader. If you plan before you start, you can set up features such as styles and templates that will allow you more easily to apply consistent formatting and layout throughout the current document and future related ones. Time spent in advance planning can also be saved many times over when using tables and other layout features, as trying to insert forgotten elements later on can lead to much tinkering (and time wasting) to achieve an acceptable result.

Before making any decisions about how to set out the document, consider its purpose. Who will use it and how? Legal documents, for instance, may have to conform to strict standards and there may be very few choices to be made. Informal documents can be much harder to plan, as the choice of styles can seem endless.

Documents that will be used several times in identical or almost identical forms can be set up as templates, or using styles. Documents that are to be given to multiple recipients may look more professional if some personal data is added to each one – a mail merge can be used for this.

PAPER SIZE AND ORIENTATION

When you have identified how the document will be used, one of the first decisions to be made is the paper size and orientation (portrait or landscape). If you change the size and/or orientation after entering some of the data, you may need to re-design the layout and font sizes.

Business documents such as letters, reports and fax cover sheets are best done on A4 in portrait set-up. 2- and 3-fold leaflets also use A4, but landscape. Simple notices (such as "More Seating Upstairs" in a restaurant) can be achieved very simply using A4 landscape. Labels, business cards and correspondence cards are available on both A4 and A5 sheets. Large posters will need A3 or bigger. If there is no printer available that can handle this size of paper, remember that each paper size is exactly half the sheet area of the previous one. Thus an A3 poster can be produced by printing each half on a sheet of A4. Flyers are often printed on A5. A5 booklets can be made by printing on A4 in landscape format and folding, but care must be taken in the sequencing of the pages.

More
Seating
Upstairs

FONT STYLES, SIZES AND ENHANCEMENT

Create a consistent style for letters and reports by using a single font style and size for the majority of the text, with 1 or 2 more styles and sizes for headings and sub-headings. Too many different fonts can create a confusing and incoherent look. Simple fonts work best, with typical examples being Times New Roman and Arial in 10pt or 12pt size for body text.

Tip

Times New Roman is a serif font. It has small 'ticks' on the ends of the letters. Some people find this style easier to read as the tick marks help the flow of the letters. Arial is a sans serif font – without the 'tick' marks. This style is often used for headings.

h – Times New Roman   h – Arial

Notices and promotional material need to have impact. Bold text in large sizes will draw the attention to that area of the page. Therefore, reserve this for the most important information. Don't have too many different font styles and colours – unless the 'busy' and confusing look is the result you are trying to achieve! And don't be afraid of 'white space' – blank areas of a document can be just as effective as the filled areas. Be consistent with text enhancements such as underlining, emboldening and italics and avoid too much, as the effect is reduced if repeated too often.

LAYOUT

The top part of a document – particularly if it is viewed on a computer screen – draws the reader's attention first and makes most impact, so try to position the most important information at the top. If using text and graphics together, it is a good idea to sketch the layout first to achieve good balance on the page.

Top margins in letters and reports can be much larger than bottom margins as the former may contain company information such as name and address, company logo, etc. This information will be included in your document if you are printing on plain paper. If you are printing on pre-printed headed paper, then the margin will simply be set to the required size and left blank. In both cases, continuation sheets will usually be on plain paper, and hence the size of the top margin on the first page will be different from that on all subsequent pages.

Margins are usually the same width on both left and right. The actual size of these margins depends on personal preference or company policy, but is usually in the range 2–3 cm. The exception to this is if the pages are to be bound together in book form, when a gutter will be set to increase the width of the appropriate margin to allow for the binding material.

Most paragraphs will fill the page width between the margins. Whether these paragraphs are left aligned or fully justified will depend on company policy. Quoted material will have the margins indented further to define the extent of this material. Lists may also be indented, or may have the numbers or bullet points in the margin area, depending on the company preference.

Body paragraphs usually have 1 blank line separating them. Lists and tables may need to be closer together to emphasise the related nature of the material within them. Using multiples of complete blank lines does not always suit the layout. Instead set the spacing between the paragraphs by using the Format, Paragraph dialog box to adjust the Spacing Before/After option. This gives you more precise control, since you can set the gap to be any number of points.

Lists of information are best presented in tabular form. Tabs and tables can be used for this. The information on fax cover sheets and at the top of memos (To:, From:, Date:, etc.) is usually considered as a list and laid out in tabular form.

If your text is presented in columns, use either full justification or have lines between the columns to improve readability.

Posters and promotional material can be much freer in format. Margin sizes often have less significance as small amounts of text will be centred on the page.

When placing graphics (pictures, charts, etc.) one of the first decisions to be made is whether the text will surround the graphic, or will break to provide a clear gap above and below.

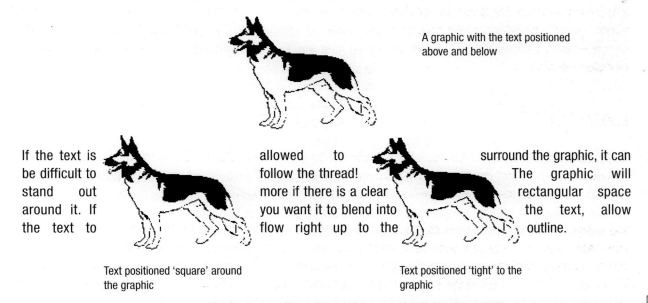

A graphic with the text positioned above and below

If the text is allowed to be difficult to stand out around it. If the text to

Text positioned 'square' around the graphic

follow the thread! more if there is a clear you want it to blend into flow right up to the

surround the graphic, it can The graphic will rectangular space the text, allow outline.

Text positioned 'tight' to the graphic

If the text is allowed to surround the graphic, it can be difficult to follow the thread! The graphic will stand out more if there is a clear rectangular space around it. If you want it to blend into the text, allow the text to flow right up to the outline.

BASIC FORMATTING AND LAYOUT OPTIONS

 Tip

A quick way to check what formatting options have been applied to existing text is to choose Help, What's This from the menu bar. The mouse pointer changes to one with a question mark attached. Clicking on any text will produce a box listing all the formatting settings. You can continue to click on other pieces of text to find their settings. When you want to return to the normal mouse pointer, press the Escape keyboard key.

The following menu commands allow you to set up basic formatting and layout.

Menu Command	Formatting
File, Page Setup	Margins, gutter, paper size, orientation and vertical alignment
Format, Font	Font style, font size, bold, italics, underlining, font colour, special effects
Format, Paragraph	Alignment, indentation, line spacing, paragraph spacing
Format, Bullets and Numbering	Bullet and numbering style

When using large fonts in particular, you may want to adjust the horizontal spacing between the characters to enhance readability or to improve the layout. This can be set from the Character Spacing tab of the Format, Font dialog box.

INSERTING HARD BREAKS

Breaks are used to separate parts of the document. This could be simply because you want the next part always to start at the top of the next page, or because there are different formatting options set for the sections. To insert a break, position the insertion point at the required place in the document and choose Insert, Break from the menu bar. Note, the position of a hard break is always under your control, unlike the soft break.

Tip

Generally, you want the text to flow from one page to another, with Word deciding when to begin the next page. This type of page break is called a soft page break. If you add or delete text, the position of the soft page break will move so that the pages do not have any gaps.

Page break	Leaves the rest of the page blank and forces the following text to the top of the next page. This type of break does not allow for different formatting, whereas section breaks do.
Column break	Used to define an area where the text is set out in columns.
Text wrapping break	Used to position text above and below a graphic or table.
Section break	Breaks the text into sections, each of which can have different formatting. For instance, if one page in the middle of a report is to be in landscape while all other pages are portrait, the report must be split into three sections.
Next page	The next section starts on the next page.
Continuous	The next section continues on the same page.
Even/Odd page	The next section starts on the next even/odd numbered page.

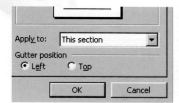

In Normal view breaks are shown by a dotted line with the type of break written in the middle.

When you have inserted section breaks and you want to apply formatting to a particular section only, ensure that the Apply to drop-down list in the formatting dialog box is set to This section rather than to Whole document.

COLUMNS

The easiest way to put text into columns is to enter all the text first, then to select the text that is to be formatted into columns and choose Format, Columns from the menu bar. The dialog box allows you to select how many columns you want, their relative widths and whether you wish to have a line between them. When you have made your choices and clicked OK, the selected text will be formatted into the columns, and a continuous section break will be inserted above and below the columns.

Tip

If you remove the columns by formatting them to a single column, you will have to remove these section breaks as well.

HEADERS AND FOOTERS

A header is text that appears in the top margin of every page. A footer is text that appears in the bottom margin of every page. Headers are frequently used to display information such as document or company name, and dates. Footers are used to display page numbers, dates and copyright information. As page numbering is so important (to detect missing pages) and done so frequently, there is a menu option available to you – Insert, Page Numbers. However, to have more control over the style and positioning of the page numbers, as well as the other information you may need to add, you can create the Headers and Footers yourself with the View, Header and Footer command.

Tip

If the Header and Footer toolbar does not automatically appear when working on a header or footer, choose View, Toolbars, Header and Footer from the menu bar.

The header area of the current page is displayed with a dotted outline and the body of the document is 'greyed out'. You can enter any text or graphics in the header and format it exactly as you would in the rest of the document. The Header and Footer toolbar provides you with buttons for commonly used automatic text such as page number, date, etc. There is also the Insert AutoText button that produces a drop-down list of more automatic data (fields) including document author (from the name given during installation of the program) and filename. Information contained in these fields can be determined by the computer's operating system, which will ensure that up-to-date values are used. For instance, if you decide to rename the file, and have used the filename field to display this information, then the new filename will be displayed. The fields can be formatted exactly as normal text.

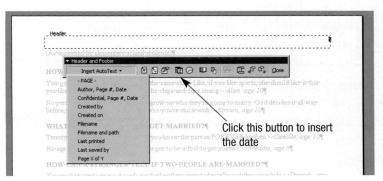

Click this button to insert the date

27

> **Tip**
>
> A most useful field is the Page X of Y. X is the page number and Y is the total number of pages in a document. This ensures that you know when you have reached the end of the document – particularly useful for legal documents, or those where the end is not obvious.

Buttons on the right-hand end of this toolbar allow you to move to the footer area of the same page, or to move to the header or footer of the next or previous section.

To move out of the header and footer area and return to working on the main document, click the Close button on the Header and Footer toolbar.

TASK

Create a new document in portrait orientation with 4cm margins all round. Add a header containing your name on the left-hand side and today's date (use automatic data) on the next line of the header in the centre. Embolden the date. Use a field to insert the filename in the footer, which should be right-aligned and in 8pt font. Key in the text of a letter to a hotel explaining that you have produced 2 designs for the required poster.

Create a second page by adding a next page section break after all your text. Set the orientation of this second page only to landscape. Save the document for a later task.

> **Tip**
>
> Once you have a header or footer, you can switch to working on it by double-clicking anywhere in a header or footer. To return to working on the main document, double-click in it.

INSERTING SYMBOLS

We frequently use signs and symbols that are not available on standard keyboards. Word has these symbols built in, and they are accessed by the Insert, Symbol menu command. When the dialog box opens, you will see a list of these symbols, containing letters with accents (such as à, ē), mathematical notation (such as ±, ∞, $1/8$) and many more (™, ©, and ♫). Select the symbol you are interested in by single clicking on it, and an enlarged picture will be displayed. To insert the symbol, click the Insert button. The dialog box remains open until you click the Cancel button, allowing you to insert several symbols.

Depending upon the installation options of your system, you may have other sets of symbols available to you from this dialog box. Click on the Font drop-down list to see the other options.

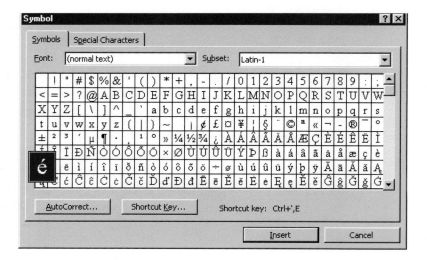

TASK

On the second page of the document you created in the previous task key in the following text – one language per line – and format it into a poster suitable to display in a hotel corridor:

Bathroom on ground floor

Cuarto de baño en la planta baja

Salle de bains sur le rez-de-chaussée

Badezimmer auf Erdgeshoß

INSERTING GRAPHICS

Inserting a ClipArt Graphic

On the principle that a picture paints 1000 words, you may want to insert a graphic into your document. Microsoft applications come with their own library of ClipArt.

Choose Insert, Picture, Clip Art. The Insert ClipArt dialog box is displayed.

The ClipArt window contains a search facility so that you can type in what you are looking for and Word will attempt to find it. Alternatively, you can browse all the different categories by selecting them.

If ClipArt contains suitable graphics that match your search criteria, they will be displayed. If there is more than one, select the graphic using your mouse; a thick border will outline the chosen graphic.

To insert the graphic, select the Insert clip icon  and then close the ClipArt window to return to your document.

Once the graphic has been inserted into your document, there is a possibility that it will be either too big or too small. Word allows you to resize the graphic by dragging on the small squares, called 'handles', that surround the image.

To keep the proportion, use the handles in the corner when dragging. Note the different arrows you get when your mouse is moved over the different handles. The corner arrows are shown here. If you use the handles on the sides or the top or bottom, you will get a stretched version.

To move the graphic, select it and drag to the new position.

Inserting a Graphic from a Stored Location

In addition to ClipArt, Microsoft applications let you insert graphics from other locations – you may have been given a graphic on a floppy disk, CD or zip disk or a graphic may be stored in a folder on the C: drive. Choose Insert, Picture, From File.

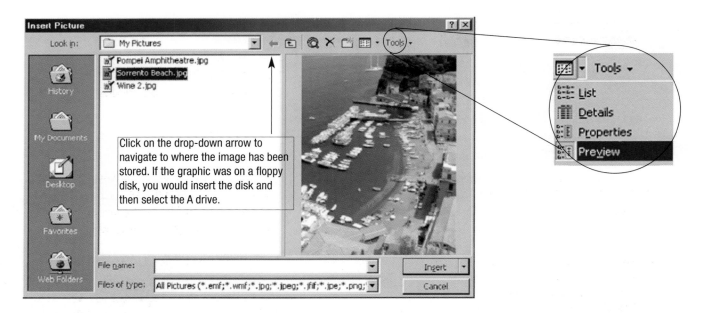

To view an image of the selected graphic, click the Views button and select Preview. This is useful to ensure that you are inserting the correct image. Select Insert to insert the graphic into your document. As with ClipArt, these images can also be resized by clicking on the image and then clicking and dragging on the handles.

Formatting a Graphic

To format a graphic, select it and choose Format, Picture from the menu bar. This opens the Format Picture dialog box. The tabs in this box allow you to add fill colours and lines of all styles around the edge of the graphic, and to position the graphic precisely on the page. The Layout tab lets you choose whether the graphic is in line with the text (i.e. the graphic behaves as if it were simply another character) or an object that can float over the text. The advanced button gives access to a few further options for the floating picture. You can set the object so that the text breaks above and below or is displayed alongside it. You can also allow the graphic to be positioned behind or in front of the text.

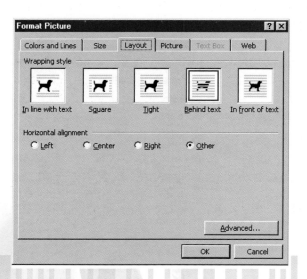

Tip

If a picture is placed so that it is completely behind the text, it can be difficult to select it. Try clicking the Select Objects button on the Drawing toolbar and using that to select the picture. You will need to click this button again or press the Escape keyboard key to return the mouse pointer back to normal.

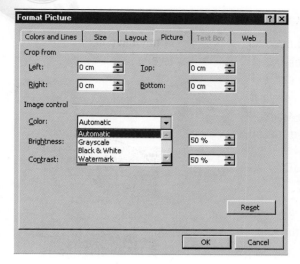

The Picture tab lets you adjust the brightness and contrast of the graphic. In particular, the Color options let you change a brightly coloured picture to Watermark, which is useful if the picture is set behind the text. This tab also lets you crop the picture if you wish to cut off parts of the picture.

TASK

Add a suitable graphic to the poster of the previous task, positioning it behind the text. Adjust any settings as necessary from the Format Picture dialog box.

INSERTING FILES

If you have some information for your document already stored as a Word file, you can insert the entire file by choosing Insert, File from the menu bar. Navigate your way to the stored file and select it. Then click the Insert button. The entire file will be inserted at the position of the insertion point. No link is maintained to the original file, so data changes in the source file will *not* be reflected in the destination file.

Tip

If only a small part of a file is to be copied into the destination file, open the source file and select the area to be copied. Choose Edit, Copy. Return to the destination file, position the insertion point at the desired location and choose Edit, Paste.

INSERTING OBJECTS

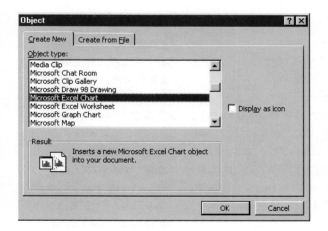

Many different kinds of objects can be inserted into a Word document. For instance, if you are producing a report and need to include sales figures, this information is often better presented as a chart or graph. Microsoft Excel is the best tool to use to produce charts from numerical data.

Choose Insert, Object from the menu bar. If you want to create a new object of a specified type, use the Create New tab of the dialog box. Select the type of object you want and click the OK button. If the object you want to insert already exists in a file, use the Create from File tab. Select the file and click OK.

Tip

Select the Link to File option to maintain a link between the destination and source files. Changes in the source file data will be automatically reflected in the destination file when that is next opened.

Order of Objects

If you have two or more objects overlapping one another, then you will need to decide which one is 'on top' of the others. Think of the objects as being in a stack. To change the order of the objects on the stack, select an object and choose Draw, Order from the Drawing toolbar. You can use the Bring Forward and Send Backward options to move the object one position in the chosen direction, or Bring to Front or Send to Back to move them to the extreme top or bottom of the stack.

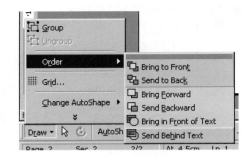

Grouping Objects

You can make a composite object from more than one by selecting all the desired objects and choosing Draw, Group from the Drawing toolbar. To select more than one object, select the first, then hold down the Shift key on the keyboard while selecting the others. A grouped object will behave as a single object. It has a single set of sizing handles, and so all the constituent parts can be re-sized together and in proportion. Also, the whole object can be moved as one, avoiding the need to re-assemble the parts.

A composite object can always be separated into its constituent parts by selecting it and choosing Draw, Ungroup from the Drawing toolbar. The objects will now all have their own individual sizing handles. To select a single object so that you can work on it, click away from the objects so that none is selected, then click on the desired object.

TASK

Create a 3rd page in your letter by inserting a next page section break after the text of the 1st poster. Set the orientation of this new page to landscape. Copy all the text and the picture from the 1st poster and paste it into the new page. Adjust the font sizes if necessary. Add a 2nd picture to this new page and place it and the 1st picture in the top right-hand corner so that they overlap slightly. Order them so that the 1st picture is on top. Group the two pictures together, re-size and re-position the grouped object as appropriate.

STYLES

A style is a collection of formatting options that you can assign to selected text in a document. Each style includes attributes such as font type, font size and enhancements, spacing, alignment, indents and tabs. You can build your own styles, and Word provides some ready-to-use ones. In fact, all text that you enter is obeying a style rule. When you open a document from the normal template, the default style that is applied to your text is the Normal style. When Word is first installed the Normal style is usually Times New Roman 10pt font. If you choose to change the default to 12pt, you are actually changing the setting of the Normal style.

Paragraph Styles and Character Styles

A paragraph style controls paragraph formatting such as text alignment, tab stops, line spacing, etc. It can also include character formatting such as bold, 12pt, etc. It affects the entire paragraph.

A character style contains character formatting such as font style and size, and affects selected text within a paragraph. Characters within a paragraph can have their own character style, even if there is a paragraph style applied to the paragraph as a whole. The character formatting will override the paragraph formatting for those selected characters.

Previewing a Style

You can use the Style dialog box to see the settings for the styles in the current document. Open the dialog box by choosing Format, Style from the menu bar. The dialog box will list all the styles in the current document in the Style list. Select one by clicking on it and the formatting options will be described in the dialog box.

Tip

Make sure the List drop-down list in the bottom left-hand corner is set to Styles in use.

Note that there are different icons for paragraph styles and character styles. In the Style dialog box, for example, the style H MAIN HEADER is a paragraph style and H Menu is a character style. The Description part of the dialog box is showing the description of the H Body style. This paragraph style was based on the Normal style, as you can see.

Within a section of text, the paragraph and character formatting options are taken from the paragraph style, except where the character style overrides them.

Applying a Style

You can apply a style by entering the text first, selecting it, and then applying the style. Or you can set the style and then enter the text. You will have to remember to set the next style when you need it.

To apply a style select the text and open the Style dialog box. Choose your style and click the Apply button.

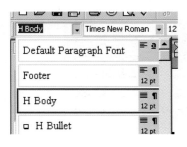

Tip

You can also apply a style from the formatting toolbar. The Style button is usually on the left-hand end of the toolbar. To apply a style, again first select the text you want to format. Then open the Style drop-down list in the formatting toolbar by clicking on the arrow. Select the style you want by clicking on it and the style will be applied to the selected text.

Built-in Styles

Word has a built-in body text format (called Normal) and several heading formats. If you cannot see them in the Style dialog box, set the List box in the bottom left-hand corner to All styles.

Creating a Style

If the built-in styles are not suitable for your document, you can create your own styles. There are two ways to do this:

By Example This is the simplest way to create a style. First, format some text with the desired style, and then select it. Click into the Styles box in the formatting toolbar to select the current style name and delete it. Key in the name for your new style and press the Enter key to add the name to the style list.

By Definition When using this method to create your new style, the easiest way is to base it on an existing one. Make sure your insertion point or your selection is in text that is using the style that is the closest to your new style. Then open the Style dialog box by choosing Format, Style from the menu bar. Click the New button to open the New Style dialog box. Enter the name for your style in the Name box and choose whether you want it to be a paragraph or character style from the Style type box. The style in the Based on box will be the one from your selection. You can change this if necessary by clicking the drop-down arrow. The Style for following paragraph (only available for paragraph styles) defines the style that will be applied to the new paragraph created when you press the Enter key at the end of a paragraph of your style. (Normally this will be the same as the style of the existing paragraph, but heading styles, for instance, often want a body style to follow.)

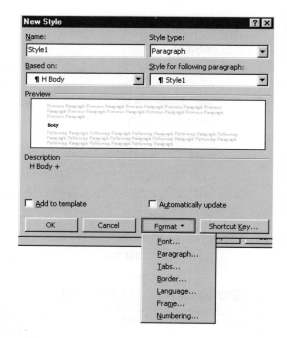

To create your style you will have to make changes to the current settings. To do this, click the Format button at the bottom of the dialog box. This will produce a menu of formatting options, such as Font, Paragraph, Tabs, etc. Clicking on an option will produce a standard Formatting dialog box for that option. Make your selections in the dialog box and click its OK button. You will return to the New Style dialog box where you can choose another option from the Format menu.

New styles are stored with the document. This means that they can be applied to any text within the document, but not to text in other documents. If you would like to use the style you have created in other documents, select the Add to template check box in this dialog box. If you do, the style will be added to the template that the current document is based on. Any future new documents based on this template will have the style available.

Tip

If you frequently create similar documents with standardised content and formatting, save your styles in an appropriate template.

The Automatically update option means that if, in the document, you change any formatting in a piece of text that has had your style applied to it, the style will be modified to include your new formatting. This can have dramatic effects on your document, so use with caution!

Modifying a Style

You can change both pre-set and user-created styles. Choose Format, Style from the menu bar. In the Style dialog box select the style you wish to modify and then click the Modify button. The Modify Style dialog box will appear. This is basically the same as the New Style dialog box, but you cannot change the style type (i.e. whether it is a paragraph style or a character style). Click the Format button to display a drop-down list of the style attributes that can be edited. After making all the desired changes, click the OK button to return to the Style dialog box. Then click the Apply button, and all text with that style will be changed.

> **Tip**
>
> One of the main advantages of using styles is that when you modify a style, all text formatted with that style will have its formatting altered to reflect the changes. Thus using styles makes it easier for you to change the look of your document in a consistent manner.

Deleting a Style

In the Style dialog box, select the style you wish to remove. Then click the Delete button.

TEMPLATES

Templates are the 'design' on which new documents are based. A template can contain formatting, styles, text, graphics, macros, customised toolbars, formulas, etc. Although you may not be aware of it, all new documents you create are based on a template. This template is known as 'Normal' and contains no data, but does contain formatting such as default margin settings, default font and font size, etc. When you create a new document by clicking the New button on the standard toolbar, Word uses this Normal template by default. There are many alternative templates available to you, and you can create your own.

Viewing the Available Templates

To see a list of templates available, choose File, New from the menu bar. A dialog box will open with an icon for each template. Note that the templates are usually grouped together in sections such as General, Letters & Faxes, etc. The normal template will appear in the General section with name Blank Document. Any icons with a 'magic wand' are templates with Wizards attached. The wizard will lead you through the creation process by asking questions and using your replies to generate the document.

Using Existing Templates

To create a document using an existing template, show the available templates by choosing File, New. Select the desired template by single-clicking on its icon and clicking OK, or double-clicking the icon. If you have chosen a wizard, you will have to complete a series of dialog boxes. If the template chosen is one of the 'built-in' Office templates, it may contain areas with instructions such as 'Click here and type name'. If so, click anywhere in the

marked area and type the desired text. If the template is a user generated one, then it will probably have just formatting and standard data in it, and you will need to position the insertion point yourself before entering the rest of the data. It may, however, also have some fields and you will be asked to supply the data for these fields in a series of dialog boxes.

TASK

Create a fax cover sheet using one of the fax templates. Invent data for each of the fields/text locations.

Tip

If you select a 'built-in' template in the New dialog box, Word will be able to show you a preview of what the finished document will look like.

Creating Your Own Template

To create your own template, start just as you would for a normal document. Enter any data that would be common to all files based on this template, and set up any desired formatting including styles. When the template is complete, choose File, Save As from the menu bar. The first field to be completed in the Save As dialog box is the Save As Type field. From the drop-down list, choose Document Template. The dialog box should change to show the relevant templates folder. (If not, you need to locate them. They are stored in a sub-folder of the Office folder.) You can select any other templates folder, or even make your own by clicking

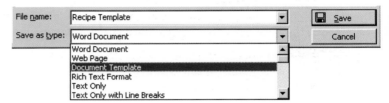

the New Folder button on the dialog toolbar. (It is best to keep all your templates in the templates folders. You can, of course, save them anywhere, but then it will not be as easy to browse through all the relevant templates when trying to choose one to use.) Having chosen a folder, key in a name for your template in the Filename box, and click Save. Then close the file. To use the new template, choose File, New and you will see an icon for your template. You can now open a document based on your template.

Tip

To locate the folder where the templates are stored, search for files of type *.dot and this will show you where these files are stored on your system.

TASK

Create a letter template for yourself with your name and address in a suitable location. Save this as a template and close the template. Create a document based on your new template. Add a paragraph of text and create a style for this paragraph. Save and close the file, saving the changes to the template when asked. Now create a second document based on your template, and check that it has your new style available for use.

USING TABS

Tabs are used to control the vertical alignment of text in a document. This is used when you want to present text in the form of a table.

Word has default tab stops set to 1.27cm, so every time you press the Tab key on the keyboard, the cursor moves 1.27cm (or 0.5 inches) to the right.

Tip

Tables are a much easier and more adaptable way of producing tabular data.

However, these settings may not be suitable for your requirements. To change the default settings, choose Format, Tabs.

The Tabs dialog box will be displayed.

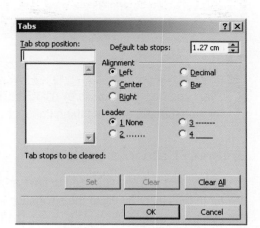

Type in the measurement of the first tab stop in the Tab stop position box, select the alignment of the tab stop, and click Set. Enter the details of the next tab stop as before. Continue until all tab stops are set. Click OK.

To remove tab stops, open the Tabs dialog box, select the tab stop that you wish to remove and click Clear. To remove all tab stops click Clear All.

Left   text is aligned evenly on the left against the tab stop

Right   text is aligned evenly on the right against the tab stop

Centre   text is centred directly under the tab stop

Decimal   data containing decimal points such as monetary values are lined up using the decimal point directly under the tab stop

Bar   places a vertical line at the tab stop

TABLES

A table is a convenient method of organising text into a neat layout. However, a table can be used for more than columns of text or numbers. It can be a simple method of creating a hanging indent, such as in the paragraph above explaining Decimal Tabs. It can also be used to provide layout for documents such as a form, and to accurately position elements such as graphics.

Tables consist of cells arranged in columns and rows. You can fill cells with text or graphics.

Inserting a Table

Example:

Supplier	Address	Telephone
Cat Flaps Inc	Leeds	0113-2221222
Collars 'n' Leads	Reading	0118-9790555

You can insert a table with the Table, Insert, Table command. In the Insert Table dialog box you must specify how many columns and rows you want. You can always add extra columns and/or rows later, or delete unwanted ones. For a simple table, leave the Column Width set to Auto. This will produce a table with equal width columns evenly distributed between the document margins. Again, you can change the column widths later.

> **Tip**
>
> It is very easy to add/delete rows later, but adding and deleting columns will mean that you have to 'fiddle about' with the table layout. If possible, calculate in advance exactly how many columns you will need.

> **Tip**
>
> You can also insert a table by using the Insert Table button on the standard toolbar . To define the size of the table you drag out the number of columns and rows you want in the grid that appears.

Entering Data in a Table

To put anything in a cell you need to have an insertion point in the cell. You can do this by clicking with the mouse pointer in the cell or by using the navigation keys on the keyboard. Once you have an insertion point in a cell, you can also move around the table by using the Tab key on the keyboard, which moves the insertion point to the next cell in the row. If the insertion point is in the last (right-most) cell of a row, it will move to the first (left-most) cell of the next row. If the insertion point is in the last cell of the last row when you press the Tab key, a new row will be created.

Entering Text in a Table

When text is typed into a cell the text wraps from one line to the next, enlarging the cell vertically as you enter more text. Pressing Return or Enter will also cause the cell to be enlarged vertically. Note, occasionally Word will try to assist you by adjusting the column widths as you type to accommodate your data. You can change the column widths yourself – see page 41.

> **Tip**
>
> **Shift + Tab** will take the insertion point to the previous cell.

Example: (*The previous table with more text than will fit in the horizontal width of a cell*)

Supplier	Address	Telephone
Cat Flaps Inc	9 Lives Lane, Leeds, LS99 2QT	0113-2221222
Collars 'n' Leads	Pet Pals House, Pedigree Lane, Lower Earley, Reading, RG17 5TY	0118-9790555

> **Tip**
>
> An annoyance can be if you want to enter in a cell text that does not start with a capital letter, but Word automatically changes it into a capital. This is an AutoCorrect option. To remove, choose Tools, AutoCorrect from the menu bar. Select the AutoCorrect tab if necessary, and remove the check mark from the Capitalise first letter of sentences check box.

Selecting Areas of a Table

In order to perform operations on parts of or a whole table, you will need to be able to select these different areas. Each cell has its own selection bar, i.e. a narrow strip down the left-hand side of the cell where the mouse pointer changes to a small black arrow pointing to the top-right. Clicking in a cell's selection bar will select the entire cell contents. You can also drag your mouse pointer to select adja-

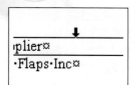

cent cells. To select an entire row, use the selection bar of the document. To do this, move the mouse pointer to the extreme left-hand side of the page until the mouse pointer changes into a white arrow pointing to the top-right. Click in this area to select the row that is opposite the mouse pointer, or drag down or up to select several adjacent rows. To select a column, position the mouse pointer above the column. It will change into a small black arrow pointing downward. A single click will select the whole column, or you can drag to select adjacent columns. To select the whole table, hover the mouse pointer anywhere in the table and a small square will appear at the top left-hand corner of the table. Click on this with your left mouse button.

Tip

The small black column selection arrow can be difficult to find. Move the mouse pointer down slowly from above the column onto the top of the column and you should see it.

It is also possible to select different areas of a table by using the Table, Select menu bar.

Formatting Text in a Table

Text inside a table can be formatted in the same way as text that is not contained in a table. That is, either apply the formatting *before* typing the text, or type the text, select it (part of a cell or entire cells) and then apply the formatting.

Selected text can have the font type and size changed from the formatting toolbar, or from the Format, Font menu. It can also be made bold, italic or underlined, and can have high-lighting applied. From the formatting toolbar it can be left-aligned, centred, right-aligned or fully justified over the column width. These options plus others such as line spacing, spacing before/after paragraph and indenting are also available from the Format, Paragraph menu option.

Example: (*The previous table with the top row bold and the right-hand column right aligned*)

Supplier	**Address**	**Telephone**
Cat Flaps Inc	9 Lives Lane, Leeds, LS99 2QT	0113-2221222
Collars 'n' Leads	Pet Pals House, Pedigree Lane, Lower Earley, Reading, RG17 5TY	0118-9790555

An extra formatting option available with tables is to adjust the cell margin. This is the space (usually called padding) between the edge of the cell and the cell contents. A default margin will be set when a new table is inserted. To change the value for the entire table, click into any cell in the table and choose Table, Table Properties from the menu bar. In the Table tab click the Options button and set the desired margins. To change the value for the selected cells only choose Table, Table Properties from the menu bar and use the Options button in the Cell tab instead.

Tip

If you have set a tab stop in a table cell, pressing the Tab key will *not* move the insertion point to it – it will move it to the next cell. To move to a tab stop in a table cell you must press Control+Tab instead.

Positioning the Table on the Page

As with other graphics, tables can be positioned anywhere horizontally across the page, and can have text wrapping around them or not. These options are available from the Table tab of the Table, Table Properties menu option.

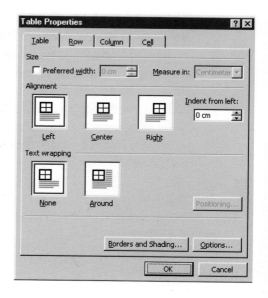

Tip

You can drag the table to its horizontal position by using the small table selector handle from the top left-hand corner of the table.

Applying Borders to Tables and Cells

The default setting for a new table is to have thin single-line borders around all the cells. To print out a table with a different style or weight of borders, or even no borders at all, select the cells to be changed and use Format, Borders and Shading from the menu bar. Make sure you are on the Borders tab of the dialog box.

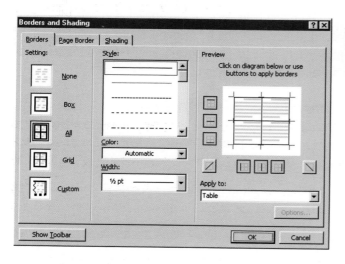

Tip

You can also bring up this dialog box by choosing Table, Table Properties from the menu bar and selecting the Table tab. This contains a Borders and Shading button.

In the dialog box, select the style, colour and width settings from the centre of the box. Then click the buttons in the Preview area to apply your chosen borders to the required sides of the selected table area. There are also some standard preset options on the left-hand side of the dialog box that you can use.

Tip

If the borders do not seem to be applied to the correct area, check the setting in the Apply to drop-down list at the bottom right-hand corner of the dialog box.

A more limited set of borders can also be applied by using the Line Style button [⎯⎯⎯ ▼] , the Line Weight button [½ ▼] and the Borders button on the Tables and Borders toolbar.

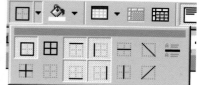

Tip

This can be displayed in the normal way from the View, Toolbars menu.

When using the toolbar, choose the style of border you want from the Line Style box and the thickness (weight) from the Line Weight box first. Then apply the border by clicking the Borders arrow down button, and choose the correct menu item for the position in which you want the border to be applied (top, outside edge, etc.). The chosen style remains the default until you next start Word.

To change border styles simply apply the new type. The new border will replace the old one.

To remove individual borders, select the cells and use the No Borders option. Apply this to the relevant edges of the selection.

Example: (*The previous table with no borders*)

Supplier	Address	Telephone
Cat Flaps Inc	9 Lives Lane, Leeds, LS99 2QT	0113-2221222
Collars 'n' Leads	Pet Pals House, Pedigree Lane, Lower Earley, Reading, RG17 5TY	0118-9790555

> **Tip**
>
> To quickly remove *all* borders from the *whole table*, select the table and use the No Border option on the Borders toolbar.

When you have a table with no borders, it can be difficult to see it on the screen. Word will provide pale grey lines, known as gridlines, to indicate the positions of the cells. Their display can be controlled by using the Table, Gridlines menu command. Note that these gridlines will *not* be printed. To print lines around the cells you must use Borders.

Applying Shading to Tables and Cells

The Format Borders and Shading dialog box has a Shading tab that allows you to apply a background colour to selected areas of the table. As well as plain colours, there are some patterns available from the Patterns drop-down list. The Tables and Borders toolbar also allows you to apply solid colours to the background of the table by using the Shading Color button . As for borders, you must select the area to be affected first. Then click on the drop-down list and select the colour or depth of grey shading you want. To take off any shading you have applied, apply No Fill.

Example: (*The previous table with a double outside border, dashed inside borders and the top row shaded*)

Supplier	Address	Telephone
Cat Flaps Inc	9 Lives Lane, Leeds, LS99 2QT	0113-2221222
Collars 'n' Leads	Pet Pals House, Pedigree Lane, Lower Earley, Reading, RG17 5TY	0118-9790555

Changing Column Width

You can change the width of columns by eye or by setting a measurement.

To change the width of a column or columns by measurement, select it/them (or click into a cell in the column) and choose Table, Table Properties. Select the Column tab if necessary and set the column width by either typing in the required value, or by using the arrows. Using this method all other columns in the table will retain their original width settings, so the right-hand edge of the table will also be repositioned.

41

To change the width of a column by eye, click into any cell in the table. Place the mouse pointer over the column edge indicator in the horizontal ruler where it will change into a double-headed arrow and you should see the tool tip 'Move Table Column'. You can now drag the column edge to give the desired width. As when using the menu bar command, all other columns will retain their original width.

Tip

If the ruler is not visible, choose View, Ruler from the menu bar. If you hold down the Alt key whilst dragging, the column widths will be displayed in the ruler.

An alternative method of adjusting the column widths by eye is to place the mouse pointer over the right-hand edge of the column in the table itself. The mouse pointer will turn into a double-headed arrow. Using this method, the right-hand edge of the table remains in place and columns to the right of the re-sized column will also have their widths adjusted to accommodate the change.

Tip

Note that if you want to change the width of *all* the cells in the column (i.e. the entire column) make sure you don't have any rows or individual cells selected. If you do, only the selected cells or the cells in the selected rows will be adjusted.

Example: (*The previous table with the widths of the second and third columns altered*)

Supplier	Address	Telephone
Cat Flaps Inc	9 Lives Lane, Leeds, LS99 2QT	0113-2221222
Collars 'n' Leads	Pet Pals House, Pedigree Lane, Lower Earley, Reading, RG17 5TY	0118-9790555

Changing Row Height

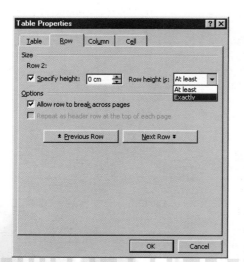

Because the default setting for the height of the rows allows them to adjust to accommodate the data, changing the height of the rows is a little different from changing the widths of the columns. However, you can do it by eye or by measurement. The bottom edge of the table will always adjust so that all other rows retain their current settings.

To change the height of a row by measurement, select it and choose Table, Table Properties. Select the Row tab if necessary. Note that the Specify height option will not be selected, which means that the row will enlarge to accommo-date the data. If you select the option you can then set a value as either an exact height (Exactly) or a minimum height (At least).

Tip

You can use any measurement unit you prefer, as long as you key in the unit as well as the measurement.

Tip

If the ruler is not visible, check that you are in Print Layout view (choose View, Print Layout). If the ruler is still not visible choose View, Ruler from the menu bar. If you hold down the Alt key whilst dragging, the row heights will be displayed in the ruler.

To change the height of a row by eye, drag the bottom edge of the row in the table itself or in the ruler. If you hold down the Alt key whilst dragging, the row heights will be displayed in the ruler.

Adjusting the row height by dragging the bottom of the row in the table is the equivalent of setting the row height to an At Least value. This allows the row height to increase if necessary, but to never go smaller than the set measurement. Exactly will mean that the row height will be fixed and any data that does not fit will not be lost but cannot be displayed. Increasing the height of the row will cause the 'missing' data to be shown.

Example: (*The previous table with the rows set to **At Least** 48 pt*)

Supplier	Address	Telephone
Cat Flaps Inc	9 Lives Lane, Leeds, LS99 2QT	0113-2221222
Collars 'n' Leads	Pet Pals House, Pedigree Lane, Lower Earley, Reading, RG17 5TY	0118-9790555

Alignment

Horizontal alignment of the data in the cells is achieved by the same methods as for normal text as described in previous sections. To align the data vertically within selected cells choose Table, Table Properties and select the Cell tab if necessary. This has 3 options to allow you to place the data at the top, middle or bottom of the cell. Note that you will only see a result if the cell height is greater than that necessary to display the data.

Example: (*The previous table with the text centred vertically in the row height*)

Supplier	Address	Telephone
Cat Flaps Inc	9 Lives Lane, Leeds, LS99 2QT	0113-2221222
Collars 'n' Leads	Pet Pals House, Pedigree Lane, Lower Earley, Reading, RG17 5TY	0118-9790555

Tip

The Tables and Borders toolbar contains a button with nine menu options combining different horizontal and vertical formatting settings.

Inserting Rows

To insert rows at the end of a table position the insertion point in the last cell and press the Tab key. This will add 1 extra row at the end of the table. You can add as many extra rows as you like using this method. To insert rows into the middle of the table, select the number of rows you wish to insert and then choose Table, Insert. You can now select either the Rows Above or Rows Below option.

Tip

It is so easy to add extra rows that you really don't need to be too concerned about setting the correct number of rows when you first insert the table.

Inserting Columns

To insert columns in a table, select the number you want to insert and choose Table, Insert from the menu bar. You can then choose either to insert Columns to the Left or Columns to the Right.

Example: (*The previous table with an extra column and the column widths adapted to fit*)

Supplier	Address	Contact	Telephone
Cat Flaps Inc	9 Lives Lane, Leeds, LS99 2QT	SM	0113-2221222
Collars 'n' Leads	Pet Pals House, Pedigree Lane, Lower Earley, Reading, RG17 5TY	IB	0118-9790555

> **Tip**
>
> Adding columns will most probably necessitate changing the column widths, so it is better to insert the table with the correct number of columns in the first place if possible.

Deleting Rows/Columns

To delete rows or columns, select them and then choose Table, Delete Columns or Table, Delete Rows from the menu bar. This will remove the rows/columns and delete the data contained in them.

Entering Graphics in a Table

The simplest form of graphics to enter in a table is ClipArt. Make sure the insertion point is in the desired cell and choose Insert, Picture from the menu bar as normal. The rows of the table will expand to accommodate the cell contents. You can change the size of the ClipArt by selecting it and then dragging one of the sizing handles. The row height will automatically adjust (unless you have set it to be an exact height).

> **Tip**
>
> Different versions of Word treat the positioning of the inserted graphic in different ways. If you find that the picture is not automatically placed in the table cell you will have to format the picture. Right click on it and choose Format Picture or Format Object from the pop-up menu. Depending on your version of Word, click on the Layout or Position tab and set the option In line with text or turn off the Float over text option.

Merging and Splitting Cells

So far all the tables we have worked with have had a regular arrangement of the cells into columns and rows. Sometimes you want a more irregular arrangement where single cells are spread over larger areas or are split into smaller cells. A common use of this is so that several columns or rows can have a heading. You can do this by either merging the heading cells, or by splitting the cells underneath the heading.

To merge cells, select them and choose Table, Merge Cells from the menu bar.

Splitting is done in the same manner using the Table, Split Cells command on the menu bar. However, you will have to specify how many columns or rows the selected cells are to be split into.

When cells have been merged or split, selecting columns and rows using the mouse pointer can become more difficult as larger cells will often be considered as being part of

> **Tip**
>
> You can also use the Merge Cells or the Split Cells buttons on the Tables and Borders toolbar .

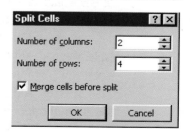

several columns or rows. It may be easier to position the insertion point in a cell in the desired column or row and to use the Table, Select menu.

Example: (*A table containing ClipArt and text, formatting and merged cells*)

Activities for Wednesday Afternoon

		Meeting Place
	Skiing	Bottom of Dry Ski Slope
	Golf	Outside Club House
	Football	Astro-turf
	Sub-Aqua	Diving Pool

TASK

Create the table shown in the above example. Note, there are six rows (Meeting Place is in the 2nd row) and three columns, with the cells of the 1st row merged. Internal vertical borders are turned off, dashed internal horizontal borders are applied to all edges except the bottom edge of the 1st row. All cell contents are centred both vertically and horizontally, and the height of the 1st row has been set to at least 48pt.

MAIL MERGE

Mail Merge is used to create documents that contain personalised data in each copy. One example is a letter that has to be sent to many people. Although the main part of the letter is the same for each person, there is also information that varies, such as the recipient's name and address. You might also want to produce mailing labels or envelopes for each recipient.

Before we start, let's cover some terminology.

Data Source A file containing the personalised data that is entered into the separate copies of the document. It can be one of many types of file, e.g. a table in a Word document, a database in an Excel Workbook, a table in an Access database, etc.

Main Document The Word document containing the fixed text, drawings, etc. and also the placeholders for the personalised data. It could be a sheet of labels or a letter, for instance.

Mailing Labels The sheets of labels produced by combining (or merging) a **Data Source** with a **Main Document** that is in the form of blank labels.

Form Letters The personalised letters that are produced by combining (or merging) a **Data Source** with a **Main Document** that is in the form of a letter.

Mail Merge The process of creating **Mailing Labels** or **Form Letters** by using a **Data Source** and a **Main Document**.

There are many methods for creating both the data source and the main document. We will start by producing a sheet of mailing labels from a data source that has been created in advance of the merge process. The data source will be in the form of a table in a Word document.

PRINTING A GROUP OF ADDRESSES CONTAINED IN A WORD TABLE ONTO LABELS

Tip

The table should be the first thing in the document (i.e. no blank lines or text above it or in front of it).

Before starting the mail merge process, you need to create a Word table containing the names and addresses you want to print.

Each row of the table should contain the information for one person (a record), and each column of the table should contain one piece of information about that person (a field). The contents of a field

Tip

The first row of the table must contain field names.

are known as a data item. Each row should have the same layout (i.e. the same fields in the same positions). You can, if necessary, leave a field blank.

An example of a table with two records, each containing five fields is given below. Note, the table has three rows, the 1st row being for the field names.

Title	First Name	Surname	Address 1	Town
Miss	Jane	Andrews	10 The Drive	Wokingham
Mr	Fred	Smith	64 Westerley Road	Leeds

Tip

If you will never need the individual parts of a data item, then you can combine them in one field. For instance, in the data source above you could have had a single name field containing the title, first name and surname. However, if you want to refer to Miss Andrews (without the Jane) then they must be separate. It is a simple task to combine individual fields – almost impossible to separate out the parts of a combined one. If in doubt, use separate fields.

Calling Up Mail Merge

Choose Tools, Mail Merge from the menu bar. The Mail Merge Helper dialog box appears. This will guide you through the merge process, and you will need to re-display it several times.

Tip

Save and close the document containing the data source before proceeding with the mail merge. Otherwise, it is very easy to confuse all the different documents you will create.

If Word does not have any documents open, you will not be able to begin the Mail Merge Process. If necessary create a new blank document.

The Mail Merge
Helper dialog box at
the beginning of the
Mail Merge Process

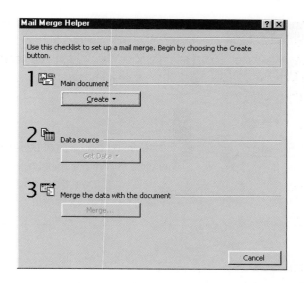

Tip

If you lose the Mail Merge
Helper from your screen, click
on the Mail Merge Helper icon
on the mail merge toolbar.
Alternatively click Tools, Mail
Merge to view the helper.

The mail merge is a 3-step process. Greyed out buttons in the Mail Merge Helper dialog box indicate that you cannot yet perform this particular step. The three stages correspond respectively to dealing with the main document, dealing with the data source, and performing the merge.

Step 1 – Creating the Main Document

The main document for mailing labels will be in the form of a table with a cell at each of the label positions of your chosen label style. Unusually for a mail merge, there is very little fixed text. Each document is a single label containing mostly placeholders for the fields in the data source.

In the Mail Merge Helper dialog box click the Create button under step 1. You will see a list of different merge types. Select Mailing Labels. The next dialog box will ask you if you want to use the Active Window or a New Main Document. **For mailing labels, always choose a new main document**. You will see a new blank document appear behind the dialog box. This will become the main document, i.e. a table with the layout of your labels, containing placeholders for your personalised data. If you look carefully, you should see that this document has the Mail Merge Toolbar in the toolbar area of the window, although most of the buttons are greyed out at this stage. You now need to proceed to step 2 of the mail merge.

The Mail Merge
Toolbar

Step 2 – Attaching the Data Source

At this stage, you need to associate the data source with the main document. Click on the Get Data button at step 2 of the Mail Merge Helper. Since your data source already exists select Open Data Source from the list of options. A standard Open dialog box opens to allow you to navigate your way to your saved data source. Select it and click the Open button. You will return to your mail merge, with a dialog box where the only option is to Set Up The Main Document. Click this button.

Setting Up the Main Document You now have to choose the type of label you want to use, and where you want your fields to be positioned on the labels. The first dialog box lets you select your label type, in a similar manner to when you are creating an individual label. When you have chosen, click OK.

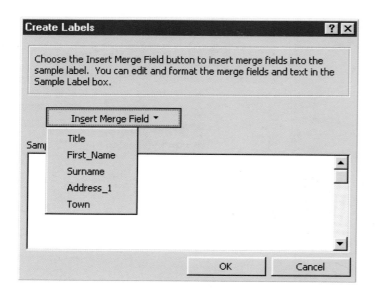

The next dialog box presents you with a blank label and only one button, Insert Merge Field. Click on this button and you will see a list of the field names from your data source.

Tip

If the Insert Merge Field button is greyed out, you have not selected your data source correctly. Cancel out of the dialog box and start again.

To insert a field, select it from the list. Continue inserting the fields in the order you want them to appear. You should put in any punctuation such as commas, spaces and return characters to separate the lines.

A label set up with three placeholders in the first line

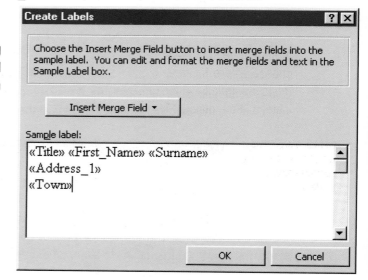

Then click OK. You will now be back at the mail merge helper, with all the buttons available to you. (If you want to change the layout of the main document or the data source, click the Edit button at the appropriate step.) Behind the mail merge helper, you should be able to see your main document with its table. In each cell there will be placeholders (field names inside double brackets) for your data. Also, every cell except the first will have a special field to move on to the next record in your data source (although you may not actually see this field until you have performed the first merge).

«Title»·«First_Name»·«Surname»¶
«Address_1»¶
«Town»¶
¶
¤

«Title»·«First_
«Address_1»¶
«Town»¶
¶
¤

«Title»·«First_Name»·«Surname»¶
«Address_1»¶
«Town»¶

«Title»·«First_
«Address_1»¶
«Town»¶

Step 3 – Performing the Merge

The diagram below illustrates what will happen during the merge process. (Note, this is a very simple data source with only one field per record.)

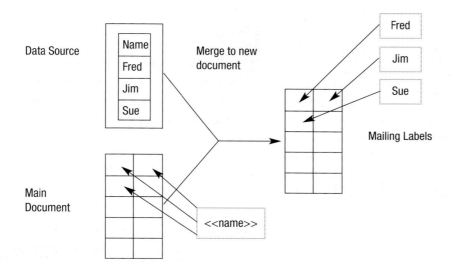

At step three in the Mail Merge Helper dialog box, click the Merge button. This opens a dialog box allowing you to choose where the output from the merge goes. You can, if you are confident, merge straight to your printer. However, initially, you will save a lot of wasted paper (and expensive labels!) if you merge to a new document instead. If the document is correct, you can always print it later.

The Mail Merge Helper dialog box when ready to perform step 3 – the Merge

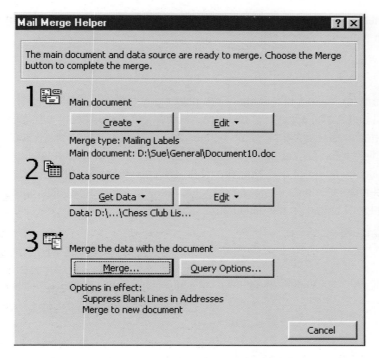

Merging to a new document will produce another new document containing the layout of your main document, but with data from your data source substituted for the placeholders. So, there should be one label for each row in your data source. Note that this is *not* your original main document. That is still open (behind the mailing labels document) and still contains the placeholders.

Printing

If your labels are correct, then you can print them by printing the document. When performing the same mail merge in future, you can merge directly to the printer if you are confident.

Saving

It is not usual to save the result of the merge process. If you were creating form letters, for instance, and you had a 2-page letter for each person, then the result of the merge process with a data source of 50 records would produce a 100-page document. You do not usually want to 'clog up' your disk with such large documents. However, as you can fit many labels onto a single page, the document resulting from a mailing labels merge is often quite a small file. If you think that the source data will not change very frequently and that you will want to print out exactly the same names and addresses again, then you could save the document containing the actual names and addresses. Save it in the normal manner. If, however, you think that your data will change frequently, do not save the document containing the mailing labels data (i.e. the actual names and addresses). In either case, always save the main document. Then you can repeat the merge process as below using the saved file, and will not have to repeat the label set-up procedure.

Formatting the Labels

The output document generated when you perform a mail merge to produce mailing labels is, in fact, a Word document containing a table. The table is set out so that the margins are the same as the margins on your sheet of labels, and there is a cell in the table corresponding to each of the labels on the sheet. (Note, there may also be other columns and rows to assist in the layout.)

As this is a table, it can be formatted in the same way as any other table. For instance, you can change the font and font size, you can apply bold, italics, underline, etc. You can align the cell contents both horizontally and vertically. You can also add extra text or pictures to each cell.

Label Types

Although the mail merge uses the term mailing labels, there are now many formats of labels that can be purchased, not just for use in the mail and not all sticky! For instance, you can purchase sheets with labels for large parcels, floppy discs, video cassettes, business cards, name badges and postcards. Often when you purchase a new type of label, there will be a disk in the packet that will enable you to install that type of label on your computer. Hence, when you want to produce labels of that type, the label reference number will be in the appropriate dialog box. Otherwise, if your label measurements do not correspond to any of the pre-installed options, you can enter the details by using the New Label button on the dialog box.

Tip

When setting up your labels, if you want to see the detailed measurements of any label type, select it and then click the Details button.

TASK

Use mail merge to create some name badges for the attendees at a conference. Follow the steps below:

1 Create a word document with a table containing a column for each field. Some fields you could include are – first name, surname, company name, conference code. Add in a few records – but don't spend too long – 3 or 4 will do.
2 Save and close this document.
3 Start the mail merge process and choose mailing labels at step 1. At step 2, associate your data source as prepared above. Choose a style of label that would give an appropriate size for lapel badges. Set up the labels to contain the placeholders in an attractive manner.
4 Merge to a new document at step 3 of the Mail Merge Helper dialog box. You will probably find that the resultant labels contain the data in the correct positions but, as they are to be lapel badges, the font will be a little small. Format the table to increase the font size and apply any other formatting you think appropriate. If you wish, print out the labels onto plain paper.
5 As the delegates to the next conference will have changed significantly, do not save the lapel badges. However, save the main document.

Now try repeating the above, but this time set up a data source containing names and addresses for the invitations to a 21st birthday party. Produce a sheet of labels of appropriate size. Again, do not spend too long creating lots of data in your data source – you can always add to it later if the mail merge works correctly. Save the main document as you will need it for a later task, but not the mailing labels.

Editing the main document and data source

If you need to correct mistakes or add data, you need to decide in which document to make your corrections. It is very unusual to make any changes in the result of the mail merge, i.e. in the form letters, the mailing labels or the envelopes. For instance, suppose your letters should have said "Yours sincerely", but actually say "Yours faithfully". If you change the form letters, you will have to change *every* letter. You would only change the form letters if only a few contain a mistake – for instance if, just after producing the letters, you discover that you have been given an incorrect address for one recipient. Normally, if there are any errors, you should discard the form letters, fix the mistakes, and then repeat the merge.

You can change the data simply by opening the relevant document and making the required changes. You can also use the Mail Merge Helper dialog box at any time to make corrections to either the main document or the data source by clicking on the relevant Edit button.

Tip

If you are viewing the main document, there is a button on the Mail Merge Toolbar that will let you edit the data source .

If you need to add or delete fields in your data source, simply add or delete columns in the table. Any new fields will be automatically included in the list of merge fields the next time you open the main document. Take care when deleting fields as these may have already been used in the main document. Renaming fields can cause similar problems.

Typical Errors in the Data Source

- Incorrect data, such as mis-spelt names, out-of-date telephone numbers.

- Inappropriate capital letters, plurals, etc. that make the merged document grammatically incorrect (e.g. "*thank you for the Hat you sent me*").

- Insufficient fields (e.g. you would like to have "*Dear Mr Jones*", but have put all the name in a single field as "*Mr Henry Jones*").

Typical Errors in the Main Document

- Incorrect spellings, punctuation and grammar in the body of the text (as could occur in any document).

- Incorrect punctuation and spaces around the fields (e.g. "*DearMr Jones ,*").

- Fields positioned incorrectly (e.g. "*Dear hat, Thank you for the Mr Jones*").

Typical Errors of Inconsistency

- Non-agreement of number in *some* records only (e.g. "*please send me a hat*", "*please send me a gloves*").

- Non-agreement of gender in *some* records only (e.g. "*Jane has achieved her Grade 3 badge*", "*Fred has achieved her Grade 1 badge*").

- Renaming, moving or deleting the data source file leads to an error message when opening the main document – click the Find Data Source button.

e-Quals
UNIT 023 SPREADSHEETS

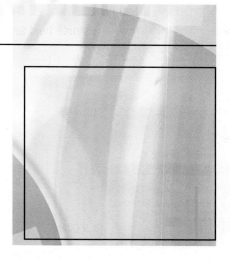

USING MICROSOFT EXCEL

Microsoft Excel is used if you need to create a file that contains a combination of text and figures, or if you wish to carry out calculations on the figures.

Excel recognises three types of cells – text cells, value cells and formula cells.

Text cells contain text and can be left aligned, centred or right aligned. You use text to type 'labels', column headings and row headings. Excel recognises text as you type it.

Value cells contain numbers. These can also be left aligned, centred or right aligned, but you would use a figure in a cell where you may wish to carry out a calculation later. **N.B. Excel can only carry out calculations on value cells**. Excel recognises a value as you type it.

Formula cells contain a calculation (formula). As soon as you type the sign =, Excel recognises that you are about to create a formula. When you have written a formula, the result of the formula appears in the cell, but the formula itself appears on the Formula Bar.

=	=B1-E2

It is important that you type the correct type of data into the cell. Cells should be formatted correctly in order that the data input adopts the right formatting.

Terminology

There are three terms that you may come across when using Excel:

Data Input   the data that is entered into a spreadsheet.
Data Output   the data that is produced from the spreadsheet (as a result of calculations carried out on the sheet).
Data Processing the name given to the act of entering and outputting data.

ENTERING DATA INTO A SPREADSHEET

If you wish to enter a 'label', column heading or row heading, you can simply type the text. Excel will recognise that this is now a 'text' cell and will apply General formatting to it. You can format your text using the Formatting toolbar or by choosing Cells… from the Format menu.

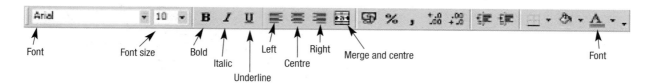

Font   Font size   Bold   Italic   Underline   Left   Centre   Right   Merge and centre   Font

Tip

SHORTCUT KEYS

Enter	Move down to the next cell
Shift+Enter	Move up to the previous cell
Alt+Enter	Start a new line in the cell
Tab	Move right to the next cell
Shift+Tab	Move left to the previous cell

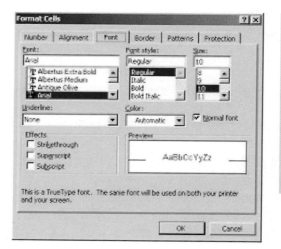

The Format Cells dialog box displaying the Font tab. On this tab you can change the font, font style and font size, choose different underline options, change font colour and add other text effects. (The Preview area allows you to see the results of your changes.)

Typing Figures as Text

If you wish to type a figure, but want Excel to interpret that figure as text (such as a part number in a heading), you can change the formatting of the cell. Click on the empty cell that you wish to type the 'text' into. Choose Cells from the Format menu and click on the Number tab.

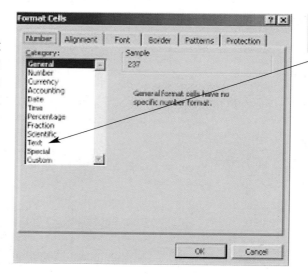

Click on Text formatting in the list and then click OK. Type the data into the cell

Tip

If you want data to be treated as text, type 'before typing the figure.

FORMATTING FIGURES ON THE SPREADSHEET

If you type a figure onto a spreadsheet, Excel will recognise that it is a value and apply General formatting. If you wish your figure to appear differently, you can use the formatting tools on the Formatting toolbar or the Format, Cells dialog box.

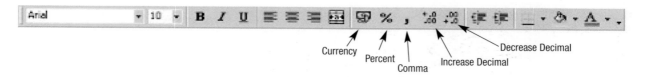

Currency Percent Comma Increase Decimal Decrease Decimal

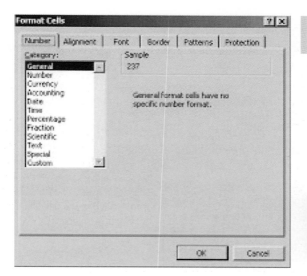

The Format Cells dialog box displaying the Number tab. On this tab you can choose from a large range of different number formats and customize them to suit your requirements.

Tip

You can press Ctrl+1 to access the Format Cells dialog box.

N.B. IT IS IMPORTANT THAT CELLS CONTAIN THE APPROPRIATE FORMAT IN ORDER THAT DATA INPUT INTO THOSE CELLS APPEARS AS REQUIRED.

Adding Borders

The lines that appear on the worksheet are called gridlines. By default, these lines do not print. If you want to have lines around your data input cells on the printed page, it is best to apply borders.

Select the cells that you wish to apply borders to and choose the appropriate option from the Border palette on the Formatting toolbar.

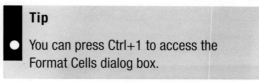

Alternatively, you can apply borders by choosing Cells… from the Format menu and clicking on the Border tab.

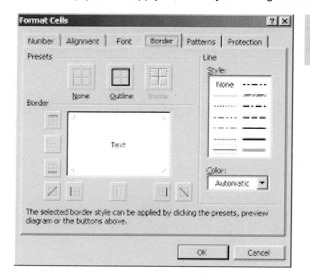

The Format Cells dialog box displaying the Border tab. On this tab you can apply borders to the cells. You can also choose the line style and colour for the border. The Text area allows you to see the results of your changes.

Applying Shading

If you wish your cells to be shaded on the printed page, you can apply grey or coloured shading.

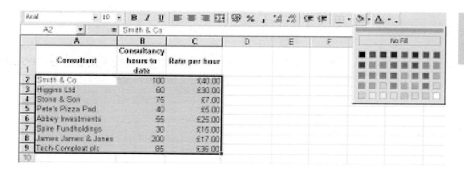

Select the cells that you wish to apply shading to and choose the shading colour from the Shading palette on the Formatting toolbar.

Alternatively, you can apply shading by choosing Cells… from the Format menu and clicking on the Patterns tab.

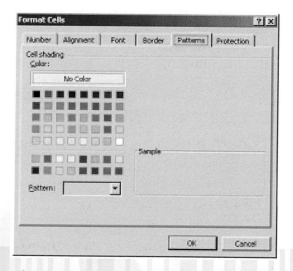

The Format Cells dialog box displaying the Patterns tab. On this tab you can apply cell colour and patterns. You can also choose a pattern colour from the second palette. The Sample area allows you to see the results of your changes.

Tip

Ctrl+B	Apply bold format
Ctrl+U	Apply underline format
Ctrl+I	Apply italic format
Ctrl+Shift+~	Apply general number format
Ctrl+Shift+$	Apply currency format
Ctrl+Shift+%	Apply percent format
Ctrl+Shift+#	Apply date format
Ctrl+Shift+@	Apply time format

REMOVING FORMATTING FROM A RANGE OF CELLS

Tip

The Delete key on the keyboard deletes the cell contents not the entire cell.

Press Ctrl+Hyphen to delete the entire cell (this will remove formatting as well as the contents).

If you have added a lot of formatting to cells, i.e. bold and underline and borders and shading, you can individually switch off each formatting. However, it is quicker to use the Clear command.

Select the cells that contain the formatting you wish to remove and choose Clear from the Edit menu. Click on Formats in the sub-menu. The formatting is stripped from the cells, but the contents remain.

SAVING EDITED SPREADSHEETS

If you use the Save command, you will overwrite the existing spreadsheet. However, if you wish to create different versions of the same spreadsheet, you should use Save As. Use a naming system that makes it easy to recognise which is the latest version, e.g. use dates in the names.

You can also use headers and footers in the spreadsheet itself to specify which version the file is. (You can use dates and version numbers in the header or footer.)

Checking Formulae

It is very important that you check any formulae that you have created on the spreadsheet. You are not checking whether Excel can add up(!), but whether you have used the right cell references in the formula.

The most effective way to test the formulae is to save the spreadsheet with a different name (i.e. test) and then enter dummy data into the spreadsheet. Check the results with a calculator to ensure that the calculations are correct.

TASK

Enter the following data onto a new worksheet:

ITEMS	BUDGET	JAN	FEB	MAR	APR
Bedding					
Cleaning					
Electricity					
Furniture					
Gas					
Catering					
Laundry					
Maintenance					

Save the workbook as Test Data Version 1.

Centre and bold the column headings. Apply currency formatting to the data cells. Add borders and shading.

Save the workbook as Test Data Version 2.

Head up two new columns – Spent and Balance. Create formulae for these calculations.

Save the workbook as Test Data Version 3.

Enter test data for each item. Use a calculator to check that the formulae are calculating correctly.

Save the workbook as Test Data Version 4. Close the workbook.

VIEWING THE SPREADSHEET

Hiding Rows and Columns

If you do not wish to view certain rows or columns on the spreadsheet, you can hide them.

To hide a row or column using the mouse, drag the resizing handle until the row or column is no longer visible on the worksheet.

To unhide a row or column using the mouse, move your mouse onto the grey column tiles (lettered) or the grey row tiles (numbered), so that it rests on the line between two column tiles or two row tiles. The white cross icon will change to a double-headed black arrow. This is the resizing handle. If you drag this, you will resize the row or column.

To reveal a hidden column, move your mouse slightly more to the right (for a column) or down (for a row). The resizing handle changes slightly to a double-headed arrow, with a double vertical line. Drag this handle to reveal the hidden row or column.

To hide a row or column using the dialog box, sit in the row or column you wish to hide and choose Column, Hide or Row, Hide from the Format menu.

To unhide a row or column using the dialog box, select the rows or columns on either side of the hidden row or column and then choose Column, Unhide or Row, Unhide from the Format menu.

Tip

To hide a row, press Ctrl+9
To hide a column, press Ctrl+0

To unhide a row, press Ctrl+Shift+(
To unhide a column, press Ctrl+Shift+)

Freezing Panes

If you have entered a lot of data onto the worksheet, you will notice that as you scroll across or down, the row or column headings scroll off the screen. If you want column headings or row headings (or both) to remain visible on the screen as you scroll around, you can freeze panes.

Click in the row below the row you wish to freeze and in the column to the right of the column you wish to freeze. Choose Freeze Panes from the Window menu. A thick black line appears on the screen to indicate that the row or column is frozen. When you scroll around the worksheet, the rows and columns you have frozen will not scroll off the screen.

Choose Windows, Unfreeze Panes to remove the freeze from columns and rows.

Splitting the Window

This features works in a similar way to Freeze Panes, but actually splits the window into two or more sections. You can then view different areas of the worksheet at the same time.

Choose Split from the Window menu. A horizontal and vertical split bar appear. Point to the bar and the mouse pointer changes to a split pointer. Drag the split to wherever you want on the screen. To remove the split, choose Remove Split from the Window menu.

Alternatively, you can drag the split bars onto the screen using the mouse. The vertical split can be found at the right end of the horizontal scroll bar and the horizontal split is at the top of the vertical scroll bar.

Vertical split

Move your mouse over the grey bar and it changes to a split pointer. Drag the split onto the screen.

Horizontal split

Working with Multiple Windows

If you wish to be able to view several sheets in your workbook on the screen at the same time, you can open the workbook into several windows and then view different sheets in different windows.

Open the workbook you wish to work with. Choose New Window from the Window menu. Repeat this to create as many windows as you wish. Choose Arrange from the Window menu, select Tiled and click OK. You are now looking at different windows of the same workbook. You can view different sheets in the different windows.

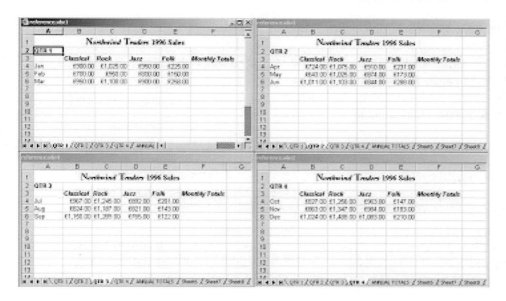

The active window has a blue title bar. Click in the different windows to make them active. Close each window in the normal way.

Show Formulae

By default, when you enter a formula into a cell, the result of that formula appears in the cell. If you wish to be able to view the formulae instead of the results, choose Options from the Tools menu, click on the View tab and check the Formulae box under Window options.

MOVING AND COPYING DATA ON THE SPREADSHEET

If you wish to move or copy data from one place to another in your spreadsheet file, you can use the Windows clipboard. The clipboard is a temporary storage area that enables you to move or copy data from one place and then paste it back at another location within the same file, into another file, or into another application. The Windows clipboard can only hold one item at a time. If there is something already sitting on the Windows clipboard and you then cut something else, this will replace the original item.

Moving Data using the Clipboard

Select the cells that you wish to move and choose Cut from the Edit menu. Alternatively, you can click on the Cut button on the Standard toolbar. A moving border appears around the selected cells. Navigate to the new location and click in the cell that will be at the top left corner of the new location and choose Paste from the Edit menu. Alternatively, you can click on the Paste button on the Standard toolbar.

Copying Data using the Clipboard

Select the cells that you wish to copy and choose Copy from the Edit menu. Alternatively, you can click on the Copy button on the Standard toolbar. A moving border appears around the selected cells. Navigate to the new location and click in the cell that will be at the top left corner of the new location and choose Paste from the Edit menu. Alternatively, you can click on the Paste button on the Standard toolbar.

Tip

You can press Ctrl+X on the keyboard to Cut, Ctrl+C to Copy and Ctrl+V to Paste.

Copying Formatting using the Format Painter

If you wish to copy formatting to other cells, you can use the Format Painter.

Select the cell that contains the formatting you wish to copy. Click on the Format Painter button on the Standard toolbar and select the cells that you wish to apply the formatting to.

N.B. All formats are copied, including borders and shading.

TASK

Open the workbook Test Data Version 2.

Using cut and paste or drag and drop, rearrange the items into alphabetical order.

Add two new rows at the bottom of the worksheet – Medical Supplies and Postage.

Use the Format Painter to copy the formatting of the existing data cells onto the cells in the new rows.

Save and close the workbook.

USING PASTE SPECIAL

Paste Special enables you to control what you paste back onto the worksheet. For example, you may have selected a range of cells, copied them to the clipboard, but only wish to paste the formats that those cells contain. Or, you may have copied a range of cells to the clipboard, but only wish to paste the formulae that are contained in those cells.

You can also use Paste Special to copy and paste any comments or validation rules contained in cells.

Copying Formatting using Paste Special

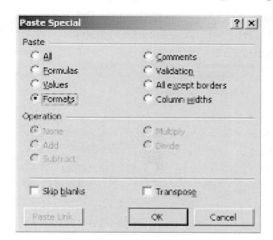

Select the cells that you wish to copy the format of and choose Copy.

Move to the new location and choose Paste Special from the Edit menu (or right-click and choose Paste Special from the shortcut menu).

Click Formats and then click OK.

Copying Formulae using Paste Special

Select the cells that contain the formulae you wish to copy. Choose Copy.

Move to the new location and choose Paste Special from the Edit menu (or right-click and choose Paste Special from the shortcut menu).

Click Formulas and then click OK.

Pasting Formulae as Values on another Sheet

Select the cells that contain the results you wish to copy.

Choose Copy.

Move to the new location and choose Paste Special from the Edit menu (or right-click and choose Paste Special from the shortcut menu).

Click Values and then click OK.

Using Mathematical Operations when copying

You can use Paste Special to paste data onto other data and carry out a mathematical operation. For example, you may have a number of sheets containing data and you wish to create a "consolidation" sheet that adds the data up.

Select the cells that contain the data you wish to add. Click on Copy.

Select the cells that contain the data you wish to add to and choose Paste Special from the Edit menu (or right-click and choose Paste Special from the shortcut menu).

Select the mathematical operation you require and click OK.

TASK

Create a new workbook and name four sheets January, February, March and Totals.

Type the following text onto the January sheet. Use copy and paste to put the same text on the other sheets.

Name	**Wages**
Bob Smith	
Penny Cooper	
Deirdre Wall	

Enter figures for January, February and March wages. Use Paste Special to add the figures together on the Totals sheet.

FIND AND REPLACE

You can search for text or data on your spreadsheet and replace it with alternative text or data.

To simply find data or text on the spreadsheet, choose Find from the Edit menu.

Type what it is you wish to find in the Find what box and choose whether you wish Excel to search By Rows or By Columns. You can also specify that it should look in Formulas, Values or Comments.

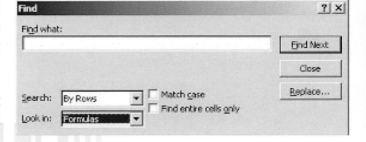

Click Find Next. Excel searches the spreadsheet and stops at the first match. Click Find Next to find the next match. Click Close to close the Find dialog box.

If you decide you need to replace text or data on the spreadsheet, you can either click on the Replace button in the Find dialog box, or choose Replace from the Edit menu.

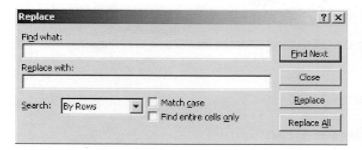

Type what you wish to find in the Find what box and type what you wish to replace it with in the Replace with box. Choose whether you wish Excel to search By Rows or By Columns.

You can ask it to match case (upper case or lower case, etc), or you can specify that it should only stop if the match is the entire cell contents.

Click Find Next to start the search. Excel searches the spreadsheet and stops at the first match. Click Find Next to find the next match or Replace to replace that occurrence with the new text or data. If you wish Excel to carry out the Find and Replace task automatically, click Replace All.

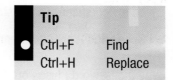

Tip	
Ctrl+F	Find
Ctrl+H	Replace

WORKSHEET PROTECTION

If you have spent time creating a worksheet containing complex formulae and functions, it is wise to protect the worksheet against being overwritten. You should certainly protect the worksheets of a workbook if that file will be used by a number of different people. It is also useful to protect the worksheets of a workbook that only you will use. You can protect individual worksheets in the workbook as there may be different areas in each worksheet that you want to have protected.

Protecting a worksheet is a two-stage process. When you switch on worksheet protection, every cell on that worksheet will be protected – meaning you will not be able to enter or edit data on that sheet. If there are cells on the worksheet that you do want to be able to work with after switching on worksheet protection, you need to unlock them first.

Unlocking Cells

Select the cells on the worksheet that you wish to be able to work with after worksheet protection is switched on.

Choose Cells from the Format menu and click on the Protection tab. Deselect the Locked box.

Click OK.

Repeat this process for each separate range on the worksheet that you wish to unlock.

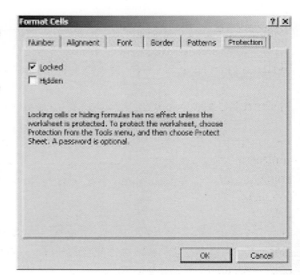

Protecting the Worksheet

Once you have unlocked the ranges on the worksheet that you do want to be able to work with, you can switch on worksheet protection.

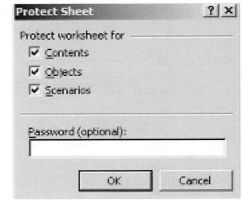

Choose Protection from the Tools menu and then click on Protect Sheet in the sub-menu.

Choose what you want to protect the worksheet for:

- **Contents** – prevents changes to cell contents or items in charts

- **Objects** – prevents deletion, moving, resizing or editing of graphic objects on a worksheet or chart sheet

- **Scenarios** – prevents changes to scenarios set up on a worksheet

Type a password (this is optional). If you do enter a password, you will be prompted to re-enter it. The worksheet cannot be unprotected without the password.

USING BUILT-IN FUNCTIONS TO PERFORM CALCULATIONS

There are a whole range of functions that you can use in Excel to perform mathematical operations. The sum function is the most commonly used function and it has already been assigned to a button (AutoSum) to make it very easy to use. To access other functions, choose Function from the Insert menu, or click on the Paste Function button on the Standard toolbar.

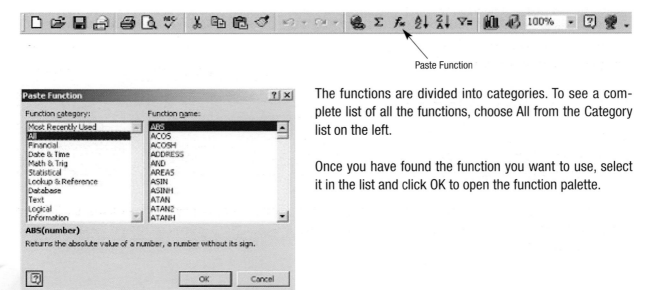

Paste Function

The functions are divided into categories. To see a complete list of all the functions, choose All from the Category list on the left.

Once you have found the function you want to use, select it in the list and click OK to open the function palette.

The Max and Min Functions

If you wish to know the maximum or minimum value in a range of values, you can use the Max or Min function.

Click in the cell on the worksheet that you wish the result to appear in and choose Function from the Insert menu or click on the Paste Function button on the Standard toolbar.

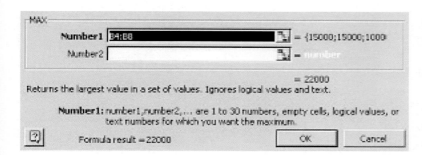

Select the Max or Min function from the list (they are both in the Statistical category) and click OK.

You will now be offered the function palette.

A cell reference or range needs to be entered into the Number1 box. (It may have already guessed what range you wish to calculate.)

If you need to see the worksheet behind the function palette, press the button with the red arrow on. This will temporarily collapse the palette. Select the range on the worksheet and open the function palette again, by pressing the red arrow. Click OK.

You can calculate the maximum or minimum of up to 30 different numbers on the worksheet. Alternatively, you can calculate the maximum or minimum of a number of ranges on the worksheet. Enter each separate range in the Number2, Number3 box and so on.

The Count Function

If you wish to count the number of values in a range, you can use the Count function.

Click in the cell on the worksheet that you wish the result to appear in and choose Function from the Insert menu or click on the Paste Function button on the Standard toolbar.

Select the Count function from the list (in the Statistical category) and click OK.

You will now be offered the function palette.

A cell reference or range needs to be entered into the Value1 box. (It may have already guessed what range you wish to calculate.)

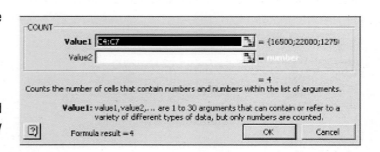

If you need to see the worksheet behind the function palette, press the button with the red arrow on. This will temporarily collapse the palette. Select the range on the worksheet and open the function palette again, by pressing the red arrow. Click OK.

The Round Function

The Round function will round a number or calculation on the worksheet to a specified number of digits.

Click in the cell on the worksheet that you wish the result to appear in and choose Function from the Insert menu or click on the Paste Function button on the Standard toolbar.

Select the Round function from the list (in the Math & Trig category) and click OK.

You will now be offered the function palette.

The number is the cell reference of the number you wish to round. The Num_digits is the number of digits you wish to round to.

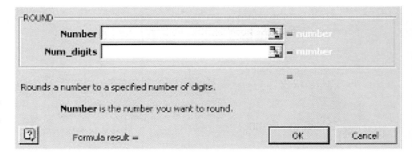

If you need to see the worksheet behind the function palette, press the button with the red arrow on. This will temporarily collapse the palette. Select the cell on the worksheet and open the function palette again, by pressing the red arrow. Type the number of digits you wish to round to and click OK.

The Date Function

Excel stores dates as serial numbers so that it can perform calculations on them. 1 January 1900 is serial number 1. 1 January 1998 would therefore be serial number 35796 because it is 35,795 days after 1 January 1900.

The Date function enables you to turn the date into its corresponding serial number, so that you can carry out calculations on it.

Click in the cell on the worksheet that you wish the result to appear in and choose Function from the Insert menu or click on the Paste Function button on the Standard toolbar.

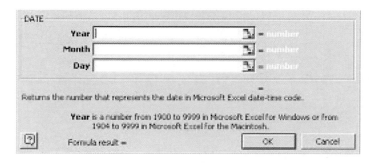

Select the Date function from the list (in the Date & Time category) and click OK.

Year – select the cell on the worksheet that contains the year that you wish to calculate.
Month – specify the number of the month you require, i.e. 1=January, 2=February, etc.
Day – specify the number of the day you require, i.e. 1=1st, 2=2nd, etc.

If you need to see the worksheet behind the function palette, press the button with the red arrow on. This will temporarily collapse the palette. Select the cell on the worksheet and open the function palette again, by pressing the red arrow. Enter the other required information and click OK.

The IF Function

IF functions are used where you want to be able to analyse data and ask Excel to perform an action dependent upon the data. For example, if different bonuses are awarded depending on sales figures, you can ask Excel to perform a test to see whether the sales figures fall into a certain band and then calculate the bonus based on this.

An IF function has three parts: a logical test to perform, what you want Excel to do if the test returns true and what you want Excel to do if the test returns false.

Click in the cell on the worksheet that you wish the result to appear in and choose Function from the Insert menu or click on the Paste Function button on the Standard toolbar.

Select the IF function from the list (in the Logical category) and click OK.

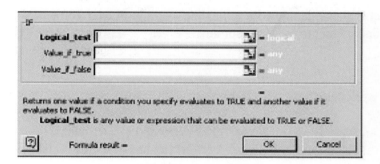

Type the logical test to perform, e.g. B3>C4. (Logical operators include =, <, >, >=, <>).

You can ask Excel to simply return an answer for true or false, or to carry out a mathematical operation. If you want an answer, type the text you want to see in the Value if true box and Value if false box. If you want to perform another calculation based on the test, type the calculations you require in the Value if true box and Value if false box. For example, B3*B5.

Logical Operators

Symbol	Meaning	Example of how used
=	Equal to	A1=B1
>	Greater than	A1>B1
<	Less than	A1<B1
>=	Greater than or equal to	A1>=B1
<=	Less than or equal to	A1<=B1
<>	Not equal to	A1<>B1

TASK

Enter the following data onto a new worksheet

Name	Age	Bowling Average
Joan Simmonds	54	250
Bill Smith	60	300
Harry Ramsden	65	300
Barbara Street	59	270
Harriet Barlow	56	240
Sid Thomas	53	340

A bowling tour is being organised, but only those people who are over 55 may go. Use the IF function to discover who can go on the bowling tour.

The criteria has now changed and only those people with a bowling average of over 250 can go. Use the IF function to discover who can go on the bowling tour now.

TASK

Enter the following data onto a new worksheet

Employee Name	Jan Sales	Feb Sales	Mar Sales	Total Qtr 1 Sales	Bonus Due
Jane Smith	15,000	16,500	18,250	49,750	
Keith Forbes	15,000	22,000	18,500	55,500	
Wendy Turner	10,000	12,750	15,000	37,750	
Dave Sutherland	22,000	27,500	34,250	83,750	

Use the IF function to calculate who gets a bonus. The employees only get a bonus if their Total Qtr 1 Sales are more than 50,000. The bonus is 10% of their total sales. Calculate this in the IF function.

CREATING CHARTS

If you wish to show your data graphically, you can easily create a chart from the worksheet data and then choose to have that chart on a sheet on its own, or on the worksheet with the data. Values from your worksheet data can be displayed as bars, lines, columns, pie slices or other shapes in the chart. The chart you create is automatically linked to the data on the worksheet. Every time the data on the worksheet is changed, the chart will update to reflect the changes.

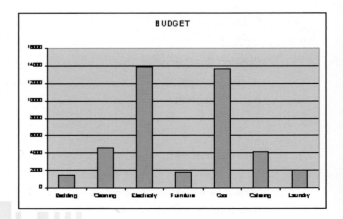

Select the data that you wish to plot onto the chart (include any column or row headings) and choose Chart from the Insert menu or click on the Chart Wizard button on the Standard toolbar.

Chart Wizard

Step 1 of the Chart Wizard allows you to choose a chart type. You can choose from a range of Standard Types including Column, Bar, Line, Pie and Scatter. There are various sub-types for each Chart Type. You can also click on the Custom Types tab and choose a custom chart.

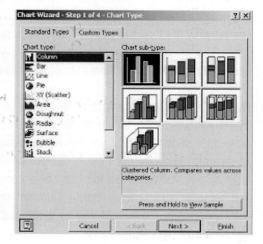

The data you wish to display will often dictate the type of chart that is best. If you really aren't sure, allow the Chart Wizard to choose for you.

You can Press and Hold the button at the bottom of this dialog box to view the chart type you have chosen.

Click Next once you have made your choice. (You can click Back at any time if you change your mind.)

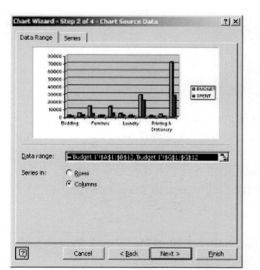

Step 2 of the Chart Wizard provides you with visual feedback of what your data will look like plotted onto the type of chart you have chosen.

You can check that you have selected the right data ranges on the worksheet. (If you discover this is wrong, collapse the wizard by pressing the red arrow button and select the right range on the worksheet.)

You can choose whether you wish the data to be displayed by rows or columns.

The preview area at the top of this step of the wizard allows you to try things out and see what they look like.

Click on the Series tab to check that the correct ranges on the worksheet are providing data for the appropriate part of the chart.

Click Next when you have made your choices. (You can click Back at any time if you change your mind.)

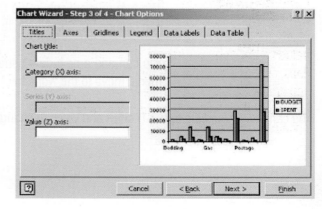

Step 3 of the Wizard enables you to add any titles you may require – Chart and axes titles.

The **Axes** tab enables you to choose what you want the axes to display. You can also switch axes on and off.

The **Gridlines** tab enables you to choose whether you wish to see major and/or minor gridlines. You can also switch gridlines on and off.

The **Legend** tab enables you to switch the legend (key) on or off. You can also choose where you want the legend to appear on the chart.

The **Data Labels** tab enables you to switch data labels on and also choose what you want the data labels to display.

The **Data Table** tab enables you to switch on a data table, which will appear under the chart.

The preview area means you can "try things out" and see what they look like before making your choices.

Click Next to move to the final step of the wizard.

The final step of the wizard enables you to choose where you want the chart to appear. You can put it on a new sheet on its own. (You are given the opportunity to name the new sheet at this time.) Alternatively, you can have the chart as an embedded object on a worksheet. Choose which worksheet from the list. (It will be displayed in a box on the worksheet.)

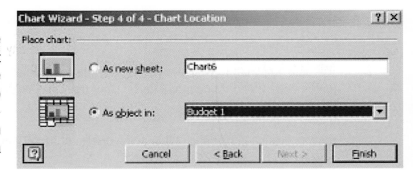

Click Finish to complete the Chart Wizard. Your chart will now be created and inserted in the location you have specified.

Tip

 To quickly create a chart sheet, select the cells on the worksheet and press F11.

THE CHART MENU

When you move to a chart sheet, or select an embedded chart on a worksheet, a Chart menu appears in the menu bar. You can use the Chart menu to make changes to your chart.

The first four options in the Chart menu take you back into a step of the Wizard. You can change the Chart Type, the Source Data, Chart Options and the Location.

You can add a new data series to an existing chart. Choose Add Data from the Chart menu, move to the worksheet and select the new range with the mouse. Click OK.

You can add a trendline to a 2-D chart and you can change the 3-D view of a 3-D chart.

Moving and Sizing an Embedded Chart

To move a chart on the worksheet, point to the edge of the chart area and click and drag it on the worksheet.

To change the size of the chart, click on the chart to select it. Black squares will appear around the 'box' that the chart appears in. Move the mouse over a black box and it will change to a double-headed arrow. Drag this resizing handle to resize the chart.

Deleting an Embedded Chart

To delete an embedded chart, click on the chart to select it and press the Delete key on your keyboard.

Editing an Embedded Chart

Excel creates a default chart. However, you can change any part of that chart: the Y-axis and Y-axis title, the X-axis and X-axis title, the data labels, the chart title, the data markers, the legend, the category names, the tick marks, the plot area, the chart area and the gridlines, etc. Even the colours of the bars, columns or pie slices can be changed.

Double-click on any area of the chart to modify it. You will be taken into the appropriate dialog box to make your changes.

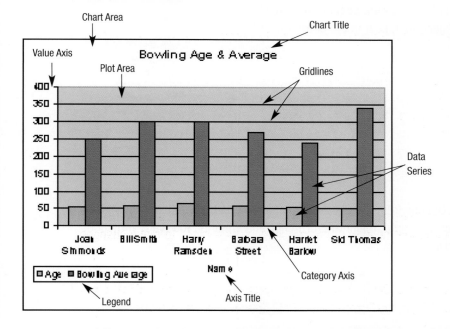

For example, to change the chart title and axes labels, double-click on the one you wish to change. The Format Chart Title or Format Axis Title dialog box will open. This dialog box has three tabs: Patterns, Font and Alignment. Make any changes you require and click OK.

To change the axes scales, point to either axis and double-click. The Format Axis dialog box will open. This dialog box has five tabs: Patterns, Scale, Font, Number and Alignment. Make any changes you require and click OK.

To edit the gridlines, point to one of them and double-click. (If you don't have any gridlines on the chart, use Chart Options in the Chart menu to add them.) The Format Gridlines dialog box will open. This dialog box has two tabs: Patterns and Scale.

To edit the legend (key), point to the legend and double-click. The Format Legend dialog box will open. This dialog box has three tabs: Patterns, Font and Placement.

To change the chart background, point to either the Chart Area or the Plot Area and double-click. The Format Chart Area or Format Plot Area dialog box will open. This Format Chart Area dialog box has three tabs: Patterns, Font and Properties. The Format Plot Area dialog box has one tab: Patterns.

Adding Data Labels

Select the data point or data series that you want to add data labels to and choose Chart Options from the Chart menu. Click on the Data Labels tab and specify what kind of data labels you want. Click OK.

Adding a Chart Title and Axis Titles

Choose Chart Options from the Chart menu and click on the Titles tab. Type which titles you require and click OK.

Adding a Legend

Choose Chart Options from the Chart menu and click on the Legend tab. Check the Show Legend box and choose where you want the legend to appear in the Chart Area. Click OK.

Adding Gridlines

Choose Chart Options from the Chart menu and click on the Gridlines tab. Specify which gridlines you want: major and/or minor and whether you want vertical or horizontal gridlines.

Working with Colours

Remember, your chart will look very colourful on a colour monitor, but if you are going to print to a black and white printer, you need to assign contrasting colours so that it will be easy to understand the legend even in black and white. Purple and dark pink might look lovely together on screen, but will appear very similar when printed in black and white.

Printing Charts

If your chart is on a separate sheet in the workbook, then you can choose to print that sheet. The chart will print A4 landscape and will fill the page.

If your chart is embedded on the worksheet, you have two choices for how you print it:

To print the chart on its own, select the chart prior to printing. The chart will print A4 landscape and will fill the sheet of paper.

To print the worksheet with the chart, click on any cell on the worksheet. By default, worksheets print A4 portrait. You will now see the worksheet data and the chart on the same page. (It is a good idea to use print preview to see how it looks prior to printing).

Tip

When creating a chart on the worksheet, make it the same width as the worksheet data, or 'centre' it under the worksheet data. It will look more effective when presenting it on an A4 piece of paper.

TASK

Enter the following data onto a worksheet:

ITEM	BUDGET	JAN	FEB	MAR	APR	SPENT	BALANCE
Printing	3100	110	29	693	244		
Provisions	72000	2305	8041	7672	9945		
Council Tax	11400	2462	0	0	413		
Sundries	5100	519	159	156	1727		
Telephone	2300	0	0	480	0		
Entertainment	7300	740	315	557	1568		
Vehicles	13000	533	1894	2697	1107		
Totals							

Calculate Spent, Balance and Totals.

Create a column chart on a separate sheet to show a comparison between the Budget figure for each item and the amount spent for each item. Insert a chart title and category and value axis titles. Format the chart text and colours.

Create a pie chart on the worksheet to show the total amount spent for each month. Insert a chart title and add data labels to show the value. Change the colours of the pie wedges and move the January wedge away from the rest of the pie.

USING ABSOLUTE CELL REFERENCES

References are usually 'relative', which means they are relative to where they are at the moment. For example, if you enter a formula that adds the contents of cells A1+B1, you can insert the answer in cell C1. If you then copy this formula into the next row, the formula will change to A2+B2. The reference of the original formula was relative.

There are times when you may need to make references 'absolute'. This means that regardless of where the formula is moved to, it will remain the same, i.e. referring to the original cells. Absolute means the formula does not change depending where it is on the worksheet. An absolute reference is denoted by placing a dollar sign ($) before the column letter and row number.

If you have a figure on the worksheet that you need to refer to for lots of your calculations, you will need to make this cell reference absolute. For example, A1+B1 will change as it is copied down through rows. However, A1+B1 will never change, regardless of where it is copied to on the worksheet.

Tip

Use F4 to enter the dollar signs in cell references.

TASK

Enter the following data onto a worksheet:

    Product   Nett Price   VAT   Total Price

Set up a worksheet listing five products with their nett price.

Type 17.5% in cell H1 on the worksheet. Create the VAT calculation referring to this cell. (You will need to make it an absolute cell reference.) Calculate Total Price.

Change the figure in cell H1 and notice how the VAT and Total Price calculations update.

Save and close the workbook.

LINKING SHEETS

There are two ways to link sheets within a workbook: by writing a formula that refers to another sheet, or by using Paste Link in the Paste Special dialog box.

3-D References

Excel calls the act of referring to a range of other sheets in the workbook, 3-D Referencing. A 3-D reference is a range that spans two or more sheets in a workbook. For example:

=SUM(Sheet2:Sheet6!A2:C5).

This formula shows a sum function on the range of cells A2 through to C5 on Sheets 2 through to 6 in the work-book. To enter a 3-D reference, you can type the reference directly, or select the worksheet tabs that indicate the beginning and ending sheets of the range and then select the cells you wish to reference.

To insert the above formula, click in the cell where you wish the answer to appear. Click on the AutoSum button to start the formula. Click the Sheet 2 tab, hold down Shift and click the Sheet 6 tab. (All the sheets from 2 to 6 are selected. You can now release the Shift key.) Now select the range of cells A2 to C5 on the current sheet. Press Enter on the keyboard to complete the formula and return you to the cell where you started.

How Deleting and Inserting Cells Affects 3-D References

If you insert sheets between the sheets that are included in the 3-D reference, any values in the referenced cell range of the inserted sheets are included in the calculation.

If you delete sheets between the sheets that are included in the 3-D reference, their values are removed from the calculation.

If you move sheets between the sheets that are included in the 3-D reference to a location outside the referenced sheet range, their values are removed from the calculation.

If you move the first sheet or last sheet of the 3-D reference, the calculation adjusts to include the new range of sheets between them.

Creating Links using Paste Special

Select the cells in the workbook that contain the source data and choose Copy from the Edit menu to copy these cells onto the clipboard. Move to the new location and choose Paste Special from the Edit menu (or right-click and choose Paste Special from the shortcut menu). In the Paste Special dialog box, click on the Paste Link button.

The data is copied to the new location and Excel automatically sets up a link between the two sets of data using a formula.

LINKING EXCEL WORKBOOKS

You can link a formula in a workbook to data located in another workbook. This means that any changes made to the source data will also be reflected in the linked formula.

An external reference is a reference to a cell or range on a sheet in another Excel workbook. The dependent workbook contains a link to another workbook and depends on that other workbook for the information. The source workbook is the workbook where the source data referred to in the external reference is located.

Creating a Link by Typing a Formula

Start to create the formula in the normal way, using =. Type the path name (drive and directory) of the workbook you wish to link to, with a backslash between. For example =C:\SALES\ (C: being the drive and Sales being the directory). Type the name of the workbook that contains the source data (enclosed in square brackets). Type the

name of the sheet that contains the source data followed by an exclamation mark. Type the cell reference of the source date.

        =C:\SALES\[Budget2002]Budget1!C3:E4

If you include the disk path or if the workbook or sheet name includes space characters you must enclose the path, filename and sheet name in a pair of single quotation marks. Type the exclamation mark after the closing single quotation mark. If you are not sure when to include single quotation marks, do it anyway. If the reference does not need them, Excel will simply ignore them.

Creating a Link by Selecting Cells

Rather than typing the formula and having to remember all the syntax, you will find it a lot easier to create the formula by selecting cells. Open both workbooks and arrange the windows (Tiled) so that you can see both work-books at the same time. Start creating the formula by typing =. Now use your mouse to navigate to the required sheet and select the cells in the external worksheet.

Creating a Link using Paste Special

Select the cells in the workbook that contain the source data and choose Copy from the Edit menu to copy these cells onto the clipboard. Move to the new location and choose Paste Special from the Edit menu (or right-click and choose Paste Special from the shortcut menu). In the Paste Special dialog box, click on the Paste Link button.

The data is copied to the new location and Excel automatically sets up a link between the two sets of data using a formula.

Saving Linked Workbooks

- Always save the source workbook before saving the dependent workbook linked to it.

- Make sure both the dependent workbook and the source workbook are open before you save the source workbook.

- Save and close the source workbook in the normal way.

- Save and close the dependent workbook.

If you do change the name of a source workbook while the dependent workbook is closed, or if you move linked workbooks to different directories or folders, you must change the links in the dependent workbook to include the new name or full path name of the source workbook. Choose Links from the Edit menu and then choose the Change Source button in the dialog box.

Opening, Updating and Changing Links

Choose Links from the Edit menu. The Links dialog box lists the workbook and sheet name for each external ref-erence used in the active workbook.

You can select a filename from the list and choose Open Source to open that file.

You can select a filename from the list and choose Update Now to update any data. If the Update Now button is dimmed it means that data is current.

You can select a filename from the list and choose Change Source. The Change Source dialog box will appear so that you can locate and open a different workbook.

Removing Links Between Workbooks

In order to remove a link in a formula you must use copy and paste to replace the formula with its current value.

Select the cell containing the linked formula and choose Copy from the Edit menu. Now choose Paste Special from the Edit menu and select Values. Click OK.

IMPORTING AND EXPORTING

Opening Files into Excel

You can easily open a file created in another program into Excel. As long as Excel has the necessary converter, it will open the file in Excel format.

Choose Open from the File menu and locate the file that you wish to open. Select it and click Open.

Importing Text Files

If you have saved a file as a text file (for example, in Word), you can import it into Excel. When you save the file in Word, choose Text Only (*.txt) from the Save as type drop-down list. In Excel choose Get External Data from the Data menu and then click on Import Text File. Navigate to where the text file is stored, select it and click in Import. This launches the Text Import Wizard.

Step 1 of the Wizard allows you to choose the original data type and which row you wish to import the data into on the spreadsheet.

Click Next.

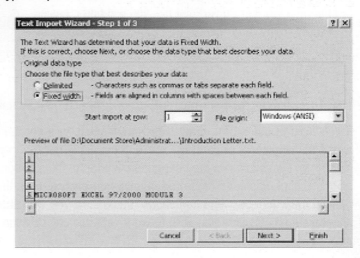

Step 2 of the Wizard allows you to set field widths by putting in break lines.

Click Next.

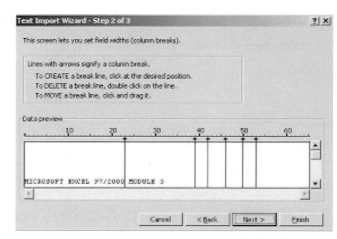

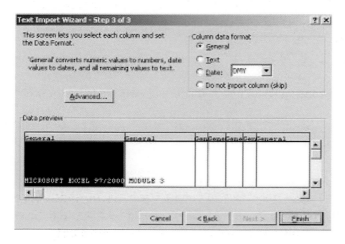

Step 3 of the Wizard allows you to set the data format for each column. Select each column in turn and choose the appropriate data format.

Click Finish.

Exporting from Excel

When you save files in Excel, you have a large range of different file types you can save into, in order that you can open that file in a different application.

Simply choose the appropriate file type in the Save As dialog box.

However, if you simply wish to use an Excel spreadsheet or chart in a Word or PowerPoint file, you will find it easier to simply copy and paste the object into Word or PowerPoint. You can also use Paste Link to set up a link between the two applications.

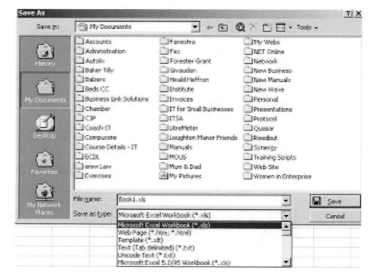

Pasting Information from Excel into other Applications

If you want to use a part of an Excel spreadsheet, or a chart, in a Word document or PowerPoint presentation, select the worksheet or chart in Excel and copy it to the clipboard. Switch into Word or PowerPoint and open the file that you wish to paste the information into. Go to the appropriate location in that file. To paste the spreadsheet or chart, click Paste. To paste the information *and* set up a link between the two applications, choose Paste Special from the Edit menu and choose Paste Link. The worksheet or chart is pasted into Word or PowerPoint as an 'embedded object'. If you wish to work with this object, double-click on it and you will be returned to Excel to make any changes.

If you have used Paste Link, you are free to work with each application separately. If you make changes to the Excel spreadsheet or chart, the next time you open the linked file, you will be prompted to update the links.

Converting a Microsoft Excel List into an Access Database

To be able to convert an Excel list to Access, you must have Access installed on your computer. You also need to install the AccessLinks add-in program (Tools menu, Add-Ins).

Select a cell in the Excel list and choose Convert to MS Access from the Data menu. If you wish to create a new Access database, click New Database. If you wish to add the list to an existing database, click Existing Database and then specify the path to the existing database. Click OK. The Access Import Spreadsheet Wizard and Table Analyzer will guide you through the steps to convert the list to Access.

Once you have converted the Excel list to Access, you can work with the data in Access. Any changes you make in the Access database do not affect the Excel list.

TASK

Create a chart in Excel. Copy and paste link the chart onto a PowerPoint presentation slide. Save and close the presentation. Make changes to the data on the Excel spreadsheet so that the chart updates. Open the PowerPoint presentation and notice the changes take effect on the chart.

TASK

Type the following text into a Word document. Save the document as a text file (*.txt).

Overheads

Expenses	Fourth Quarter	Third Quarter	Change
Payroll	330,485.00	289,800.00	14.04%
Taxes	35,500.00	12,075.00	194.00%
Rent	29,600.00	29,600.00	0.00%
Telephone	26,277.50	17,803.50	47.60%
Total/Change	421,862.50	349,278.50	20.78%

Use the Import Text Wizard in Excel to bring the Word document onto an Excel spreadsheet.

UNIT 024 DATABASES

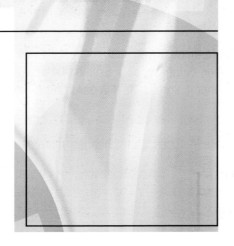

WHAT IS A DATABASE?

If you need to store information about customers, suppliers, products, etc., and want to be able to pull out any of the information stored, in different orders and formats, you need to store the information in a database. A database is similar to a comprehensive list. However, each record in the list can be stored in such a way that individual parts of that record can be extracted without having to pull off the whole record.

Most computerised databases are 'relational'. This means that you create a number of tables containing different areas of information. These tables are then related to each other. This is more efficient than creating one huge table containing all the information that needs to be stored in the database.

DATABASE DESIGN

Designing Databases

Before you use Microsoft Access to actually build the tables, forms, and other objects that will make up your database, it is important to take time to *design* your database. Good database design is the keystone to creating a database that does what you want it to do effectively, accurately, and efficiently.

Determine the purpose of your database

The first step in designing a database is to determine its purpose and how it's to be used. You need to know what information you want from the database. From that, you can determine what subjects you need to store facts about (the tables) and what facts you need to store about each subject (the fields in the tables).

Talk to people who will use the database. Brainstorm about the questions you and they would like the database to answer. Sketch out the reports you'd like it to produce. Gather the forms you currently use to record your data. Examine well-designed databases similar to the one you are designing.

A database consists of four basic features:

Tables   These create the basic framework of the database and are where the data resides. You create fields in your table and can assign properties to those fields, to control what data is allowed to be input and how it appears.

Forms   These are a user-friendly way of inputting data into the database. Rather than the data inputter keying information directly into the table, they would enter the information into a form that was easily navigable. Forms customise the way data contained in tables or queries is viewed and displayed on screen; also used for entering new data and modifying existing data.

Queries   If you wish to extract information from the database, you create a query. This lists the fields you wish to extract information from and also sets conditions that must be met for the information to be extracted. For example, the last name and first name of all people who are aged 21 and over. Because the result of a query is actually a dynamic set of records, called a dynaset, based on your table's current data, data in a query result can be updated.

Reports   Although tables, forms and queries can all be printed, you can produce more professionally displayed output by using reports. You can base a report on a complete table, or on a query you have already created. Reports can be produced on portrait or landscape paper and the text in the report can be formatted to suit your requirements.

TABLES

Before any information can be input into a table, it needs to be designed. Once you have established what tables you will need in your database, you can create a list of the fields that are required for each table.

The database window contains a list of the different objects down the left side: Tables, Queries, Forms, Reports, Pages, Macros and Modules.

The main part of the window displays all Tables, Queries etc when the appropriate object type is selected.

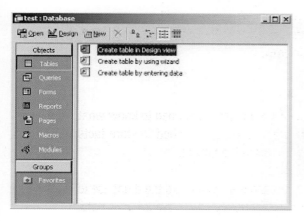

At the top of this list you have options to create a new table (or query, or form, or report). You can create a table by using Design view or by using the wizard. If you choose 'Create table by entering data', Access creates the table for you and simply numbers the columns.

> **Shortcut**
>
> Alt+D   Open the selected table (or a new table in design view)
>
> Alt+N   Opens the New Table dialog box

Creating a Table using the Wizard

If you would like some help to get started with your table, you can use the wizard. Double-click on 'Create table by using wizard' in the list.

Step 1 of the wizard allows you to choose a sample table to base your table on. You can choose from a range of Business tables (business-related subjects) or Personal tables (personal-related subjects).

You are then offered a list of sample fields. Select the field in the Sample Fields list that you wish to have in your table and click on the arrow button (>) to put it into the Fields in my new table list. Repeat this process for each field you wish to include in your new table.

Click on Next.

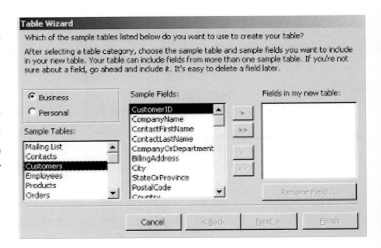

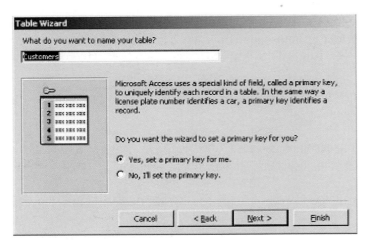

Type a name for your table and specify whether you wish Access to set the primary key for you, or whether you wish to set the primary key yourself.

Click on Next.

The final step of the wizard asks you whether you wish to modify the table design, enter data directly into the table, or enter data into the table using a form that the wizard can create automatically.

Click on Finish once you have made your choice.

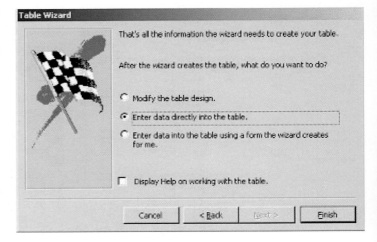

Creating a Table in Design View

Rather than using the wizard, you may prefer to create your table by going into design view and typing the field names in yourself.

Double-click on 'Create table in Design view' in the database window.

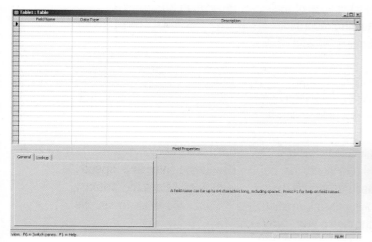

The top part of the Design grid allows you to enter field names and to specify the data type for that field. You can also type a description (optional).

This description will appear in the status bar when the cursor is moved into this field, either in the table or its associated form.

Tip

Table names can be up to 64 characters.
Field names can be up to 64 characters.
Field descriptions can be up to 255 characters.

Data Types

The data type you select for each field can greatly affect the performance and functionality of your database. Several factors should influence your choice of data type for each field in your table.

Field type	Appropriate uses	Storage space
Text	Data containing text, combination of text and numbers, or numbers that do not need to be included in calculations; examples are names, addresses, department codes and phone numbers.	Based on what is actually stored in the field; ranges from 0 to 255 bytes
Memo	Text and numeric strings up to 32,000 (64Kb) long; examples are notes, synopses and descriptions.	Ranges from 0 to 64,000 bytes
Number	Any numeric data (other than currency) on which you are likely to perform calculations. You can include whole numbers or fractional values (using decimals) and negative values can be preceded with a minus sign or placed in brackets; examples are ages, quantities, exam results or payment amount.	1, 2, 4, or 8 bytes, depending on the field size selected
Date/Time	Includes automatic validation of entries (you cannot enter invalid dates or times like, for example, **31/02/94** or **17:30AM**), allows you to perform calculations (for example, subtracting one date field from another gives the number of days between them); examples are date ordered, birth date.	8 bytes

Field type	Appropriate uses	Storage space
Currency	Any numeric data that represents monetary values, includes by default 2 digits after the decimal point and displays the currency symbol as set in the Windows Control Panel; examples are amount due, price.	8 bytes
AutoNumber	Automatically inserted unique sequential values for each record, which can be used as a *Primary Key* because of their uniqueness. If a record is deleted, the remaining records are not renumbered; examples are invoice numbers, project numbers, Customer ID.	4 bytes (16 bytes for replication ID)
Yes/No	Logical fields containing either of two conditions that are mutually exclusive (yes/no, true/false, on/off or a Boolean entry such as −1 for yes and 0 for no); examples are paid, tenured, passed, available.	1 bit
OLE Object	Any objects created in other Windows applications (pictures, graphics, documents, spreadsheets, sound and video) can be *linked* to or *embedded* in an Access database using this data type field. In Datasheet View Access displays only information about the *type* of the OLE object; viewed through a Form, you can see either the actual linked or embedded object itself, or its representation; examples are employee reviews or employee photos.	0 bytes to 1 gigabyte depending on what is stored within the field
Hyperlink	Text or combinations of text and numbers stored as text and used as a hyperlink address. A hyperlink address can have up to three parts: *display text*: the text that appears in a field or control, *address:* the path to a file or page (URL), *sub address*: a location within the file or page. The easiest way to insert a hyperlink address in a field or control is to click Hyperlink on the Insert menu. A hyperlink address may also contain more specific address information (for example, a database object, Word bookmark, or Microsoft Excel cell range that the address points to). When you click a hyperlink, your Web browser or Microsoft Access uses the hyperlink address to go to the specified destination.	
Lookup Wizard	Creates a field that allows you to choose a value from another table or from a list of values by using a list box or combo box. Clicking this option starts the Lookup Wizard, which creates a Lookup field. After you complete the wizard, Microsoft Access sets the data type and storage space based on the values selected in the wizard.	

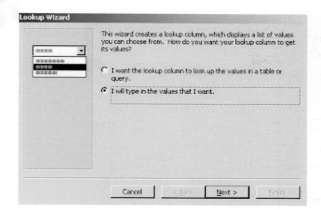

Using the Lookup Wizard

Choose whether you want the wizard to look up values in another table or query in the database, or whether you will type the list of values you want.

Click on Next.

The next step of the wizard will vary according to what you choose in the first step. If you chose 'I will type in the values that I want', then the second part of the wizard enables you to type the values you want in the list in a column.

Click on Next.

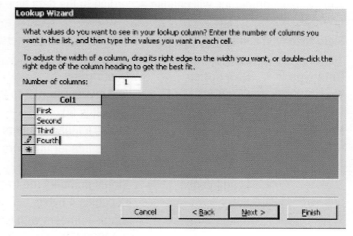

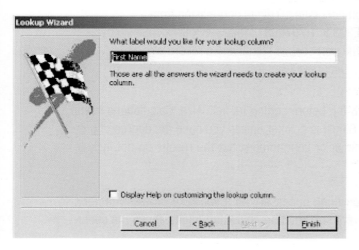

The final step of the wizard asks you what label you want for your lookup column. This label will usually be the same as the field name, e.g. First Name.

Click on Finish.

Field Properties

As well as specifying field names and data types, you must also set the Properties for each field, i.e. how much can be typed into the field (field size), the format of the field and whether you wish to set validation rules, etc. The Field Properties area is at the bottom of the table design grid.

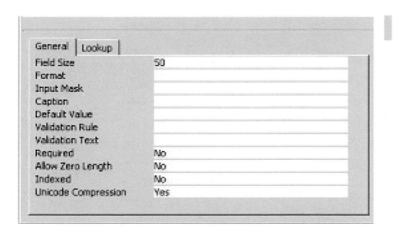

Field Properties box showing the properties for a text field

Shortcut

Use F6 to switch between the top and bottom areas of the table design grid.

The available properties will change according to the data type of the field.

Field Size you can specify the maximum number of characters/digits that will be allowed in the field.

Data type	Size option	Description
Text	0 – 255	Any number from 0 to 255 can be specified for the length of the field. The default is 50
Number	Byte	Stores integer numbers (no fractions) from 0 to 255. Occupies 1 byte
	Integer	Stores integer numbers (no fractions) from –32,768 to 32,767. Occupies 2 bytes
	Long Integer	Stores numbers (no fractions) from –2,147,483,648 to 2,147,483,647. Occupies 4 bytes
	Single	Stores numbers with 6 digits of precision from -3.402823E38 to 3.402823E38. Occupies 6 bytes
	Double	The default. Stores numbers with 10 digits of precision from –1.79769313486232E308 to 1.79769313486232E308. Occupies 8 bytes.
	Replication ID	A unique number for the purposes of identifying a record when a database is replicated. Occupies 16 bytes

You need to think about what you want to use a number field for, before setting its field size. Calculations using Double will be slower because of the precision of the results. Single is quicker unless you need the degree of precision that Double offers. Calculations are much faster on Integer or Long Integer, but the results do not include any decimals.

You should adjust the field size to as small a number as you think necessary as it will take up less memory. However, remember not to make it too small as this will prevent you entering characters/digits above the specified number.

Format the format field will offer different choices, depending what type of field you are working on.

For a text field you can create custom settings by using the following symbols in the format field:

Format	Explanation	Example
@	Text character (character or space) required	
&	Text character not required	
>	Forces all characters to be upper case	smith displays as SMITH
<	Forces all characters to be lower case	Smith or SMITH displays as smith
@>	First character must be a text character or a space and the entire field will display in upper case	smith displays as SMITH *jones would be disallowed as the asterisk is not a text character sMITH displays as SMITH 293a displays as 293A
@;;"N/A"	Text entries must begin with a text character, zero length entries display blank. N/A is displayed if the field is left completely empty	a skipped entry would display N/A
@@/@-@	If four characters are entered, the other two literals are automatically placed in the field	12GX displays as 12/G-X

For a number or currency field, there is a range of predefined number formats you can choose from:

Format	Explanation	Example
General Number	The default. The number is displayed as entered	28765.386 displays as 28765.386
Currency	Follows the pre-set Windows default: inserts a currency symbol, a thousands separator and a decimal point and rounds the number to two decimal places	28765.386 displays as £28,765.39
Fixed	Fixed number of digits with no currency symbols or comma separators (default is two decimal places)	28765.386 displays as 28765.39
Standard	Fixed number of digits with no currency symbols but *with* comma separators (default is two decimal places)	28765.386 displays as 28,765.39
Percent	Multiplies the value by 100 and appends the % symbol. (Default is 2 decimal places)	0.5672 displays as 56.72%
Scientific	Forces exponential scientific notation with one digit displayed to the left of the decimal point	28765.386 displays as 2.88E+04

TIP

Decimal precision can be governed using the Decimal Places property.

For a Date/Time field, there is a range of predefined date/time formats you can choose from:

Format	Explanation	Example
General Date	The default. If the value is date only, no time is displayed; if the value is time only, no date is displayed	6/10/94 9:30:00 AM 6/10/94 9:30:00 AM
Long Date	Same as the Long Date setting in the International section of the Windows Control Panel	Thursday, October 6, 1994
Medium Date		06-Oct-94
Short Date	Same as the Short Date setting in the International section of the Windows Control Panel.	06/10/94

> **TIP**
>
> The Short Date setting assumes that dates between 1/1/00 and 12/31/29 are 21st century dates (that is, the years are between 2000 and 2029). Dates between 1/1/30 and 12/31/99 are assumed to be 20th century dates (that is, the years are between 1930 and 1999).

Long Time	Same as the Long Time setting in the International section of the Windows Control Panel	09:30:00 AM
Medium Time		09:30 AM
Short Time	Same as the Short Time setting in the International section of the Windows Control Panel	9:30 ('Military Time')

For a Yes/No field, you can choose from three predefined formats:

Yes/No
True/False
On/Off

Input Mask sets controls as to how data elements entered in Text and Number fields appear and restricts entries to exact, user-defined formats, by employing various combinations of generic placeholders and literal characters (shown below) to arrive at specific display formats.

The following table shows a list of the placeholders and literal characters with a description of what they mean when used in the input mask property field:

0	Digit (0 to 9, entry required, plus and minus signs not allowed)
9	Digit or space (entry not required, plus and minus signs not allowed)
#	Digit or space (entry not required, plus and minus signs allowed)
L	Letter (A to Z, entry required)
?	Letter (A to Z, entry optional)
A	Letter or digit (entry required)
a	Letter or digit (entry optional)
&	Any character or a space (entry required)
C	Any character or a space (entry optional)
<	Causes all characters to be converted to lowercase

>	Causes all characters to be converted to uppercase
!	Causes the input mask to display from right to left, rather than from left to right. You can include the exclamation point anywhere in the input mask
\	Causes the character that follows to be displayed as its literal character (for example, \A is displayed as just A)

If you need to create a commonly-used input mask, such as a telephone number, driving license, post code or social security number, it is probably easiest to use the Input Mask Wizard (this works only with Text and Date/Time fields). Select the Input Mask you require from a pre-defined list and answer the remaining questions regarding how you wish the data to be stored.

Caption overrides the field name. If you don't enter any value in the Caption property, Access uses the name of the field as a label. Captions are typically used to provide more thorough explanations of fields to users in database applications and can include up to 255 characters.

Default Value Specifies a default value for a field, which will be automatically placed in that field when a new record is added. For example, in a database of addresses you could specify *London* as the default value for the *City* field; this will appear automatically whenever a new record is added. You can leave this value unchanged or enter the name of another city. Default values can be set for all field types except OLE Object and AutoNumber fields. In Yes/No fields Access sets automatically the default value to No; you can change this to Yes if most of your records are likely to have a Yes value stored in this field.

Validation Rule defines an expression that is evaluated when existing data in the field is changed or new data is added. The new data is compared to the Validation Rule and if it conforms, Access allows you to include it in the field, but if for some reason it breaks the Validation Rule and does not satisfy the specified conditions a standard Access message is displayed.

Validation Text if you set a validation rule, you should use this property to set the message that you would like to appear if the validation rule is broken. Both the Validation Rule and the Validation Text help to ensure that the data entered is valid and maintains the integrity of your tables.

Required this field property simply specifies whether entry is required in a field. It can be set to Yes or No.

Allow Zero Length determines if a zero-length data entry is considered valid by Access, with Yes and No options and the latter as the default. By setting this property to Yes you can differentiate between unknown values (null value) and non-existent values (zero length values). During the data entry process zero-length settings are entered in fields by typing a set of double quotation marks (""). For example, you can enter two double quotation marks "" in a Mobile Phone Number field, to indicate that a contact does not have a mobile phone number, or leave it blank to indicate that a contact may have a mobile phone number but it is unknown.

Indexed you can use this property to set an index on the field. Indexing speeds up queries run on the field, as well as sorting and grouping. For example, if you have a Last Name field that you will probably be using a lot in queries, you can set an index on the field to speed up searching for a specific name. It can be set to No, Yes (No Duplicates) or Yes (Duplicates OK).

Once you have created all your field names, specified the appropriate data type and set any field properties, you can close the table. You will be prompted to save the table. Give the table an appropriate name.

Tip

If you wish to switch between design view (the view for designing your table) and datasheet view (the view for inputting data into the table), you can press the first button on the toolbar.

Modifying Table Design

Inserting and Deleting Fields In the table design grid, insert a row where you want the new field to appear and type your name field name. Set its data type and properties.

New rows are always inserted above the row you are currently sitting in. To insert a row, click in the row below where you wish to insert the row and choose Rows from the Insert menu.

To delete a field, you can simply delete the field name and type a new field. (Remember to amend the data type and properties if necessary).

Alternatively, if there is to be no replacement field, you can delete the whole row from the table design grid. Select the row by clicking on the grey tile to the left of the row and press Delete on the keyboard.

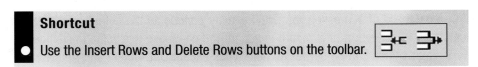

Modifying Data Types It is a good idea to create a backup of your database before changing data types (in case this results in data loss).

In the table design grid, click in the field you wish to change the data type of and choose the new data type from the drop-down list.

If the change in data type will result in a loss of data in that field, Access will display the following message:

Click on Yes or No depending whether you wish to proceed with changing the data type or not.

Modifying Properties To change field properties, click in the field in the top part of the design grid and then switch to the field properties area of the design grid (bottom).

If changing a field property is going to impact data that you have already entered into the database, you will receive the following message when you try to save the table:

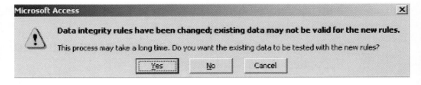

If you do want the fields in the table to be tested with the new rules, click on Yes. Access will go through the table, testing the new field property against the existing data. Any existing data that doesn't comply with the new rule will be deleted. You will receive the following message:

Click on Yes or No depending whether you wish to proceed with changing the field property or not.

Removing the Primary Key Sometimes, it may be necessary to remove the primary key temporarily to enable you to work with duplicate records. Once you have removed (or changed) the duplicate records, you can apply the primary key again.

Select the row that contains the primary key icon by clicking on the grey tile to the left of the row. Click the primary key button on the toolbar.

Copying a Table Structure If you have already created one table in your database and now wish to use the same structure for another table or database, you can simply copy the rows from the design grid and paste them into a new design grid. (This will copy the field names, data types and field properties).

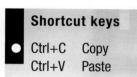

Shortcut keys

Ctrl+C   Copy
Ctrl+V   Paste

Once you have copied the structure, you can then modify it to suit the new table. This is often a lot quicker than starting a new table completely from scratch.

Select the rows in the table design grid of the existing table. Choose Copy from the Edit menu or click on the Copy button.

Create a new table in design view. Choose Paste from the Edit menu or click on the Paste button.

Saving Table Structures Every time you make a change to the table design, you will be prompted to save the table when you close the table or switch into datasheet view.

TASK

Create a new database and name it Vaccination Records.

Design a table to include the following field names:

> **Child's First Name**
> **Child's Last Name**
> **Parent's First Name**
> **Parent's Last Name**
> **Date of Birth**
> **Date of Appointment**
> **Time of Appointment**
> **Location**
> **Was appointment attended?**

Assign appropriate data types to the fields and set any necessary field properties.

WORKING WITH THE DATASHEET

Part of the editing process is finding the data you need to edit. Choose Edit, Find or click on the Find button on the toolbar to display the Find and Replace dialog box.

Here you can specify any text you wish to find and your search can be further refined by the following options:

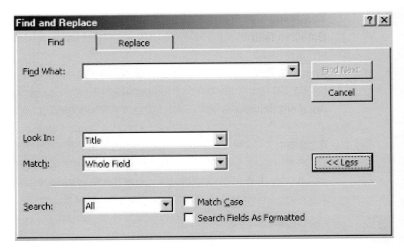

Find What	Here you enter the string of text you wish Access to find. You can use wild-card characters to make the search more general: entering Wil* will find all occurrences of William, Wilkins, Williams, Williamson, Willis, etc.
Match	Clicking on the drop-down arrow displays a list of all possible search locations, with the following options: Any Part of Field – searches for any occurrence of the text string: searching for col will find Coleman, Malcolm and protocol; Whole Field – recognises a match only if the searched-for string matches the entire contents of the field; and Start of the Field – searches for the text string at the beginning of the field only (e.g., searching for col will find Coleman but not Malcolm or protocol).
Look In	Selecting this option will cause the search to be conducted only in the current field. Deselecting it will conduct the search in the entire datasheet.
Match Case	Select this option only if you wish Access to search for the text string exactly as you typed it in the Find What section. For example, searching for *Road* will find all occurrences of *Road* but not *ROAD* or *road*.
Search Fields As Formatted	Select this option if you wish to find data based on its display format. For example, although dates in a database are stored as date/time values, they may be displayed in a particular format, such as *19 Jan 45*. To search for records in September of the year 1963, you could turn on this option and specify *Sep 63.

Access also enables you to search for specific text strings and replace them with other strings. The strings can include a phrase, a word or part of a word and as with the Find command, you can include wildcard characters to make the search more general. Clicking on the Find Next button finds the first and any subsequent occurrences of the searched-for text. Clicking on the Replace button replaces the found text with the text in the Replace With box, clicking again on the Find Next button finds the next occurrence of the search text without replacing the previously found occurrence and clicking on the Replace All button replaces all the occurrences of the searched for text without confirmation.

Selecting Records in a Table

The following table details how to select different parts of your table. It shows the mouse technique and the keyboard shortcut:

To select:	Mouse	Keyboard
Data in a field	Drag across the data	Hold down Shift and use the arrow keys to indicate the direction you wish to select
An entire field	Click on the left edge of the field – ✚	Move the cursor into the field and press F2
Adjacent fields	Click on the left edge of the field and drag across the fields	Press F2, hold down Shift and use the arrow keys to indicate the direction you wish to select
A column	Move to the top of the column. Click when the black arrow appears	Press Ctrl+Spacebar to select the current column
Adjacent columns	Click and drag when the black arrow appears	Press Ctrl+Spacebar, hold down Shift and use the arrow keys to indicate the direction you wish to select
A record	Move to the left of the record. Click when the black arrow appears.	Press Shift+Spacebar to select the current record.
Multiple records	Click and drag when the black arrow appears	Press Shift+Spacebar, hold down Shift and use the arrow keys to indicate the direction you wish to select

Deleting Records in a Table

Select the record that you wish to delete and then choose Delete Record from the Edit menu or press the Delete Record button on the toolbar.

Sorting Records in a Table

Access sorts data contained in different types of fields in different ways:

Text fields – can be sorted alphabetically in *Ascending Order* (from A to Z) or in *Descending Order* (from Z to A).
Number fields – can be sorted numerically in *Ascending Order* (from lowest to highest) or in *Descending Order* (from highest to lowest).
Date/Time fields can be sorted chronologically in *Ascending Order* (from earliest to latest) or in *Descending Order* (from latest to earliest).

To conduct a sort based on a single field, place the insertion point anywhere in the field you wish to use as the basis for your sort (you can also select the field by clicking with your mouse pointer over the field selector) and, depending on the sort direction you wish to effect, choose Records, Sort/Ascending or Records, Sort/Descending. Alternatively click on the Sort Ascending or Sort Descending buttons on the toolbar.

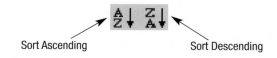

Sort Ascending   Sort Descending

Sorted data is not saved. When you close the table, the records are returned to their original order unless you press Save.

Extracting Data from an Existing Table and Appending it to Another Table/Database

If you are updating an old version of a database, it is useful to copy the structure and data of the old database into a new database, so that you can save the old database in case you need to refer to it again. You are then free to update and amend the new database to suit the way you wish to work in the future.

If you wish to copy data from an existing table and put it into another table or database, it is as simple as copying and pasting.

Select the records in the existing table that you wish to copy. Choose Edit, Copy, or press the Copy button on the toolbar, or press Ctrl+C.

Open the other table in datasheet view. Select the rows and then choose Edit, Paste, or press the Paste button on the toolbar, or press Ctrl+V.

Shortcut keys for working in datasheet view	
Ctrl+;	Insert the current date
Ctrl+:	Insert the current time
Ctrl+'	Insert the value from the previous record
Ctrl++	Add a new record
Ctrl+-	Delete the current record
Shift+Enter	Save changes to the current record
Ctrl+Enter	Insert a new line in the current field

TASK

Open the table and input the following records:

Child's Name	**James Marsden**
Parent's Name	**John Higgins**
Date of Birth	**01/01/02**
Date of Appointment	**15/04/02**
Time of Appointment	**2.00 pm**
Location	**Heart Health Centre**

Child's Name	**James Butler**
Parent's Name	**Anne Butler**
Date of Birth	**05/02/02**
Date of Appointment	**15/04/02**
Time of Appointment	**2.15 pm**
Location	**Heart Health Centre**

Find and Replace the word Heart with Diamond.

Practice selecting different fields, rows and columns in the datasheet.

Sort the records in the table in Descending order.

FORMS

Database tables are the most important elements of a database, as this is where the information resides.

However, it is not always easy to enter information directly into a table. If you are designing a database for some-one to input data into, it is easier for the user to input information through a form. It is easier to navigate around a

form and you can make the controls on the form the appropriate size to accommodate what will be input into them. Forms also enable you to use colours and borders, which make it more professional.

A form is made up of two elements – labels and controls. The label is what the user would see on the form, prompting them to enter the appropriate data. The control will be a blank box, which is where the user enters the data.

In the database window, click on the Forms button in the Objects list on the left.

Click on New

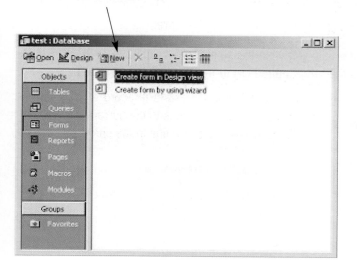

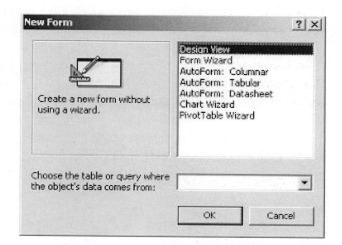

Creating a Form in Design View

Choose Design View from the list in the New Form dialog box. Choose the table or query that the form will be based on from the drop-down list. Click on OK.

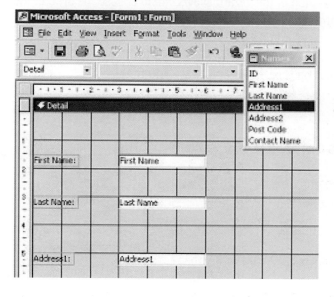

You will be taken into the form design grid. The field list will appear. Drag the fields from the list and drop them onto the design grid.

Two elements will appear – the label and the control.

Creating a Form using the Wizard

Choose Form Wizard from the list in the New Form dialog box. Choose the table or query that the form will be based on from the drop-down list. Click on OK. This will launch the wizard.

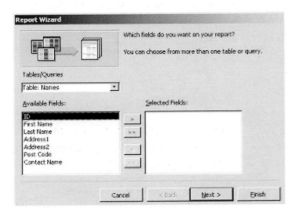

The first step of the wizard asks you to select which fields from the table you wish to put onto the form. (It is not always necessary for the user to see every field in the table. For example, if the ID field is simply set to AutoNumber and this number doesn't need to be known, you do not need to include this field on your form.)

Click on the field you wish to use in the Available Fields list and press the arrow button (>) to move it into the Selected Fields list.

Click on Next.

The next step of the wizard enables you to choose the layout you would like for your form. Choose the different layouts to see a preview of what that layout looks like.

Click on Next.

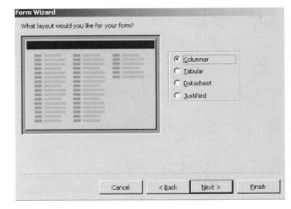

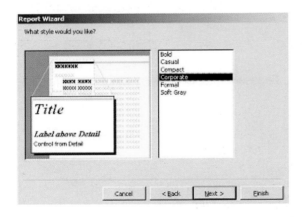

This step of the wizard allows you to choose the style of the form (background look). Click on a style in the list to see a preview of that style.

Click on Next.

The last step of the wizard allows you to give your form a name.

You can choose to open the form so that you can start entering data, or you can go into the form design grid, to make further modifications to the design.

Click on Finish.

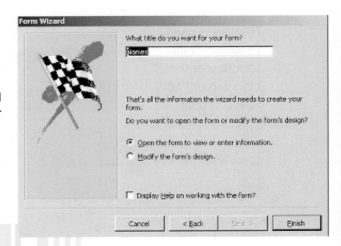

Working with Form Design

The form design grid allows you to resize the form itself, to move the labels and controls on the form, to resize the labels and controls and to add formatting. The grid itself enables you to line up objects in a uniform manner.

To resize the form horizontally – point to the right edge of the grey area of the form. The mouse pointer changes to a resizing handle. Drag to the right to enlarge the form area. To resize the form vertically – point to the bottom of the grey area of the form. The mouse pointer changes to a resizing handle. Drag down to enlarge the form area.

To move the label and control together – point to the label or control. A black hand appears. Click and drag to move the label and control.

To move the label or control separately – click on the object you wish to move. Selection 'squares' appear around the object. Point to the larger square at the top left of the object. The mouse pointer changes to a pointing finger. Click and drag to draw the object. (Note that the matching label or control does not move with it.)

To resize a label or control – click on the label or control to select it. Move to one of the corner 'handles' (squares). The mouse pointer changes to a resizing handle (double-headed black arrow). Drag this arrow to resize the label or control.

To format a label or control – click on the label or control to select it. Use the Formatting toolbar to make changes to the selected object.

Object – an alternative way to navigate around your form is to choose the object name from the drop-down list on the Formatting toolbar.

Font – you can choose from a list of available fonts.

Font Size – you can choose from a list of available font sizes.

Bold – press this button to embolden the text in the selected label or control.

Italic – press this button to italicise the text in the selected label or control.

Underline – press this button to underline the text in the selected label or control.

Align Left – press this button to align the text in the label or control to the left.

Centre – press this button to centre the text in the label or control.

Align Right – press this button to align the text in the label or control to the right.

Fill/Back Colour – use this drop-down palette to fill the selected object with a colour.

Font/Fore Colour – use this drop-down palette to change the colour of the text.

Line/Border Colour – use this drop-down palette to change the colour of the lines around objects.

Line/Border Width – use this drop-down palette to change the width of the lines around objects.

Special Effect – use this drop-down palette to add a 'special effect' to the selected label or control.

Alternatively, you can right-click on an object on the form design grid and choose Properties from the shortcut menu. Changing an object's properties will change the way it looks and behaves.

To select multiple objects, hold down Shift as you click on each object in turn. Alternatively, you can drag a selection area around the objects that you wish to select. (The objects must be completely within the selection area you drag in order to be selected).

Saving the Form

Every time you make a change to the form design, you will be prompted to save the form when you close the form or switch to form view.

> **TASK**
>
> **Design a form based on the database you have created.**
>
> **Move the labels and controls on the form.**
>
> **Format the labels and controls on the form.**
>
> **Save the Form as Vaccination Details.**

Inputting Data into a Form

Data is entered into each control on the form. (Remember, the form is based on a table, so the data type and properties set in the table still apply.)

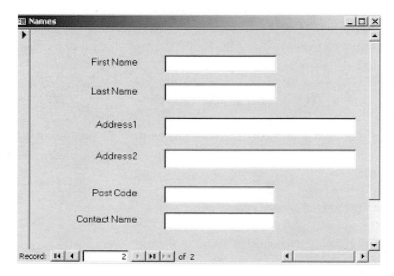

You can use Tab or Return to navigate through each field.

When you press Return on the last field, you are taken onto a new record.

To navigate through the records of the form, you can use the Record Navigator at the foot of the form.

 First record in the table.

◀ Previous record in the table.

▶ Next record in the table.

▶❙ Last record in the table.

▶＊ New record in the table.

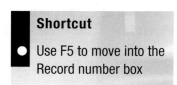

Shortcut

Use F5 to move into the Record number box

98

If you know the record number that you wish to move to, you can click in the number area itself and type the record number and press Enter.

N.B. Records are automatically saved as soon as you move to the next record. You will not be prompted to save a form when you close it unless you have changed the form design.

Editing Data in a Form

If you wish to amend a record, use the record navigator to navigate to the record you wish to amend. Click in the control that you wish to change, delete the existing entry and type the new entry. (Or use backspace and/or delete key to amend the entry).

The record is amended as soon as you move onto a new record.

Printing Forms

Print   Print Preview

If you wish to print a form for every record in the database, press the Print button on the Standard toolbar. (You may wish to use Print Preview first).

If you wish to specify which records of the database you want to print the form of, select the records first using the Record Selector. (This is the bar down the left side of the form in form view).

Choose Print from the File menu and choose Selected Records under the Print Range.

Click on OK.

TASK

Open the form and input the following records:

Child's Name	Kate Grant
Parent's Name	Mary Grant
Date of Birth	06/12/01
Date of Appointment	16/05/02
Time of Appointment	2.00 pm
Location	Willow Medical Centre
Child's Name	Lee Smith
Parent's Name	Chris Smith
Date of Birth	21/09/01
Date of Appointment	16/05/02
Time of Appointment	2.30 pm
Location	Willow Medical Centre

Print a form for each record in the database.

SEARCHING FOR RECORDS

You can search for records based on information in a field you specify. You can use Find or Find and Replace in datasheet view or form view.

Click in the field you wish to use as your search criteria and click on the Find button on the toolbar.

Type what you want to find in that field and click on Find Next.

Use Find Next to move through the records that match your search criteria.

Using Wildcards when Searching

There are various 'wildcards' you can use when searching. Using wildcards enables you to search for field contents that partially match your search criteria.

Below is a table of wildcards you can use:

Character	What it does	Example
*	Matches any number of characters	*ml** in a town field would find Milton Keynes, Middlesborough, Mimms, etc.
?	Matches any single alpha character	*f?ll* finds fall, fell and fill
[ ]	Matches any single character within the brackets	*f[ae]ll* finds fall and fell but not fill
!	Matches any character not in the brackets	*f[!ae]ll* finds fill and full but not fell or fall
#	Matches any single numeric character	*2#3* finds 203, 213, 223

FILTERING RECORDS

If you wish to view a subset of records in your database (that match a specific criteria), you can filter the records in the table or form.

Filter by Selection

Click in the field in the table that shows the information you wish to filter the rest of the records by. For example, if you only want to see records that have Smith as the last name, click in the last name field of a record that contains Smith.

Click on the Filter by Selection button.

The records are filtered according to this selection. At the bottom of the table the record navigator indicates that you are viewing a set of filtered records.

Record: |◀ ◀ | 1 | ▶ ▶| ▶* | of 2 (Filtered)

When a filter has taken place, the Filter button will be in "on" mode. To remove the filter and return the table to its unfiltered state, release the Filter button. ▽ This button toggles between 'Apply Filter' and 'Remove Filter'.

Filter by Form

If you wish to be able to filter using more than one criterion, you can use Filter by Form.

Press the Filter by Form button on the toolbar. You will be offered a blank table.

Use the drop-down list in the field to choose what criteria you wish the records to be filtered against. (You can have more than one criterion.) Click on Apply Filter. You are returned to the table screen, with the filter applied.

To remove the filter, click on the Remove Filter button.

N.B. These filter buttons can be used in exactly the same way to filter records in form view.

> **TASK**
>
> **Find all records in the database where the Last Name begins with G.**
>
> **Filter the records so that you are just viewing the records for Diamond Health Centre. Remove the filter.**
>
> **Filter the records so that you are just viewing the records for Willow Medical Centre for appointments on 16 May 2002.**

QUERYING DATA IN THE DATABASE

Filtering enables you to view records in a database that match certain criteria. You can print your filtered list.

However, if you wish to create a subset of records based on a certain criteria, or you wish to extract records from the database to use in a report, you need to create a query.

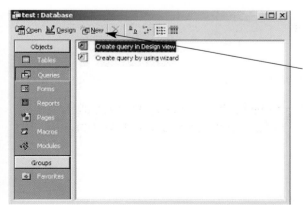

In the database window, click on the Queries button in the Objects list on the left.

Click on New

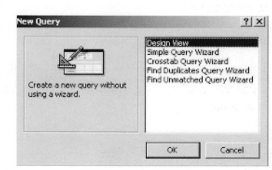

Creating a Query in Design View

Choose Design View from the list in the New Query dialog box. Click on OK.

Add the tables that you wish to extract data from to your query design grid. Click on the table name and click on Add.

Do this for each table you wish to add.

You can close this dialog box once you have added the tables.

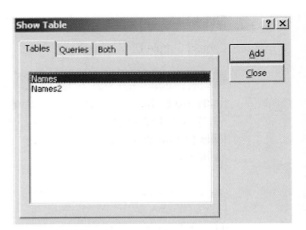

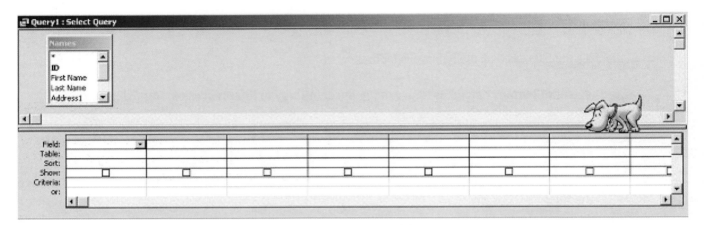

The list of field names from the tables you have added appear in the top part of the query design grid. (This list can be resized by dragging the resizing handle on the right border.)

Design your query by placing the appropriate fields (i.e. the fields you want in your query) into the bottom part of the query design grid. Point to the field in the list at the top and double-click. This will put it into the first column in the grid at the bottom. (Alternatively, you can click and drag the field name from the list at the top onto the grid at the bottom.)

You can sort by any field in the query. In the Sort row for that field, choose Ascending or Descending from the drop-down list.

To run the query, press the Run button on the toolbar.

To switch between datasheet view and design view, use the first button on the toolbar, which changes according to which view you are currently in.

Creating a Query using the Wizard

Choose Simple Query Wizard from the list in the New Query dialog box. Click on OK. This will launch the wizard.

The first step of the wizard asks you to select which fields from the table you wish to include in your query. You can choose fields from more than one table by choosing the table from the drop-down list at the top.

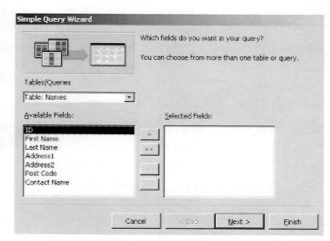

Click on the field you wish to use in the Available Fields list and press the arrow button (>) to move it into the Selected Fields list.

Click on Next.

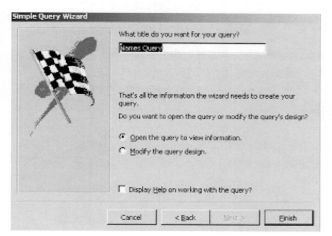

The last step of the wizard allows you to give your query a name.

You can choose to open the query so that you can view the extracted information, or you can go into the query design grid to make further modifications to the design.

Click on Finish.

Setting Criteria in Queries

You can set criteria for one or more fields in your query design grid. For example, to extract only records where the Last Name field is Smith, type the word Smith in the Criteria row of that field in the query design grid. (You will notice that Access will add words and symbols to help it match your criteria. For example, if you type Smith in the name field, it will add the word 'Like'.)

And You can set more than one criterion for extracting data (known as multiple criteria). For example, to extract only records where the Last Name field is Smith *and* the town is Manchester, type these criteria into the appropriate fields on the query design grid. Criteria that is on the same row acts as "and" criteria. This means that the record must match *both* criteria to be extracted.

If To extract only records that have the Last Name of Smith *or* the town of Manchester, type the first criterion in the first line of criteria in the design grid and the next criterion in the next row down. Criteria that are on different rows in the design grid acts as 'or' criteria. This means that the records must match *either* criterion to be extracted.

Not You can also use an expression 'Not'. If you type Not Smith in the Last Name field, any records that have Smith in the Last Name field will *not* be extracted.

Null If you wish to find records that don't contain any value in the field, you can type 'Is Null' in the criteria line.

Current Date If you wish to find fields that have the current date in, type Date() in the appropriate field in the query design grid.

Setting One Condition

In the query design grid, choose the fields in the table list at the top that you wish to include in your query. (Double-click on these fields to put them into the bottom part of the design grid.) Click in the Criteria line of the field you wish to set the condition on. Type your condition.

If your condition is in a text field, type the word you wish it to find. If you wish it to match only part of the field contents, use the wildcard. For example, L* will find all fields containing L+anything. If you wish to find fields from C onwards to the end of the alphabet, type >C*.

If your condition is in a date field, type the date you wish it to find. The date must be typed in the same format as it appears in the database and must have a hash (#) at either end of it. For example, #1/6/01#. If you wish to find a date range for a field, you need to type both dates using the hash key (#). For example, Between #1/1/00# and #30/6/02# will find all records from 1 January 2000 until 30 June 2002.

If your condition is in a number field, type the number you wish it to find. If you wish it to find numbers greater than or less than a certain number, use the > or < operators. (You can use >= and <= if you also wish to include the number you specify in the search.)

Setting Multiple Conditions using And

In the query design grid, choose the fields in the table list at the top that you wish to include in your query. (Double-click on these fields to put them into the bottom part of the design grid.) Click in the Criteria line of the first field you wish to set a condition on. Type your condition. Click in the Criteria line of the second field you wish to set a condition on. (Make sure you are on the same line as the first condition.) Type your condition. Continue in this way, setting criteria for each field. If all the criteria are on the same line, they will be treated as 'and' criteria – the record must match *all* of the criteria to be extracted.

Setting Multiple Conditions using Or

In the query design grid, choose the fields in the table list at the top that you wish to include in your query. (Double-click on these fields to put them into the bottom part of the design grid.) Click in the Criteria line of the first field you wish to set a condition on. Type your condition. Click in the Criteria line of the second field you wish to set a condition on. (Make sure you are on the next line down from the first condition). Type your condition. Continue in this way, setting criteria for each field. If all the criteria are on subsequent lines, they will be treated as 'or' criteria – the record must match *any* of the criteria to be extracted.

N.B. You can mix 'and' and 'or' criteria by placing the criteria on appropriate lines in the design grid.

Using =, >, <, <=, >= and <> to set Criteria for Ranges of Data

You can use logical operators for text and numbers. For example, >D* will return all records beginning with D through to the end of the alphabet. <=500 will return all records less than or equal to 500.

Using Wildcards when setting Criteria

You can use the same wildcards as you use for searching when setting criteria for fields. For example, L* in the Town field, will find all towns that start with L.

TASK

Create a query to show Child's First Name, Last Name, Date of Birth and Location for all records.

Create a query to show Parent's First Name, Last Name and the Date of Appointment for all records.

Create a query to show only those children attending Willow Medical Centre. Save the query.

Create a query to show only those children born between December 2001 and January 2002. Save the query.

Create a query to show only those children attending Diamond Health Centre who were born during January 2002.

CREATING REPORTS

Whilst you can print tables, forms and queries in your database, if you wish to present data so that it can be formatted on an A4 page, you should produce a report.

A report can be based on a table or on a query that you have run in order to extract the appropriate records from the database.

In the database window, click on the Reports button in the Objects list on the left.

Click on New

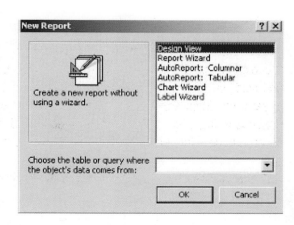

Creating a Report in Design View

Choose Design View from the list in the New Report dialog box. Choose the table or query that the report will be based on from the drop-down list. Click on OK.

You will be taken into the report design grid. The field list will appear. Drag the fields that you require from the list and drop them onto the appropriate section of the design grid.

Two elements will appear – the label and the control.

Creating a Report using the Wizard

Choose Report Wizard from the list in the New Report dialog box. Choose the table or query that the report will be based on from the drop-down list. Click on OK. This will launch the wizard.

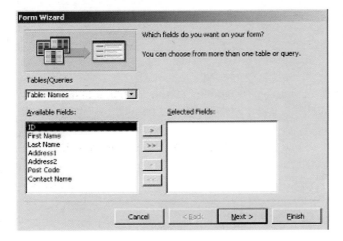

The first step of the wizard asks you to select which fields from the table or query you wish to include in the report.

Click on the field you wish to use in the Available Fields list and press the arrow button (>) to move it into the Selected Fields list.

Click on Next.

The next step of the wizard enables you to choose any grouping levels you might want in your report. (This creates sub-headings within the report and the data is grouped under that heading.)

Click on the field that you wish to make a sub-heading and click on the > button to group the report by that heading.

Click on Next.

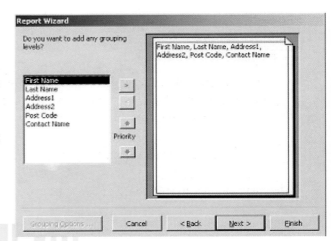

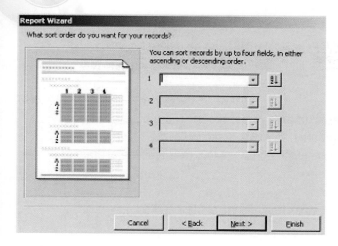

This step of the wizard allows you to sort the records on the report (if you haven't already sorted them in the table or query).

You can sort by up to four fields, in ascending or descending order.

Click on Next.

This step of the wizard enables you to choose a layout for your report and the page orientation.

Click on a layout to preview what that layout looks like.

Click on Next .

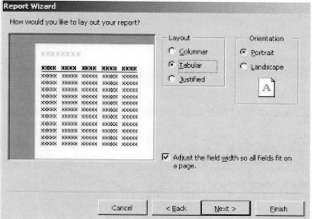

This step of the wizard enables you to choose a style for your report.

Click on a style in the list to see a preview of what that style looks like.

Click on Next.

The last step of the wizard allows you to type a title for your report. (This will appear at the top of the report on the printed page.)

You can choose to preview the report ready for printing, or you can go into the report design grid, to make further modifications to the design.

Click on Finish.

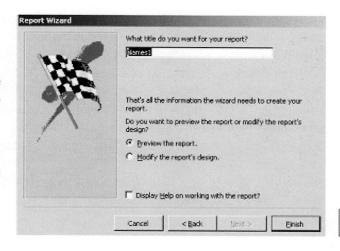

Working with Report Design

The report design grid is divided into sections: Page Header, Detail, Page Footer. You can resize each section of the report, move the labels and controls on the report, resize the labels and controls and add formatting. The grid itself enables you to line up objects in a uniform manner.

To resize the report horizontally – point to the right edge of the white area of the report. The mouse pointer changes to a resizing handle. Drag to the right to enlarge the report area. To resize a section of the report vertically – point to the bottom of the white area of that section. The mouse pointer changes to a resizing handle. Drag down to enlarge that report section.

To move a label and control together – point to the label or control. A black hand appears. Click and drag to move the label and control.

To move a label or control separately – click on the object you wish to move. Selection 'squares' appear around the object. Point to the larger square at the top left of the object. The mouse pointer changes to a pointing finger. Click and drag to draw the object. (Note that the matching label or control does not move with it.)

To resize a label or control – click on the label or control to select it. Move to one of the corner 'handles' (squares). The mouse pointer changes to a resizing handle (double-headed black arrow). Drag this arrow to resize the label or control.

To format a label or control – click on the label or control to select it. Use the Formatting toolbar to make changes to the selected object.

Object – an alternative way to navigate around your form is to choose the object name from the drop-down list on the Formatting toolbar.
Font – you can choose from a list of available fonts.
Font Size – you can choose from a list of available font sizes.
Bold – press this button to embolden the text in the selected label or control.
Italic – press this button to italicise the text in the selected label or control.
Underline – press this button to underline the text in the selected label or control.
Align Left – press this button to align the text in the label or control to the left.
Centre – press this button to centre the text in the label or control.
Align Right – press this button to align the text in the label or control to the right.
Fill/Back Colour – use this drop-down palette to fill the selected object with a colour.
Font/Fore Colour – use this drop-down palette to change the colour of the text.
Line/Border Colour – use this drop-down palette to change the colour of the lines around objects.
Line/Border Width – use this drop-down palette to change the width of the lines around objects.
Special Effect – use this drop-down palette to add a 'special effect' to the selected label or control.

Alternatively, you can right-click on an object on the report design grid and choose Properties from the shortcut menu. Changing an object's properties will change the way it looks and behaves.

To select multiple objects, hold down Shift as you click on each object in turn. Alternatively, you can drag a selection area around the objects that you wish to select. (The objects must be completely within the selection area you drag in order to be selected.)

Grouping Records on a Report

You can group records in a report by up to 10 fields.

In Design View, click the Sorting and Grouping button on the toolbar.

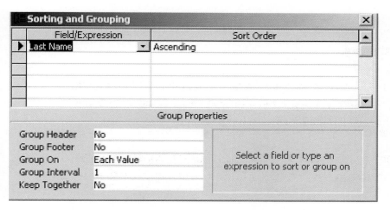

Choose the Field that you wish to set sorting and grouping on.

Choose the Sort Order for this field.

In the bottom part of the dialog box, set the Group Properties. You must have a Group Header or Group Footer to create a separate group on your report. (Change one of these to Yes.)

Choose how you want the values to be grouped. This will depend on the data type of the field you are grouping on.

Choose a Group Interval (if appropriate for that field).

Choose what you want Access to do when it prints the report. You can specify that the group is kept on the same page.

Adding Headers and Footers to a Report

In Design View, choose Report Header/Footer or Page Header/Footer from the View menu. (A Report Header or Footer will appear only once at the top or end of the report. A Page Header or Footer will appear on every page in the report).

A header and footer area appears on the report. You can drag fields from the field list and drop them into the header or footer area.

If you wish to place text in either of these areas, choose the Text Box tool from the toolbox and drag a box in the header or footer area. Type your text in the box. The Text Box can be formatted using the formatting toolbar.

Saving Reports

The first time you close the design view of your report, you will be prompted to save your report and give it a name. You will be prompted to save the report again each time you make changes to its design.

Printing Reports

There are two ways to view a report – design view and print preview. Print preview allows you to see the report exactly as it will look when printed.

Before you print the report for the first time, you might want to change margins, page orientation and other page setup options. (File menu).

You can choose File, Print or simply press the Print button on the toolbar when you are ready to print the report.

TASK

Design a report to show the data from the last query.

Move the labels and controls on the report.

Format the labels and controls on the report.

Add a footer to the report with your own name in.

Save the report design.

Print the report on A4 landscape.

USING INDEXING IN A DATABASE

Indexing speeds up searching and sorting in a database. The primary key field is automatically indexed. Some fields can't be indexed because of their data types.

Creating a Single-Field Index

Open the table in design view and click in the field you want to index.

In the Field Properties area at the bottom, click in the Indexed box and choose Yes (Duplicates OK) or Yes (No Duplicates) depending whether duplicates are allowed in that field.

Creating a Multiple-Field Index

Open the table in design view and click the Indexes button on the toolbar.

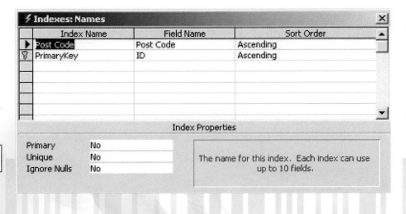

The dialog box shows you which fields are already indexed. In the next blank row of the Index Name column, type a name for the index.

In the Field Name column, choose the first field name from the drop-down list. In the next row down, choose the next field name from the drop-down list. Repeat for every field name you wish to include in this index. (You can have up to 10 fields.)

The default sort order is Ascending. Change this to Descending if you wish. Close the Indexes dialog box.

CREATING BACK-UPS

Just as you would backup any other file on your computer, it is important to backup a database, because of the amount of data that can be contained in it.

Close the database and use Windows Explorer to copy the database file (*.mdb) to your backup medium. (You will probably not be able to backup to a floppy disk as the database will probably be larger than a floppy disk.)

(If you wish to backup individual objects within the database, e.g. tables, queries, etc., create a new blank database and import the object from the original database.)

UNIT 025 USING THE INTERNET

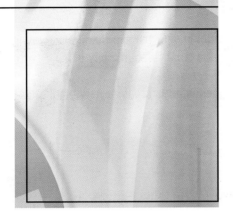

CUSTOMISING YOUR BROWSER

A browser is a computer program that facilitates access to the Internet. It is a Graphical User Interface (GUI) program that presents options in the form of clickable icons and pictures rather than being Command-Driven. (Command-Driven programs need you to type in text codes to tell them what to do.)

Browsers tend to fall into two main commercial formats:

(a) Microsoft
(b) Netscape

Both have strengths and weaknesses, but most people use Microsoft, or Microsoft-compatible browsers, because they co-ordinate with a range of other Microsoft Company off-the-shelf programs.

It is also the case that many ISPs (Internet Service Providers) provide their own proprietary browsers but for the sake of generality we will almost always use the standard Microsoft browser Internet Explorer 5 (IE5) throughout this unit.

On your Desktop and in other GUI situations, it is likely that IE5 will be represented by a blue 'e' orbited by a blue ellipse as shown below:

Make sure you are connected to the Internet, if necessary by calling-up your own ISP, perhaps AOL or FreeServe. If you are a broadband user, explicit ISP call-up may not be necessary.

Click on the blue 'e' icon to invoke the IE5 browser.

Choosing a Web Page as a Home Page

The Home Page is the screen which we always see when we call up the IE5 browser. This can be changed to suit your requirements or personal preference.

On your Desktop, right-click on the blue 'e' icon and select **Properties**.

Click on the **General** tab if the general tab contents are not already displayed. At this stage you should see:

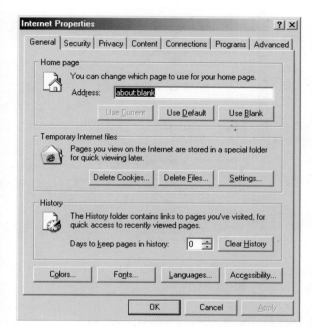

Click in the **Address** text bar and replace "about:blank" with the address of the new home page, such as http://www.hotbot.com.

We will now see the screen every time we go online through the browser.

How to Enable and Disable the Acceptance of Cookies

If you have returned to your Desktop, right-click the blue 'e' again.

When you are viewing the IE5 **Properties** window, left-click on the **Privacy** tab.

Cookies are small data files which some Web pages create and store on *your* hard disk. These Web pages, and potentially others, do however retain access to your cookies, if those cookies exist. Usually these cookies contain innocuous personal details such as your preferred background screen colour and the like. But cookies are sometimes generated which contain more sensitive details such as your address or credit card number. Because of the potential which cookies afford for privacy violations, especially if they are read by third parties, Microsoft, Netscape and your ISP all give you facilities to delete or restrict cookies or even bar their creation in the first place.

The IE5 Privacy slider allows you to choose the extent of the vetting to which you wish to subject cookies.

There are six broad options:

1 Block All Cookies

2 High

3 Medium High

4 Medium   (default)

5 Low

6 Accept all Cookies

Drag the slider with the tip of your mouse pointer, keeping the left mouse button depressed. When you have selected the level of cookie activity you consider permissible click **Apply** and **OK**.

Enabling and Disabling Image Presentation

In certain circumstances you may wish to disable the display of images on Web pages. This is often the case if you wish to speed-up Web page downloads on a narrowband portal when you are only interested in the textual content of the site; or if you wish to file large amounts of Web text that is mixed with pictures, and especially if you are going to copy those downloads uncompressed or on small media.

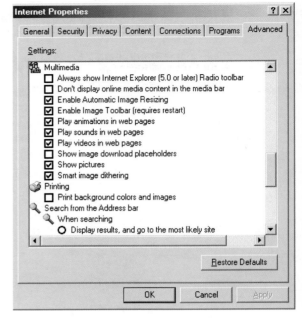

Again, right-click the blue 'e' and select **Properties** and click the **Advanced** tab.

Use the scroll bar to scroll down to Multimedia. You can select or des-elect various types of images, both still and video, and also audio, by clicking in the boxes.

If a multimedia component is selected a tick (check-mark) appears in the box. The check-box is a toggle system: click in the box once with the tip of your mouse pointer to get the tick, click again to turn it off.

To turn off still pictures, click the box 'Show Pictures' to remove the tick. Click again to restore the display of pictures. Click OK.

Cache Settings for the Internet

A cache is a storage area set aside for the more or less temporary holding of work-in-progress.

In the Internet browsing context, it is a disk directory (folder) which is kept for the storage of downloaded Web pages. This directory is on *your* hard disk.

The advantage of keeping pages in a cache is that the computer does not have to waste time re-downloading frequently-consulted pages every time you want to view them. The disadvantage is that the saved pages can quickly clutter part of your disk if you do not manage them effectively.

Part of the cache management can be organised through cache **Settings** which you can alter via the IE5 **Properties** window we access by right-clicking the blue 'e'.

Broadly you can set the cache size to any capacity between 1Mb and 32000Mb. It is usually wise to keep the cache small. If you are a broadband user it will be difficult to economically-justify keeping a page cache. Anything you really want to keep should be transferred to topic folders set up by you with due respect to copyright.

To alter cache settings select **General** on the **Properties** window and then the **Settings** button under the Temporary Internet Files heading. The cache is referred to as the "Temporary Internet Files folder" on the next window. Select the desired storage level with the slider bar and press OK.

Configuring Web Page Access Restrictions

If your workstation is used by children or other third persons you may wish to implement website access restrictions. For your own peace of mind you may also wish to do so even if you are the sole user.

Access restrictions typically vet these categories of undesirable material:

(a) Offensive Presentations

(b) Potentially Fraudulent Web Offerings

(c) Malicious Code including Viruses

Note that you most emphatically should install a reputable anti-virus software system before you connect to the Internet and not rely upon luck, clean working or general browser settings.

To modify Category (a) access settings in the IE5 context again right-click on the blue 'e' and select the **Content** tab of the **Properties** window.

From the **Content Advisor** section click on the **Enable** button.

A slider bar will now enable you to select the affective level of permitted presentation explicitness under the following sub-categories: Language, Nudity, Sex and Violence.

Click one of the four genres and then use the slider bar. For example, in the case of Language the four selectable levels range from Level 0: Inoffensive Slang to Level 4: Explicit or Crude Language.

Clearly, these **Content Advisor** options are most effective for personal protection and would easily be defeated by a knowledgeable or persistent child. Where effective protection of third parties is needed you should install a reliable nanny program.

When you have made your selections click OK.

Part of your Category (b) protection can be addressed by the **Certificates** section where selection of the **Publishers** button allows your approved verification authorities to be logged.

Within Publishers you can specify both your own and trusted third-party certification authorities, whose job is to facilitate the encryptive guarantee of reputable goods and service providers, including possibly yourself.

Rearranging Browser Toolbars

Toolbars are sets of icons for command selection, usually displayed at the top of GUI screens including those of browsers. The selectable commands are grouped by functional area, e.g. file control, drawing, etc. From within a browser you can move, modify or re-arrange a selected toolbar.

First of all, enter the IE5 browser by double-clicking the blue 'e' icon on the Desktop.

When the browser screen comes up, click **View**, **Toolbars**, **Lock the Toolbars** so that the tick (check-mark) beside the **Lock the Toolbars** option disappears.

Then use the tip of the mouse pointer cursor, with your finger pressing the left button, to drag individual toolbars around. Use the pointer to select the upright shaded line handles at the left of the bars.

A possible configuration is illustrated below. When you are satisfied with the arrangement, and if you wish to freeze it for further sessions, re-check **Lock the Toolbars**.

TASK

Open the browser software.

View the security settings that you have on your machine. Make any necessary changes that you feel appropriate (if in a College, Library or open access environment do not make any changes unless pre-agreed).

Rearrange the toolbars and position in the most suitable location for you and lock in position.

Close the browser and re-open to check the position of the toolbars. Close the browser.

COMPRESSING AND DECOMPRESSING FILES

Creating Compressed Archive Files

Mathematically-speaking, much of the recorded code of ordinary computer files consists of redundant 'fresh air'.

This redundant code space eases the algebraic manipulation of computer data but occupies relatively large amounts of disk space and wastes time and money when transferred electronically, especially when transferred over the analog public telephone system.

Using special compression programs it is possible to re-arrange the internal code of files to weed-out semiotic padding, making programs and other files smaller and thus easier to store and cheaper to transmit. Before they can be used, however, the original code patterns must be restored by decompression at the receiving end.

Proprietary browsers, such as the AOL browser, will often automatically compress and decompress transmitted files under certain circumstances, for example if more than one file is sent as an email attachment. Alternatively, you can use dedicated software, such as WinZIP, to compress and decompress whichever files you wish, and as implied you can shoehorn several at a time into the same compressed file for sending.

When you install WinZIP it usually consigns itself to a subdirectory of the standard Microsoft Programs folder, but it also installs a shortcut icon on your Desktop for convenient access. This icon looks like an old-fashioned carpenter's clamp compressing a wooden filing cabinet.

Descriptive Example of File Compression and Decompression

The files and directories discussed below are *not* available on your hard drive but your tutor will be able to help you find or create other files and folders on which you can practice your file compression and decompression skills. There is of course no reason in principle why you could not work through the example as given or modify it to reflect your own interests.

For example, in the folder COMPRESS on my hard disk C: there are four files relating to the Poussin painting sometimes known as *Et in Arcadia Ego* or *The Shepherds of Arcady*.

There is a short text file and three graphics files of the famous masterpiece in three alternative formats, and it is these graphics files which will be preposterously big. The graphics files are a .mix file for use with Microsoft PhotoDraw; an already part-compressed photographic .jpg file; and thirdly a tagged graphics format .tif file.

The respective sizes of the four files are 1209 Kb, 1253 Kb and 1824 Kb for a total of 3287 Kb. This amount of data could easily take hours to download on a slow narrowband link.

These four files will be compressed into a single archive file called ETINARCA.zip which I will put in another folder called DUMP (though there is no reason why it should not be dumped in COMPRESS).

First double-click the WinZIP Desktop icon and then click File and New Archive. When the directory explorer dialog window appears, navigate to DUMP and then enter the archive name to be created as ETINARCA.zip and select OK.

WinZIP now offers the opportunity to Add files selectively (from COMPRESS) by clicking the filenames and the Add button on the Add window.

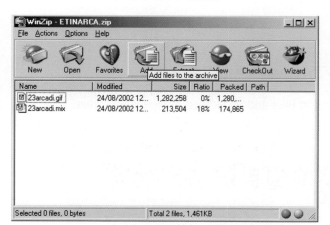

Each time the Add button is clicked WinZIP will revert to the main window display as shown here.

Add the third and fourth files by clicking the toolbar Add button on this **'WinZIP – ETINARCA.zip'** window to go back to the Add window.

When all four files have been selected complete the generation of the compressed archive file ETINARCA.zip in directory DUMP by selecting File and Close Archive from the **'WinZIP – ETINARCA.zip'** main window.

Decompressing Archive Files

ETINARCA.zip in DUMP has a size of 2638Mb, a 19.75% size saving.

To reconstitute the four original files in DUMP reverse the process by again invoking WinZIP by double-clicking the icon and then selecting File and Open Archive.

This gives us the archive contents screen **WinZip – ETINARCA.zip**.

To complete the process click the Extract toolbar icon taking care to identify the desired DUMP folder. When the required directory has been chosen select the Extract button on the Extract window.

LOCATING KNOWN SITES WITH YOUR BROWSER

If you know the unique URL (Universal Resource Locator) address for the website you wish to view you can type that address directly into the browser Address Bar and click on Go.

For example, you wish to read the website "Some Studies of the Historical Time Series of British and European Lead Mine Production" and you know that its URL is http://www.miningstatistics.com:

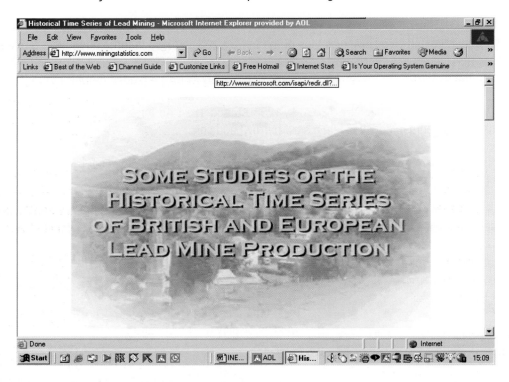

The text of the site includes textual hyperlinks: phrases marked-out in blue and underlined in blue which when selected jump to another location on the page or subsidiary pages.

USING SEARCH ENGINES TO LOCATE UNKNOWN SITES ABOUT A DEFINED TOPIC

Search engines are Web-resident programs designed to comb the Internet looking for websites relevant to a particular subject which you define by typing keywords into a text box.

There are many thousands of available search engines. But most of us are content to use proprietary, 'free' offerings that are more than adequate for most purposes.

There are two main types of search engine: automatic ones which look for relevant words embedded in the actual site content and programming; and semi-automatic structured search catalogues like Lycos which are partly moderated by human editors.

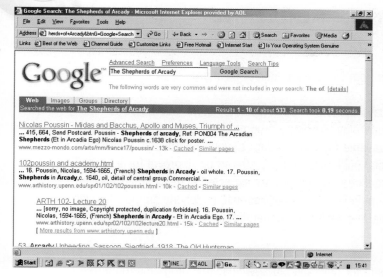

Apart from Lycos, the principal worldwide search engines include Google, HotBot, AltaVista, GoTo and Ask Jeeves, the last being a semi-taxonomic natural language engine.

We will concentrate on using Google which can be addressed at http://www.google.com

Type your search words into the text box, such as 'The Shepherds of Arcady' and click on the Search button.

The sites are ranked in order of relevancy as computed by Google based upon our selection of keywords, of which only "shepherds" and "Arcady" count, because "the" and "of" are discarded as trivial.

For many purposes we would have enough to be going on with research-wise, but if we have a yet more specialised enquiry we can employ an **Advanced Search** in which we can not only use more and better-chosen keywords, but also specify selection criteria such as the site language, the site ages (i.e. submitted since such-and-such a date) and the number of sites to report. Some engines will also allow the selection of Web elements which are wholly or partly pictures or audio presentations. The keywords themselves can be all mandatory, some mandatory or exact phrases.

In our advanced search we will select the first 100 sites (or less if there are insufficient worldwide) which contain all the words 'geometric iconography Nicolas Poussin'.

This yields-up a list of leads guaranteed to contain each and all of the four words in quotes.

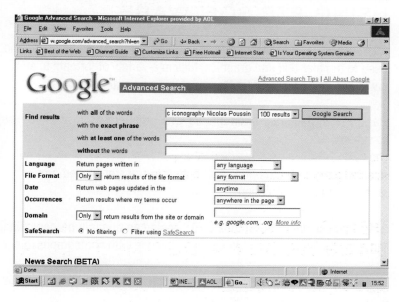

TASK

Open the browser software.

Using a search engine locate information about a subject of your choice. Access a suitable website and use the hyperlinks available to navigate the site.

Close the browser.

LOCATING SHAREWARE AND FREEWARE PROGRAMS ON THE NET

Sometimes you can obtain useful programs as downloads from websites at little or no charge.

Freeware programs are free to the user and are often Java applets or other code snippets distributed for specialised applications or are other highly sector-specific offerings. Freeware programs are offered 'as is' and are almost never supported, though source code may be available for you to adapt to your own needs. Shareware programs are typically older editions of minor commercial packages and are offered on approval for a limited period. If you like the downloaded program and wish to continue using it you are expected to pay a small, or even nominal, fee for a perpetual licence and this will often entitle you to a small manual, telephone support forever and even maybe a promotional newsletter. Much shareware is somewhat unhelpful but occasional gems can be detected and acquired by the outlay of a few dollars.

You can search the Internet for download sites. A good site for new and old downloadable programs (both freeware and shareware) is www.download.com. This site allows you to find specific software or trawl through the vast amount of software available. Always ensure that you check the file size before downloading, in some instances this may take many hours. Follow on screen instructions for downloading files.

USING FTP SOFTWARE

FTP is short for File Transfer Protocol. The FTP code convention, and its associated program tools, are usually used to transfer text and graphical files in a variety of formats to and from Web servers, though the system is versatile enough to be used for file transfers in several contexts.

Basic FTP systems are often offered with proprietary ISP browsers, especially those which offer free Web space to subscribers.

You are expected to use this FTP option to transfer limited amounts of HTML code and JPEG or GIF pictures to your free Internet allocation.

More professional free-standing FTP tools can cheaply be downloaded from the Internet and used to transfer large amounts of HTML or other mark-up code with photographs, diagrams and video or audio clips.

These tools are typically relevant to uploading your own website designs to previously-purchased site addresses.

We will briefly look at the FTP tool packaged with the AOL ISP portal.

This is accessed via **INTERNET**, **FTP** from the AOL Home Page.

This then displays the **FTP Transfer Protocol (FTP)** guidance window.

Use of the **Upload** function then permits you to send pre-existing material to the Net.

CHAT PARTICIPATION

Chat rooms are online Web facilities which mediate real-time text message communication on a scrolling screen.

Actually, the chat is hardly real time because the vagaries of the public telephone systems and disparate personal computer systems conspire to shuffle the order of the typed messages in an often disconcerting manner, to the embarrassment of speed typists at least.

Like voice telephone, and ad-hoc conferencing in general, Internet chat demands special skills and the average person is best advised to stick to a medium where he or she has the time to frame their thoughts. Therefore special care must be afforded to respecting confidentiality, protecting one's own privacy, and choice of language if chat is to be enjoyable. Children should never be allowed to chat unsupervised: an Internet chatterer is not necessarily invulnerable.

For example, I want to chat about art and in particular ask 'Does anyone know where I can find information about the mathematical basis of the iconography of seventeenth-century French painting?'

This may not be your idea of chat or even my idea but it is an interesting question and someone worldwide can answer it. But that person is of course most unlikely to be online in my chosen chat room at this time. And I have to accept that I may get some brusque or downright rude answers, whether couched in academic or non-academic language.

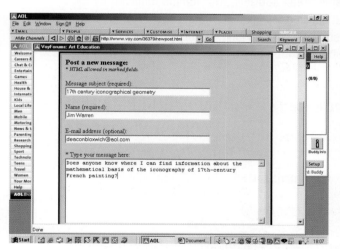

As a first step you need to enter the keyword/s into a search engine e.g. Google, which will then display some links that may provide a suitable chat room. Click on the most suitable link. You can then post your message via a form as shown on the left.

When you click the gray Send button at the top your message is then 'posted' and a screen notifies you of this.

This bulletin board method posts a semi-permanent message on a server which can be accessed over weeks or months. This has the advantage over live chat in that it gives respondents the opportunity to consider their replies and even maybe do a spot of research.

Later, you can re-enter the site and check whether anyone has answered your message. This screen, accessed eight days later, shows this message in a list of others.

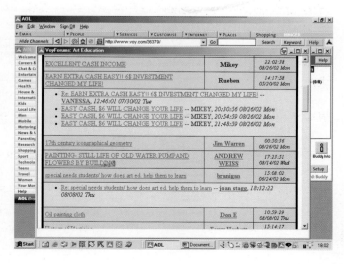

If the respondent clicks on the "Jim Warren" link he or she gets a direct email letter form to type in and send to the email address.

To participate in real-time chat about a subject you will need to log in through a series of forms. You must be prepared to divulge your name and email address to the chat room host.

However, never divulge your personal details when participating in a chat room. You do not know who you are talking to. We cannot be held responsible for the content within a chat room. If you do not like the chat content or feel at all uncomfortable about the questions being asked, log off and locate an alternative chat room.

USING AN INTERNET SERVICE TO CREATE A WEB-BASED EMAIL ACCOUNT

Creating a Web-Based Email Account

We will use the Microsoft Hotmail service to create and manage an email account. It offers basic correspondence facilities independently of your particular ISP platform.

Prepare for registration by selecting a distinctive and memorable email address. Your initials followed by the name of your village is likely to be sufficiently memorable without causing rejection due to duplication of an existing name. Secondly, decide upon a memorable password at least six characters long. Thirdly prepare an answer to the question "What is your favorite pets name?": your reply should not be any of your *actual* pets' names but something that you will remember.

Enter www.msn.co.uk in the Address bar of the Internet browser. Click on the Hotmail link.

Select the New Account Sign Up tab (if not already selected).

Enter your particulars in the Registration Screen. Read the Users' Agreement and click the **I Agree** button.

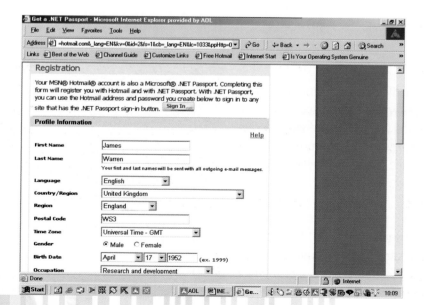

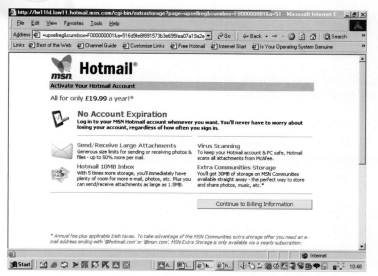

The following screen gives you different types of account available, with various fees. To sign up for a paid service scroll to the small print at the bottom of the page and read the part that says 'click here to sign up for a 2MB account'. Click on the blue underscored <u>click here</u>.

The following screens may ask you if you want to sign up for junk mail – choose carefully if at all, you may easily fill your 2Mb account with unwanted junk mail. Continue through these screens.

You will eventually meet the Hotmail home screen illustrated below:

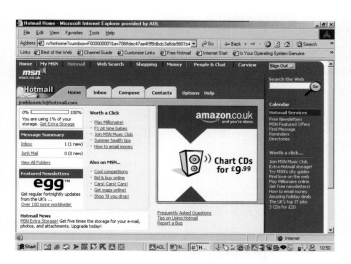

Click the Inbox tab and on the next screen click the orange "Hotmail Staff" text to read your introductory circular from Hotmail.

Create, Send and Receive Email Messages

Click the Compose tab and fill in the recipient's email address and enter a suitable subject heading (to describe the basic content of the email to the recipient).

Then type your message in the text box and click the Send button.

Click on the Inbox tab to check for any new messages. If any have appeared click on the orange text to open and read the message.

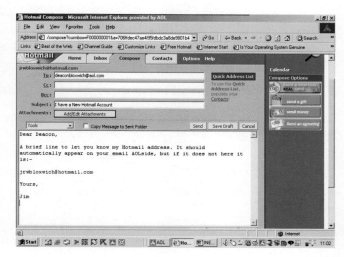

Configuring Automated Replies

Hotmail does not have this feature available.

Automated replies can be configured using stand-alone email mediation software such as Microsoft Outlook and Microsoft Outlook Express. This has been covered within the email section of level 1.

Maintaining an Address Book

It is possible to set up and use a simple address book from within Hotmail. This address book can be used conveniently to store the email addresses of your contacts enabling the accurate and efficient call-up of communications particulars.

Click the Contacts tab, and then the New Contact button. Fill in the particulars of your new contact on the Create New Contact form.

When you have added enough detail click the OK button at the bottom of the page to add your new respondent's handle-name and primary email address to the address list.

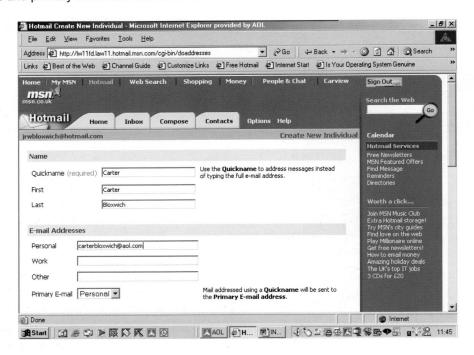

Editing and Deleting Respondents' Particulars

To do this simply click on the quickname and then edit the particulars on the succeeding View/Edit Individual form.

To remove someone from the address book click the checkbox to the left of the name whereupon a black tick mark appears. Click the Delete button and click OK on the deletion confirmation window. The details are then removed.

Creating and Addressing Groups

It is possible to corral selected email addresses into groups. This may be relevant if for example you wish to classify your church friends into a collection which you can then circulate with an email about a change in the venue for next Sunday's meeting, without bemusing business clients with cryptic messages about such matters.

To add a group click the New Group button, and fill in the Create New Group form.

After filling in these details click OK and the new group is logged.

To send a suitable circular to this group only, click Send Mail, then on the message composition screen click Show All, then on the following selection form check the tick box under To: to the left of the group quickname. Complete and send the email as normal.

> **TASK**
>
> **If you have the available access, sign up to a free web-based email account. Manage an address book and send some emails to groups of family or friends.**
>
> **Sign up to enter a chat room (we cannot be held responsible for the content of any chat room visited).**

ACCESSING A CONFERENCING PROGRAM

Many commercial conferencing programs are on the market and are readily identified using appropriate searches but in this unit we will look at Microsoft NetMeeting because it is available free and reliably contains many of the basic useful features we expect.

Broadly, a conferencing program allows two or more people to hold a real-time conversational meeting whilst physically stationed at Internet portals anywhere there is a public telephone connection. It goes beyond text chat by adding audiovisual analog media like live Webcam links so you can see each or all of the other delegates and also sound systems so that you can hear them and they can listen to you.

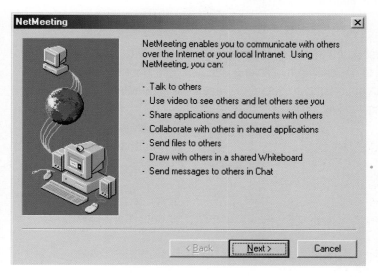

Accordingly, full functionality demands physical cameras, microphones and speakers at every station, as well as the mediative modem and microprocessing hardware (graphics and sound cards) and thus has stringent cost, organisational and hardware platform demands.

If you are a Windows 2000 user NetMeeting is already installed. You can access it through Start, Programs, Accessories, Communications and NetMeeting.

If you are *not* a Windows 2000 user summon http://www.microsoft.com/windows/netmeeting/ and follow the onscreen download instructions.

On pressing Next you will be guided through setting-up your identity information, followed by an independently-invokable Audio Tuning Wizard. To independently invoke the Audio Tuning Wizard at some later time select Tools from the top toolbar and then Audio Tuning Wizard.

On completing these initialisations you will be presented with the NetMeeting home window shown below:

Making a Conference Call

Click Call on the top toolbar and select New Call from the drop-down menu.

The Place a Call window will appear.

Enter the name, email address, computer name, computer IP address *or* telephone number of the person you wish to call.

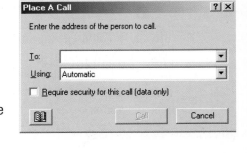

If you wish to host a new meeting involving several people it could be more convenient to set one up by clicking Call and then Host Meeting. This then gives an opportunity to define the meeting's parameters using the Host a Meeting window.

Receiving Conference Calls

There are several active and passive ways to receive conference calls.

One active way to join a meeting in progress is to call any existing participant though if you do so you will lose your connection when he logs off. Therefore, it is safer, as well as more reliable, to call the actual host of the meeting.

You can also configure your system passively to accept incoming summonses by clicking Call on the top menu and then Automatically Accept Calls. A confirmatory check will appear beside Automatically Accept Calls that can later be toggled off if required.

When someone calls you an Incoming Calls dialog box appears. To respond to this invitation either click Accept or Ignore.

Transfer a File to a Connected User

To send a file or files first click the **Transfer Files** button at the far bottom right of the NetMeeting window.

Click on the **Add File** button.

Then select the files you want to send, followed by the recipient's name or **All** for distribution to all members of the meeting. Finally click the **Send All** button. (Note that the **File Transfer** window is grayed-out and inactive until you are actually in a call.)

To take receipt of files sent to you, click **Accept** in the pop-up box which appears when a file is transmitted to your computer. To view received files, click on the fifth button on the **File Transfer** window (the one that looks like a yellow tabbed manila folder) and inspect the **Received Files** folder.

Using the NetMeeting Whiteboard

The whiteboard in a conferencing program is a blank window in which delegates and the host can sketch free-hand diagrams, insert text or paste pre-drafted images including charts, photographs and equations.

To invoke the NetMeeting whiteboard select **Tools** from the top toolbar, followed by **Whiteboard**.

You are then presented with an ordinary PAINTBOX bitmap drawing window which you can paint or composit. If however you choose to save the result it will be recorded as a NetMeeting Whiteboard image with a .NMW extension.

The whiteboard and its current contents are shared by the host and delegates and can be viewed and manipulated at any station by clicking the **Whiteboard** button third along the bottom in the NetMeeting window.

Note that because of its fundamentally bitmapped character, the whiteboard will remove special formatting from transferred text, making the conservation of font stylistics problematical. If the artistic style of the text is important it may be valuable to pre-prepare the copy into a graphics file, though Whiteboard is unable to accept normal bitmaps, JPEGs or GIFs. Text generated in a second saved whiteboard using whiteboard-permitted fonts can however be cut and pasted into the active whiteboard. Clearly, real-time graphics transfers to and from the whiteboard will need careful prior planning and agreement.

The result of such a mediated pasting event is illustrated here.

Exiting a Conference Call Correctly

To leave a conference call (subsequent presumably to the normal courtesies) click on the **End Call** hang-up button visible on the NetMeeting window as a little telephone handset with a red arrow underneath.

This apparently does nothing, but it terminates your participation in the current meeting.

NetMeeting now waits for you to join or convene another meeting.

To finish with NetMeeting altogether you must click **Call** on the left of the top toolbar and choose the **Exit** option at the bottom of the drop-down. If you have been using the whiteboard and you are the last to leave you may well be invited to save the contents by a normal Microsoft Save Current File window. Click the **Yes** button and NetMeeting will close.

USING SOME SECURITY FEATURES ON THE INTERNET

It is difficult to overstress the crucial importance of adequate security measures and personal virtual hygiene when using a connection to the Internet.

It is not enough to rely upon the fact that you correspond only with men and women of honour, or that you only visit respectable sites.

You must subscribe to a reliable, reputable and continuously-updated anti-virus service before you use the Internet, preferably by CD-ROM before physical connection.

Remember that the data you create is amazingly more valuable than your hardware, both in cash and in hard labour, and is virtually irreplaceable.

Passwords

Passwords are one of the weakest security devices and need both frequent changes and intelligent construction. If you share your computer with others always protect the confidentiality of your files, and your Internet access, with a password but do not rely upon it exclusively.

With regard to Internet access the particulars of password access will vary between ISPs.

In the case of AOL single users often log on with a stored password for convenience but this of course must change for shared systems.

Note that it is possible to password-protect individual files created with Microsoft tools, as well as many other kinds of data objects, and of course you can password-protect your own object programs in several different ways of varying security and reliability.

Digital Signatures

Digital signatures are secret code structures encrypted from confidential personal or company data by trusted third agents. An example of a specialist signature agent is the Thawte Corporation.

Digital signatures are typically used to certify the identity of those who send you files, including email letters, over the Internet.

Obtaining a Digital Signature A digital signature is an encrypted (scrambled) message which is attached to an email message as a means of "authenticating" the identity of the sender. This is not a password in the usual sense and I cannot stress too highly that whatever the number-theoretical indications of security it is foolish to place too much, and especially a long-lasting, faith in *any* security code.

Digital signatures can be ordered over the Internet from proprietary suppliers. Microsoft's preferred supplier is Verisign.

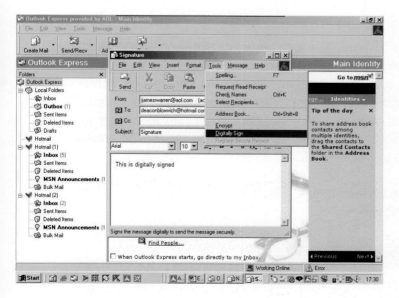

This is a generally lengthy procedure involving a lot of confidential personal information and it is a good idea to assign half a day to the process.

You are likely to be made to traipse around a lot of cyberspace dead letter-boxes. **Do not attempt this process in a college, library or other semi-public place**.

Attaching a Signature to Email Messages When you have successfully acquired your digital signature tool you may implement it using **Tools** and **Digitally sign** before Sending your message. This is illustrated here.

Locks

Locks in the context of software security measures are computer programs that enable you selectively to prevent the re-naming, moving, copying or editing of files or whole directories (folders).

They can be configured to protect individual hard-disk or floppy resources or entire networks and are therefore very useful for the protective management of academic or corporate systems.

On Guard is an example of a Windows-compatible file-locking system and is available from http://ww.nowsoft.com/products/onguard from where it may be downloaded across the Internet.

A single-user licence costs $59.95 (about £40) and it may be tested on 30 days approval (December 2002).

Other offerings may be identified with the Google Advanced Search on 'software security locks'.

Virus Protection

Good virus protection, both curative and preventative, is offered by a number of proprietary anti-virus packages. These scrutinise incoming emails, Web pages and other downloads, including file transfers from disk, in order to identify "hostile code". This hostile code may take the form of viruses, trojans or worms designed secretly to intrude into your disk storage. Once present, these hostile code fragments may be hardly noticeable, or may on the contrary reduce machine performance or even wreak wholesale destruction in your file stores. Hostile code fragments are often self-replicating (hence the comparison with organic viruses) and can infect other peoples' systems via disk transfers or the Net.

All good packages reside on your hard drive and transfer active agents to central memory at boot time. From there they intercept incoming traffic and alert you to any suspicious entry. When the potentially hostile carrier is identified the anti-virus software invites you to ignore, quarantine or destroy the incoming message. For a small annual fee you can subscribe to automatic ongoing updates to enable your system to cope with the latest threats. These updates are sent down the Internet link as and when needed, but new updates arrive every ten days or so. Anti-virus packages such as Norton also contain curative 'disinfection' facilities that find and destroy viruses which already inhabit your disk system.

Some packages offer email alerts, and alerts regarding the identity, date, effects and defence against each new virus variant are always posted on the various brand websites.

Occasionally you will see obvious hacker damage on websites, even highly-professional maintained sites like that of the Google search engine. This is seldom a cause for alarm (unless of course it has happened to *your* site!) and will usually disappear when the webmasters have had time to restore the integrity of their presentation.

CodeRed, SirCam, Nimba and Similar Viruses

These use innocent email as transport and employ your Address Book entries to infect others. They will even infect critically important Windows programs and as usual the infected user remains ignorant of his own infectiousness.

Trojans

These are apparently-useful programs which carry a sequence of destructive code that is activated upon a specific date or upon a specific condition, perhaps when a remote operator transmits an activation code.

They are designed to cause Denial of Service, and are very insidious, some even masquerading as Windows programs. Some of them can be cleaned of their contained viruses.

INTERNET CONNECTION TYPES AND SPEEDS

POTS

Analog transmission is slower than digital. The analog data transmission speed aimed for today is 56Kbps (Kilo bits per second).

POTS (Plain Old Telephone System) conveys both voice and data signals as analog waves over phosphor bronze wires. You can use this for narrowband data exchange at up to 56Kbps. As with all analog communication, environmental noise interference can be a problem.

Your computer will need a modem to handle such traffic.

Simultaneous voice and data use is not practicable with POTS.

Wireless

Wireless connection can be via:

- Mobile Telephone
  This incurs air time as well as ISP charges and data storage is limited

- Wireless ISP
  Depends upon short-range transceivers in metropolitan areas. More a medium for Local Area Networks (non-Internet)

ISDN (Integrated Services Digital Network)

This allows simultaneous voice, fax and data transmission on the basis of a single 128Kbps connection.

It is not available everywhere and is higher in cost than POTS, but more convenient with more reliable transmission.

ADSL (Asymmetric Digital Subscriber Line)

This is a development of the ISDN concept which also offers simultaneous voice, fax and data use but at much higher data speeds (typically 0.5Mbps or about half a million bits per second). Also it is less prone to degeneracy (data congestion delays) than POTS or other slow systems due to greater bandwidth (more available channels). It is often described as broadband in contrast to the slow and limited narrowband system of POTS.

It is 'asymmetric' (lop-sided) because the data speed is slower for you to send information to the server (host computer) than for it to download data to the client (your computer). It is relatively expensive, but available in most urban areas of the UK.

Cable

Data transmission speeds downstream to the client are often very fast due to the optical fibre transmission media, but some forms are not duplex (configured for two-way traffic) and thus rely upon slow analog responses from your computer. The asymmetry may be as much as 3Mbps/128Kbps. Though prone to local degeneracy, cable still achieves speeds much better than normal wire-based services. You need to have cable installed in your street if this is to be a viable option.

Leased Line

Corporations like large companies or ISPs can often employ one or more varieties of privately-leased telephonic line using traditional twisted-wire technology.

The US T1 system is rated at 1.544Mbps; The T3 standard is fibre optic and runs at 45Mbps. BT has similar facilities on the market.

Typical Modem Speeds

The table below contains the typical download times for three sorts of software through four speeds of data channels:

Type of Data	File Length	28.8K Modem	56K Modem	ISDN 128Kbps	DSL 1.5Mbps
Internet: 25 pages of text with graphics	2.5Mb	18mins	8mins	2mins	13secs
20 second video	8Mb	36mins	18mins	8mins	43secs
Download all IE4 software	25Mb	150mins	75mins	26mins	2.2mins

Different kinds of ISPs

From the point of view of Web access speeds there are basically two kinds of ISP companies:

(a) Narrowband

These service data rates up to 56Kbps using POTS, typically for domestic users or low-volume small businesses. 'Free' providers may charge for telephone connection, and at a premium rate if you ring them for voice advice. Paid providers will charge about £15 per month but allow you to access the Web using 0800 freephone numbers which they will divulge when you subscribe. You may need to install the more local of these numbers yourself using their software: this is not technical, their software tells you exactly how to do it. Again, paid ISPs may or may not charge over the odds for ringing-up a human advisor.

If you use the Net to any degree, especially in office hours, paid providers like AOL or BT Online may prove better because you can access the service on a 24/7 basis (i.e. anytime) and service is more prompt both to log on and to access material because fewer people are competing for the same bandwidth (channels).

(b) Broadband

Public broadband services like BT Openworld and TeleWest BlueYonder utilise ADSL technology employing either copper wire (in practice phosphor bronze is tougher, so it's that which tends to get strung up on poles) or fibre optic cable. The latter is limited to the major urban areas.

With ADSL connection you are always logged online even when you are not physically working on your system. So there are no connection delays and data transmission is at least three times as fast from your client computer to the Web and ten times as fast (about 0.5 Mbps) downstream.

A further advantage of broadband is that you can use voice telephone, the Web and even fax all at once. Narrowband connection cuts off your phone which is only restored when you log off the Internet.

On the minus side you pay £250 for ADSL installation followed by a typical £40 per month line charge (December 2002). From 1 April 2002 non-BT ADSL ISPs will offer services over BT infrastructures for a typical £30 per month with a £60 set-up fee. AOL will offer 'free' set-up but subscribers must commit to a minimum twelve-month contract. With fibre optic cable you may or may not get television channels thrown in.

ADSL is worth considering if you are a business or a data professional working from home.

Either kind of ISP will offer:

(a) Web Surfing (consulting websites already in existence including possible trade or polling interaction)

(b) Email and Messaging

(c) Upload of Web Pages

   Sensible design involves programming pages offline using a browser and then using the FTP (File Transfer Protocol) to upload them to a pre-arranged domain (a named Web compartment hosting the website).

   A protocol is an internationally-agreed computer code format to permit the exchange of data between different systems.

(d) News, Weather and Online Advice

Enabling fast connection

Identify a suitable ISP by consulting friends or purchasing one of the Internet magazines that publish classified tables of 'free' and paid narrowband and broadband providers. The magazines tabulate the following details:

(a) Name of ISP

(b) ISP Website URL

(c) ISP Voice Telephone Number

(d) Connection Charge (if any)

(e) Monthly Line Charge (if any)

(f) Web-access Call Charge per minute (if any)

(g) Voice Advice Call Charge per minute

(h) Number of Permitted Screen Names

(j) Number of Permitted Email Addresses

(k) Web Space Available to User (if any)

(l) Other features

Obtain the ISP's connection software. It is sometimes feasible (but potentially expensive) to download this online if you have an existing Internet connection. But the best thing to do is to ring your chosen ISP and order a CD-ROM: this will be 'free'. Popular ISPs sometimes give away CD-ROMs in supermarkets or phone shops.

Check you are wired to the phone line!

Start your computer and place your CD-ROM in its drive. Wait passively for the ISP's registration process to start itself. If the process fails to start you may have to 'run' the CD-ROM via Windows or your usual operating system. If this is necessary the ISP's printed instructions will talk you through the process.

The ISP's software may ask you for technical information about your connection and modem, but this is unlikely with modern programs that can 'feel' your system's characteristics for themselves.

What you will need to sort out for yourself are a Username and a Password to access the system. It is also wise to pre-decide a selection of Screen Names, usually one for each person who will access the Net. Very often you will want to tie each Screen Name to an Email Address of the format screenname@ispname.com.

The Password must be chosen with great care and changed frequently. Avoid any choice which involves use of the following:

(a) Personal Names or their Diminutives

(b) Social, Sporting, Religious or Political Allegiance

(c) "genius", "passwd", "letmein", "secret" or any other Unoriginal Combination

(d) Any Dictionary Word

(e) Any Place Name

On the other hand the password must be memorable to you.

Bulletin Boards

These are similar in concept to a newsgroup's Message Board except that the emphasis is not so much on sharing information as passing down messages on a one-to-many basis.

Bulletin Boards and Message Boards are always themed, usually password or username accessible for enhanced privacy, and will be regularly edited for content and currency.

Audio Conferencing

Audio Conferencing is live voice chat between two or more people mediated via a WAN (Wide Area Network). The Internet, of which the World Wide Web is a part, is a WAN system, but there are many other private and leased line WANs present upon the international telecommunications system.

In such contexts, pre-booked satellite links can be invoked to connect participants separated by oceans. A properly organised audio conference can be more efficient than telephoning and vastly cheaper than physically gathering and accommodating delegates who have arrived by air.

Video Conferencing

Video Conferencing utilises television cameras as well as microphones in order to convey 'body language' to a meeting of remote participants. Traditionally, this was highly expensive, but often cheaper than physical meetings in big, sparsely populated countries like Canada, Sweden and Russia. Now that there are Webcams and the Internet, low-quality types of video conference are more widespread.

Successful video conferencing demands high-quality dedicated broadband connections which are still costly. Normal connections introduce unacceptable delays in frame refreshment (updating the picture) as well as in image quality.

Data Conferencing

Data conferencing is one of the more practicable conversational modes with normal narrowband networking like the domestic Internet.

It can be either synchronous (live) or asynchronous (reliant upon recorded materials you can display later).

In the static, asynchronous context a wide variety of computer data files, including documents (typed reports), spreadsheets (tabulations) or indeed ordinary programs can be exchanged as email attachments or by explicit use of FTP tools.

In live, synchronous working you can share a document or spreadsheet (or other suitable resource) with other co-workers over the Net and they can contribute information from their own keyboards and computers to help you update the file in real time. This has obvious potentials for showing people how to use such software. The completed task can be saved (recorded on disk) and emailed to each member of the group concerned after the session. This synchronous data sharing is sometimes called Desktop Sharing.

E-COMMERCE

e-Commerce is the use of Net pages (especially websites) for buying and selling.

The Net must of course rely upon parcel delivery services physically to get purchases of goods to the customer. Certain services are, however, ideally suited to the Net because the data and instructions submitted by the customer can be electronically relayed to databases which execute the order promptly.

Accordingly the Net is currently most successful for selling:

- Services
  (a) Financial Services, including Banking, Stockbroking and Insurance
  (b) Holiday and Transport Bookings

- Consumer Durable Smallwares
  (a) Books
  (b) Jewellery and Giftware

- Auctioned Smallwares

- Highly-Specialised Capital Goods and Services

The first three direct selling consumer sectors are facilitated by HTML forms which appear on the screen and are filled with address delivery and product details by the customer who is invited to add his credit card details to the form using a secure sub-process. Some traders restrict orders to registered customers who log in with a username and password. This policy is to enhance security and consolidate gathered market intelligence.

When the customer clicks a submit button on the screen, the form details are uploaded to a secure server CGI-bin (a special file directory for gathered data uploads). The secure connection is then terminated and the details relayed to a product management database for subsequent order processing.

The capital goods sector rarely sells products online. Its websites are used purely as 'shop windows' for prospects who then contact the vendor by email, telephone or packet post.

INTELLECTUAL PROPERTY AND THE INTERNET

Traditional English copyright was assumed to be a title of possession attaching naturally and without any registry or licence to the author of a written or drafted work, published or unpublished. It resided in the authors estate until the fiftieth anniversary of their death, but could be assigned to others (usually for a fee).

Copyright was intended to prevent the plagiarism (copying) of printed works and was first internationally addressed by the Bern Convention of 1887. The US, however, refused to sign the Bern Convention and took the view that foreign work in English (i.e. British production) was 'fair game', achieving copyright protection within American territory only after typesetting in the US. The actual (and intended) effect of this apparently bizarre anomaly was to partition the English-speaking market between American and British interests for a hundred years. In 1952 the Universal Copyright Convention attempted to bring America into co-ordination with international practice. To an extent this was both a cause of and a solution to the long-term decline of British publishing, especially in the scientific markets.

A developing legal distinction is forming around the concepts of:

(a) Copyright: a contractual maxim designed to prevent financial damage to a publisher's interest due to plagiarism.
(b) Moral Right: an ethical maxim in respect of an author's human right to be credited with the origination of his own work.

Broadly speaking, UK and US courts focus on copyright principles, whereas French and Continental courts view Moral Right as taking precedence over commercial issues.

English Copyright law is governed by the Copyright Act of 1988, but the position is further confused by the global primacy of US, European and Treaty law, and the technical behaviour of computer systems that automatically copy human work as part and parcel of Internet presentation.

Many Web programmers try to prevent plagiarism and other forms of theft by technical means, the ultimate expression of which is currently encryption (data scrambling) by the use of sophisticated mathematically-based passwords called Public and Private Keys.

Realistically, however, all such defences can be broken through given time and ingenuity. So the sensible policy is to make such break-ins (sometimes called "hackings") commercially uneconomical and to review, monitor and change safeguards frequently.

Fair Play

As far as ordinary Web users, including researchers, are concerned a great deal of responsible and mutually-profitable work can be achieved by the exercise of good manners and academic professionalism.

US law has attempted to codify good Internet practice in terms of principles of 'Fair Use':

1 You are permitted to reproduce reasonable amounts of relevant copyright material for purposes of:

    (a) Criticism
    (b) Comment
    (c) News Reporting
    (d) Teaching
    (e) Research
    (f) Scholarship

2 Fair Use will implicitly be construed as non-profit use in normal circumstances.

3 Fair Use may vary with the Nature of the Work copied as well as the amount.

4 Due regard must be paid to the effect of copying upon the potential market for, or the value of, the copyright work.

Fair Use applies both to published and unpublished work. Work that appears only on the Net is 'unpublished' in the eyes of US and UK law.

Note that UK judgments tend to the view that multiple copies for classroom teaching infringe copyright whereas US adjudications support such copying; a professional tutor would disdain photocopy plagiarism to support his own lectures.

Good manners and professionalism dictate:

A   Always include full bibliographic details (i.e. title, author, and source of the original book, magazine or paper you quote) in your own material. This obviously includes Net URLs. Clearly, this also allows your readers to track-down further information.

B   Never run down another contributor. Fair Use criticism is always impersonal, well-researched and academic, emphasising the importance of your 'victim's' contribution to culture and analysing the work's shortcomings in a constructive way. After all, you will never talk about unworthy work on the Net.

Intellectual freedom

As we have seen, legal concepts like copyright overlap with issues of morality and honour, and morality is especially to the fore in questions of intellectual freedom, or Freedom of Speech.

The global reach of the Internet has revitalised cultural and national differences in thinking about freedom.

In much of Europe and North America it is a matter of principle that anyone can publish writings and images about their political, religious and social beliefs, as well as any scientific or mistakenly-scientific theory.

Some countries and communities attempt, however, to censor Net offerings about such issues, just as they censor printed sources. Islamic countries take a dim view of overtly Christian websites whilst Singapore actively polices incoming Communist or 'decadent' information. Other countries like the UK attempt to ring-fence pornography, whereas some countries like Japan or Nordic nations take a more liberal stance on titillation. The UK and some other countries are also very sensitive to terrorist or bomb-making websites, often with good cause.

Even within the US there is debate about whether certain ideological offerings on the Net should be censored, not just rabid or obscene race hate, but more 'academic' anti-Semitism sites.

Currently much responsible publication depends upon personal honour, taste and decency with respect for others based upon respect for self.

COMPUTER MISUSE

Computer misuse is another concept with multiple facets, different motivations and varieties of both unsophisticated and highly technical methods.

Misusers of the Net fall into three main categories.

Idle or Immature Persons

This most easily deterred group will attack computer systems just to prove they can do it, or get away with it, or just for the kick of applying a covert power.

In practical terms their intended or accidental effect exists in Denial of Service. The US law concept of Denial of Service has two facets:

(a) Actual Computer Service Interruption: this is usually short term but expensively disruptive.
(b) Deterrence of Legitimate Network Use: respectable users are made shy of using resources in case their own computer systems are damaged.

Idle abusers usually make small, home-made programs propagate across the Net before becoming destructively active. Such programs include viruses, technically 'self-propagating, autonomous code fragments' which propagate through the booting (start-up) of computer operating systems, and worms which are 'self-replicating complete programs'.

Viruses and worms can be intercepted or even 'disinfected' from already-corrupted systems by remedial code downloaded from specialist software providers.

Criminals

Professional criminals are interested in financial gain through theft and will wish to evade detection for as long as possible; they therefore avoid Denial of Use crises.

Typical Net crimes are commonly:

(a) Theft of Copy
Agencies very often copy advertisements from other traders, and the (unattributed) creation of academic presentations from Net sources (for personal advancement) is also very common.

(b) Fraudulent Interception
This focuses upon attempts to steal credit card codes and other instruments of exchange relayed electronically, for resale ("fencing") or direct theft of cash. This can be mitigated by code encryption (scrambling), statistical vigilance in customer or basket (purchase history) analysis, and by supplementary user or password registrations.

(c) Misrepresentation
This crime uses transient websites to invite customers to send money (by credit card or otherwise) in exchange for non-existent or very inferior goods and services.

(d) Purveyance of Illegal Materials
This involves fulfilled or unfulfilled promises to supply hard pornography or banned materials (e.g. firearms, drugs, ivory) at inflated prices.

All crime requires specialist, full-time prevention and detection and is deterred both by probability of punishment and by economic deterrents.

Governments and other Ideological Agencies

As noted, governments may impose censorship of Net traffic and may also covertly exploit the Net to gather both fiscal (tax and customs) and political intelligence about groups and individuals.

The extent to which this is an infringement of liberty or an actual crime varies from regime to regime.

International treaties and the invigilation of Net use by semi-official groups such as W3C (the World Wide Web Consortium) as well as traditional human rights charities can mitigate some state-sponsored Web abuse.

Although government abuse can ultimately be deterred by threat or economic sanctions, widespread bad publicity is usually a more effective deterrent against democratic regimes because of its electoral and trading effects.

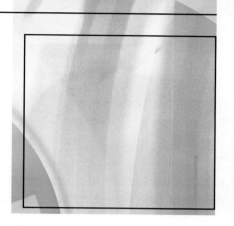

e-Quals
UNIT 026
PRESENTATION GRAPHICS

MICROSOFT POWERPOINT

Microsoft PowerPoint is a flexible and powerful presentation software package with which you can create professional looking presentations in various formats and for different purposes. Its ease of use and intuitive interface, similar to that of Microsoft Excel and Microsoft Word, Microsoft PowerPoint's two stable-mates, make it attractive to millions of users. With PowerPoint you can create:

- On-screen presentations
- Web pages
- Colour and Black and White overheads
- Colour and Black and White paper printouts
- 35 mm slides
- Audience handouts
- Speaker notes

CREATE AND SAVE A NEW PRESENTATION/ SLIDESHOW TEMPLATE

Load the Software and Select a Blank Template

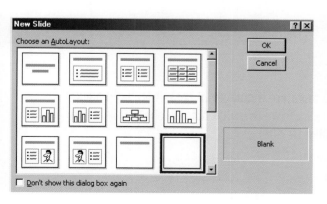

Start the presentation software by clicking on the Start menu, then Programs and choose MS PowerPoint. The New Slide dialog box will appear. Choose the slide you want to use from the default slides available. A thick blue border indicates the slide that has been selected. Then click OK. This will bring up a blank slide for you to work with.

The PowerPoint New Slide dialog box consists of twenty-four different default slide layouts, with pre-set and pre-formatted placeholders for text and most other graphic objects that can be included in a presentation.

Change the Background Colours

To change the colour of the background for your slide, click on the Format menu and then choose Background. The Background dialog box will appear. You can choose which colour you would like to make your background colour, by clicking on the drop down menu, and selecting either from the most recently used colours, or from the PowerPoint palette.

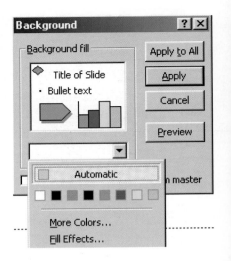

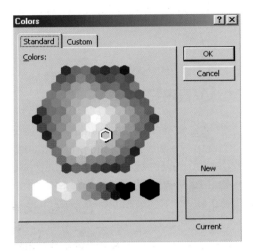

If you click on the More Colors option, the PowerPoint palette brings up the range of colours to choose from. Select the colour you prefer, and then click OK.

From the Background dialog box, you can also create fill effects, should you want to make your background more interesting. The options available to you here are Gradient, Texture and Pattern.

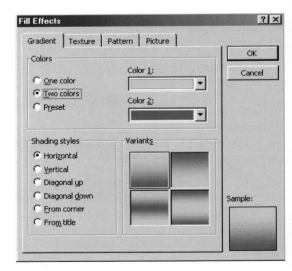

Under Gradient, you can choose one or two colours and create a gradual flow of one colour into the other. There are a number of shading styles to choose from.

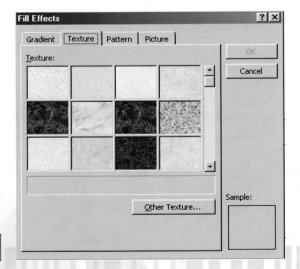

Under Texture there are a number of default-textured backgrounds to choose from. If you do not see one you like, you can click on Other Texture.

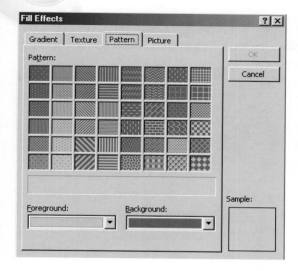

Under Patterns, there are a number of different types of pattern, such as brickwork or lines, which are available. You can choose which colour to have as foreground or background colour.

Once you have chosen your desired background colour and fill effects (if any) click on OK. The Background dialog box gives you the option to apply this background colour to all slides (Apply to All) or just to the current slide (Apply). Once you have applied the background, you can change it.

TASK

You will be able to use your previously acquired level 1 knowledge to complete this task.

As the manager of the Downtown Internet Café, you are required to create a presentation to show to employees about the various blends of coffee that the café offers. The purpose of the presentation is to answer the many questions customers have about the types of coffee available. The first slide should be a title slide. The title of the presentation is Coffee Talk. The subtitle should read Downtown Internet Café. Adjust the slide background to that of your choice.

Change Default Text Attributes

To change any of the text attributes, go to the Format menu and click on Font. This will bring up the Font dialog box.

Make the changes to the text, as you require. If you would like the Font, Font Style, Size, Colour and any effects to be the same for the entire presentation, click in the Default for new objects box. This sets the default so that every time you create a new text box, the text will be formatted in the same way, without you formatting it every time.

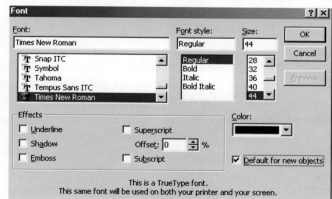

TASK

Change the title text to Westminster, Size 44, colour blue.
The sub title text should be Arial Narrow, size 28, colour blue. Make this the default for all new text objects.

Ensure that the background colour, pattern or texture does not clash with the font colour.

Adding Footers, Slide Numbers and Dates

To insert a header or footer containing text, the slide number or even the date, click on the View menu, and select Header and Footer. The Header and Footer dialog box will appear.

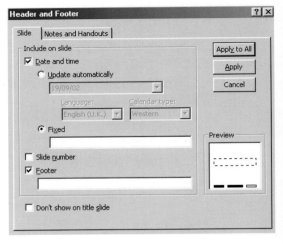

You can add headers and footers to the slides, or to the notes you are creating. For now, let's just look at adding headers and footers to the slide.

To insert the date simply click in the check box next to Date and Time. If you want the date to update every time the document is opened, then click on the radio button next to Update Automatically. This will ensure that when the date changes, the date on the slide will reflect this. If you do not want the date to change, click on the radio button next to Fixed.

You can also include the slide number by clicking in the check box next to Slide number.

To add any other information you would like, click in the check box next to Footer, and then in the space underneath type the details. You can make sure that the details do not show up on the title slide by clicking in the check box at the bottom: Don't show on title slide.

To the right you can see a preview of what the header or footer will look like.

You can choose to apply the changes to all the slides (Apply to all) or just the current slide (Apply).

> **TASK**
>
> **Add the date and the slide number to every slide in your presentation, except the title slide. Place the name of the café in the centre, at the bottom of the page. Make sure that the date of the presentation does not automatically update.**

Change the Default Format of the Blank Presentation

You might want to change the default format of the blank presentation if, for example, you always use a certain colour scheme or if you want the logo of your company in every presentation.

A master or template is a model publication that you can use as the basis for creating a new publication. A template can contain the basic layout and formatting, text and graphics, as well as layout guides, text styles and background elements such as page numbers and rules, that can be re-used in future publications. To make a template, create a publication and save it as a template. Then open it any time you want to base a new publication on it. Once you have designed the perfect publication you may wish to use it again for further publications. To save yourself the extra work of creating your design again, simply save the publication as a template. This will be very useful if there is little change between the design elements of the publications. Using a template also helps to carry the house style throughout all your publications.

Many organisations specify a house style for their documents, which you should follow closely. The idea of a house style is to produce a standard, easily recognisable look for an organisation's documents. This look or image gives the customers and staff a sense of organisational unity and efficiency, and of everyone working together to produce a high-quality product or service.

Say for example that you are given an assignment from a company or client that requires you to set up the page in a specific way – with defined margins, gutters and page orientation, and that requires you to use a particular background and colour. If these elements are the same no matter what type of publication you create for this company or client, then this is called a house style.

A house style ensures that presentations from two different people at the same organisation will have the same look, as the dates and references are all in the same position, and that the font that is used is the same in all the documents. The same is true for logos – these are always in exactly the same place, and exactly the same size and colour on every document.

To create a template:

1   Open an existing presentation or create a new one.

2   Change the presentation to suit your needs.

3   On the File menu, click Save As.

4   In the Save as type box, click Design Template.

5   In the File name box, type Blank Presentation, and then click Save.

6   If a message box is displayed, click Yes to replace the existing blank presentation.

WORKING WITH TEXT

Cutting and Pasting Text into Outline View from Another Source (Importing Text)

In level 1 you learnt how to insert text boxes using the text box tool and add text to your presentations. But you can also copy and paste text into your presentation from another source, such as a text processor or Web browser (from the Internet). This is easy using the outline view option available in PowerPoint. To switch to outline view, click on the outline view icon at the bottom of the screen.

The screen layout will change and look as the screen print (Left).

Draw a text box on your presentation slide. To copy text from a text processing package such as WordPad or Word, or from a Web browser simply select the text in the source, then copy it using the Edit menu. Open your presentation in PowerPoint, and switch to outline view. Click on Paste from the Edit menu. The text will be pasted with the formatting from the source, so you may need to re-format it so it fits in with the rest of your text and into the text box. This may require resizing the text box, and changing the size of the text.

Manipulating Text in Text Boxes

If you change the size of the text box by dragging on the handles (square markers on the edges of the text box that show up when selected), the text inside will automatically adjust to the new size (this will only happen if you have marked the auto wrap check box in the format text box dialog box). This is called wrapping. Just make sure that the text still makes sense!

Select the object you want to resize.

1 On the Format menu, click the command for the type of object you selected – for example, AutoShape or Text Box – and then click the Text Box tab.

2 Select the Resize AutoShape to fit text check box.

If the Resize AutoShape to fit text check box is selected and you later try to make the shape smaller, the shape will resize only to where the text still fits within it.

To rotate text within a text box, click on the Rotate icon on the Drawing toolbar.

The corner handles on the object will become lime green circles. You will note that the shape of the mouse cursor also changes to arrows.

To rotate the text, click on one of the green rotate buttons, and drag the text box to the left or right. This will rotate the text as much as you move the box.

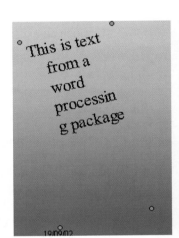

Changing Text Box Properties

To change the style, colour and size of the border of the text box, click on the Format menu, and choose Placeholder. The Format AutoShape dialog box will appear.

From this dialog box, you can change the colour of the line and the background colour of the text box. Choose from the palette of PowerPoint colours, or patterned lines (for the line) or colours and fill effects (for the background).

You can also decide if you would like the line to be solid, dashed or dotted.

The Style drop down menu offers a selection of single lines, double lines and ornamental lines of differing widths.

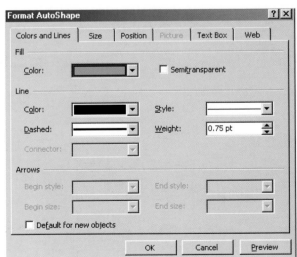

The Weight relates to the thickness of the line. The higher the point size, the thicker the line.

Select the style that you want from these four options and click OK.

If you are creating a house style, you have the option of setting a default for new objects as before.

Click on the Text Box tab to make changes to the text box, including auto wrap, auto size and auto rotate.

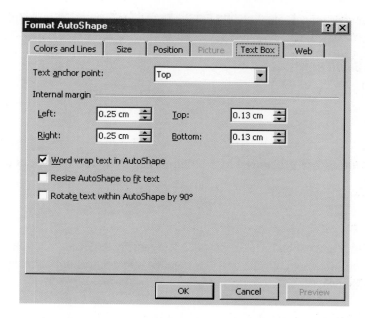

Spell-checking your Slides

Click on the Tools menu and then select Spelling. Let the spell checker take you through your presentation, highlighting any words that may be misspelled. Add any new words to the dictionary, when given the option, and change those that are spelled incorrectly.

Bulleted or Numbered Lists

This is automatic if you choose the Two Column Text, Text and Chart or Clipart and Text slides from the AutoLayout screen when starting a presentation. But you can also add bullets to your text. This may be useful if you are creating lists, or have abbreviated information, which the presenter will explain in more detail.

To add bullets to text:

1   Select the text or placeholder you want to add bullets or numbering to.

2   On the Format menu, choose Bullets and Numbering. Choose which bullets or numbering you require.

Or you could:

1   Add bullets by clicking Bullets 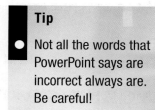 .

2   Add numbers by clicking Numbering 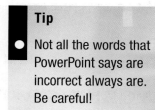 .

In level one you will remember learning how to change the appearance of the bullets and numbering.

> **TASK**
>
> The third slide in your presentation should list the topics for discussion in the presentation, as follows:
>
> **Regular Roasts**
> > **Central and South American**
> > **East African**
> > **Indonesian**
> **Other Offerings**
> **Coffee Terms**
>
> **Make sure the topics are presented in a bulleted list. Change the bullets so that they reflect the topic of the list.**

Using WordArt

WordArt is also known as graphical text. This is because it is usually larger than normal text, and is used mainly for creative headings. WordArt should only be used for creative effect and is not normally accepted for more professional looking presentations.

To use WordArt simply click on the Insert menu, select Picture and choose WordArt. The WordArt gallery will appear, offering the different styles of text available.

In level 1 you dealt with using WordArt, and manipulating the style to suit your presentation.

WORKING WITH GRAPHICS

Inserting Graphics

To improve the quality of your presentation, you may want to include some photos or images that you have saved onto your hard drive or network drive, from a CD-ROM or directly from the Internet or company Intranet. You may also want to include graphical objects such as drawings or charts. PowerPoint also offers the option of inserting graphics from scanner or digital camera.

To do this use the Insert menu, select Picture and then choose From File, Autoshapes, Organization Chart, or From Scanner or Camera. If you choose From File, PowerPoint will prompt you to select the area where the file is saved. Find the correct file and then click OK. A graphical box will automatically be inserted, which you can manipulate, resize and crop as required, using the picture handles and the Picture toolbar.

> **TASK**
>
> **Insert a suitable, coffee related graphic into slide 3. Make sure that it does not displace the text in the bulleted list.**

To insert Autoshapes, follow the steps as above. There are a number of Autoshapes to choose from which are all available on the Autoshapes toolbar.

You can use Autoshapes to insert lines, basic shapes such as squares and circles, arrows, callout boxes and stars and banners.

To add text to these shapes, draw a text box over the shape, type in the text and click off the box. To make sure that the shape is still visible, make sure that there is no fill colour on the text box. Alternatively, right click and select Add Text.

You can modify the colour and line style of the shape clicking on the Format menu, and choosing AutoShape. Remember to select the shape first. The Format Autoshape dialog box is the same as the Format Placeholder box discussed before.

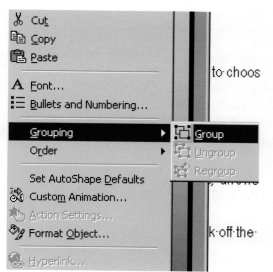

To group objects so that they form a more cohesive look and are easier to move around and copy, click on the first object. Holding the Shift key down, click on the second object. Then right click and choose Grouping. Click on the option to Group. This will 'merge' the two objects so that they can be manipulated as one. If at any point you want to separate these objects, follow the same procedure, but choose Ungroup.

If you want to insert a picture from the Internet, the best method is to save the picture first to your hard drive or network area, and then insert from file as above.

You can also duplicate and delete objects, as discussed in level 1, as well as copy objects to other slides, using the copy and paste commands on the Edit menu.

If a chart is required as part of your presentation, then choose the Chart slide from the AutoLayout screen. You can, however, insert a chart as part of an existing slide.

To insert a chart or graph, click on the Insert menu, and then select Chart. A default chart will be inserted into your presentation, together with a table in which to enter the data to be charted.

As you enter the data into the table, the chart should change.

When finished entering your data, click outside the chart area and only your chart will be left on the slide.

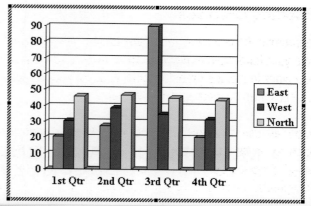

If at any time you wish to make changes to your chart, double-click on the chart area.

If you want to change the chart colours or fonts, select the chart and then double-click it. The Format Chart Area dialog box will appear.

This box offers options to change the colour and pattern of the chart bars, as well as format the font used.

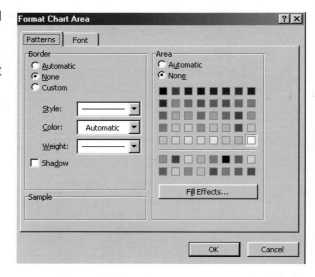

Select a Different Chart Type

For most 2-D charts, you can change the chart type of either a data series or the entire chart. For bubble charts, you can change only the type of the entire chart. For most 3-D charts, changing the chart type affects the entire chart. For 3-D bar and column charts, you can change a data series to the cone, cylinder, or pyramid chart type.

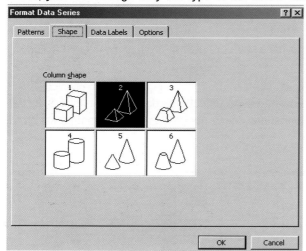

1 In PowerPoint, double-click the chart you want to change.

2 To change the chart type of a data series, click the data series in the chart.

3 To return to PowerPoint, click outside the chart.

ADD MULTIMEDIA AND ANIMATED OBJECTS TO A PRESENTATION

Insert Sound and Animated Objects

To insert either a sound or an animated object into your presentation, use the Insert menu and choose Movies and Sounds. There are several options available to you at this point.

You can choose to insert either a movie or sound from the PowerPoint gallery, or from a file you may have previously saved.

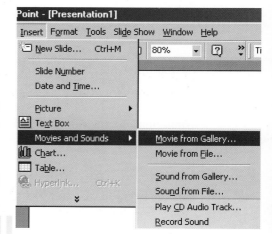

If you would like to insert a movie or sound from the gallery, click on the appropriate option on the menu. The Insert Movie or Insert Sound dialog box will appear. This shows all the categories to choose from. Here you can search for a specific word, or go through the categories until you find something you want. If you do not have any Movie or Sound files to choose from, select Clips Online and follow on-screen prompts to download suitable selections.

The Insert Movie and Insert Sound boxes look similar.

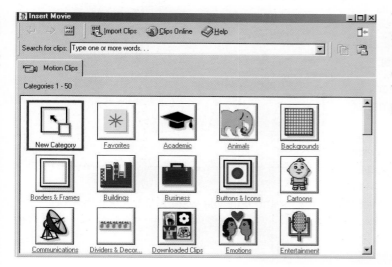

The thick blue border indicates which category has been selected. When you click on a category, all the available movies or sounds in that category will be listed. To insert, click on the movie or sound and then use the Insert icon. You can also play the movie or sound to check if it will fit in with the style of your presentation.

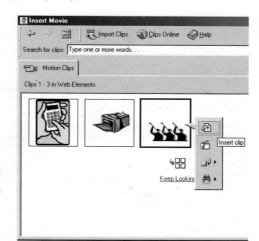

When you choose to insert sound into your presentation, once you have selected the relevant sound and inserted it, the following prompt will appear:

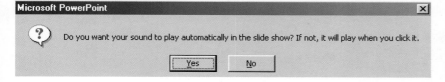

If you click on yes, then the sound will play in the background throughout your presentation. Be careful not to choose anything too annoying.

Tip

If you add background music to your presentation do not use any other sound effects as they will clash and sound awful!

To choose a movie clip or sound that you may have previously saved, choose the Movie From File, or Sound From File option on the menu. This will prompt you for a search of your hard drive or network drive to retrieve the saved file.

TASK

Insert a sound into your presentation. Make sure that the sound you choose matches the coffee theme, or choose something that will not be too distracting. The sound should be background music to play throughout your presentation.

Animated Sequences for Text and Graphics

You may wish to make your presentation more interesting by adding animations to text and graphical objects. This may also be useful if you want to discuss a line of text at a time, and not the whole page. To animate text or graphics

in an existing presentation, click on the Slide Show menu and then choose Custom Animation. This allows you to choose different animations for each part of your slide, and presentation. The first tab deals with the order and timing of the elements.

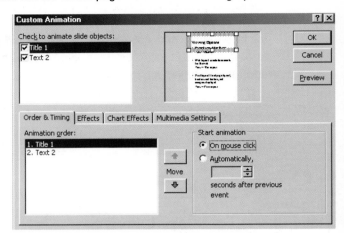

1 Custom animation lists all the elements of your slide, click in the check box next to the ones you want to animate.

2 The elements will be listed in the Animation order box as you click on them. Here you can change the order of the animations.

3 You are given the option to start the animation on a mouse click, or automatically after the number of seconds you input.

The Effects tab deals with types of animation, the entry of the elements and how you want to introduce the animated element.

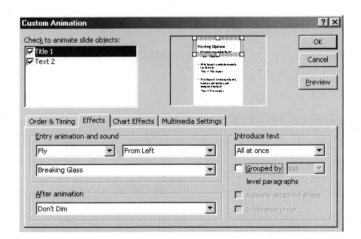

From this dialog box you can choose:

1 The type of animation, for example Fly, Blinds and Spiral.

2 The entry of the element – bottom, top, left, right or any combination of these.

3 What happens to the text after the animation – should it dim, disappear, or change colour?

4 To introduce the text all at once, or by word and even by letter.

The entrance of the element can also be announced with sounds such as breaking glass, applause or the sound of a cash register.

Once you have decided on the options for animated elements, you can check that they all work as you have planned by previewing the presentation. When happy, click OK.

REFINE AND STANDARDISE SLIDES FOR A PRESENTATION

Working with Margins, Tabs and Indents

MS PowerPoint doesn't have fixed margins as in word processing programs. You can place text and objects right up to the edges of a slide. You can align objects by resizing their placeholders on new slides or resizing objects on existing slides. To help you align objects, you can position guides on a slide in place of margins.

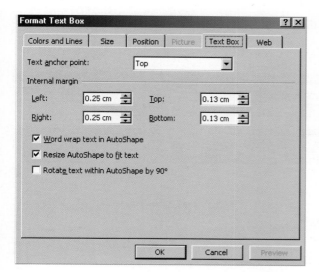

To change the margins around text in an object:

1 Select the object that has the text whose margins you want to change.

2 On the Format menu, click the command for the type of object you selected – for example, AutoShape or Text Box – and then click the Text Box tab.

3 Select the Resize AutoShape to fit text check box.

4 Under Internal margin, adjust the measurements to increase or decrease the distance between the text and the object.

The size of the object increases or decreases to accommodate the new margins.

To change the tabstops for text:

1 In the slide pane, select the text where you want to set or clear tab stops.

2 If the ruler isn't displayed, click Ruler on the View menu.

3 To set a tab stop, click the tab button at the left of the horizontal ruler to display the type of tab you want, and then click the ruler where you want to set the tab.

4 To clear a tab stop, drag the tab marker off the ruler.

There are different types of tabs to choose from the most popular of these are shown below:

Tip

You can set as many tabs as you want; default tabs in front of tabs you set are cancelled.

To Align	Click	To Align	Click
Left edge of text with tab	⌞	Right edge of text with tab	⌟
Center of text with tab	⊥	Decimal points in text with tab	⊥∙

You can click on the tab button to change it to the different types of tab.

If tabs are not what you want you can set indents for the slide. Indents are the distance that the text is from the edge of the page. There are different types of indent to choose from. These are First Line Indent, Hanging Indent, and Paragraph Indent. The indents are on the ruler, so make sure that you can see the ruler (as before).

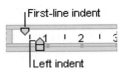

1 To set the indent for the first line of a paragraph, drag the upper indent marker. (First Line Indent)

2 To set the left indent for other lines in a paragraph, drag the lower indent marker. The rectangular part of the lower indent marker also moves with it. (Hanging Indent)

3 To maintain the relationship between the first line and the rest of the paragraph, move both markers by dragging the rectangular part of the lower marker. (Paragraph Indent)

Using Guides

We have already shown how to use the ruler to help you to align text and graphic objects in your presentation, but if you want to align elements perfectly you may want to use the guides.

To see the default guides that come with PowerPoint, click on the View menu and choose Guides. The dotted lines will appear on your slide. To add more guides, hold the control key down and click on an existing guide.

The distance between guides is measured as you drag, so you can accurately space the guides. Each new guide will show up as a dotted line on your slide.

These guides are only visible on the screen – they do not print.

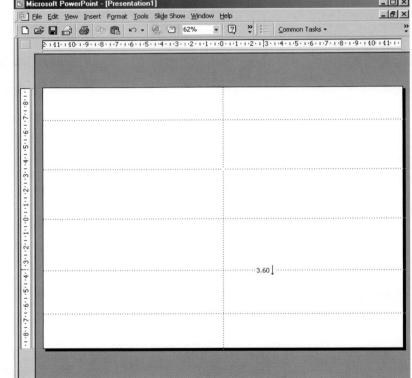

Aligning Text

You can use the horizontal and vertical rulers to move and align objects precisely. If the rulers aren't displayed, click Ruler on the View menu. When displayed, the rulers appear at the top and left side of the slide pane. When you move the pointer or a drawing tool, its movement traces on the rulers to show you precisely where you are on the slide.

The appearance of the ruler changes depending on what you select on the slide. When you select a picture or an AutoShape, the ruler's origin is at the centre. When you select text, its origin is at the left. When you select text inside a text box, the ruler displays the indent markers and tabs for the text. Each text box has its own ruler and its own indentation and tab settings.

You can also use the guides to align text and graphics, as discussed before. Simply drag the text box or placeholder to where you want to start aligning, and add guides as necessary.

Grouping Text and Graphical Objects

In PowerPoint it is possible to group objects or elements on your presentation so that they form one cohesive object. This makes it easy to manipulate objects that will always be placed together. It is possible to combine text and graphics in this way. One of the most common reasons for combining text and graphics is where the text is used as a label or annotation for the graphic, as shown in the diagram.

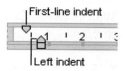

To create the text you will need to insert a text box for each item of text, i.e. one for the First-line indent label, and one for the Left indent label. These two text boxes can be combined with the graphic (the ruler picture) and the lines to create one object.

Repositioning and resizing grouped objects is achieved in the same way as you would reposition or resize a single object.

Before you group objects together, you may wish to change the stacking order of the objects. This can be done by right clicking on the object and choosing Order. Ordering objects was discussed in full in level 1.

There is also the option to rotate the object, either left or right, or using the free rotate tool. You can also flip the object vertically or horizontally, and invert the grouped object. These options are all available on the Draw toolbar.

PRODUCING A HARD COPY OF YOUR PRESENTATION

When you have completed your presentation, you may wish to keep a hard copy of the presentation, print off just one slide, or print off handouts for your audience to use while you are presenting the slides. You can also print a copy of the presentation for yourself, with the notes you have made, to help you when presenting. All these options are available on the Print dialog box, from the File Menu.

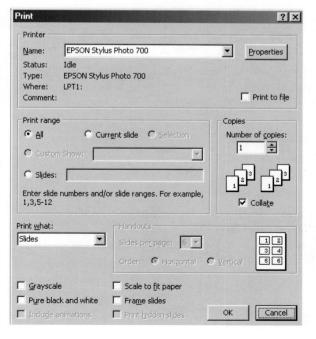

To print the entire presentation:

1   Click on the File menu and choose Print.

2   Under the Print range, click in the radio button next to All.

3   Make sure that under Print what you have selected Slides.

4   Click OK.

5   This will print all the slides in your presentation.

To print off a particular slide, make sure that the slide is selected. Follow the steps as above, except under Print range click in the radio button next to Current slide. You can also input the numbers of the slides you wish to print in the space next to Slides, under Print range. This will print only the selected slides.

To print handouts for your audience to use:

1 Click on the File menu and choose Print.

2 Under Print what select Handouts.

3 Then choose the number of slides you want on the page, and whether the layout should be vertical or horizontal.

4 You can also choose to print a colour presentation in black and white or greyscale to save on colour ink and reduce printing costs.

5 Do not forget to change the number of copies.

6 Click OK.

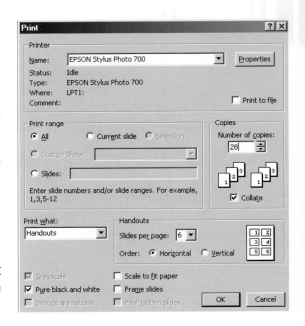

To print the entire presentation, with all the notes you have made, select Outline view from the Print what drop down menu. To print only the notes, select Notes from the drop down menu.

TASK

When you have finished designing your presentation, print out a set of handouts for your employees to follow when you make the presentation. Print six slides per page. You also need to print out a set of slides to keep in your management file. You only have a monochrome printer at the café, so you will have to set up to print the slides accordingly.

RUNNING A SLIDESHOW

Using the Slide Sorter View

You can change the view to slide sorter view so that you are able to view all slides in your presentation at once. In this view it is very easy to change the order of the slides, or duplicate and delete slides.

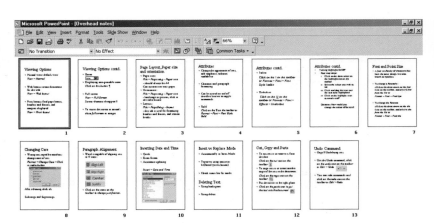

To switch to Slide Sorter View, click on Slide Sorter on the View menu. This will change your screen so that it shows all slides.

To duplicate a slide:

1 Click on the slide to select it – the slide will have a blue border around it when selected.

2 Then click on the Edit menu, and select Duplicate. This will make an exact copy of the slide.

3 The duplicate slide will appear to the right of the original.

4 You can move the slide to a new location by dragging it.

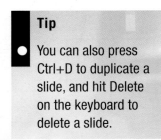

Tip

You can also press Ctrl+D to duplicate a slide, and hit Delete on the keyboard to delete a slide.

To delete a slide:

1   Click on the slide to select it.

2   On the Edit menu, choose Delete.

3   All the slides will shift to the left.

To move slides into sequence:

1   Click on the slide to be moved to select it.

2   Hold down the left mouse button and drag the slide to its new location.

3   Drop the slide where the grey line indicates between two slides.

4   The slide will be moved to its new location.

Setting up the Slideshow

Transition is the word that PowerPoint uses to describe how slides arrive on screen. To set up the transition between slides, you will need to decide what type of slide show you are presenting. If it is a professional presentation, you may want to limit the noises and special effects, or at least link them to the subject of your presentation. Transitions between slides can be set up to be mouse controlled or automatic. When setting up automatic timings remember there may need to be some extra time included for questions from the audience. This can all go wrong if your new slide comes up before you've had a chance to explain the previous slide!

To select types of transition between slides, click on the Slide Show menu and choose Slide Transition. The Slide Transition dialog box will appear.

This dialog box offers the opportunity to choose the effect and the speed that the effect will appear.

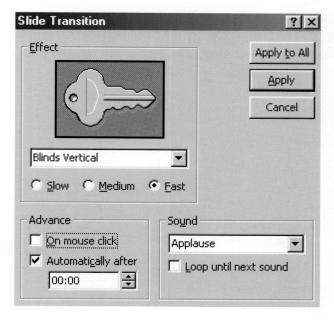

It also gives you the option of choosing whether to move to the next slide On mouse click, or Automatically after the number of seconds you input.

The sound drop-down menu offers a range of sounds such as breaking glass, applause and cash register to greet your new slide. You can also loop the sound, which means the sound will play continuously.

These options are either applicable to one slide only (Apply) or to all the slides in your presentation (Apply to All).

To set up your slide show, choose Set Up Show from the Slide Show menu. This dialog box will give you the option of setting up your show to perfection, deciding who will be using the show, and creating looped presentations.

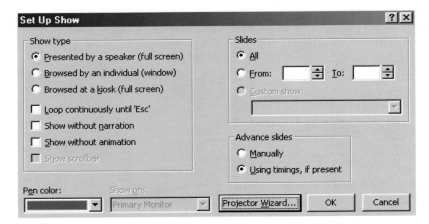

Once you have created your presentation, you need to decide what type of show you have created the presentation for. If you (or someone else) are going to present the slideshow, then you will choose the option Presented by speaker. This will ensure that your slideshow is presented full screen.

If you have designed the presentation to be viewed by an individual – say for an insurance salesman to take around with him to clients – then select the option Browsed by an individual.

Finally, your slideshow may have been designed to show at an exhibition or awards evening, and will need to show continuously unaided for a period of time. If this is the case, then choose Browsed at kiosk, and click in the check box next to Loop Continuously until 'Esc'.

You will need to make sure that all slides are included, by clicking in All, and that you are using timings, by clicking in Use timings if present under Advance Slides.

To add a bit of spice to your show, you may want to draw on the presentation while you are delivering it. You may want to underline certain words or areas to add emphasis. To do this you can use the pen option. You can choose the pen colour to contrast with your slide show by clicking on the drop-down menu under pen colour. To draw with the pen *during the presentation*, follow these steps:

1 Right click and choose Pointer Option and Pen from the shortcut menu.

2 The pointer changes to a pen.

3 Drag the pointer to draw lines and shapes on-screen.

4 Press 'Esc' when you have finished using the pen.

Once you have completed your set up, click OK.

Dress Rehearsal

Before you give a presentation, it is advisable to practise it a few times. As you dress rehearse, check the timings to see how long the slides stay on-screen, and time the presentation to see how long it takes. Just in case, you may want to include a couple of hidden slides that you may choose to show if your presentation runs short.

To dress rehearse your presentation:

1 Switch to slide sorter view.

2 From the Slide Show menu, click Rehearse timings.

3 The first slide fills the entire screen. In the lower right hand corner of the slide the rehearsal dialog box shows how long the first slide in the presentation has been on-screen, and how long the slide show has taken so far.

4 Pretend you are giving the presentation, and go through all the slides, discussing everything you are planning to say in relation to each slide. Click on the arrow button to move to next slide. Pause as necessary, and when you think the slide may start a discussion, leave that slide on-screen for longer.

5 When you click the arrow button after seeing the last slide, a message box will appear on-screen. This box tells you how long the presentation has taken, and asks if you want to record the new slide timings and use them in the slide show.

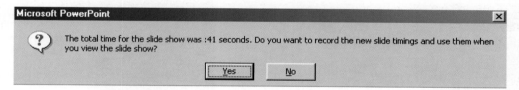

TASK

Run through your completed presentation. Check the timing of each slide, and the time taken to present the entire slideshow.
Enter the total time the slideshow took to present here: ....

PACK AND GO: VIEW YOUR PRESENTATION ON ANOTHER COMPUTER

When you want to run a slide show on another computer, you can use the Pack and Go Wizard to pack your presentation. The wizard packs all the files and fonts used in the presentation together on a disk or network location.

When you intend to run your show on a computer that doesn't have PowerPoint installed, you have the option of including the PowerPoint viewer. You can include linked files as part of your package, and if you use TrueType fonts you can include them as well. If you make changes to your presentation after you use the Pack and Go Wizard, just run the wizard again to update the package.

After you pack the presentation, you can unpack the presentation to run on another computer.

To pack up a presentation

1 Open the presentation you want to pack.

2 On the File menu, click Pack and Go.

3 Follow the instructions in the Pack and Go Wizard. See the steps shown below:

Step 1

Step 2

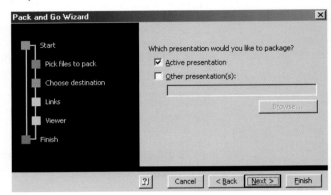

Step 3

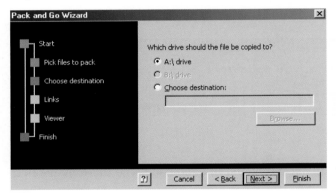

Step 4

Step 5

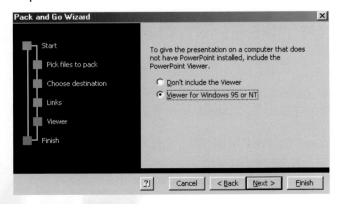

Step 6

4 If prompted, insert another disk.

To unpack the presentation on the destination computer:

1 Insert the disk or connect to the network location you packed the presentation to.

2 In Windows Explorer, go to the location of the packed presentation, and double-click it.

3 Enter the destination you want to copy the presentation to.

If you have packed the viewer, you will have the option of unpacking it with the rest of your presentation.

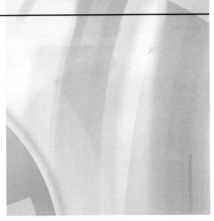

UNIT 027 COMPUTERISED ACCOUNTS

USING THE OPERATING SYSTEM

Introduction to Sage Instant Accounts

Any computerised accounting system should allow you to record, control and examine finances more easily than traditional manual systems. Whenever an invoice, credit note or journal is created, it should update all the appropriate records. Invoices and credit notes can be printed from within the system. All the information can be set up and recalled by the appropriate transactions.

Getting Started

This section explains how to access Sage Instant Accounts.

After turning on your computer, you can access the accounting software using three different methods:

1 **Programs**
   - Search for the software name
   - Then click on it

2 **Shortcut**
   - Click on the icon

3 **Search facility**
   - Search for the appropriate accounting software with the correct suffix
   - Double-click on the software application

Entering your Environment Settings

From within the system you are able to personalise the accounting system to your own working environment.

To set your environment defaults from the Options window:

- Click the Environment tab – the Environment information appears.

- In the boxes provided enter the function key information.

- To save any changes and exit – click OK.
- To exit without saving – click Cancel.

Function Keys

Function keys can be used to call up any program that you need quickly.

The following function key information can be entered:

F11 Key The F11 key is automatically set to run CONTROL.EXE. This is the Windows' Control Panel which lets you change your Windows system settings such as the date and time, printer fonts, colours and so on. For further information about the Control Panel, see your Windows User's Guide.

F12 Key This key is set up to run REPDES.EXE. This is the Report Designer, which you can use to create and edit all your reports and layouts.

Accounting System Requirements

All accounting systems should be integrated so that you only need to enter and update once for all changes to be effective throughout. This provides you with the advantage of input at any level in the business.

You set up processes and procedures, which are then followed by all within the business. All double-entry book-keeping is done for you by the system.

Keeping track of all trading is made easy through graphs, tables and built-in reports. These features allow you to see where your money is coming from and where it is going.

When setting up any accounting system you need to make certain decisions before transactions can be recorded. Each business has its own needs and time constraints but with implementation of any new system it should be introduced at the business's own pace.

If it is a new set up for a business, you will need to go through the following stages step-by-step:

- Set up and check your nominal account structure.
- Enter your customer records and their opening balances.
- Enter your supplier records and their opening balances.
- Enter the opening balances for your nominal ledger.
- Enter the opening balances for your bank accounts.
- Enter your product details.

About this Guide

Sage Instant Accounts is fully compatible with Windows. If you are familiar with the terminology of Windows this will be helpful. You can decide whether to use the keyboard or the mouse to work the system.

This course will provide you with an introduction to computerised accounts and how to operate within this type of environment.

There are many different types of accounting packages available; most of them will tend to use similar terminology and rules to record transactions. In this particular course we shall be using **Sage Instant Accounts**. The course will show you how computerised accounts packages work and how they can be tailored to suit individual company accounts.

Prerequisites The majority of computerised accounts packages tend to be Windows based; therefore you should be competent in using a computer including the mouse and keyboard.

This course covers many aspects of accounting and bookkeeping including the following:

- Customers under the sales ledger

- Suppliers under the purchase ledger

- Nominal ledger

- Bank transactions

- Products

- Invoicing including credit notes

- Financials section to cover accounting aspects

- Period ends

Introducing Sage Instant Accounts

When opening Sage the following screen will appear:

The screen below provides a background to the structure of the set up within the Nominal tab. Working within the Nominal tab is covered later in this chapter.

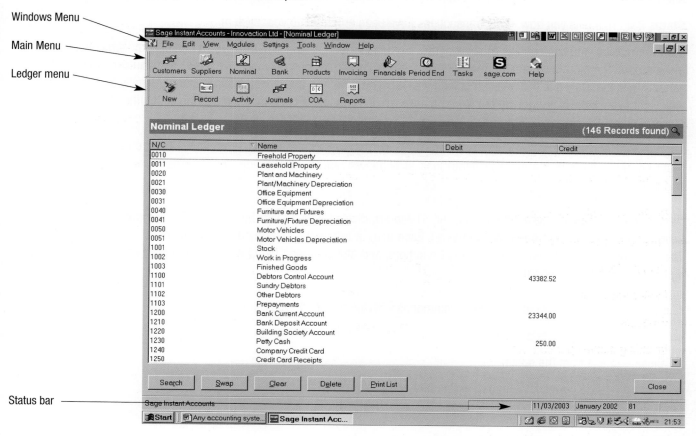

As you can see it is a Windows-compatible system with large amounts of information within it. The normal Windows type toolbar shows:

- File

- Edit

- View

- Modules

- Settings

- Tools

- Windows

- Help

Accounting System Menu To open an option, point the cursor on the icon you want and click the mouse. Alternatively you can choose the required option from the Options menu.

Status Bar This tells you how many transactions have been entered into your system.

Using Windows You can open as many windows from the system as you like. However, it can become difficult to move around the system without getting confused. It is advisable to open only those windows that you can reasonably manage. Only one window can be active at any one time. The active window is coloured (usually blue) while inactive windows are greyed out. When more than one window is open they will overlap each other, but the active window will always be in front.

Sage Instant Accounts has the same functionalities as Windows where document windows can be minimised, restored, resized etc. For a more in-depth look at Windows refer to your guide from Microsoft for navigation and training.

Data is entered into the system using 'forms'. These are divided into smaller boxes and data is input using the keyboard or by selecting from a list of choices. Each item of information recorded in the system is called a field. There are numeric fields, which only accept numbers, and alphanumeric fields which accept both numeric and alpha keys from the keyboard.

Menu Commands You are able to select commands with the aid of a keyboard or a mouse.

- Save – to accept the data entered.

- Close – to exit from the option.

- Discard – to clear any data entered in the data entry boxes from the screen.

- OK – to save, process the data and exit the option.

- Cancel – to act as the Discard button and also exit the option.

Using Drop-Down List Boxes Some fields have a drop-down list box. Drop-down lists are indicated by a down-pointing arrow in a small box at the right-hand end of the field. When you click onto the down arrow it offers a selection. Click on any item to display that option on your screen.

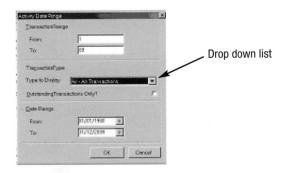

Drop down list

Radio Buttons Radio buttons allow you to select an item from a list. If you wanted to select from the list offered for printing, for example, then the Output box is displayed with options, which you select from. Only one option can be selected.

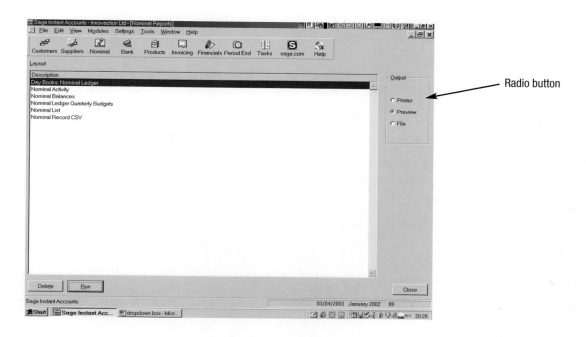

Radio button

Check Boxes Check boxes allow you to select one or more actions from a selection. See below for an example of a check box:

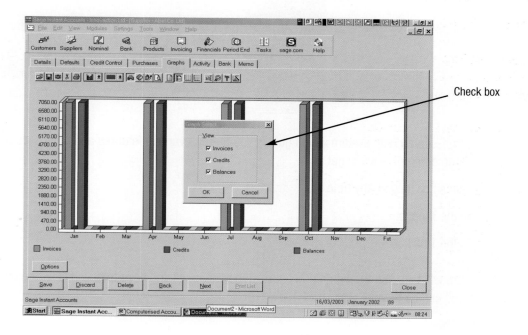

Check box

To access the screen shown above do the following:

1   In the Suppliers tab choose Record.

2   Select any supplier record.

3   Choose Graph.

4   This will allow the following views:
   – Invoices
   – Credits
   – Balances

Function Keys Function keys provide shortcuts to fields that are used frequently. An example of a function key is the F1 key. Pressing F1 accesses Sage Instant Accounts' on-line help. You should take the time to familiarise yourself with the following function keys:

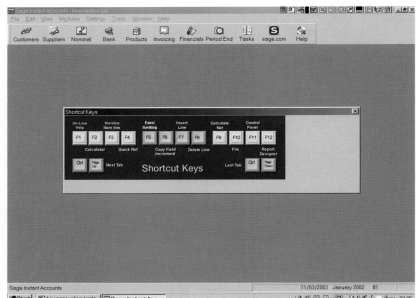

F2	Calculator
F3	Invoice item line
F4	Quick reference
F5	Spelling
F6	Copy field
F7	Insert line
F8	Delete line
F9	Calculate Net
F10	File
F11	Control Panel
F12	Report designer

Getting Help There is an on-screen Help system which guides you through various features and processes of the program. There are three different ways to get help:

● Press F1 for context-sensitive help at any time.

● Click the Help icon on the Toolbar.

● Click the Help icon on the Title bar.

Wizards A Wizard program will take you through a procedure step by step. All you have to do is follow the on-screen instructions. Wizards can be found:

● Under Modules on the Title bar.

● In Tools on the Title bar under Global Changes.

- In upgrade Program and Convert data.

- In the Bank Transfer window.

Virus Checker

Virus checks should be made on a regular basis and before you back up any data. There are a number of virus detection software packages available. Running virus checks ensures that any programs you run are protected from corruption.

You should also follow internal procedures specific to your workplace for opening emails or email attachments as these can also contain viruses. There are further warnings on macros used in Windows software. There is no special anti-virus software required for this package other than the one already in use on your computer.

Tip

1   Never download files from unknown or suspicious sources.

2   Avoid direct disk sharing with read/write access unless there is absolutely a business requirement to do so.

3   Always scan a floppy disk from an unknown source for viruses before using it.

4   Back-up critical data and system configurations on a regular basis and store the data in a safe place.

5   When the anti-virus software is disabled, do not run any applications that could transfer a virus, e.g., email or file sharing.

6   New viruses are discovered everyday so it is important that you periodically check for any updated versions of anti-virus software.

7   Always run the corporate standard anti-virus software.

8   NEVER open any files or macros attached to an email from an unknown, suspicious or untrustworthy source.

Developing a Backup Strategy

It is essential that you regularly back up your data. Even though complete disaster is rare, the importance of backing up your data cannot be emphasised enough. This software has Backup and Restore facilities which can be accessed from the File menu.

The safest strategy is to back up your data every day and before processes such as global updates and the Month/Year End procedures. These processes affect several files simultaneously so an error can cause widespread discrepancies in your data. An up-to-date backup will restore the original data in a few minutes.

Every business should do daily backups. However, if you are inputting large amounts of invoices every few hours then you should back up your files more often. The most significant criterion for determining the frequency of your backups is the importance of the data. If the data is vital to the running of your business, you should make a backup as often as practicable.

After you have decided how often to back up you, need to consider how many backups you are going to take. It is not uncommon for backup disks to become corrupted. A method commonly adopted is son, father and grandfather (notations used with at least three backup files). One of the files in the above method should be stored off site, in case of fire or other disasters.

Every three months it is advisable to replace your backup disks with new ones, because of the likelihood of faults occurring through general wear-and-tear.

Selecting Files for Backup

Some systems will automatically backup your data files using the floppy disk drive A. However, you can choose to backup all your files, your report and/or layout templates, your product images or just your data files.

Files that you are backing up must have a correct file extension otherwise they will not be included in the backup. For example, if you are backing up layout templates all of the files must have the file extension .SLY, while image files must have the extension .JPG or .GIF.

Backing Up your Data

The amount of disk space required depends on how much data you have saved in your program. If you are backing up to floppy disk make sure you have a set of blank disks ready.

Do not forget to label your disk(s) with the date and file name. If you use more than one disk, you should also number the disks sequentially indicating how many disks there are in total, for example 1 of 4, 2 of 4 etc.

You should also write on the label the files that you have backed up – data files, layout templates, report templates or all files. Therefore, if you only need to restore specific files, you know which disk to use.

To backup a file do the following:

- Open the File menu and choose Backup.

  A message appears asking you if you would like to check your data. It is recommend that data is checked before it is backed up.

- To check the data click on Yes.

  However, if you are confident of the data then click No. This option will be available in all accounting systems that are available as off the shelf packages.

- Normally a display appears on the screen to show you what is taking place and to what degree the checking has progressed.

After the process is complete a report will appear providing you with output.

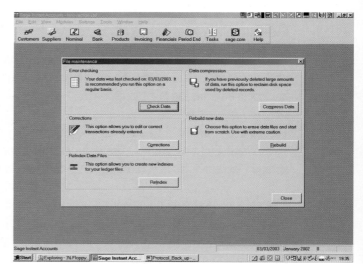

If any errors or warnings appear, you should fix them before continuing with the data backup.

- To continue with the backup, click Close.

- The Previous Paths drop-down list shows the location of your previous backups. If you want to back up your data to one of the previous locations, select the path you require from the list.

  Alternatively, enter the drive, directory and file name you require in the boxes provided.

> **Tip**
>
> *By default the backup will be saved onto your C drive in the path C:\Program Files\Sage\Accounts in a file called SAGEBACK.001.*

You should use a simple and appropriate description for your backup, for example Week 1 dated 25/03/2002. Type the text you require in the Description box.

1 Select the type of data that you want to backup from the File Type check boxes. Choose from:
   - All Files
   - Data Files
   - Report Templates
   - Layout Templates
   - Image Files

2 To proceed with the backup, click OK.

   If you do not want to continue with the backup, click Cancel.

3 If you have chosen to overwrite an existing backup a warning message appears informing you of this.

   To overwrite the file, click Yes.

   If you do not want to overwrite the file, click No.

4 The Backup window appears, showing the details of the backup as it proceeds.

   If you are backing up onto floppy disk you are prompted to replace each disk, as it becomes full.

5 When the backup is finished, a message box appears telling you whether the backup has been successful or not. Click OK to acknowledge this message.

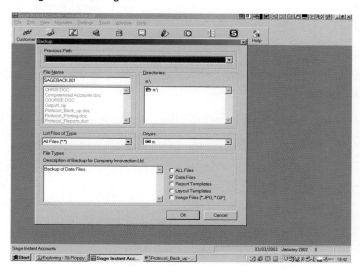

To Restore Data from Backup

If an error has occurred and you need to restore a previous backup, do the following:

1. Open the File menu and choose Restore.

   The Restore window appears:

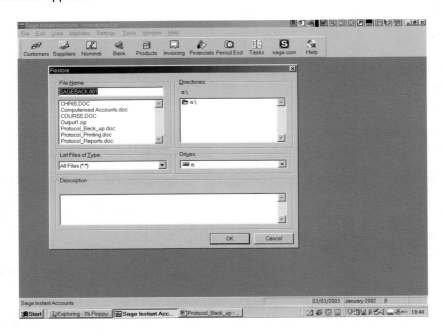

2. Locate the file you want to restore and click OK.

NB: You must restore all of your data. It is vital that you do not restore data selectively. For example, you cannot restore assets.dta in isolation from other data files or use the MS-DOS copy command to restore individual files. If you do a mismatch between the ledger data may result and your data will become corrupted.

The Restore procedure automatically restores all of your backed up data, if you choose to use another method ensure that you restore the full data set.

A message appears informing you that you are about to restore data and that the current data within your company will be overwritten. To continue click Yes or, if you wish to exit from the procedure, click No.

When the restore is finished, a message box appears telling you whether the restore has been successful or not. Click OK to acknowledge this message.

After successfully restoring your backup data use the Check Data option from the File Maintenance window to make sure your data is not corrupt.

Changing your Backup Utility

If you use an alternative method of backing up your data, for example an external zip drive or tape-stream, you can set it up using the Backup option.

1 Open the Tools menu and choose Options.

   The Options window appears, showing the Toolbar tab.

2 Click the Backup tab.

3 In the Backup box enter the full path for the backup utility you require.

   Click Browse to help you find the path.

4 To save your settings click OK.

Access Rights

The Access Rights feature lets you set individual passwords for each person who has access to the accounting software. You can even restrict which ledgers, menus and windows each user can use and you can hide your bank and nominal balances from certain users if you wish. You can also choose to restrict access to reports, assign Access Rights to Options and restrict which options and menus a user can access from the main window.

For example, you can limit a user to have access only to the Customers and Suppliers options or to give the accounts manager sole access to your financial information.

NB: If you remove a user's access to reports, that user will not have access to any ledger letters, statements or any ledger reports. This user will also be unable to access any of the reports in the Financials option (for example, the balance sheet and profit and loss reports).

Changing the Access Rights for Windows

You can restrict the windows in each option for different users.

For example, a user with access to the Customers option may only need to be able to access the Records, Letter and Labels windows.

Tip

The Bank and Nominal options also contain a window called Balances. If you deny a user access to Balances the user will be unable to see the balances of either the bank accounts or the nominal accounts.

1 From the User's list on the User Access Rights window, select the user whose access rights you wish to change.

2 Click Details; the Access Details window appears. Select the option you require then click Dialogs. The Dialogs window appears listing all of the modules that belong to the option selected and showing their current access status. To see the modules that the user can currently access for an option, double-click on the required option icon from the Access Details window (or highlight with the arrow keys then press the Spacebar). The Access Details list expands to show the access rights status of each module.

3   Change the access rights for the windows listed by selecting the module(s) you require then clicking either the Full Access or No Access button.

4   To accept your new user details click OK or, to clear the details and start again, click Discard. To exit without saving click Close.

5   To view the modules you have just set up, double-click on the Option icon in the Access Details window.

Creating a New User

1   Open the Settings menu from the main menu bar and choose the Access Rights option. The User Access Rights window appears listing all of the available users.

2   Click New. The Create New User window appears.

3   In the boxes provided, enter the logon and password information.

    Indicate the overall access you are giving this new user by selecting one of the Access Rights option buttons.

4   To accept your new user details click Save or, to clear the details and start again, click Discard.

5   To exit the Create New User window click Close. The New User name now appears in the Users list box on the User Access Rights window.

Deleting a User

1   Select the user to be deleted from the User's list box on the User Access Rights window.

2   Click Delete. The Delete User window appears asking you to confirm deletion.

3   If you wish to delete the user access rights click Yes. If you do not wish to delete the user access rights, click No. You are then returned to the User Access Rights window.

Editing a User's Password

To change a user's password select the Edit button. A Manager could use this if a user had forgotten his (or her) password or to change users' passwords on a regular basis.

You can also use this option to change a user's access rights to 'Full' or 'None'.

Networked Systems

Each company buying any accounting software will have its own environment set up. Both single and multiple users can be networked to a server. However, it is only usually multiple users that need Sage installed on their server. A single user would have the software installed on his or her computer.

With the multi-user option the setup of networking access and sharing files is paramount. Normally, each individual follows procedures in accordance with their job role.

As many users will be accessing the system, the database should be installed onto the server with the appropriate access available for each user. This way the viewing option is available to all who do not have the authority to update any record or transaction.

As an individual you would access your section of the system and record information as normal. If this were to be shared then access to other users would be made available. The only problem with this situation is the updating of records by two or more users simultaneously. This may block the record being updated.

Sharing files is down to the access path to the server. Usually the profile of an individual will allow that person the access and the sharing facilities on the network.

Printing

To print a document select the Printer option then click Run.

The Print window then appears. This allows you to choose how many copies to print and what specific pages you want to print etc.

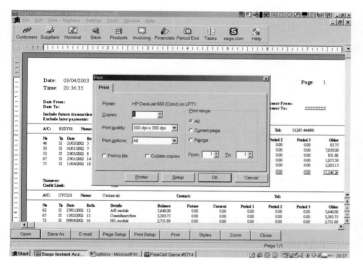

When you print certain documents, such as Customer reports, the Criteria window appears for you to select the information that you want to include in a particular report or document.

Report layout files control the appearance of your reports or stationery. When you print a fixed report, the default Windows printer is loaded. If you have created your own layout files you can assign the report to a printer. It is this printer that is loaded for you. If that printer is not available the Windows default printer is used automatically.

Sage has a Print Manager facility. This is very useful as it allows your document to be held in a queue until the printer becomes available.

Changing the Default Printer

1   Choose the Printer button. The Printer Setup window appears.

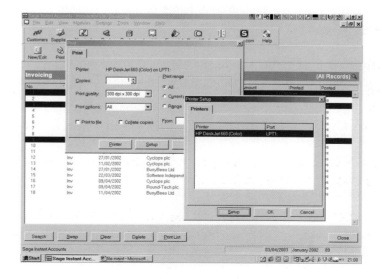

2   Choose the printer you require from the list of available printers.

3   To change the print options, such as intensity control, click Setup.

Printing 'Batched' Invoices and Credit Notes

Use this function when you want to print or spool (save to file to print later) a copy of one or more invoices or credit notes. By 'batching' invoices or credit notes in this way you can make sure that the correct stationery is in the printer and you can then print out all your invoices at once.

The layout of the invoice or credit note document is dependent on the stationery layout file selected. Both the layout and the content of the document is determined by the stationery layout file used.

If you want certain fields included or removed from a document you will need to amend the existing layout or create an alternative document.

Standard invoice layouts have been designed to fit the stationery supplied but for other systems you can edit these and create your own.

To print or 'spool' invoices or credit notes:

1   First select the relevant records from the Invoicing list window by highlighting the required invoices with your mouse . You can use the Search button if you wish to print a selection.

2   Having identified the invoice(s) or credit note(s) to be printed, click Print.

All invoices and credit notes that have been printed will be flagged in the list displayed in the Invoicing window, but can be reprinted if required.

You can reprint your invoices as many times as you wish.

Immediate Printing of Product Invoice or Product Credit Note

When you create an invoice you have the choice of either printing it straight away or saving it to print later in a 'batch'.

The layout of the invoice and its content is dependent upon the stationery layout file selected. If you want certain fields included or removed from a document you will need to amend the existing layout or create an alternative document.

Accounting standard systems have standard invoice layouts, which have been designed to fit the stationery supplied but you can edit these and create your own.

You can reprint your invoices as many times as you wish.

Printing Problems

This section explains the various problems that you may encounter when printing.

Nothing prints on the page

1 Check the printer is turned on and that the 'On-line' light is on.

2 Find out how the printer is attached to the machine:

 – Is it attached to the local machine directly? If so, to which port? This is usually LPT1.
 – Is it attached via a network? If so you will need to know the network path to your printer and how to re-establish it. If you do not know the path or how to set the link then seek help from your network support engineer.

3 If the printer is installed as a local printer and it appears to be printing to an incorrect local port then you must connect the printer driver to the correct port.

4 Once you have checked all of the above, try to print again.

Strange characters print on the page

● You may be using the wrong printer driver

● The printer may have been interrupted half way through printing and is resuming the print job.

To fix the problem do the following:

1 Check the model of printer and the printer driver being used and see if they are compatible.

2 If not then install the correct printer driver from the Windows Installation disks. Refer to your Windows manuals for instructions on how to do this.

3 If the printer driver is correct for the printer then make sure that there are no jobs in the print queue.

4 If there are print jobs in the queue then reload the program and try to print a short report/invoice again. If not, close Windows and reboot the machine, then try printing.

5 If you have tried all of the above points and you still have no success printing, load up another program (e.g. WordPad if you are using Windows 95) and try to print using this programme. If this also prints incorrectly then refer to your hardware documentation.

Printing your Layout File

1 From an open report, select the Report Designer's File menu and choose the Print option (or click Print from the main toolbar).

 – The Print window appears. From here you can confirm or change your printer selection. The printer that is displayed is the one that has been selected using the Report Designer's Printer Setup option.
 – To change the printer you require, click Printer. To amend the controls of your printer, click Setup.

2 In the boxes provided, enter your printing requirements.

3   From the Print Options drop-down list select how you want to print your report.

The All option uses true type fonts and is the slowest of the four options in this list. The quickest method of printing is to use the Quick Text option. This automatically selects the quickest font suitable for your printer. From here you can also set your Print Quality.

4   Click OK to print or click Cancel to return to your report.

Alternatively click Printer and select the printer you wish to use (if it is different from your default printer) or click Setup to change how you wish the printer to print your report. (For more information on the Printer and Setup options, please refer to your Windows documentation).

Creating a Report

1   From the appropriate window e.g. Invoice Reports, Customer Letters, Nominal Reports etc, click New. Alternatively from the Report Designer window, open the File menu and choose the New option.

2   The Report Wizard then appears to guide you through the early steps of creating your own report/layout. Follow the Wizard's on-screen prompts and instructions. When the Wizard is finished the Report Designer appears with the new report/layout already open for you to work on.

3   You can now either save your new document, preview or print it.

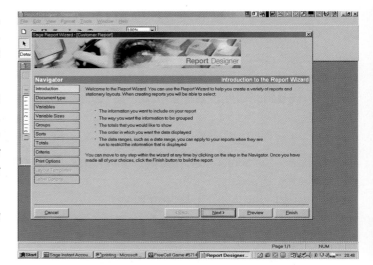

To Print an Audit Trail Report

1   From the main toolbar, click Financials.

2   Click Audit (or click Reports) then choose the report you require. The Audit Trail Report window appears.

3   Select the type of audit trail you require from the option buttons provided i.e. Brief, Summary, Detailed or Deleted Transactions.

4   Select whether or not you want to print the report in landscape or portrait format by selecting the relevant text box.

5   Select the type of output you require from the Output option buttons provided i.e. Printer, Preview, File or E-mail.

6   Click Run. The Criteria window appears.

7   If you want to restrict the Audit Trail report to display specific ranges of transactions, enter the range criteria in the boxes provided. The criteria that you can set here vary according to the Audit Trail report you selected. You can amend the Audit Trail report layout if necessary.

8   To generate the report, click OK.

9   To exit click Cancel.

File Maintenance: Problem Files

This window shows any comments, errors or warnings that have arisen as a result of the data check. The Summary tab lists these findings.

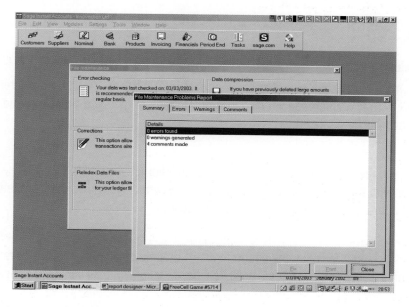

To view the comments, warnings or errors, choose the appropriate tab.

The three categories represent different types of data inconsistency:

Comments are the least serious of data problems and do not necessarily require correction. Nevertheless, they do indicate minor inconsistencies in the data, which you should consider investigating. For example, the Comments report will indicate when your month's turnover is negative, highlighting potential problems for your business.

Warnings Like comments, warnings do not necessarily require use of the fix option, however they do indicate quite serious problems that you should attend to promptly.

Errors indicate data problems. To rectify Errors use the Fix option, which can correct most of the problems highlighted in the Errors report.

Fix Option If you have any data errors you can Fix them using the fix option or you can print out a report showing the errors.

To print a report, choose the tab you require from the File Maintenance Problems Report then click Print.

Different Layout Types

Four different types of layouts make up the stationery and reports supplied in Sage Instant Accounts. Although these different types of layout each have their own separate features they work in very much the same way. Once you have become familiar with one type of layout file the others will be easy to use.

The different layout files and their unique features are listed below:

- **The Report Designer**

  The Report Designer includes a special Report Variable List option that controls how variables are sorted and how they filter the data they receive. The Report Designer also includes the ability to insert graphic objects, such as rectangles and lines.

- **Stationery Layouts**

  Stationery Layout files are designed to handle your every day stationery using pre-printed forms, such as 3-part invoice paper. They include special layout template files to give you a background image of the Sage stationery that they will be printed on.

- **Letter Layouts**

  The Report Designer gives you standard customer and supplier letters, which you can use at any time. As you get more familiar with the Report Designer you may wish to create your own standard letters, which incorporate data from the boxes in your customer or supplier records.

- **Label Layouts**

  The Label Report Designer includes the option to insert graphic objects. Also included is a special tab in the Page Setup option that lets you choose the specific type of stationery label you want to use.

Storage of Reports

By default all reports are stored locally on your computer's hard disk. However, you can choose to store the reports centrally on the network drive.

Sage Instant Accounts has an extra setting within Company Preferences called 'Use Data Path for Reports'. If this option is checked (the default) the program will always use the program path to find its reports (i.e. reports will be held locally on each computer).

If this option is unchecked, it will use the data path instead (i.e. reports will be held on one computer and all other computers linked to this one will use these reports).

Tip

If the Use Data Path for Reports option is enabled and you edit a report layout, it will only change the report held on the computer you are using. If you want the new report to be accessed by other PCs, either uncheck the Use Data Path for Reports or copy the new report onto the PC that is used to store the reports centrally.

To save your report/layout to a different file:

1 Open an existing layout or report file and make your changes.

2 Open the Report Designer File menu and choose the Save As option. The Save As window appears.

3 Enter the new name in the Filename text box.

It is good practice to save all layout files of the same type under one directory and give them the same file-name extension. By default, the layout files are stored in the following directory structures.

If you are using a program directory other than the default c:\Program Files\Accounts\, replace Accounts with your own directory name. See the following section for a further explanation of file extensions.

4 Click OK to save your report to a different file name or click Cancel to return to your report without saving your changes.

File Extensions

Stationery Layouts have the extension *.SLY and are found in the Program files\Accounts\Layouts directory.

Report Layouts have the extension *.SRT and are found in the Program files\Accounts\Reports*DIRNAME* direc-tory, where *DIRNAME* is the type of report, e.g. Customer for a customer report.

Label Layouts have the extension *.SLB and are found in the Program files\Accounts\Labels directory.

Letter Layouts have the extension *.SLT and are found in the Program files\Accounts\Letters directory.

All default layouts have the extension *.SLY or *.SRT.

Stationery Templates have the extension *.STM and are found in the Program files\Accounts\Templates directory.

Rebuilding Data Files

You can create new data files for all or selected parts of your accounting system. For example, if you have been using dummy data to familiarise yourself with the program and wish to clear your files prior to using it properly.

Alternatively, you may want to rebuild your audit trail but leave the accounts untouched because of data corruption.

Exiting Sage Accounts Instant

You should follow the correct procedures to exit Sage Instant Accounts otherwise your data and files may get damaged. To exit Sage Instant Accounts do the following:

1 Close all windows that are open.

2 The system will ask if you want to save the data. Respond Yes or No (any new file layouts that you have cre-ated will produce a prompt to save).

3 Ensure that all other users have finished (applies to applications where there are multiple users who likely to corrupt the data being saved). This will not apply in Sage Instant Accounts as there is only one user able to access the system.

4 Backup your files on the server or computer.

5 Select File, Exit.

6 Switch off your computer.

It is recommended that you follow the backup procedures mentioned previously in this section.

ENTERING AND RECORDING DATA

Advantages and Disadvantage of Computerised Systems

The use of a computerised accounting system such as Sage Instant Accounts has many advantages over a manual system. The advantages are listed below:

- It can be a more efficient, faster way of recording many transactions.
- The computer performs the calculations, so accuracy is guaranteed.
- You can use operators without any accounting knowledge for basic input.
- You can control accessibility to different levels set up by administration.
- When any general defaults are changed, such as VAT rate changes, the system will automatically re-calculate.
- Financial reports (B/S and P&L) are automatically generated.

There are also numerous disadvantages inherent within a computerised accounting system such as Sage Instant Accounts.

- It is expensive to install and implement.
- The recording of transactions is only as accurate as the operator who enters the data.
- Systems are reliant on constant power supply, any failure will lead to loss of data.
- You need to backup the computerised system regularly to ensure against corruption of data, or computer malfunction.

Manual systems have some advantages over accounting computerised systems, these include:

- Entries are all well understood.
- The audit trail is easy to follow.

Disadvantages include:

- It is very labour intensive.
- Changes in VAT rates or terms means changes to individual records.
- Storage of records takes up valuable space.
- Continuity is difficult; you require staff with the correct qualifications.

Customers

The customer option allows you to enter details of each customer and keep a track of what sales you make.

You can post any number of invoices and/or credit notes that are used to build reports. The activity screens will tell you when payments are due and when they are overdue.

Invoices are raised by using the information within the system. However, there are occasions when errors creep into the system and a reversing of the transaction is required, for this you will need to use a credit note.

It is always recommended that to reverse any incorrect entries or errors it is better to use the function that shows the opposite and equal entry. It further helps to keep the audit trail consistent and easy to read.

This section describes how to set up your customer records. It is very important that you plan the codes you will use for your customers. They all require a unique reference to identify them. It is recommended that you choose a meaningful code.

Tip

You need to make sure that you allocate a unique account code for each of your suppliers and customers. This will allow you to identify them easily when you record transactions against them, including their balances, activity and payment history.

For example, you could use the first six letters of the customer name. You should try and incorporate both letters and numbers into your code structure, as you may have customers with the same name, e.g. Mr Jones. You could set the code up as JONES01, so that a second Mr Jones could be identified as JONES02 and JONES03.

If you include numbers into your codes then you must include preceding zeros, as this helps to keep the sorting in the correct order.

Two examples of a coding structure for customers or suppliers are shown below.

Customer name	Code
Abel Co. Ltd	ABEL01
Abel Supplies	ABEL02
Gogetit	GOGE01

Customer name	Code
Abel Co. Ltd	00001
Abel Supplies	00010
Gogetit	00050

Customer Defaults It is useful to set up defaults within the system as this will save time if many of your customers have similar terms and conditions. The defaults will then appear automatically every time you create a new customer record, but can be amended to allow for any minor differences that there are.

To set up customer defaults:

1 Click on the Settings menu and choose Customer Defaults:

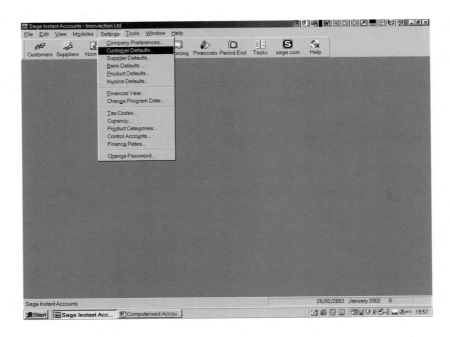

2 In the Record tab, fill in the following fields:

- Credit limit
- Payment due date
- Settlement discount
- Settlement due date
- Terms

3 Now complete the following fields:

- Currency
- Standard tax rate
- Default nominal code
- Descriptions for Invoices, Credits, Discount and Payments
- Ageing (options for calendar or period ageing and whether to include future totals in balances)

4 Once you have filled in all the required fields click OK.

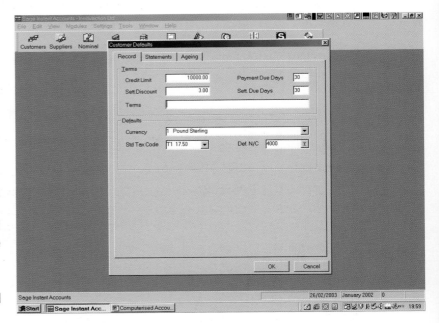

Creating a Customer Record Firstly click on the Customers icon, then click on the Record icon – the following window will appear:

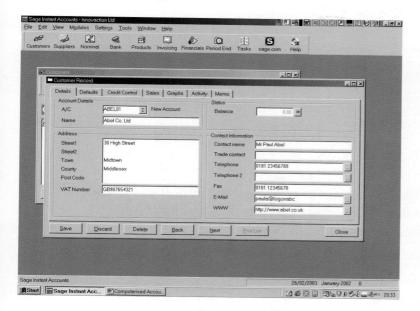

Use the Details tab to complete all the basic information needed for your customers.

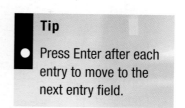

Tip

Press Enter after each entry to move to the next entry field.

- The Defaults tab allows you to edit/amend the automatic defaults you originally entered.

- The Credit Control tab allows you to enter or edit your credit control details.

- The Activity tab shows all the transactions you have against the customer.

- To save any changes, click on the Save button. If you do not wish to save the changes, click on the discard button.

Creating a Supplier Record

The supplier option allows you to enter details of each supplier and keep a track of what purchases you make.

You can post any number of invoices and/or credit notes that are used to build reports. Activity screens will inform you of payments that are due and when they are overdue so the appropriate action can be taken.

These invoices and credit notes are entered into the system when received from a supplier. However, as with your customer records there are occasions when errors creep into the system and you will need to reverse a transaction. Again, you would need to use a credit note. When reversing any incorrect entries or errors it is better to use the function that shows the opposite and equal entry. It further helps to keep the audit trail consistent and easy to read.

It is very important that you plan the codes for your suppliers. They all require a unique reference to identify them. It is recommended you choose a meaningful code.

You could for example use the first six letters of the supplier name. You should try and incorporate both letters and numbers into your code structure, as you may have customers with the same name, e.g. Bell Company. You could have the code set up as Bell01, so that a second Bell Company could be identified as Bell02 and Bell03.

If you include numbers into your codes then you must include preceding zeros, as this helps to keep the sorting in the correct order.

Two examples of a coding structure for suppliers are shown below.

Supplier name	Code
Clean Up	CLEA01
Power Supplies	POWE01
Smith & Jones	SMIT01

Supplier name	Code
Clean Up	00001
Power Supplies	00010
Smith & Jones	00050

Supplier Defaults It is useful to set up defaults within the system as this will save time if many of your suppliers have similar terms and conditions. The defaults will then appear automatically every time you create a new supplier record, but can be amended to allow for any minor differences that there are.

To set up supplier defaults:

1 Click on the Settings menu and choose Supplier Defaults.

2 In the Record tab, enter the terms required by your suppliers by completing the following fields:

   ● Credit limit
   ● Settlement discount
   ● Payment due days
   ● Settlement due days
   ● Terms

   Other defaults include:

   ● Currency
   ● Standard tax code
   ● Default nominal code

3 Then click OK to save.

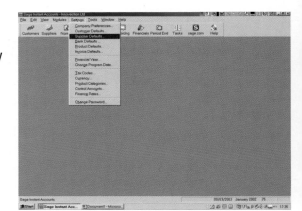

You need to be aware that there are dangers associated with data entry within a computerised system. If you enter incorrect data as a default setting, for example, on customer's terms of payments or on the cost of products, then this error will intensify if it is unnoticed. This will lead to many customers taking longer to pay their invoices, leading to serious cash flow implications for the company. If products have been incorrectly priced on the system, this too will lead to errors when invoicing the products to customers. It is vital that checks and controls are in place to prevent and correct these errors.

Creating a New Supplier Account

Creating a new supplier account is similar to creating a customer account:

1 Click on the Supplier icon.

2 Click on the Record icon.

3 This will bring up the Supplier Record window, shown opposite:

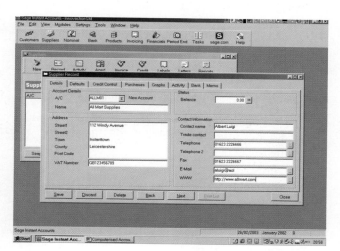

- Use the Details tab to complete all the basic information needed for your suppliers.
- The Defaults tab allows you to edit/amend the automatic defaults you originally entered.
- The Credit Control tab allows you to enter or edit your credit control details.
- The Activity tab shows all the transactions you have against the supplier.
- To save any changes, click on the Save button. If you do not wish to save changes, click on the Discard button.

Printing Out Customer and Supplier Details

You can print your customer's details by clicking on the Customers icon and then the Print List button. This will print out a list of customers showing their account codes and the balance on their account.

You can print out a supplier's details by clicking on the Suppliers icon and then the Print List button. This will print out a list of suppliers showing their account codes and the balance on their account.

Tip

You can use your arrows on the keyboard to scroll up and down and pressing the Spacebar to select the record or records you want.

You can also print out labels for your suppliers and customers by clicking on the Labels icon. This will print out the following:

- Contact name
- Company name
- Company address

For each customer or supplier label needed:

1 Highlight those customers or suppliers required.

2 Click on the Label icon.

3 Choose the type of label required.

4 Choose your output (it is always wise to preview your printing before you print).

5 Press Run.

You can edit the label size to fit different labels by selecting the Edit button.

There are advantages to having the facility to design the layout of forms:

- You can have different designs for your customers and for your suppliers
- You can make changes to reflect a change in the company's image
- The use of colours could be introduced
- You can design reports as and when required
- It works out less expensive than to keep on changing stationery
- Global changes to all months and headings are easily done

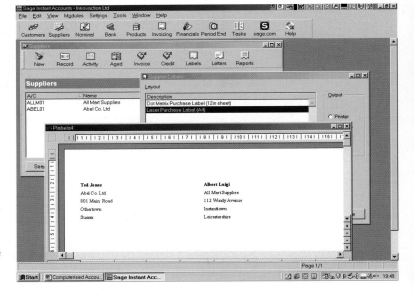

Nominal Accounts

All transactions made by the company are recorded in the nominal ledger accounts. This ledger summarises the sub ledgers:

- Accounts receivables
- Accounts payable
- Capital expenditure

e-Quals

- Cashbook

- Accounting entries made at month end and year end via journals.

When Sage is first installed, a standard set of nominal accounts is already available for immediate use. Certain nominal accounts (inclusive of control accounts) must be set up before any transactions can be recorded on the accounting system.

By clicking on the nominal icon you can view all the nominal ledger accounts that are currently set up. The Record option lets you add, edit and delete nominal accounts. With this option you can change the name of the account if necessary.

> **Tip**
>
> It's a good idea to look at the default set of accounts and their codes. By doing this you will get used to the accounts, their names and layout. You can do this by clicking on the Nominal button and viewing the list.

The Activity option lists all of the nominal account balances and the individual transactions that have been posted to make up these balances.

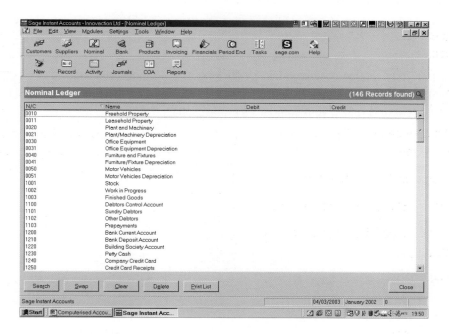

If the existing set of nominal accounts is not suitable or cannot be amended to suit your requirements, then you can create your own set of nominal accounts to cater for your business.

The nominal records have been set up in groups within certain number ranges; these groups fall into the categories required by a simple Trial Balance, from which the Profit & Loss Statement and the Balance Sheet can be derived.

189

Grouping	Number range 'from'	Number range 'to'
Sales	4000	4999
Purchases	5000	5999
Direct Expenses	6000	6999
Overheads	7000	7999
Fixed Assets	0001	0999
Current Assets	1000	1999
Current Liabilities	2000	2299
Long term Liabilities	2300	2999
Capital & Reserves	3000	3999

As you can see from the table above, you can have as many sales accounts as you want, as long as the account coding for these falls between 4000 to 4999.

As long as your sales accounts are numbered to fall within this range, then the balances from those accounts will be shown within the Sales group. If you allocate the code 5001 to a sales account, then the balance of that sales account will be shown within the Purchases section. Obviously this will cause errors in your financial reports so you need to be extremely careful when allocating codes to your nominal accounts.

It is worthwhile making a printout of the number ranges for your nominal accounts groupings to keep for future reference.

The same applies to other groups or categories. By sticking to the ranges allocated to each group, you can be certain that your Trial Balance will balance and that your other reports, the Profit & Loss Statement and your Balance Sheet, will accurately reflect your company's transactions.

The previous table shows the default set of nominal ranges. You can, of course, choose your own set of categories and number ranges to apply to those groups – just make sure that the groups are consistent with any legal requirements for sets of accounts.

> **Tip**
>
> Accounts are numbered in sequence, but gaps are left purposely to allow further records to be created as the company demands.

Control Accounts These are used by Sage accounts to allow automatic double-entry postings, they include:

- Debtors Control
- Creditors Control
- Bank
- VAT on Sales
- VAT on Purchases

- Sales Discount

- Purchase Discount

- Retained Earnings

- Default Sales

- Bad Debts

- Mis-postings

- Suspense

The control accounts in the default set of accounts are listed under Settings on the toolbar under Control Accounts.

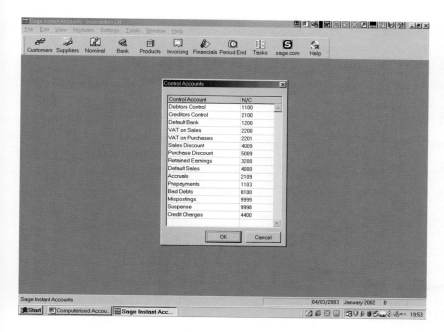

All of these control accounts will fall into one of the groups noted above; if you are creating your own chart of accounts, then you will need to create control accounts. These are allocated by selecting a nominal ledger account as a control account.

Deleting or Amending Nominal Account Records To delete nominal records that are not required, click the Nominal icon, highlight those accounts no longer needed, then click Delete.

It is not possible to delete a nominal record if it has any of the following properties:

- Transactions on it

- A balance

- It is a control account

To edit nominal records, click the Nominal icon, then the Record icon. Next select the nominal record that you want to change from the drop-down list (shown below):

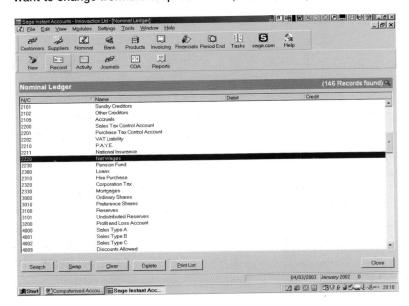

Then type the new name over the original name.

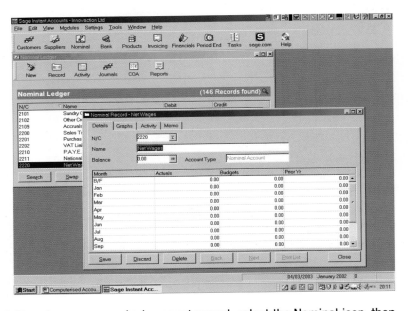

Adding a New Nominal Account Record To enter a new nominal account record, select the Nominal icon, then click on the Record icon. The Nominal record window will appear.

In the details tab, you need to enter the following:

- Nominal account number

- Account name

- Balance – this is zero until transactions are posted against it

● Account type

To create the new nominal account code, click on Save, then Close to return to the main Nominal window.

Opening Balances

When you first set up your accounts on a computerised system you will need to enter opening balances onto the system.

If you are starting a new business, then your opening balances will be made up of your start-up costs e.g. costs of any assets, bank balance, share capital. You will need to enter an opening balance for each nominal account code that has a value and is on your trial balance.

If you are transferring your accounts from one computerised system to another, then the opening balances will be the balances from your trial balance. Ideally this should be at the end of an accounting period.

Note: If you are transferring your accounts at the beginning of your financial year, the only balances, that will need transferring, will be your balance sheet values. This is because the Profit & Loss account is calculated on a yearly basis and at the end of each year any profit or loss is transferred automatically to Retained Profit within Reserves in the Balance Sheet.

> **Tip**
>
> Once nominal codes have been set up, it is recommended that customer and supplier details are entered with their opening balances. Only after they have been entered should opening balances on nominal accounts be entered. This avoids duplicating entries to debtor and creditor control accounts.

To Enter Opening Balances

1 Click on the Nominal icon.

2 Select (highlight with your mouse) the nominal account codes that have opening balances and then click on Record.

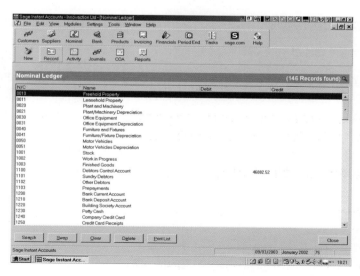

3 Click on the OB button (shown below)

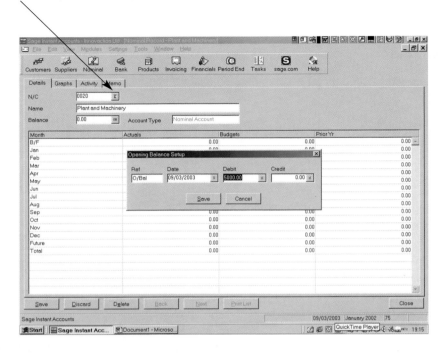

4 The Opening Balance Setup window will appear as shown above.

5 Enter details as required from your trial balance.

- **Ref:** O/Bal is entered here as a default, but you can choose any description you wish. This description will appear on the audit trail and will help with identification.

- **Date:** Enter the last date of the previous accounting period.

- Either:

  - **Debit:** enter the debit value, or,

  - **Credit:** enter the credit value

6 Then click on Save, to save the opening balance or, to exit without saving, click on Cancel.

7 Repeat these steps for the rest of your opening balances.

The opposite side of any opening balance entry is the Suspense account. If you are entering opening balances from a trial balance, after all opening balances have been entered, the suspense account will come back to zero. You will need to confirm this is the case before you continue.

If you enter opening balances without a trial balance, then you will be left with a balance on the Suspense account. This should not be a problem until you get to the end of the year when you will be able to clear your figures.

USING THE SALES AND PURCHASE LEDGERS

Introduction

Once the customers and suppliers have been set up with the following:

- Account codes
- Defaults
- Company name
- Company address
- Contact details
- VAT number (if applicable)
- Credit limit

We can then start to enter invoices and credit notes onto the system.

There are two ways in which we can record invoices within Sage.

The first method is via the Invoice button within Customers and Suppliers. This method can be used to record any invoices or credit notes that do not require any printed documents (i.e. to send out to customers). This process is mostly used to record invoices and credit notes received from suppliers.

The second method involves the Invoicing option. This is the preferred option for customers.

Sales Ledger

The most commonly used method is via the Invoicing option, whereby you can produce printed invoices and credit notes to send to your customers.

It is wise to remember that when you are raising invoices, you are creating a legal document between your company and the customer, this has a variety of implications. It is a document which formalises a contract by the company to provide certain goods or services at a certain price, at a particular time, subject to a set of payment terms – all of which the customer has agreed to.

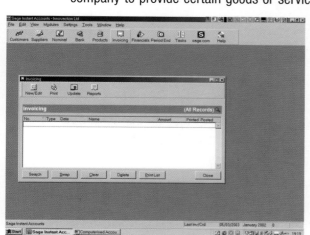

This method is preferred for raising invoices and credit notes to send to your customers.

NB: You can use this facility at any time.

> **Tip**
>
> By pressing F1, you will get Help related to the window that you are in.

Using the Invoicing Option To raise invoices or credit notes to your customers you need to select the Invoicing tab.

The Invoicing option is linked to:

- The Customer
- The Supplier
- The Nominal accounts

An invoice or credit note is raised; they are automatically updated when the invoices are updated.

There are two types of invoices/credit notes, which can be raised on this software:

- Service – where you are providing a service to your customers and you need to invoice them for it.
- Product – where you are selling products (goods) to your customers and need to invoice them.

To raise an invoice or credit note to a customer:

1   Click on the New/Edit button in the Invoicing option.

2   The following screen will then appear:

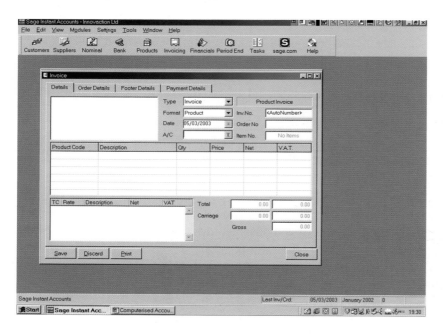

3   Click on the dropdown arrow in Type. Select either:
    –   Invoices, or,
    –   Credit notes

4   Click on the dropdown arrow in Format. Choose between product or service invoices.

5   Enter the tax date of the invoice in the Date box – this may or may not be the same date as the date on which you are actually raising the invoice. This is important, as the date will identify which period the invoice will fall in and will also identify the period in which the sales are recognised in the nominal ledger and in the financial statements.

6   Access the calendar by clicking on the option.

7   Enter the account code for the customer you are raising the invoice to: you can type the code directly into the box. Alternatively you can use the finder button. The customer's full name and address will appear in the box on the left hand side of the screen.

Creating a product invoice

To create a product invoice do the following:

1   Choose Product in the Format box.

2   Use one line of the invoice for each product type to enter product information.

3   Either enter the product code or use the finder button to locate the product code. The description will appear when the product code is entered – this can be changed if required.

4   Then enter the quantity, which you are invoicing; by default, 1 unit of the product is entered automatically.

5   The price of the product also appears automatically – you can amend this value if you wish.

6   The net value is calculated automatically and cannot be amended.

> **Tip**
>
> If you press F5 when your cursor is in a monetary field, then the Euro-Calculator will appear.

7   The VAT value appears automatically and cannot be amended from here.

8   You can continue entering the rest of your product lines as required.

Once you have finished invoicing that particular customer:

● Click on the Save button.

● If you do not wish to save your invoice click Discard and start again as desired.

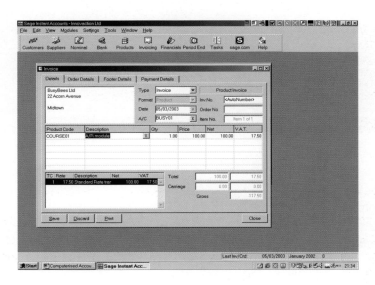

Creating a product record

1   Enter products using the Products option.

2   Click the Record button.

3   Enter a note of the following:

- Product code
- Description – it is important that the description entered is as accurate as possible in order to make proper identification of goods or services sold.
- Location
- Price – you will need to confirm that the price, which is brought up by entering the Product code, is the price quoted to your customer. An incorrect price will be compounded by the quantity invoiced out to the customer.

> **Tip**
>
> By pressing F6, you can copy data from the box above, this helps in speeding up data entry.

Note: *Any incorrect entries on the pricing of products will lead to the same incorrect price being applied to all invoices, selling those products. This can lead to serious consequences for the company and its customers. If the customers have been undercharged then the company will not achieve its expected margins. If it has over-charged on the invoices then credit notes will have be raised, leading to extra administration costs and bad relations with its customers. The same applies if quantities are incorrectly entered.*

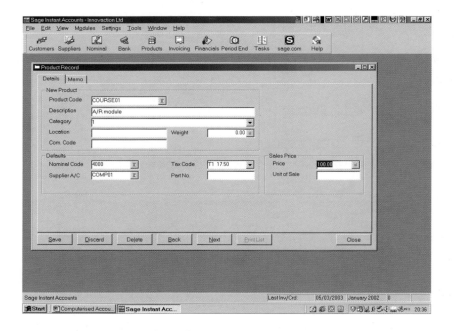

Printing an invoice

To print your invoice immediately:

1   Click on the Print button.

2   Choose the invoice layout you require.

3   Click on the Run button.

4   Close to exit out of that screen.

Updating the ledgers

To update your invoice to the customer and the nominal ledgers you will need to run an update:

1   Click on the Update button.

2   The following screen will appear:

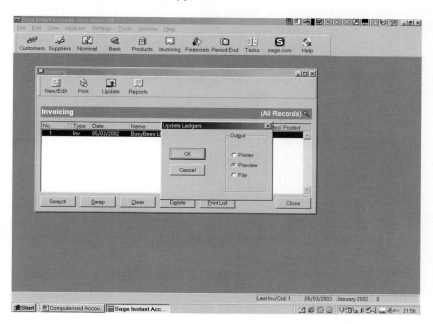

3   Select your output to printer.

4   Click on OK.

5   The update of the following will now happen:
    – Your invoice.
    – The Sales account and the VAT nominal accounts will be credited.
    – The Debtors account will be debited.

Creating a service invoice

A Service Invoice and Service Credit Note are raised similarly by going into the Invoicing option. This time:

1   Click on Service in the Format box.

2   Choose either to raise an invoice or credit note to your customer.

3   Decide on the tax date.

4   Choose the account code for the customer that you are raising the invoice to.

5   You can now enter whatever description details that are required in the Details tab.

6   Then enter the unit price for the service.

7   The net price is calculated automatically.

8   The VAT is calculated automatically.

> **Tip**
>
> A spell checker that can be used in any text box is included. Place your cursor in the text box to be checked and then press F5.

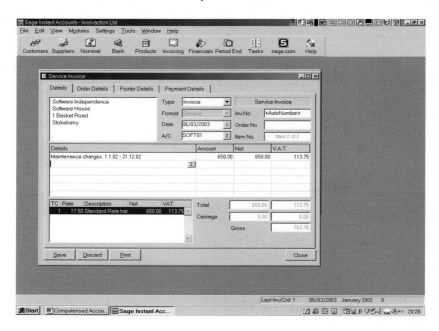

9   You can now choose to either:

- **Save:** save the invoice raised
- **Discard:** cancel and do not save the invoice
- **Print:** print the invoice

Again you will need to update the invoice for it to debit and credit the relevant codes in the debtors and nominal ledgers.

It is vital when using computerised accounts packages, that certain items are entered when creating an invoice or a credit note, these are:

Date – the date entered on an invoice will tie it into a particular period, this is especially important if the system used is date sensitive (where the date entered will register the invoice as being part of a particular period's transactions). If the invoice is raised selling goods on a certain date, you need to make sure that you have reflected the equivalent cost of selling those goods.

Invoice number – this is an automatically generated unique number that allows you to identify a particular invoice. The invoice number allows you to record, track and identify each sale, invoice by invoice.

Nominal account reference code – by entering the reference code for the nominal account, you are telling the accounts system where to record the credit (if we are raising a sales invoice), or where to record the debit (if you are raising a credit note).

Item description – by entering the item description, you are identifying the goods/products being sold or credited clearly to our customers so that they are precisely aware of what they are purchasing. This is an important point and there should be no dispute or lack of clarity in the item description. After all an invoice is a legal document recording a sale.

Item cost – you need to record the unit price on the invoice, this will be used in different variance analyses of the item.

Item VAT rate – you need to record the item VAT rate in order define what the VAT will be on that item. This will obviously be subject to VAT rules and regulations – further information on this is available from Customs and Excise.

Discounts allowed – this item should be recorded, discounts can be given for bulk purchase, prompt payment and can be set at different percentage levels for each customer with varying reason codes.

Showing customer account transactions

You need to be in the Customers option.

1   Highlight the customer you wish to print out transactions for.

2   Click on the Activity button on the Customers toolbar.

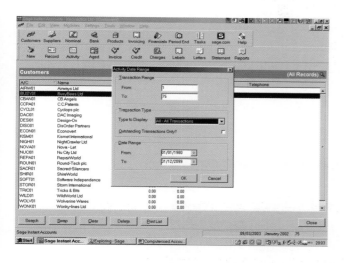

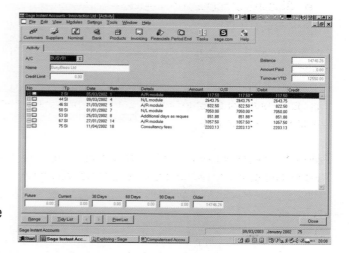

3   Enter the date range required.

4   Click OK.

5   The following screen will appear showing the customer's account transactions.

Printing out customer transactions

To print out the transaction list, click on the Print List button.

Reversing incorrect invoices

If you have raised an incorrect invoice and it has been updated to the ledgers, you will need to reverse this by raising a credit note of the same value and to the same customer.

This is done in the same way as for raising invoices:

You need to be in the Invoicing option, then select Credit in the Type box.

Note: *You must make sure that you raise the credit for the same value as the original invoice. It must be to the same customer and use the same VAT code in order for the reversal to be made correctly.*

Purchase Ledger

To enter supplier invoices:

1 Click on the Suppliers icon. Your list of suppliers entered will be displayed on the screen with the outstanding balance.

2 Now click on the Invoice icon, this will bring up the Batch Supplier Invoices screen. This is the screen you use to enter purchase invoices onto the system.

3 The cursor will be automatically be flashing on the A/C column – this is a prompt to enter the supplier code that you wish to post the invoices to. You can do this by clicking on the drop-down menu in the A/C column, this will then display all the suppliers, from which you can select the one you want by highlighting it and clicking OK.

The selected supplier will then appear in the A/C column and the cursor will have moved over to the next column.

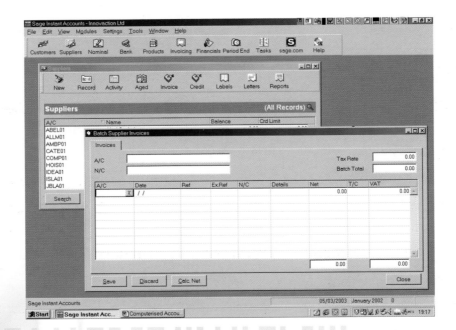

Another way of selecting a supplier is by entering the code if you know it. As you start typing in the first characters of the code the drop-down menu will appear automatically and you will see the supplier selected.

4 Once you have selected the supplier you can then continue and complete the other fields.

The amount of detail entered is up to the individual, but it is important to remember that if you enter minimal information, then when the reports are run, that is all that will be shown.

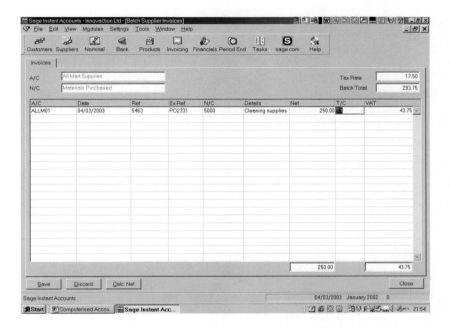

As you can see from the screen above we have completed each field.

● The Date will automatically come up as the current date, but this can be changed to show the date of the invoice.

● The Ref. is the invoice number

● The Ex.Ref. is any additional reference required, in this instance we have input a purchase order number.

● The nominal code (N/C) will come up automatically as the default code set up when the supplier was initially created.

● The Details column is used as a note of the goods or services purchased.

● The Net is the net amount before VAT from the invoice.

● The tax code (T/C) will come up automatically with the default that was set up when the supplier was created.

● From the tax code the amount of VAT is automatically calculated by the system.

203

If your invoices are simple, then you can use this screen to enter a number of invoices, one invoice per each row, as a batch input.

If, however, the invoices you are inputting are complex and involve a number of different nominal account codes and tax rates, then it is wise to enter only one invoice at a time and then check your net, tax and gross amounts.

Once you have added in all the appropriate information click the Save button.

If you receive a credit note from a supplier, then you need to open up the Batch Supplier Credits window.

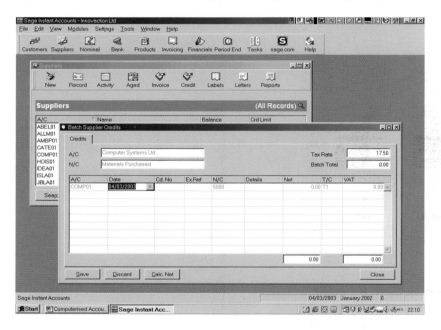

As you can see from above, the screen on which you enter credit notes into the system is exactly the same as the previous Invoice screen. The only difference is that everything appears in red type to indicate credits.

The same type of detail needs to be entered as in the case of invoices:

● Account code

● Date

● Credit note number

● Ex ref – any other reference you wish to enter

● Nominal ledger code

● Details – description

● Net value of credit note

● VAT

Printing out supplier transactions

You will need to be in the Suppliers option. Then:

1 Highlight the supplier you wish to print out transactions for.

2 Click on the Activity button on the Suppliers toolbar.

3 Enter the date range required.

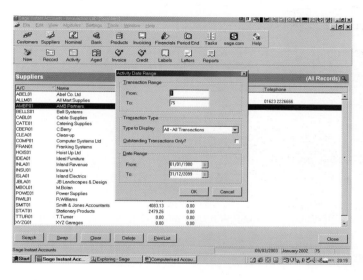

4 Click OK.

5 The following screen will appear showing the supplier's account transactions:

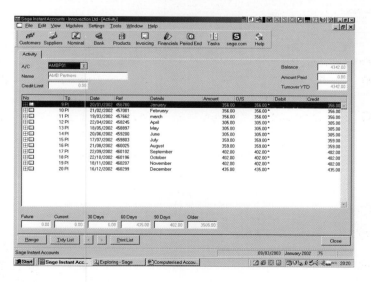

6 Print out the transaction list by clicking on the Print List button.

Allocating Receipts and Payments

To allocate receipts or payments to your customers or suppliers you need to go into the Bank option.

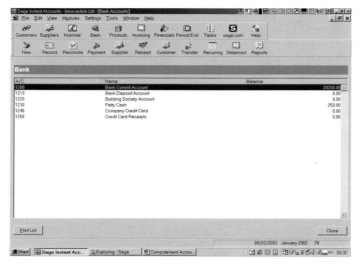

Allocating Customer Receipts

1   Select the bank account from the list – this is the account, which will be paid into (debited) with the customer receipt.

2   Click on the Customer icon from the Bank toolbar.

3   The Customer Receipt window will appear, as well as the name of the selected bank.

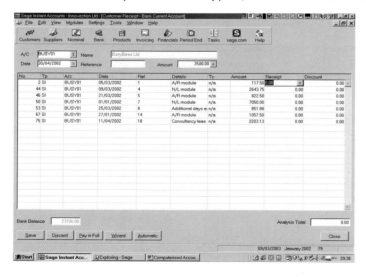

4   Enter the account code of the customer required – all outstanding, unpaid amounts will appear.

5   Enter the date of receipt in the date box.

6   Enter the reference number as required in the reference box.

7   Enter the gross amount in the amount box.

8   Allocate the money by clicking on the Pay in Full button at the bottom of the screen; the amount needed to pay the invoice is then allocated automatically.

9 Continue allocating the money until the amount in the analysis box in the bottom right hand side of the screen is the same as the value in the amount box you are paying.

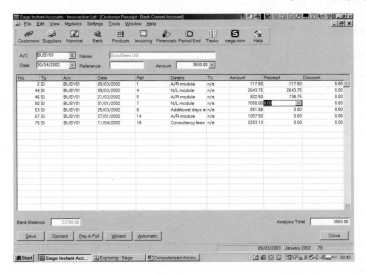

10 To process this customer receipt click on the Save button.

Note: We can allocate sales receipts automatically by clicking on the Automatic button. This has the benefits of very quickly allocating all the cash received against invoices. This is useful if you often have large receipts against a great many invoices. However, the cash is allocated to invoices in date order – this may not be a problem, but if the cash receipt was for a particular invoice, this could cause problems in agreeing outstanding invoices with your customers.

Allocating Supplier Payments

1 Select the bank account from the list – this is the account from which the supplier will be paid.

2 Click on the Supplier icon from the Bank toolbar.

3 The Supplier Payments window will appear, as well as the name of the selected bank.

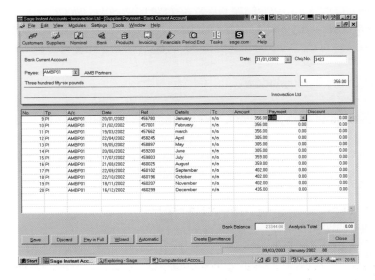

4 Enter the account code of the supplier required – all outstanding, unpaid amounts will appear.

5 Enter the date of the payment in the Date box.

6 Enter cheque number as required in the Cheque No. Box.

7 Enter the gross amount in the Amount box.

8 Allocate the money by clicking on Pay in Full at the bottom of the screen; the amount needed to pay the invoice is then allocated automatically.

9 Continue allocating the money until the amount in the analysis box in the bottom right hand side of the screen is the same as the value in the amount box that you are paying.

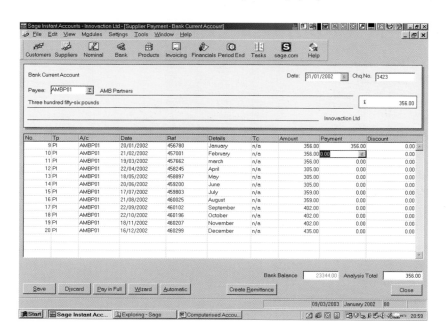

10 To process this supplier payment click on the Save button.

Note: *We are able to allocate the payment to our suppliers either manually by clicking Pay in Full against each invoice as required or we can click the Automatic button and the payment is allocated automatically. Once again this is a much faster way of allocating payments but not necessarily the most accurate method as it may leave part paid invoices or may not make use of credit notes that have been received at a later date against disputed invoices.*

Posting an adjustment in the bank window

As you have raised cheques to your suppliers, you will have recorded the transaction in the bank nominal account. This shows as a credit to the bank nominal account and a debit on the suppliers account. There will be other transactions which will appear on your bank statement such as bank charges and interest payments which will need to be recorded onto the nominal account in the system. We do this by posting an adjustment in the bank window:

1 Open the Bank Reconciliation window.

2 Click Adjustment.

3 Enter the following details:

- Nominal code
- Date
- Reference
- Tax code
- Payment or receipt amount

Printing Out a Remittance Advice Note

1 Click on the Create Remittance button at the bottom of the Supplier Payment screen (see the previous screen shot).

2 Choose the layout required for the remittance note, either 11" Layout or A4 Layout.

3 Then choose the output:

- Print
- Preview
- File

4 Then click on the Run button to produce your Remittance Advice Note.

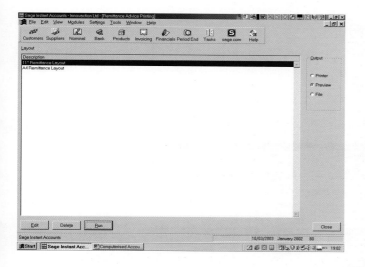

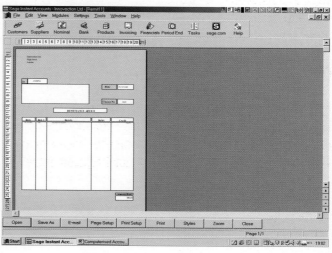

Creating a Customer Statement

1 Go into the Customers option.

2 Highlight the customers that you wish to produce statements for.

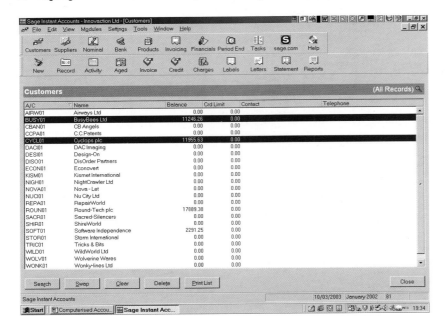

3 Click on the Statement button on the Customers toolbar.

4 Choose the statement type as required.

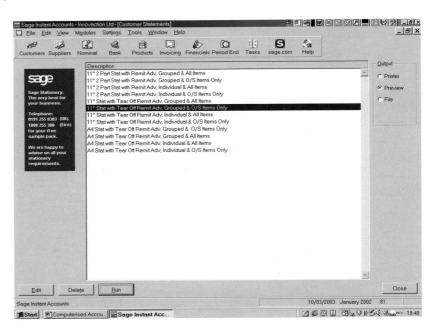

5 Now press the Run button after choosing your output option (file, preview, print).

6 Select the dates that you require for your statement and click OK.

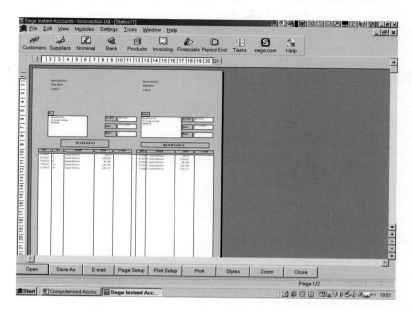

Printing Out Account Histories

Customer account history

To print out an account history for your customers, do the following:

1 Go into the Customers option.

2 Click on the Reports button on the customer's toolbar.

3 Highlight the report Customer Activity (Detailed).

4 Select your output options and click on the Run button.

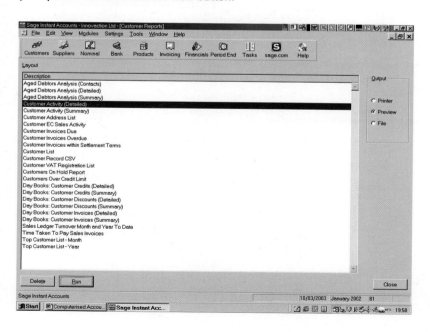

5   Select the customers and dates for which you wish to run the report and click OK.

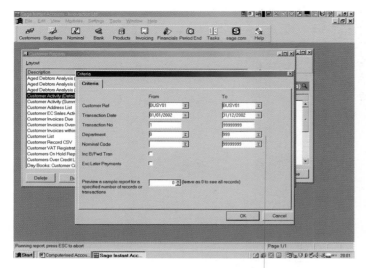

The customer's detailed activity is now available to be printed out.

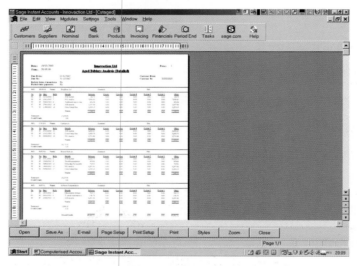

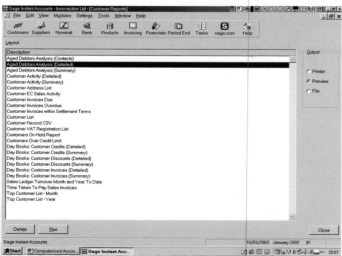

If you wish to print out an Aged Debtors Analysis, then you just need to select that report from the list within Customer Reports.

Again you will need to select the date range required and click OK.

The following Aged Debtors Report is ready for printing as required.

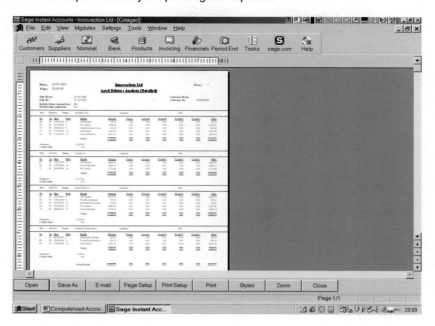

Supplier account history

1   Go into the Suppliers option.

2   Click on the Reports button on the supplier's toolbar.

3   Highlight the report Aged Creditors Analysis (Detailed).

4   Select your output options and click on the Run button.

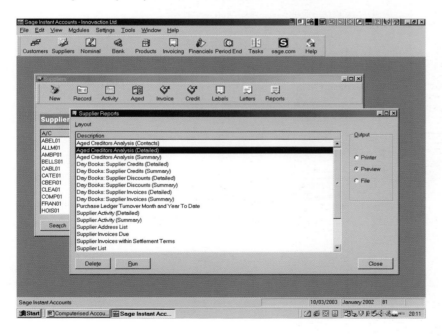

5   Select the date range for your report and click OK.

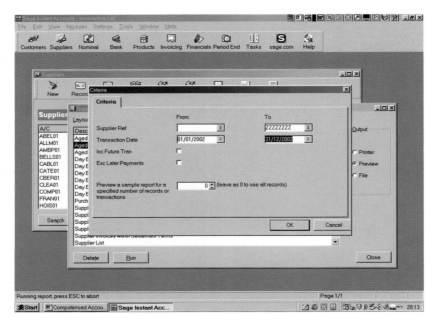

The Aged Creditors Analysis will then be available for you to print out.

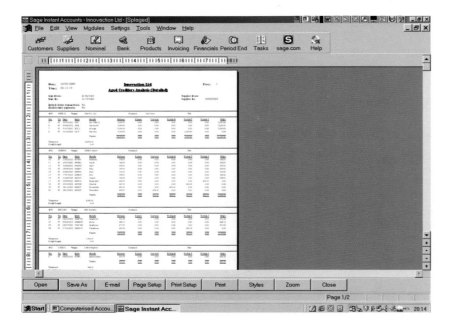

USING THE NOMINAL LEDGER

Introduction

The nominal ledger is affected by all transactions posted in Customers (sales ledger) and Suppliers (purchase ledger).

Balances from the nominal ledger form the trial balance; from this the Profit and Loss account and the Balance Sheet are extracted.

The only ways in which we can affect the balances on the nominal ledger are via postings from:

- Sales ledger
- Purchase ledger
- Journal entry
- Cash book

Journal Entry

You use journal entries for the following types of transactions:

- Opening Balances
- Depreciation
- Accruals
- Prepayments
- Wages/Salaries
- Correction of mis-postings

To make journal entries, you need to open up the Nominal window by doing the following:

1   Click on the Journals icon

- The Nominal Ledger Journal window opens up – you will need to adhere to basic double-entry bookkeeping principles when posting journals, where the value of all debits needs to equal the value of all credits.
- The boxes at the top of the journal show the following details:

    - **Reference:** enter a unique identifier here for your journal.
    - **Date:** the system date will appear, but change this as required to reflect the period in which you want your journal to effect changes.
    - **Balance:** as you enter your debits and credits, the difference remaining is displayed.

2   In the N/C column enter the nominal code you require, or use the Finder button to select the nominal code you require.

3 In the Details column enter an identifying description – remember this is what you will see in the activity report of your nominal ledger.

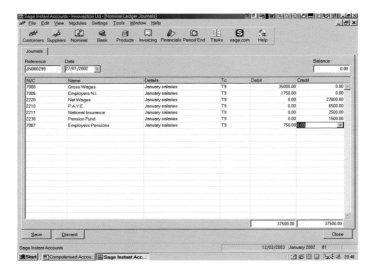

The T/C (tax code) for journals tends to be T9 as it involves the movement of amounts that do not involve VAT.

Note: *This may not always be the case – you may use a journal entry to post petty cash, and some of the items may be subject to VAT.*

4 The debit and credit columns need to be entered as necessary.

5 To post the journal – click on Save.

6 To cancel the journal – click on Discard.

7 To return back to the main Nominal Ledger window – click on Close.

> **Tip**
> If you press F2, the calculator will appear.

In the previous screen, we have posted a salaries journal, which, as you can see, affects various accounts with debits and credits which all balance back to zero.

After posting the salaries journal, which will put all the necessary entries through onto the correct nominal codes, you need to put through the bank payment that makes the actual net salary payment to the employees.

Bank Payments

1 Open up the Bank option.

2 Click on the Payments icon from the Bank toolbar.

3 The Bank Payments window appears with the following details which need to be completed:

- **Bank**   enter the bank nominal code, or use the finder button
- **Date**   the system date will appear, you can change this as required
- **Reference** enter your reference
- **N/C**   enter your nominal code, or use the finder button to select the code required
- **Details**   enter whatever detail or description is required
- **T/C**   enter T9 code (non-Vatable tax code)

4 Click on the Save button to record this payment.

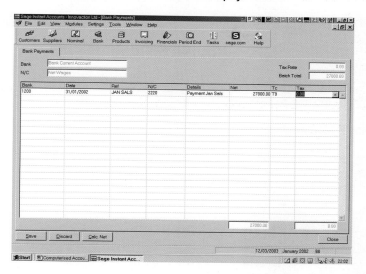

Bank Receipts

1 Open up the Bank option

2 Click on the Receipts icon from the Bank toolbar

3 The Bank Receipts window appears with the same details as in the Bank Payments, which again need to be completed:

- Bank
- Date
- Reference
- N/C
- Details
- T/C

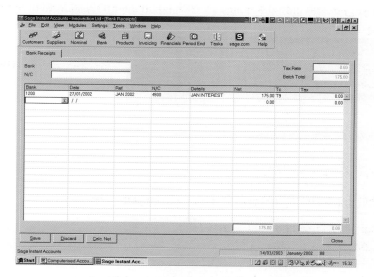

In the screen shot above you can see that interest received into the bank has been entered onto the relevant nominal account code.

Nominal Account Transaction History

In order to print out the transaction history of a nominal account, you need to first open up the Nominal Ledger window.

1 Highlight the nominal accounts required.

2 Click on the Activity icon in the Nominal Ledger toolbar.

3 You have the option to select the Transaction Range required.

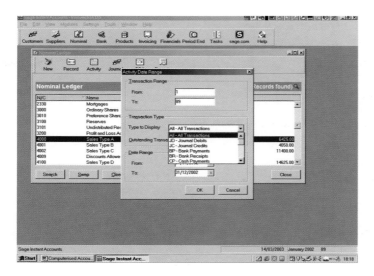

4 There is also the option to select the Transaction Type required, from the drop-down menu.

5 Select the dates required for the transaction history.

6 Click OK.

The following activity screen will appear which you can print if required by clicking on the Print List button.

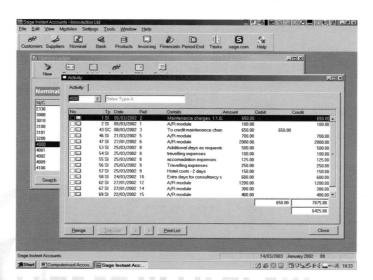

Using the Memo Tab

A note facility is an important tool to have available on computerised accounts; it allows you to add any extra information that is related to that account.

On each of the ledgers (nominal, customers and suppliers), you have the facility of a memo tab, where there is a blank screen available to enter whatever free format text you wish.

- The Memo tab is found by going into any of the ledgers and then clicking on the Record icon.

- In the Nominal Ledger you may wish to make notes on the following accounts as examples:

  - **Depreciation accounts** – depreciation method and procedure in use.
  - **Bank accounts** – you may wish to note the name of the bank manager or the contact name. You may also wish to note any overdraft limits or perhaps the bank address.
  - **Petty cash account** – you may wish to note the float limit.

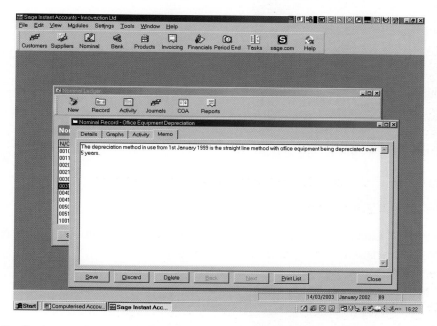

On the Customers Ledger, the Memo tab is available for each individual customer. You may wish to use the note facility for some of the following reasons regarding customers:

- Payment history

- Discounts that the customer is eligible for

- Detailed delivery address notes

- Any disputed invoices

- Update on latest outstanding invoices

- Other comments such as – 'do not work with this customer until further notice'

On the Suppliers Ledger, the Memo tab is again available for each individual supplier. You may wish to use the note facility for some of the following reasons:

- Disputed invoices

- Preferred supplier as additional bulk discounts given

- Notes regarding the performance of the supplier

- Whether they regularly make under or over supplies

- Whether they ship on time

- Condition of goods when received

PRODUCE REPORTS AND TRANSACTION DETAILS

Introduction

There are various reports that you may wish to produce for a variety of reasons:

- To keep track of your trading

- To find out what your profits or losses are

- To see how the business is performing

- To provide audit reports

- To provide VAT reports for Customs and Excise

In order to keep a track of how your sales and purchase accounts are doing, you can print out a report of all transactions for whichever sales or purchase accounts you wish to specify. To do this:

1   Open up the Nominal window.

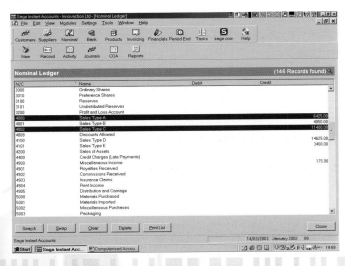

2   Highlight the sales accounts required.

3 Click on the Activity button.

4 Select the transaction range as required.

5 Select the date range as required.

6 Click OK.

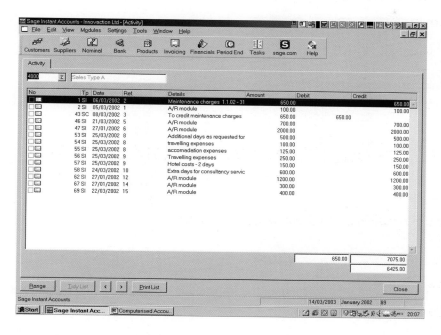

7 Click the Print List button to print out the report listing all the transactions associated with the sales accounts selected.

If you wish to print out a list of all transactions associated with your purchase accounts:

1 Open up the Nominal window.

2 Highlight the purchase accounts required.

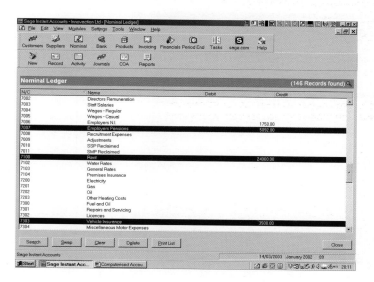

3   Click on the Activity button.

4   Select the transaction range as required.

5   Select the date range as required.

6   Click OK.

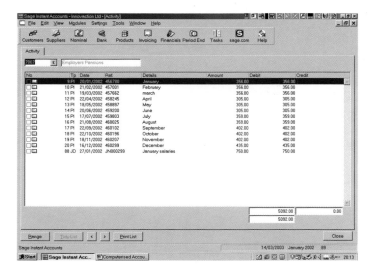

7   Click the Print List button to print out the report listing all the transactions associated with the purchase accounts selected.

To print out a list of your customer details:

1   Open up the Customers option.

2   Click on the Reports button.

3   Select the report you wish to print out.

4   Click on the Run button.

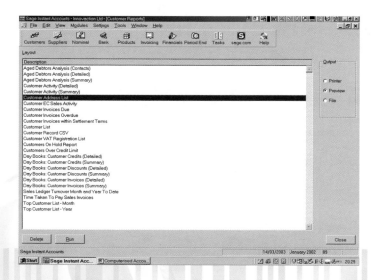

5 Select the range of customers you need.

6 Click OK.

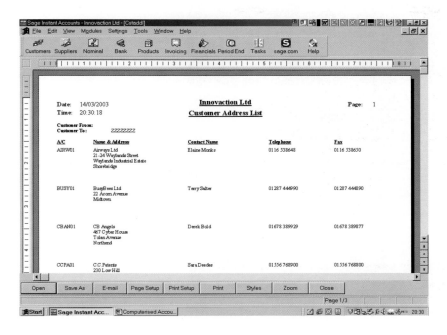

Printing Out a List of Debtors and their Current Balances

1 Open up the Customers window.

2 Click on the Reports button.

3 Select the report required – in the example below, Detailed Aged Debtors Analysis has been selected.

4 Click on the Run button.

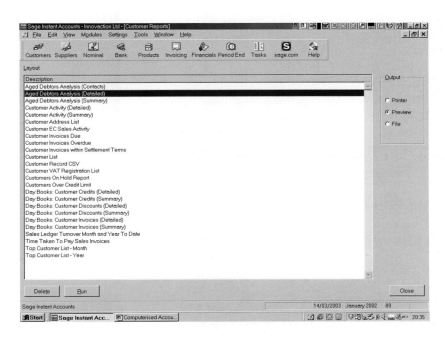

5 Select the date range and the customer range required.

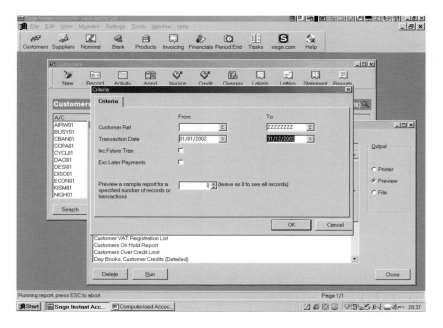

6 Click OK.

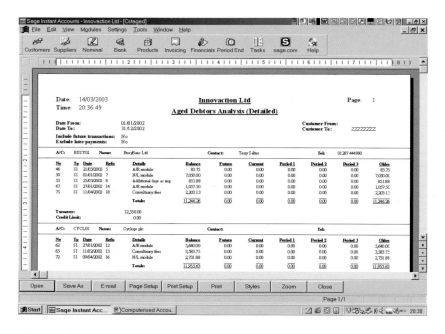

7 Click on the Print button to print out.

Printing Out a List of Creditors and their Current Balances

1 Open up the Suppliers window.

2 Click on the Reports button.

3   Select the report required – in the example below, Detailed Aged Creditors Analysis has been selected.

4   Click on the Run button.

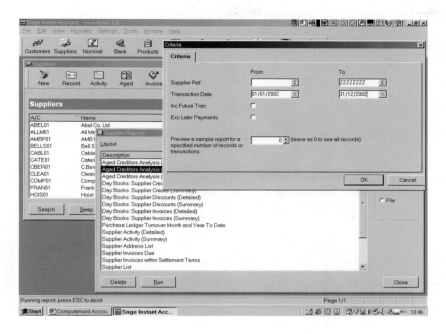

5   Select the date range and the supplier range required.

6   Click on OK.

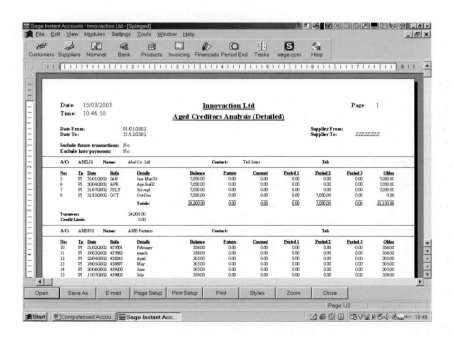

7   Click on Print.

Printing a Range of Customer Invoices and Credit Notes

1 Open up the Invoicing window.

2 Click on Reports.

3 The Reports window will appear with a range of reports available

- Invoice Summary
- Invoices not posted
- Invoices not printed

In this instance the Invoice Summary report is selected. In this particular system, invoices and credit notes are batched together.

4 Click on Run.

5 Click on Print.

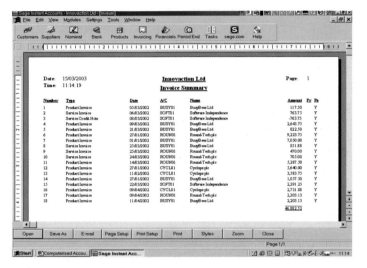

Printing Financial Statements

In order to print out any of the Financial Statements for your company using Sage, you need to go into the Financials window

Open the Financials window, as shown below:

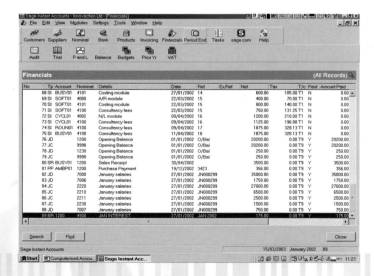

A number of icons are displayed on the toolbar, including:

- Audit
- Trial
- P and L
- Balance
- Budgets
- Prior Year
- VAT

Trial Balance

1 Click on the Trial icon.

2 Select the month you wish to run the trial balance up to.

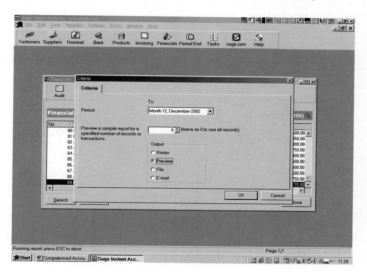

3 Click on OK.

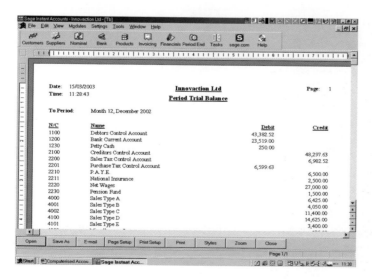

4 Click on Print.

Profit and Loss Account

To print out the profit and loss account for your company, you need to stay within the Financials window.

1 Select the P and L icon.

2 Select the range of months for which you wish to run your profit and loss account. You should choose to run the report from the start of the financial year to the month on which you are reporting – this will give you a profit and loss account which includes year-to-date figures.

3 Click on OK.

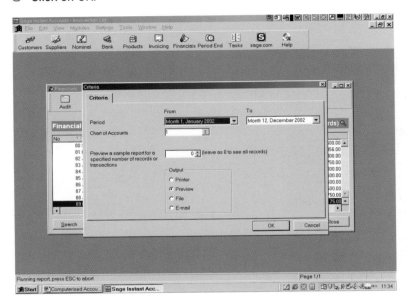

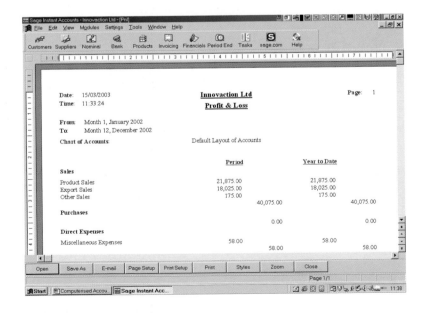

4 Click on Print.

Balance Sheet

To print out the Balance Sheet for your company, you need to stay within the Financials window.

1 Select the Balance icon.

2 Select the range of months for which you wish to run your Balance Sheet. As with your Profit and Loss Account you should choose to run the report from the start of the financial year to the month on which you are reporting – again this will give you a Balance Sheet which includes year-to-date figures.

3 Click on OK.

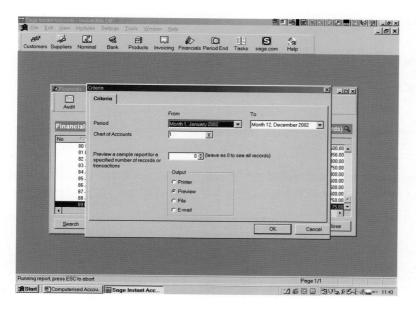

4 A preview of the Balance Sheet is shown below.

5 Click on the Print button to send the Balance Sheet to the printer.

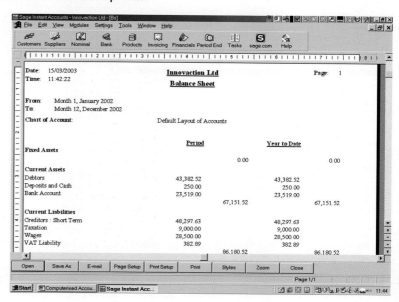

VAT Return Analysis

Each time you have entered any transactions, such as raising invoices or credit notes, or posted any purchase invoices or credit notes, you have been prompted to select the relevant tax code. By doing this, the system can then locate each transaction by searching for the relevant tax code.

Once you have recorded all of the transactions for a particular accounting period, you are ready to run the VAT return.

In order to produce a printout of the VAT return analysis, you need to remain within the Financials window.

This time you will be selecting the icon titled VAT.

- As you can see from the screen below, it looks just like the form which is submitted to Customs and Excise.

- You need to select the date range for which you wish to run the VAT return; this will be done on a quarterly basis.

- Each company's VAT dates for the returns will depend on the financial year and are dictated by Customs and Excise.

Now click on the Calculate button on the bottom left hand side of the screen. The system works through all the transactions, which have been recorded for the dates that were selected – it then automatically calculates the figures for the VAT return.

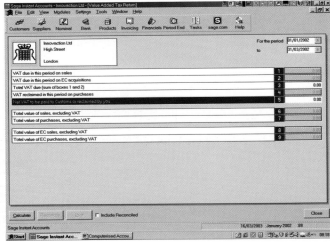

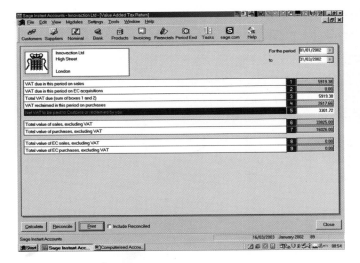

As you can see, the figures have automatically appeared in the relevant boxes, after Calculate has been clicked.

Now click on the Print button to print out the necessary reports for backup and for confirming the figures calculated by the system.

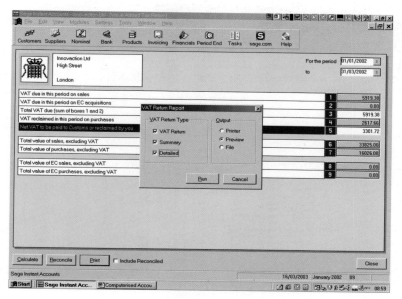

The following VAT Return Report dialog box will appear, giving the option for various reports:

1　VAT Return

2　Summary

3　Detailed

You should take prints of all three reports noted above.

A preview of part of the Summary VAT return is shown here, there is a separate page for every amount recorded in each of the boxes on the VAT return itself – here we can see the value recorded in Box 1 of the VAT return.

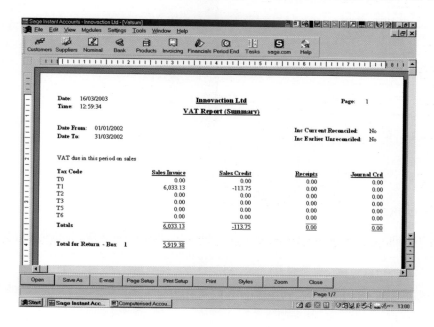

A preview of the Detailed VAT return is shown below, this shows the detail behind the totals in the Summary VAT return.

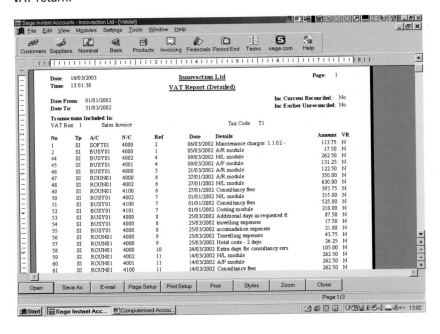

There is a drill-down facility on the on-screen VAT return.

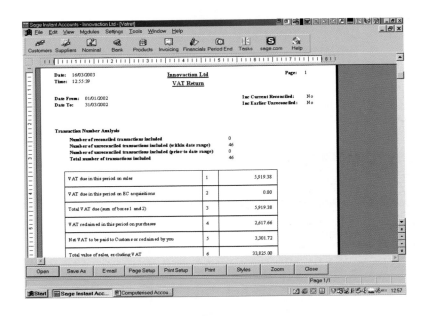

Nominal Day Books

A day book lists all transactions in the order in which they were recorded. There are usually day books associated with each of the ledgers – Sales (Customers), Purchase (Suppliers) and the General (Nominal) ledger.

These day books are sometimes split again between debits and credits, with a separate day book for each.

You will normally need to take printouts of these when you have completed entering all transactions for an accounting period.

The day books will then form a complete, itemised record of all transactions within a particular period.

1   Open up the Nominal window.

2   Click on the Reports icon on the Nominal toolbar.

3   Highlight the report – Day Books: Nominal Ledger – and click on the Run button.

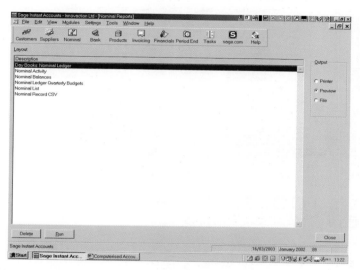

4   Select the options as required for your day book:

- Dates
- Transaction numbers
- Nominal codes

5   Click OK to run the report.

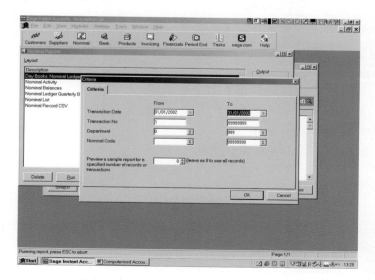

6 A preview of the nominal day book is shown below. Press the Print button to send the report to the printer.

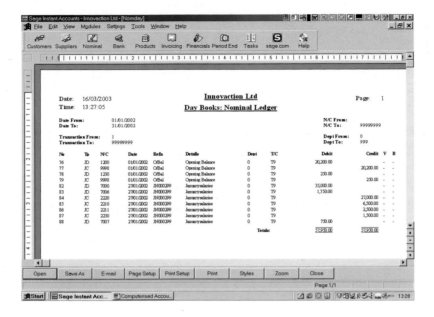

USING AUDIT TOOLS, MANAGEMENT CONTROLS AND CURRENCY

The Audit Trail

The audit trail is so called because it is a complete record of your transaction activities and is often requested by auditors during their investigations. Use this option to regularly (e.g. Monthly) print out a listing of this audit trail for reference purposes.

You can periodically clear down this audit trail. This removes those transactions that have been fully reconciled with your banks, for VAT and where appropriate, are fully paid (e.g. invoices). Before you do 'clear down', it is recommended that you take a backup and print out a copy first.

Note: *When you clear transactions from the audit trail, the details are removed but the balances they contained are kept and carried forward as opening balances so that your financial reports are all still accurate and up-to-date.*

You can store a large number of transactions in the audit trail (given enough computer memory and disk space) so you never actually need to clear down transactions from the audit trail if you do not want to.

However, the more transactions you leave on the system the longer it will take to sort through the list and calculate the values for reports. The choice is yours, but will depend on just how many transactions you enter per month.

Clear Audit Trail The Clear Audit Trail option can be run as part of the Month End and Year End routines. It is a way of clearing down paid and reconciled transactions prior to a specified date. This way you can decide how long you keep individual transactions live on the system.

It is recommended that you take a printout of your audit trail with a date range that includes your current month's transactions, before you clear your audit trail.

When you clear the audit trail, it will remove each transaction that meets the following criteria:

● It is fully paid.

● It is fully reconciled for VAT purposes, if applicable.

● It is reconciled with the appropriate bank account, if applicable.

Any transactions that do not meet all of the above criteria are not cleared from the audit trail.

When you clear the audit trail, any customer and supplier transactions dated before the specified dates are brought forward as items. Similarly, transactions on the nominal ledger are brought forward as the opening balances for the new financial month.

Note: *If you clear down your audit trail, any cleared transactions will not appear in the transactional-based management reports or in any 'brought forward' statements.*

Clearing your audit trail

1 Make sure you have a back-up of your data before running the Clear Audit Trail option.

2 Open the Tools menu, then choose Period End, then Clear Audit Trail.
The Clear Audit Trail window appears.

3   In the Date box provided, enter the date up to which transactions are to be cleared.
Transactions will be cleared from the audit trail only if all of the following conditions are met, up to and including the date you entered in the Date box:

–   Bank transactions have been reconciled with the appropriate bank account. These transactions are flagged in the audit trail with an R in the Bank column.
–   Transactions with VAT have been reconciled on the VAT return. These transactions are flagged in the audit trail with an R in the VAT column.

4   To carry out the Clear Audit Trail procedure, click OK. If you do not want to continue with the Clear Audit Trail procedure, click Cancel.

Your audit trail has now been cleared.

After your audit trail has been cleared, you will find that:

1   If any transactions have been removed, transactions on the audit trail will be renumbered.

2   All fully paid, allocated and reconciled transactions are removed from the audit trail.

3   Unreconciled and unallocated customer and supplier transactions dated before the specified date are brought forward as outstanding items.

4   Customer and supplier transactions dated after the specified dates are carried forward as outstanding items.

5   The opening balance on each nominal ledger account history is the value of all reconciled transactions that have been removed.

6   Unreconciled transactions on the Nominal Ledger are brought forward as outstanding items.

7   Any transactions dated before the Clear Audit Trail date, that have not been paid (i.e. they are outstanding or unallocated) or unreconciled, are not affected by the Clear Audit Trail option.

Note: *If transactions are not cleared when you run the Clear Audit Trail option, check the audit trail to see if the VAT and Bank columns of these transactions are flagged as R for reconciled. You can only clear transactions that have been reconciled for both VAT and the Bank. Transactions on the audit trail that have the flag of a hyphen, means that bank reconciliation or VAT reconciliation is not applicable for that transaction.*

Printing an audit trail report

1   From the main toolbar, click Financials.

2   Click Audit (or click Reports), then choose the report you require.
The Audit Trail Report window appears.

3   Select the type of audit trail you require from the option buttons provided, i.e. Brief, Summary, Detailed or Deleted Transactions.

4   Select whether you want to print the report on landscape or portrait format by selecting the relevant check box.

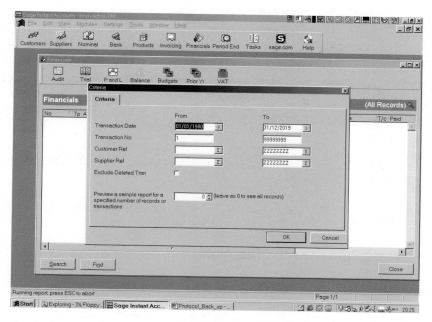

5 Select the type of output you require from the Output option buttons provided: i.e. Printer, Preview, File or E-mail.

6 Click Run.
The Criteria window appears.

7 If you want to restrict the Audit Trail report to display a specific range of transactions, enter the range criteria in the boxes provided. The criteria that you set here can vary, according to the Audit Trail report you selected. You can amend the Audit Trail report layout if necessary.

8 To generate the report, click OK.

9 To exit, click Cancel.

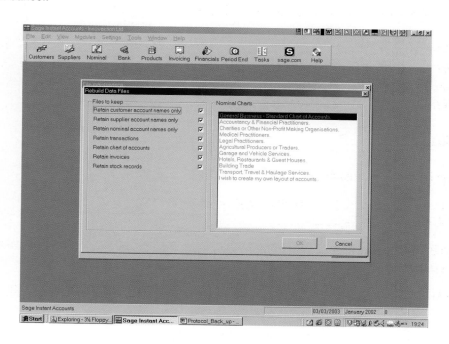

Preparing Statements for Despatch

Preparation of statements is a crucial process for the accounts receivable department of your business. Statements are run off at an agreed time (usually month-end), put into envelopes and sent by post to the appropriate customers. However, the facility is available to send statements out on request to customers or internal requests.

The following is an example of how this process can be done:

● Raise all invoices during the period

● Ensure all credit notes have been included

● Ensure that stock reconciles – all stock movement out or in should have appropriate invoice or credit notes raised

● Ensure any errors are rectified before running any reports

● Run the Aged Debtors report

● Run the statements

● Send by post – in the future there is the potential to send by email

Look at the example of the aged debtors report below. You can run this report and check for any minor errors or any disputed items, which you may want to remove. Once these have been corrected the report should be run.

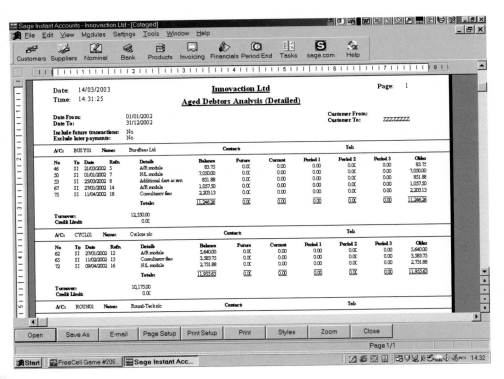

Now that you are satisfied with the data within the report, you can run the statements to pick up the information relating to the appropriate transaction date that you require with the range of customers. The output will show your details at the top of the statement and the invoices and credit notes detailed below in invoice/credit note number order.

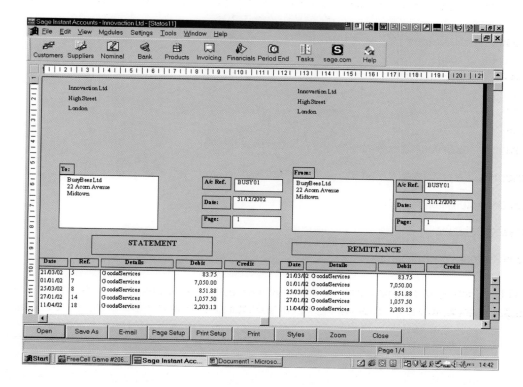

Preparing Accounts Letters for Despatch

There are many ways that you will be communicating with both your customers and suppliers. Furthermore there will be occasions when information or data will have to be shared with Government and other agencies. However, within this section you will see more day-to-day communications. You will contact your customers and suppliers when account details change over the years, or when information is requested.

Customer communications

- Account maintenance

- Marketing

- Product costs update

- Confirmation of order receipts

- Statements

- Dunning letters

- Year-end

239

- Period end

- Sales orders

- Invoices

- Credit notes

Supplier communications

- Account maintenance

- Year-end situation

- Periodic contact – build relationships

- Purchase orders

- Purchase requisitions

- Payments

- Requests for information

We will now look at two examples of letters to be sent out. Each of the above has a process and procedure behind it; however, we will look at dunning letters and change of address for a customer. It should be noted that each of the above can be set up in either the customer or supplier sections. They can be formatted according to individual needs.

Dunning letters These are letters sent to customers advising them of outstanding balance of payment on their invoices. The process involves invoicing customers for the goods and services, providing a credit note facility when there is a dispute, ensuring that payments are allocated when cash is received, all these occurring within the agreed commercial payment terms.

Once all of the above and other reconciliations have occurred, the customer is notified of the amounts of money outstanding (outside payment days). Normally, there are three letters (it could be more – depends on each individual company) which are used to notify customers, each more severe than the previous to ensure that payment is settled. Letter 1 will be a gentle reminder, the second one might be like the one shown in the screen shot and letter 3 would warn of legal consequences and outcomes of court proceedings. Each letter is sent a certain time span after the previous but the aim is to settle in an amicable way.

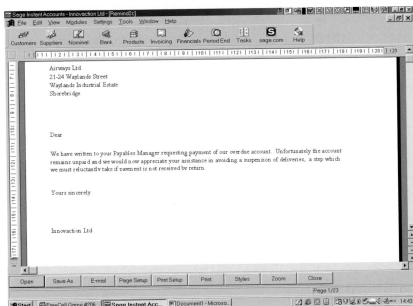

Change of address The example below shows the communication when there is a change in address or any other aspect. It is always advisable to update your customer's details and ask them to do the same when circumstances change. Again access will be either in the customer or supplier tab through means of letters. Once the letter is communicated changes to the record can be made.

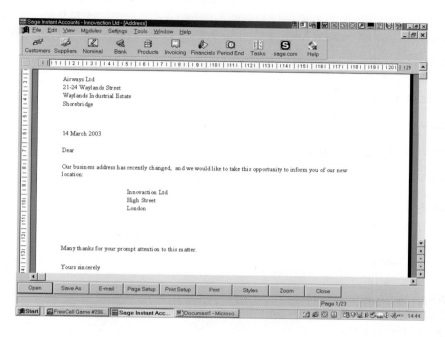

Dealing with Disputed Invoices

Your customers can dispute your invoices and you can dispute invoices from your suppliers.

Disputed customer invoices This involves analysing and reviewing customer queries with invoices and payments. These disputes include price changes, order changes, returns that have not taken effect at the right time and waiting for credit notes.

Example Process:

- Deliver goods

- Send Invoice

- Query through communications:

  - Under delivered
  - Over delivered
  - Price on the order against price on the invoice
  - Wrong products
  - Writing letters

- Mismatch invoice and order

- Give timescales within which to resolve query

- Communication between sales department and account manager

- Look for credit note

Disputed supplier invoices You will have some invoices for whatever reason through errors or procedural issues that will be disputed. These include price changes, order change, returns that have not taken effect at the right time and waiting for credit notes to allow netting so that you have enough credit to buy more goods.

Example Transactions:

- Receive goods

- Receive invoice

- Query:
  - Under delivered
  - Over delivered
  - Price on the order against price on the invoice
  - Wrong products

- Give timescales within which to resolve query

- Mismatch invoice and order

- Communication between purchase department and supplier account manager

- Look for credit note

- Hold all invoice payment until all disputes are cleared

Bad Debt Write Off

Bad debts are amounts of money that your company is expecting from a customer but no payment has been received according to the payment terms set. From an accounting perspective there should be build up of reserves to cater for the future losses of non-payments.

Over a period of time a policy may well be developed to take certain amounts from the sales to cover any bad debts that may arise. This policy depends on each company's customer profile. For example, in retail, bad debt is less likely as a majority of the transactions are cash related but there may well be high bad debts where a major-ity of the transactions are based on payment by account. Within your accounts, reserves are built up to cover any bad debts anticipated (you may want to reserve up to 1 per cent of your sales as bad debts).

In accounting systems such as Sage the following steps should be taken and records set up:

- Check credit limits (outside system)

- Sales order raised (outside system)

- Delivery made (outside system)

- Invoices raised

- Check individual customer account periodically

- Run aged debtors report for checking

- The older invoices are checked after payment received (internal process)

- Make business aware of non-payment (no further sales made)

- Send dunning letters

- Attend debtors meetings (legally set by customer)

- Take legal proceedings

- Make decision to write off bad debt (authority required)

- Raise journal entry to write down debtor balance

- Raise journal to charge amount to nominal ledger

- Mark the customer as not to be worked with until advised

Paying Bills

Paying bills is the passing of payments to your suppliers after authorisation has been received from the appropriate manager.

Before any authorisation can take place, the manager with authority requires proof of receipt of goods, the purchase order that has been raised for the goods, and that there are no discrepancies in the process.

A list of all invoices and payments is printed and provided as a back-up for the payment run. Once this list is authorised then the final payment run can take place. However, there is one further check required. The finance manager will need to ensure that there is enough money in the bank to clear cheques, BACS or bank transfers. A remittance advice note will accompany payments.

After all this has happened the bank account must be reconciled to make sure that appropriate clearance has happened in case there is query over non-payment.

In all accounting systems such as Sage the following steps should be taken and records set up:

- Set up supplier in the purchase ledger

- Raise purchase order (outside the system)

- Receive goods (outside the system)

- Receive invoice

- Log invoice onto system

- Approve payment of invoice by appropriate manager – payment could relate to one order or many orders

- Issue the list of invoices to be paid

- Pass the payment authorised for payment run

- Finance check to ensure cash flow will cover the payment run

- Select payment types: cheque or BACS or bank transfer

- Print remittance advice

- Manual cheque written

- Send to supplier the appropriate payment

- Reconcile the money in the accounts for cash flow purposes

Currency

Computerised accounting programs should automatically create currency records for the fifteen EU countries. You can then edit these currencies as required to enter the correct currency conversion rates.

Your program can handle transactions involving the euro. All you need to do is set up the correct currency rates.

You can also add other non-EU currencies. You can create up to 99 currencies in total and then assign one to each customer, supplier and bank record.

Euro calculator example: You receive an invoice from your suppliers in euros. Your base currency is pounds sterling. You need to record the invoice in your base currency to ensure that your accounts are correct. To do this you can use the euro calculator.

1 Ensure that your currencies and exchange rates are set up correctly and that your base currency is set to pounds sterling.

2 From the main toolbar, click Suppliers.

3 From the Suppliers window, click Invoices.

4 From the Batch Suppliers Invoices window, enter the following invoice details as you would normally:

- Account
- Date
- Reference
- Ex Reference
- Nominal Code
- Department
- Details

5 In the Net text box, enter the net amount of the invoice. This figure is in euros. You now need to convert this to your base currency – pounds sterling.

6 With your cursor in the Net text box, press the F5 function key.
The euro calculator appears showing the figure you entered in the Net text box.

7 From the drop-down list, select the currency you are converting from. In this example, select euro.
The converted value appears in the To text box. This shows the value in your base currency.

8   To copy this figure back to the Batch Supplier Invoices window click OK.
    You have now converted your invoice from euros to pounds sterling.

9   To accept your entries click Save. The details are 'posted' instantly to update the Nominal Ledger and the relevant supplier's details.

If you do not wish to save this batch, then click Discard to clear the data and start again. The Discard button does not cancel any batch details you have already saved.

Adding a Currency

1   From the menu bar, open the Settings menu on the menu bar and choose Currency.
    The Currencies list box appears.

2   From the Base Currency drop-down list, select your company's base currency.

3   Select the currency you wish to change, then click Edit.

4   To exit from the Currencies list box, click Close.

The Euro and your Business From 1st January 1999, the euro was introduced as the single currency unit of European Economic and Monetary Union (EMU).

Initially the euro was only used for cashless transactions, but euro notes and coins are now available. The introduction of the euro as the single European currency will affect the way you do business with your customers and suppliers.

Although the United Kingdom is not participating in the initial entry to the euro, trading will still be affected. For example, some large UK companies have announced that they will trade in euros.

This will work its way down the supply chain affecting many smaller businesses. UK exporters and importers may also be required to deal in euros. There will also be many indirect effects on UK businesses as the euro becomes a major world currency and as more and more companies within EMU start to expand their trading areas.

Using computerised accounting provides you with the ability to trade in this new European currency.

All you need to do is enter your currency rates.

Editing a Currency

1   Open the Settings menu on the main menu bar and choose Currency.
    The Currencies list box appears.

2   From the Base Currency drop-down list, select your company's base currency.

3   Select the currency you wish to change, then click Edit. The Edit Currency window appears.
    You can also double-click on any line of the table to bring up the Edit Currencies window.

4   In the boxes provided, enter the currency details.

5   To save your entries click OK, or to abandon your entry click Cancel.

6   To exit from the Currencies list box, click Close.

Setting the Base Currency

1   From the menu bar, open the Settings menu and choose the Currency option.
    The Currencies window appears.

2   From the Base Currency drop-down list, select your base currency for example pound sterling.

3   To return to the main desktop, click Close.

Tip

If your Regional Settings for your PC are set to English (Ireland), the base currency will automatically be set to euros. Any other regional setting will set the default base currency to pound sterling.

UNIT 028 DESKTOP PUBLISHING

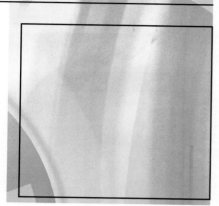

BEFORE YOU START: CHECKING YOUR SYSTEM FOR COMPATIBILITY

As discussed in level 1 it is important to check your system for compatibility. You will need a colour monitor (VDU) to see your design in full colour, a PC-compatible mouse and keyboard, a hard disk to save your designs to, and a floppy disk drive to transport any work to an outside printer if necessary, and to keep backup copies of your designs.

Remember to check how much storage space you have on the hard disk where you are going to be saving your DTP file. This is to ensure that the file saves properly. Lack of storage space affects the overall performance of your system.

To check the amount of available storage space, double-click on My Computer.

Right-click on your hard drive (usually C:\) and select Properties.

A pie chart will display how much free space you have left on this drive. Ideally you should have around 500 MB free.

A CD-ROM is necessary to install the software onto your system, and may be useful for extra ClipArt or fonts that you may wish to use. A colour printer may also be useful if you wish to print your designs yourself in full colour.

Remember you will also need to check the RAM (Random Access Memory) of your PC. You will need more RAM to work more efficiently with photo files and high-resolution graphics. 32 MB is a minimum and 64 MB or more is recommended for best results.

1   To check your system's RAM, right click on the My Computer icon on your desktop.

2   Select Properties.

3   Your system's RAM will be displayed under the General tab.

MANAGING DIRECTORIES/FOLDERS AND FILES

The easiest way to manage your directories (also called folders) and files is through Windows Explorer, which can be accessed by clicking on the Start button, then choosing Programs, then Windows Explorer. These steps are illustrated in the diagram to the right. Windows Explorer may also have an icon located on the desktop, which can be double-clicked to open the program.

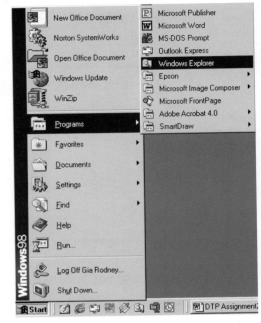

Windows Explorer is the computer's filing system. Here you will be able to divide your work or information into different areas called folders or directories. A yellow icon in Windows Explorer shows these folders. Folders contain the files you have created, including all your DTP files.

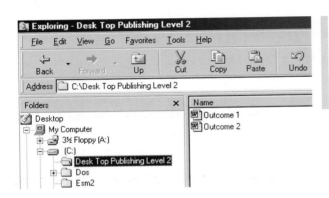

As shown a folder has been created on the c:\ drive called Desk Top Publishing, containing two files called Outcome 1 and Outcome 2.

Creating a Folder

1 Click the drive in Windows Explorer where you want to create the new folder.

2 On the File menu, point to New, and then click Folder.

3 The new folder appears with a temporary name.

4 Type a name for the new folder, and then press enter.

Note:
If you want to create a new folder within a folder, click the folder and then follow steps two, three and four above.

The use of Windows Explorer to create folders is a very useful method of organising your work so that it is easy to find at a glance, and so that your hard drive does not appear cluttered.

> ### TASK
>
> **On your system open Windows Explorer. On your local drive C or a networked drive, create a folder called Unit 028 – DTP Level 2.**
>
> **Within that folder create a subfolder for each of the outcomes in this level, for example, Outcome 1, Outcome 2, etc. There are five outcomes, so you should have five sub folders within your DTP Level 2 Folder.**
>
> **Create a separate sub folder called The Computer Organisation Newsletter.**

USING A WORD PROCESSOR OR TEXT EDITOR TO CREATE, EDIT AND SAVE A TEXT FILE

Using Notepad

You can use Notepad to create or edit text files that do not require formatting and are smaller than 64Kb. Notepad opens and saves text in text-only format. Notepad saves files with the .txt extension. This means that the files are purely text files.

To create or edit files that require formatting or are larger than 64Kb, use WordPad.

You can start Notepad by clicking Start, pointing to Programs, pointing to Accessories, and then clicking Notepad.

Using WordPad

WordPad is a text editor for short documents. You can format documents in WordPad with various font and paragraph styles.

You can start WordPad by clicking Start, pointing to Programs, pointing to Accessories, and then clicking WordPad.

Using MS Word

MS Word is a word processing program that allows you to create documents with various fonts and paragraph styles, as well as create WordArt and insert pictures. It is much more powerful than a text editor.

You can start Word by clicking Start, pointing to Programs, and then clicking on Microsoft Word.

Both WordPad and Word save files with the .doc extension.

Creating a Text File

To create a new text file, open the relevant software package as described above. A new blank document will automatically be opened. Once you have created your new document save it using the File menu (File, Save As). Remember to give your file a relevant name. To edit your text file, open the saved document (File, Open), make changes, and then save again (File, Save). The document will be saved into the directory or folder you specify.

.rtf – rich text format. Rich text format saves all formatting, and converts formatting to instructions that other programs, including compatible Microsoft programs, can read and interpret. This is useful when using different versions of word processing software, or if you need to work on two different computers that have different software installed.

USING A GRAPHICS EDITOR TO EDIT AND SAVE A GRAPHIC FILE

Microsoft Publisher recognises pictures with the following extensions: .bmp, .gif, .jpg, and .tif, as well as vector graphics. These are explained below.

.bmp – Bitmap files. These files are exactly what they sound like – they are maps made up of small dots or bits. A bitmap, especially a colour bitmap, can use up more RAM and disk space than other file types and that can slow down the display and printing of your DTP file. Enlarging a bitmap can also affect the quality of the picture as the bits become more visible.

.gif – Graphic Interchange Format files. This file format means that pictures can only use 256 colours and are therefore better for diagrams and drawings.

.jpg – Joint Photographic Experts Group files. JPEG files can usually provide the same graphics quality as a GIF file, at a smaller file size. JPEG format uses 16 million colours and is therefore more suitable for photographs.

.tif – Tagged Image File. TIF files are compressed and therefore can be minimised without degrading the quality. This is a good file format to use for screen dumps.

Vector – vector graphics are often called object-oriented graphics. They are seen as a collection of lines rather than as patterns of individual dots. Vector images are described mathematically as a set of instructions to create objects in the image. This makes it easier to magnify, rotate, and layer object-oriented graphics than bitmap graphics.

Using Paint

You can use Paint to create, edit, and view pictures. You can paste a Paint picture into another document you've created, or use it as your desktop background. You can even use Paint to view and edit scanned photos.

You can start Paint by clicking Start, pointing to Programs, pointing to Accessories, and then clicking Paint.

Once you have opened the graphics editor, you can open your picture file (File, Open) to edit it and make changes. Once complete save your edited picture to your specified file (File, Save As).

IMPORTING TEXT AND GRAPHICS INTO A NEW DTP FILE

Importing a Whole Text File

You might find that working in a word processing program to create your text is easier and faster than using Publisher. To include text files created elsewhere, you can import the text into a DTP file. Publisher can import text files created in many programs.

If you're adding text to an existing frame, click where you want to put the new text or create a new text or table frame.

To insert a new text frame, use the text frame tool **A** to create a text frame. Then click on the Insert menu, and select Text File.

Click on the file you want to import. If you do not see the name of the file you want to import text from, you may need to change the folder or drive. Then click OK.

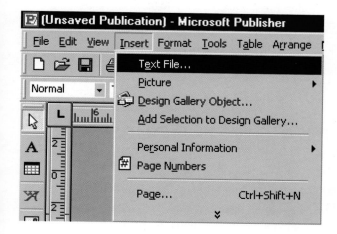
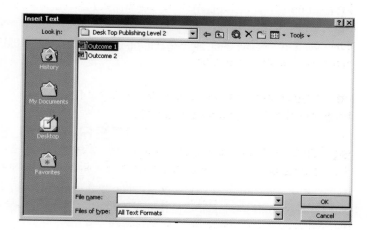

If the text you're importing doesn't fit in the text frame, Publisher may ask if you want to create text frames for the remaining text. This feature is called autoflow. Autoflow will create a new frame to accommodate all your new text.

Imported text from most word processing programs usually retains the formatting it had in the word processing program and any text styles will also be included with the text.

Importing a Picture File

If you're adding a picture to an existing frame, click where you want to put the new picture or create a new picture frame.

To insert a new picture frame, use the picture frame tool 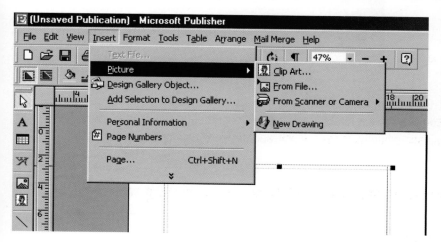 to create a picture frame. Then click on the Insert menu, and select Picture. This will give you an option to choose ClipArt, a picture from a file, or an image from a digital camera or scanner. Select which type of picture you want to import. If you choose From File a dialog box will open displaying the pictures you have saved. Click on the file you want to import. If you do not see the name of the picture file you want to import, you may need to change the folder or drive. Then click OK.

SAVING A DTP FILE TO A SPECIFIED LOCATION

To save your DTP file to a specified location you will need to use the Save As command on the File menu. This will bring up the Save As dialog box.

In the Save In box choose the location where you would like to save your DTP file by selecting from the drop down menu.

If you wish to rename your file this can be done by typing the file name in the File Name box.

When complete click on Save.

Tip

Remember where you have saved the file and what you named it!

SETTING UP A MASTER STYLE IN A GIVEN HOUSE STYLE

A master or template is a model publication that you can use as the basis for creating a new publication. A template can contain the basic layout and formatting, text and graphics, as well as layout guides, text styles and background elements such as page numbers and rules, that can be re-used in future publications. To make a template, create a publication and save it as a template. Then open it any time you want to base a new publication on it. Once you have designed the perfect publication you may wish to use it again for further publications. To save yourself the extra work of creating your design again, simply save the publication as a template. This will be very useful if there is little change between the design elements of the publications. Using a template also helps to carry the house style throughout all your publications.

Creating a Template

1 Create the publication you want to use as a template.

2 On the File menu, click Save As.

3 In the File name box, type a name for the template.

4 In the Save as type box, click Publisher Template.

5 Click Save.

Changing the Page Setup to Suit a House Style

Many organisations specify a house style for their documents, which you should follow closely. The idea of a house style is to produce a standard, easily recognisable look for an organisation's documents. This look or image gives the customers and staff a sense of organisational unity and efficiency, and of everyone working together to produce a high-quality product or service.

Say for example that you are given an assignment from a company or client that requires you to set up the page in a specific way – with defined margins, gutters and page orientation, and that requires you to use a particular background and colour. If these elements are the same no matter what type of publication you create for this company or client, then this is called a house style.

A house style ensures that letters from two different people at the same organisation will have the same look, as the addresses, dates and references are all in the same position, and the font that is used is the same in all the documents. The same is true for logos – these are always in exactly the same place, and exactly the same size and colour on every document.

To set up the margins for a template as given in a house style, start a new publication, which you will use as your template. Use the Arrange menu and Layout Guides to change the margins, as covered in level 1. You can change the size of left, right, top and bottom margins, as well as the gutter margins. Remember that gutter margins allow a little extra space to the inside margins of a booklet to make room for binding. You may not always need to use them.

Tip

Layout guides are visible on the screen but they do not appear when you print.

The layout guides not only define the margins, but also define other sections of the page and help you to align elements on the page with absolute precision. You can add or reposition layout guides to accommodate any design you want to work with.

To change the page orientation according to what is required by the house style, use the File menu and choose Page Layout. Here you can change the page orientation from portrait to landscape.

TASK

You have been asked to design a template for The Computer Organisation to use as a newsletter. The marketing department of The Computer Organisation have given you the specifics of their house style. The document must be A4, with the following specifications:

Margins:
Left – 2cm
Right – 2cm
Top – 3cm
Bottom – 2.25cm

Binding Multi-Page Documents

If your publication is more than one page and closer to being a booklet, you may want to consider binding it. The size of your finished publication is what determines whether you fold the pages or not. Fold the pages if you want the finished size to be half the size of the printer paper, use unfolded paper for a booklet that is more than half the size, or the maximum size of the printed paper.

If you decide to make a folded booklet, the Two Page Spread option is automatic, for an unfolded booklet you can use the Two Page Spread option under the View menu, to help you see the booklet as it will look when opened. Looking at the spread will help you make sure that the content and layout design work across the two pages.

If you want to, you can take the extra step and make sure that the pages mirror each other. With mirrored pages you can set up a little extra space to the inside margins to make room for the binding. This is called a gutter margin. This gutter margin can be set up by using the Arrange menu, then clicking on Layout Guides. Click in the check box Create Two Backgrounds with Mirrored Guides, then increase the Inside margin to create a gutter.

You can also position the page numbers to be on opposite corners as in a book.

Using the Background

Every page of a publication has a background and a foreground. Most of the time, you are working on the foreground of the page, and anything you place there appears on that page only. The background lies under the foreground. You can see everything on the background while you're working on a page, but to add, delete, or change any of the background elements, you must switch from the foreground to the background.

The background is most useful for placing:

1   Page numbers – Publisher automatically puts the correct number on every page.

2   Running headers or footers – text at the top or bottom of a page that provides information about the publication. The page number is often included in the running head or footer.

3   Rules – straight lines, often stretching horizontally across the top of a page to separate text from running heads.

4   Company names, logos, and graphics – recognisable symbols to identify the source or subject of the publication.

5   Watermark graphics – faint graphics that you can see through the text that have some relevance to your publication. For example, you can place a graphic, or a word such as "Confidential," on the background of a publication, so that it appears behind text on the foreground. You can shade the watermark a certain colour to match the colour scheme given in the house style.

If a company or a client has a particular logo, they may wish it to be shown on every page. This is easiest using a background. To create a specific background for a house style, follow these steps:

1   On the View menu, click on Go To Background.

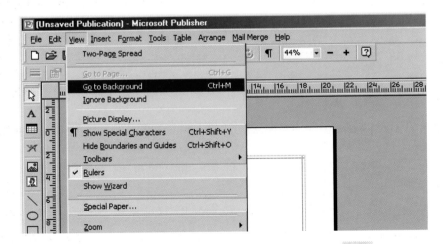

2   The page navigation button at the bottom of the screen will change to ▨R to remind you that you are working on the background.

3   Any items you place on the background will appear on every page of your document. These can be graphics, text, page numbers and so on.

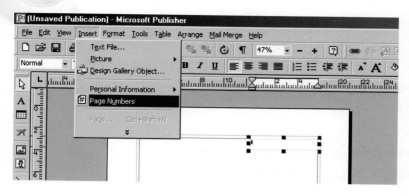

Page numbers To insert page numbers make sure that you are on the background. Then insert a text frame using the text frame tool. Place the text frame where you would like the numbers to appear on every page. Click inside the text frame so that the handles are visible and the cursor is flashing. Then from the Insert menu, click on Page Numbers, as shown.

The number of the page will automatically be placed in the text frame. You can format the page number as you would normal text.

Running headers To insert a running header or footer on the background, first insert a text frame, and then type the text you would like to appear on every page. You may be given a particular logo or company header which may need to be included as part of the house style. You can format this text as required.

Graphics and watermarks To insert a graphic as a background or watermark on every page, insert a picture frame using the picture frame tool. Then insert either a picture that you have previously saved or ClipArt. This graphic will show up in the same place on every page of your document. If you need to change the picture colour to match a house style colour scheme, click on Recolour Picture from the Format menu. Click OK.

Horizontal rules To insert a rule onto the background, or anywhere on your publication, insert a ClipArt frame, and then a rule from the Dividers and Decorations category in ClipArt. A rule is a good way to separate the headings from the body text of your publication, or to divide up the page. In the same way borders can be used to define the header or footer on a page.

Tinted backgrounds To change the background colour and create some effects, draw a text box big enough to colour the entire page of your publication. Then on the Format menu, choose Fill Colour. This will give you the options to choose a colour, either from the most recently used colours or from the colour palette. This dialog box will also give you options to create tints/shades, patterns and gradients with your fill colours as the primary colour and white, or any other colour you choose, as the secondary colour. This tool gives you the freedom to create interesting backgrounds for your publication.

Once you have made your changes to the background, go back to the foreground.

TASK

The Computer Organisation has asked you to add the following details to their template. Should the document be more than one page, The Computer Organisation insists the following details be on every page:

● **The name of the organisation (The Computer Organisation) must be at the top of the page. Font is Algerian, size 36, colour Black, centred.**

● **The name must be separated from the rest of the newsletter by a horizontal rule. Choose a suitable divider.**

● **The names of the directors of the organisation must be shown at the bottom of the page. Font Arial, size 14, colour Black, centred. The names of the directors are M. Chip, A.E. Newman and W. Gates.**

● **The company logo must be placed on the document in the centre as a watermark. (Assume the logo is any computer related picture from ClipArt.) The watermark must be grey to match the colour scheme of the house style.**

It is also possible at this point to set up columns on your template or master that may need to be the same on every page. To do this click on the Arrange menu and choose Layout Guides. This will bring up the layout dialog box. Under Grid Guides, choose the number of columns you want your DTP file to have.

After choosing your columns you can insert text and picture frames to suit your publication.

TASK

The Computer Organisation have requested that their newsletter contain two columns.

Save the publication as a template called 'The Computer Organisation Newsletter'.

When designing your template, take into consideration the impact of the layout. Use the margins, line spacing and indents to make space around your text and graphics. There should also be spacing around, but not below your heading, in order to distinguish the heading from the body text. This is called white space. White space is used to distinguish between unrelated items in a publication; less space between elements means there is a relation between these elements.

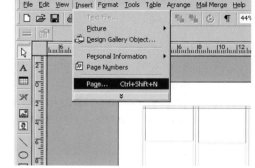

Once you have designed your template, you can save it.

Adding Pages

As you add content to your publication, you may wish to add more pages. The pages that you add to a template or master file will have the same layout guides and background components that the original page has, and they will have the same arrangement as the existing page. To add more pages click on the Insert menu and choose Page.

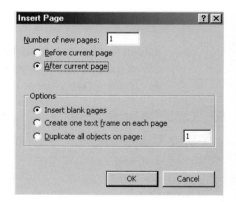

The Insert Page dialog box will appear, which indicates the options you have when inserting pages. These will include how many pages to insert, where to put the new pages, how the new pages will be structured, and which page to duplicate (if necessary).

Using Colour

Colour is an essential part of your publication or DTP file. It is important to use colour to grab attention and to bring excitement to your publication. It can also break up large areas of black and white text, and can be used to enhance pictures. Although it is good design policy to use colour sparingly, you can colour almost any part of your design. There are two main types of colour: full colour and spot colour. Full colour is used to colour the entire publication, spot colour is used to colour only certain elements of your publication.

Publisher makes it easy to choose colour and apply it to different areas of your design, by using the Font Colour (for text) on the Format toolbar and Recolor Picture (for objects and pictures) on the Format toolbar. Make sure you have selected the text you wish to recolour, then click on the Font Color icon on the Format toolbar and select a colour from those shown. If the colour you want is not shown, click on More Colors.

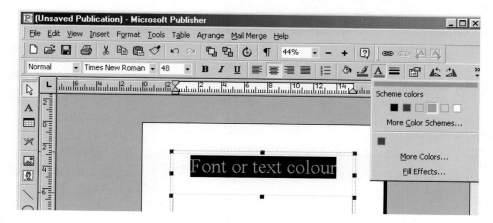

To recolour the picture, select the picture frame to be changed, the choose Recolor Picture from the Format menu, as discussed before.

You can also create tints/shades, patterns and gradients of your chosen colour. These can be changed using the Fill Effects option as shown above. Patterns and gradients are only available when filling an object.

Colour Matching with Full Colour

Sometimes the colour you have chosen and that is displayed when your design is seen on-screen may be different to the colour on your printed output. This could simply be because of the quality of paper you are using. A more complex and more likely reason may be because the printer and monitor work with slightly different ranges of colour. This is a reason why it is important to check them for compatibility before you start.

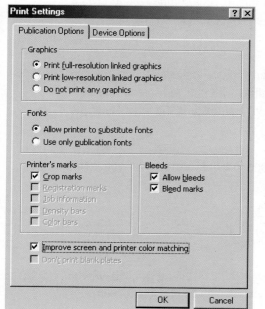

Publisher has tried to fix this problem through using Windows Image Color Matching, which tries to get your monitor and printer to agree on the appearance of colours. Even if Windows Image Maker cannot get the two devices to agree exactly, it will get them to agree that they are as similar as possible. So red will be red, not orange.

You can also make sure that your printer and screen colour are similar by ticking the improve screen and printer colour matching check box in the print settings dialog box. To do this first choose the printer you will be using, then choose Print from the File menu. Click on the Advanced Print Settings button at the bottom of the screen. The Print Settings dialog box will appear.

Click in the Improve screen and printer color matching check box to select it. Then click OK. This will ensure that your screen and printer see colours as similarly as possible.

When printing in full colour, the printing process uses four ink colours and combines them in different proportions to create the colours you specify. These four colours are cyan, magenta, yellow and black, usually known by the abbreviation CMYK (K represents black, so as not to be confused with blue).

Colour Matching with Spot Colour

Remember you can apply spot colour to most design elements including borders and text. You can also recolour your pictures to include the spot colour.

> **Tip**
>
> If you do not recolour your picture it will be printed in black and white (grayscale).

With spot colour it is difficult to match the colour you see on the screen with the colour that is printed. This is especially true if you send your printing to an outside printer. Before you choose a particular colour, it is advisable to check with the printers to make sure that the colour is available. You choose the closest available screen colour from Publisher's palette, and then choose the actual ink colour from a swatch book that your printer will supply. The colours will probably be from the Pantone Color Matching System (PMS), which is the printing industry's standard system of ink colour specification. Each of the approximately 500 colours has its own reference number.

Before you specify Pantone Colors in your publication, ask your printing service if they support the Pantone matching system. If they do not, ask them how they want you to specify colours in your publication. If they do support the Pantone matching system, use the following tips to decide which colour library to use:

If you're designing a publication that uses black plus one or two other colours, choose Pantone Solid Colors. Pantone Solid Colors are also referred to as spot colours.

If you're designing a publication that uses colour photographs or art, choose Pantone Process Colors. These colours are created by combining the four standard process inks – cyan, magenta, yellow, and black (CMYK).

If you're designing a process-colour publication and want to match an object that uses a spot color, you can convert a Pantone Solid Color to the nearest matching process colour. For example, if your company logo uses a Pantone Solid Color and you want to print that logo in a process-colour brochure, you can convert the logo's solid color to a Pantone Process Color that closely reproduces it.

If you cannot find the perfect colours for use in spot colouring your design, then you can make your own. You can create your own colour by specifying the hue, saturation and luminosity values (HSL); or red, green and blue values (RGB). In the HSL colour system, hue is the name of the colour, e.g. red; saturation is the intensity of the colour and luminosity indicates how light or dark the colour is.

In the RGB colour system, you can mix the three colours in various proportions to achieve the colour you want. Remember there are over 16 million colour possibilities.

MANIPULATING TEXT

As mentioned above in 'Changing the page setup to suit a house style', you can use the layout guides to align text perfectly on your page. There are lots of other ways to manipulate the text on your design so that it is unique.

e-Quals

Using Different Text Layouts: Bulleted and Numbered Lists

Creating a bulleted list

Position the insertion point where you want to start typing the list, or position the insertion point in existing text you want to format as a list.

1 On the Format menu, click Indents and Lists.

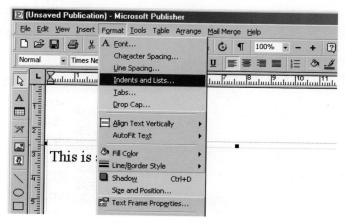

2 Under Indent settings, click Bulleted List.

3 Click the bullet you want.

4 Click OK.

5 If you haven't already typed the text, type the first item in your list.

6 To start a new line with a bullet, press ENTER.

7 To start a new line without a bullet, press SHIFT+ENTER. The line is still indented with the rest of the list.

8 To end a bulleted list, press ENTER twice.

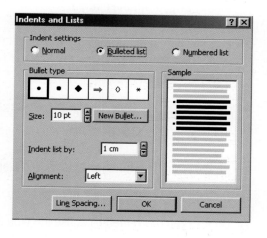

Changing the look of bullets

Highlight the entire bulleted list to select it.

1 On the Format menu, click Indents and Lists.

2 Under Indent settings, click Bulleted list.

3 Under Bullet type, click New Bullet.

4 Click the character you want.

5 If you don't see one you want, in the Font list, click a different font. Click the character you want.

6 Click Insert.

7 Click OK.

259

Creating a numbered list

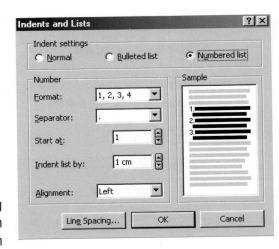

1   Under Indent settings, click Numbered List.

2   Click the number format you want.

3   Click OK.

4   Then follow steps 5 to 8 as above for creating bulleted lists.

Using Different Text Layouts: Indents

You can create space in your design and change the horizontal positioning of text on a paragraph-by-paragraph basis by setting indents for each paragraph. The paragraph indent is the horizontal distance from the margin to the text in a paragraph. There are different types of indenting that you can apply.

This is an example of a first line indent where the first line is further away from the margin than the rest of the lines.

This is an example of a hanging indent, where the first line is against the margins, but the following lines are slightly away from the margin.

This is an example of a paragraph indentation, where the each line of the paragraph is the same distance away from the margin. Both the left and right margins have been indented. In Publisher this is known as Quotation indenting.

To create an indent position the insertion point where you want to start typing with the indent, or position the insertion point in existing text you want to indent.

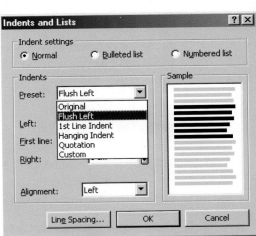

1   On the Format menu, click Indents and Lists.

2   Under Indent settings, click Normal.

3   On the drop down menu, choose the type of indenting you require.

4   Click OK.

Using Different Text Layouts: Side Bars

A sidebar contains information that isn't vital to understanding the main text, but adds interest or additional information.

It's best to put the sidebar within a page or two of the related text. Use the same font and size as the body text uses, or use the same font the caption uses, but in a larger size.

To create a sidebar, insert a textbox where you would like the sidebar to go. Type in and format the text as required. Set the sidebar off from the text by placing a border around it, or shading the background of the box, or both.

Using Different Text Layouts: Banner Headlines

To create a really effective banner headline for a newsletter or poster for example, use WordArt. Insert a WordArt frame where you want the banner headline to go on your page. Use WordArt to create larger text, with special effects and colours. WordArt can also be used to create a fancy first letter for your publication. Resize your WordArt frame to fit across the top of the page to create a banner effect.

Using Different Text Layouts: Callout Boxes

A callout box or pull quote is an excerpt from the main text that adds visual interest to the page and attracts the reader's attention. When you create a pull quote, use a large, bold font to make it really stand out from the rest of the text. You can also add shading behind the text, add a decorative border above or below the text, or create hanging quotation marks around the text.

To create a pull quote, insert a text box where you would like the quote to go. Type in the text and format it as required. Set pull quotes or callout boxes apart from the rest of the text by surrounding them with white space, and maybe including a border above or below the quote for emphasis.

You can use WordArt to flip text, rotate text or skew text in any way you like. You can also use WordArt to put white text on a black or coloured background (reverse text). Once you have created a WordArt frame and designed your text, select the frame and, on the Arrange menu, choose which effect you would like.

Play around with the effects to see what they do!

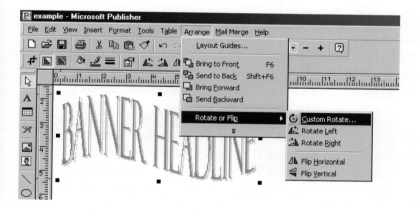

Blurb blurb

"This is where the pullout quote may be placed"

This is the sidebar. See how it is set apart from the text, yet is related.

This newsletter contains a banner headline, a pull out quote separated from the body text by a horizontal rule, as well as a sidebar and some graphics dispersed among the text.

Blurb blurb

TASK

The marketing department of The Computer Organisation would like both columns of the newsletter to contain space for text. This must be formatted to reflect a first line indent on every paragraph, font Arial Narrow size 10, colour black, justified.

There must also be space in the left column to accommodate a picture – square, no bigger than the width of the column, and space in the right column to accommodate a sidebar. The font for the side bar is Arial Narrow, size 10, Italic, colour Black, left aligned.

There should be allocation in the sidebar for a bulleted list. Any bullets can be used for the list. The watermark must still be visible on every page.

Copy Fitting Text

Copy fitting the text involves getting the text you have to fit into the space you have, or changing the space. If you are given a particular space to fill as part of a house style then you will need to manipulate the text so that it fits. There are a number of ways that this is possible.

1 Rewrite the text to include more or less words as necessary.

2 Adjust the spaces between letters. You can squeeze together or move apart all the letters or characters in a block of text. This is called tracking. Or you can squeeze together or move apart selected characters. This is called kerning.

3 Change the space between lines and between paragraphs. If the text is too long, reduce the vertical space between paragraphs. Stretch this space a bit if the text is too short. Be careful not to affect the readability of your design. Changing the line spacing is a useful copy fitting technique. You can change the line spacing to 1.5 points or double spacing if you want the text to take up more room. This space between the lines is called leading.

4 Hyphenate the text. Hyphenation is the main tool for adjusting the edges of paragraphs, or to repair justified lines where there is too much white space between words. It is a good idea to hyphenate manually where you need to. Make sure the hyphenation is correct – it is sometimes different for the same word, depending on where the word is used. Also be careful that there are not too many lines that end in a hyphen. This can make the text difficult to read.

To hyphenate text, click the text or table frame that contains the text you want to hyphenate.

- On the Tools menu, point to Language, and then click Hyphenation.

- Click the Automatically hyphenate this story check box to remove a check mark, if a check mark is there.

- Click Manual.

- Publisher will display the first word requiring hyphenation. A suggested hyphen will be highlighted in the dialog box.

- To accept the suggested hyphenation, click Yes or highlight the hyphen you want, then click Yes to continue.

- Repeat this step until you have finished hyphenating your story, or click Close at any time to stop hyphenating.

MANIPULATING GRAPHIC OBJECTS

Using a Scanner

If your scanner and scanning software support the TWAIN standard (check the manual for your scanner if you are not sure), you can place a picture directly on the scanner and scan it directly from within Publisher.

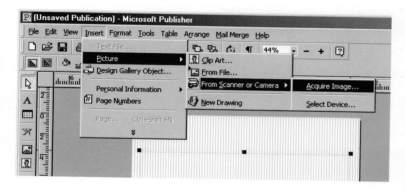

To scan directly, draw a Picture Frame. Make sure that the Picture Frame is selected. Then Click on the Insert menu, choose Picture, choose From Scanner or Camera, and then select Acquire Image.

Publisher will switch over to your scanning software and give you the options for scanning your picture.

If your scanning software does not support the TWAIN standard, then you will not be able to scan from within Publisher. You will need to scan your picture into a graphics editing application, save it as a file, and then import the picture file. This is the method that was discussed before in Importing Graphics Files.

To scan into graphics editing software, first place the picture you want to scan face down onto the scanner.

- Open the scanning software. This will normally be on the Start menu, under Programs.

- Choose the option to scan the image (acquire, get or similar).

It is an idea to preview the picture before scanning it to see how it looks, and to adjust the resolution and quality for scanning. When you preview the image, guides appear to indicate the area to be scanned. This is a quick method of cropping the picture to only scan the bits you need.

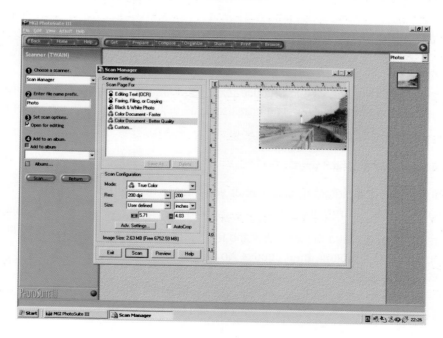

- Once you are ready to scan, click on Scan or Acquire or similar. A progress bar will appear to indicate the progress of the scan.

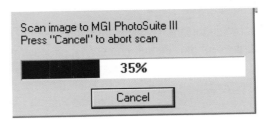

- Once the picture has been scanned, you will be able to use the graphics editing software to adjust the brightness and contrast and apply any special effects.

Using Layout Guides

You can use the layout guides to ensure that your graphics fit perfectly on pages containing text. The layout guides can be vertical and horizontal across the publication to ensure that placement of graphics is accurate.

When dealing with graphics remember that you can change the size, shape and position of the graphic on the publication, as well as change the border or background of the graphic. All of these options are available under the Format menu. Cropping and scaling are also available tools on this menu. The graphic can also be flipped, mirrored or rotated using the Arrange menu.

A graphic can also be modified to suit a house style by changing the colour, fill colour and style. This can all be achieved from the Format menu. To add a border to a graphic to set it off from the text, simply use the Line/Border style option under the Format menu.

If you would like to add a caption to a graphic, simply draw a text box where you would like the caption to go, and type the text as normal. Make sure that the style of text used for the caption fits the publication, and set it apart so it is not confused with the body text; the text should be smaller than the body text. A caption may be very useful to grab the attention of your reader, but need not always be used. Use your discretion.

Layering Objects

You can create some eye-catching effects and produce text over an image by using layering. Layering involves placing a framed object on top of another one and organising the objects so that they are in the most effective position. To move text over graphics:

1 Drag the text frame over the graphic frame.

2 If the text frame is behind the picture or shape after you release the mouse button, click Bring to Front on the Arrange menu.

3 To see the picture or shape through the text, click the text frame, and then on the Format menu choose Fill Colour, then choose No Fill, to make the text frame transparent.

Tip

These icons will also help you arrange your frames: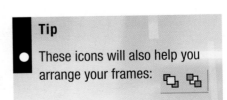

Do not confuse layering with moving between the foreground and background on your publication.

PRODUCING PRINTED AND FILE OUTPUT

Previewing your Publication

When using Publisher it is important to check that the publication or design is suitable for printing. To see how your publication will look when printed use the preview facility.

1   On the View menu, point to Zoom, and then click Whole Page.

2   On the View menu, click Hide Special Characters.

3   On the View menu, click Hide Boundaries and Guides.

4   To display special characters again, click Show Special Characters on the View menu.

5   To display boundaries and guides again, click Show Boundaries and Guides on the View menu.

Proofing

Before you print your file for final proofing, you may want to run the Design Checker to alert you to any possible design mistakes. To run the Design Checker:

1   On the Tools menu, click Design Checker.

2   To check your entire publication, click OK.

3   To check specific pages, click Pages, and then type the page numbers in the From and To boxes.

4   Click OK.

5   Publisher checks the design and displays a dialog box if it finds a problem.

6   To fix a problem, go to your publication and make your changes; you don't have to close the Design Checker dialog box. When you've finished, click Continue to have Publisher go on checking.

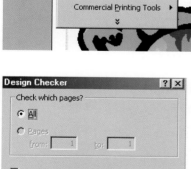

7   If you don't want to fix a problem, click Ignore or Ignore All. Then click Continue.

8   When Publisher finishes checking the design, it asks if you want to check the publication again to make sure that all problems have been corrected. Click the option you want.

9   Click the Explain button for additional information about design issues.

You can also run the spell checker, to highlight any spelling errors.

The point of proofing your publication is to check for any design flaws, or spelling errors, but also to see what your publication looks like when it is printed out. You can, and should, also print colour separations to check that the colours look right, and print in the right place on your publication.

Printing

Publisher provides advanced print settings so you can specify publication options and output device options for the specific printer you will print a publication on. These settings are categorised into publication and device options.

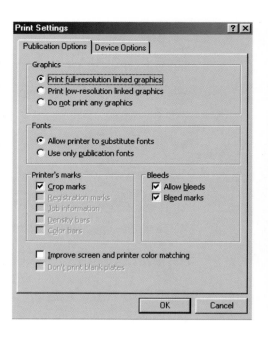

Publication Options You can print low or high-resolution linked graphics, or not print any graphics; specify font substitution; and choose printer marks, bleeds, and colour-matching options.

Printer's marks are marks printed outside the printable area on each page of your publication to help you or your commercial printing service trim, align, and control colour in your publication. In Publisher, you can choose printer's marks based on whether your publication is set up for desktop or commercial printing.

Printer's marks include:

1 Crop marks to show the final page trim edges.

2 Registration marks to precisely align colour separations for commercially printed publications.

3 Colour and density bars to monitor colour on colour separations.

4 Job information that includes the publication name, page, date and time of printing, page number, and plate name.

5 Bleed marks to show the edge of where images, objects, or text extend beyond the trim boundaries of the page.

Device Options Default device options are provided by Publisher or by the selected PostScript printer driver. You can accept default settings or customise them for your output device. Options include film orientation and output, resolution, and per-plate settings for screen frequency and angles.

To modify settings, be sure the publication is set up for the type of commercial printing you want, that the PostScript printer driver for the output device you're using is installed, and that you've selected the output device in the Print dialog box (File menu).

To get help on dialog box options, click the question mark button, and then click the option you want help on.

To print a small scale version of your publication, click on the Print option on the File menu and go to Properties. There should be a fit to page option, which will reduce your publication proportionately to A4 size. Check with your printer's setup to make sure this option is available. To reduce your publication from A4 to say A5, you would need to use the custom option, and reduce the paper size chosen. Or you could change the Page Setup to reflect the smaller size.

To print with any of the above items, choose Print from the File menu, and then click on Advanced settings. All of these options are available on this dialog box.

And Finally.....

Types of Paper

To complete your publication to perfection, you need to choose the right type of paper.

Some considerations you will need to take into account when choosing the type of paper are how you are going to reproduce your publication, your budget, the function and shelf life of the piece and the right paper to suit the mood.

You also need to match the paper with the purpose of the document. Here are some brief examples of types of paper and publications for which they are most commonly used.

Bond – bond or writing paper is the everyday paper commonly used with a personal printer or copier. Business papers are usually printed on bond paper.

You can use bond paper with different textures or finishes to create special looks especially for letterhead stationery. Laid or linen textured paper works well for more conservative looks, while for creativity go for flecked or parchment finish paper.

Book – book is a general-purpose paper used for brochures, newsletters, booklets, and any printed piece that requires light to medium weight paper.

Cover – is heavier than bond or book papers and is used for brochures, presentation folders, business cards and other projects requiring sturdy paper.

Bristol – Bristol is the heaviest type of paper and is usually reserved for printing posters, signs and packaging.

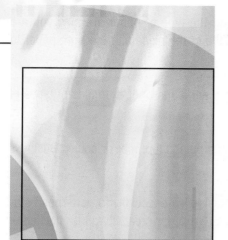

e-Quals
UNIT 029

INTEGRATED APPLICATIONS

Microsoft Office provides a suite of applications that will enable you to carry out all your general office tasks. You need to choose the appropriate tool for the job. For example, if you need to create a letter or report, then you would choose Word. If you need to set up a table of figures and carry out calculations on those figures, then you would choose Excel. If you need to create a chart based on the figures, you would also probably do this in Excel. If you need to store information about clients, suppliers, etc., then you would use Access.

However, what if you want a chart in a Word report, or spreadsheet data in an Access database? Microsoft Office makes it very simple to integrate applications so that you can use the application that does the job most efficiently and then use that information in another application.

CREATING MAILSHOTS IN WORD

If you need to send the same letter to a number of different people, you can use the Mail Merge feature in Word to do this.

You create a letter, labels or envelopes as the 'main document' and put all the names and addresses (and any other variable information) into the 'data source'. Having created these two separate files, Word can then merge the two files together to create personalised letters.

If you already have the name and address information stored in an Excel list or an Access database, then you can choose to use this as the data source for your main document.

Creating Mail Merge Letters in Word

Choose Mail Merge from the Tools menu.

The Mail Merge Helper dialog box opens. This will guide you through the three steps of Mail Merge.

Click on Create and choose Form Letters…

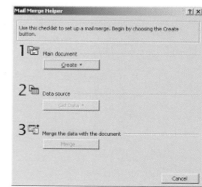

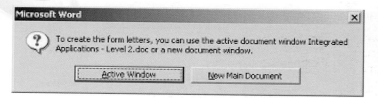

Choose whether you wish to create the letter in the Active Window (i.e. the current window) or a new document window.

The next step of the Mail Merge is to specify a data source. Click on the Get Data button.

If no data source exists, choose Create Data Source. If the Data Source already exists in Excel or Access, choose Open Data Source. (You can also use an Address Book from Outlook or Schedule+).

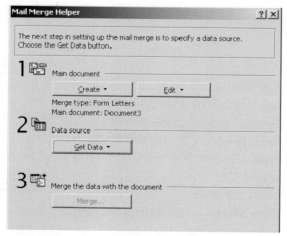

Creating the Data Source A data source has a header row which contains the field names (i.e. what information will go into that field).

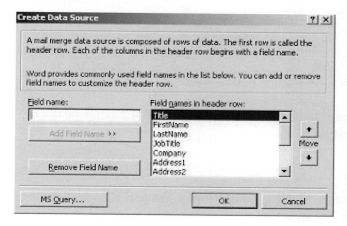

A list of field names is already offered to you for the header row. You can remove field names from the list by clicking on each one in turn and clicking Remove Field Name. You can add new field names to the list by typing the field name in the Field name box and clicking on Add Field Name. Rearrange the field names in the list by clicking on the Move arrow buttons to the right of the list.

Once you have set up all your field names, click OK.

Tip

Do not use spaces in field names.

You will now be prompted to save the data source.

REMEMBER, the data source you are currently saving is empty and must be saved again after entering name and address details.

Once you have saved the data source, you will be prompted to edit the data source. Click on the edit data source button.

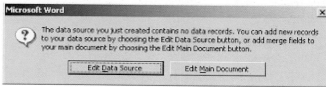

A data form now appears on the screen with the field names that you specified.

Enter the appropriate information into the fields. You can use the Enter key or the Tab key to move from field to field in the data form.

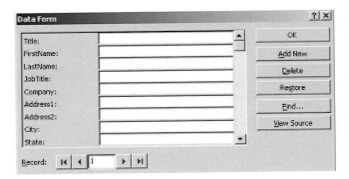

Add New – click this button to start a new record. (Once you reach the last field of the current record, you will automatically be offered a new record).

Delete – you can delete a record by navigating to it and then clicking on the Delete button.

Restore – this will undo any changes you have made to the current record.

Find – this enables you to find records in the data source. Type what you want to find and specify in which field it will appear. Click on Find First to start the search.

View Source – this displays the data in a Word table in a separate window. (If the data is not a Word table, a copy of the data is displayed, e.g. the Excel list or Access table).

Record Navigator – this appears at the foot of the dialog box. You can use this to navigate through the records in the data source.

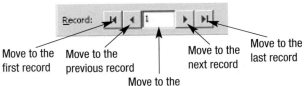

Move to the first record   Move to the previous record   Move to the next record   Move to the last record

Move to the specified record

Click on OK once you have finished entering the data.

Creating the Main Document You will now be returned to the main document window. The Mail Merge toolbar appears across the top of the screen under the Formatting Toolbar.

Type your letter in the normal way, inserting the appropriate Merge Fields where the variable information will appear in the merged letter.

The Mail Merge Toolbar

Insert Merge Field – click on this button to open the list of available merge fields (taken from the data source). Insert the appropriate fields into the letter.

Insert Word Field – click on this button to open a list of Word fields which you may wish to use when creating a mail merge. For example, the Fill-in field prompts the user for information during the mail merge. (You can add other information to the letter that is not stored in the data source).

View Merged Data – this allows you to see the main document and data source merged together on the screen; it is a good way of checking that the merge will carry out correctly.

Record Navigator – once you have switched on View Merged Data, you can use the Record Navigator to navigate through your letters. It works in the same way as in the data form.

Mail Merge Helper – this opens the Mail Merge Helper dialog box again.

Check for Errors – reports any errors in the main document or data source that will prevent merging.

Merge to New Document – carries out the merge and places the merged letters into a new document window.

Merge to Printer – carries out the merge and sends the merged letters to the printer.

Start Merge – opens the Merge dialog box so that you can choose options for merging.

Find Record – opens the Find in Field dialog box so that you can find records in the data source.

Edit Data Source – opens the data form so that you can enter new records, find records and delete records.

The Merge Dialog Box

In the Merge dialog box you can choose whether you wish to merge to a new document or merge directly to the printer.

You can choose whether you wish to merge all the records in the data source, or you can specify a record range.

You can specify how Word should treat blank lines in the data source.

Carrying out the Merge

Once you have set up your Main Document, click on the View Merged Data button on the Mail Merge Toolbar to check that your letters will merge successfully with the data source. You can use the record navigator to view each letter.

If you discover there is an error in the letter (main document), click the View Merged Data button again to switch back to the form letter and make any necessary amendments.

If you discover there is an error in the data source, click the View Merged Data button again to switch back to the form letter and then press the Edit Data Source button at the end of the Mail Merge toolbar. This will open the data form. Navigate through the records and make any necessary amendments.

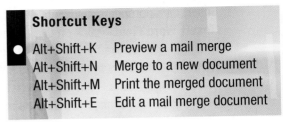

Shortcut Keys

Alt+Shift+K	Preview a mail merge
Alt+Shift+N	Merge to a new document
Alt+Shift+M	Print the merged document
Alt+Shift+E	Edit a mail merge document

Once you are happy that the merge is correct, you can choose to merge the letters into a new document window or directly to the printer. If you wish to set any other options, click on the Start Merge button to access the Merge dialog box.

Saving all the Files

If you have merged directly to the printer, then you will have two files that require saving: the main document (letter) and the data source. (Remember, when you saved the data source initially it was prior to inputting all the records.)

If you have merged to a new document, you will have three documents to deal with: the merged file containing a letter for each record in the data source, the main document (unmerged letter) and the data source. It is not necessary to save the merged file – the form letter and data source will be saved should you need to merge them again.

Save the main document (letter) in the normal way. When you close this file, the following message will appear:

BE CAREFUL – this message is prompting you to save the data source. If you have just spent hours inputting records of data, then you need to choose Yes at this prompt!!

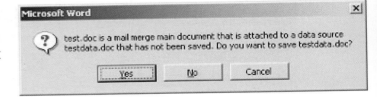

Creating Labels

Choose Mail Merge from the Tools menu.

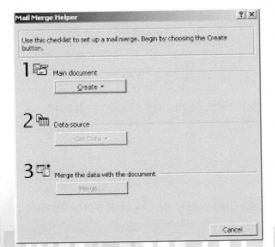

The Mail Merge Helper dialog box opens. This will guide you through the three steps of Mail Merge.

Click on Create and choose Mailing Labels.

Choose whether you wish to create the labels in the Active Window (i.e. the current window) or a new document window.

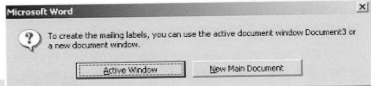

The next step of the Mail Merge is to specify a data source. Click on the Get Data button.

If no data source exists, choose Create data source. If the data source already exists in Excel or Access, choose Open Data Source. (You can also use an Address Book from Outlook or Schedule+).

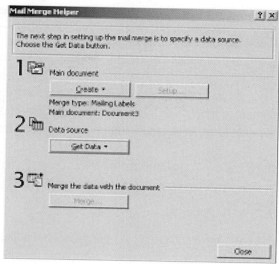

Setting up the Labels Once you have created or opened the data source, you will be prompted to set up the main document.

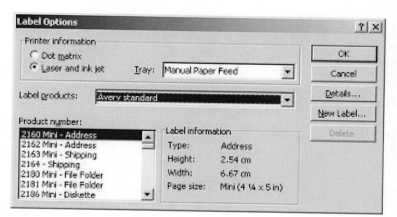

You need to choose the label product that you wish to print onto. Choose your label product from the list, e.g. Avery Standard, and select the Product number.

If you do not find your label product in the list, choose a label product that matches the dimensions of your labels.

Click OK.

Insert the Merge Fields at the appropriate place on the label.

Click OK.

A page of labels will appear in the document window and the Mail Merge helper will open.

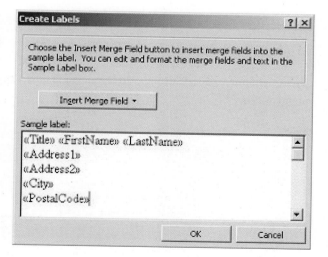

Carrying out the Merge To view how the labels will look when merged, click the View Merged Data button.

If you discover there is an error in the label, click the View Merged Data button again to switch back to the unmerged labels and make any necessary amendments.

If you discover there is an error in the data source, click the View Merged Data button again to switch back to the unmerged labels and then press the Edit Data Source button at the end of the Mail Merge toolbar. This will open the data form. Navigate through the records and make any necessary amendments.

Once you are happy that the merge is correct, you can choose to merge the labels into a new document window or directly to the printer. If you wish to set any other options, click on the Start Merge button to access the Merge dialog box.

Once you have completed the merge, save the files that you may wish to use in the future.

Creating Envelopes

Choose Mail Merge from the Tools menu.

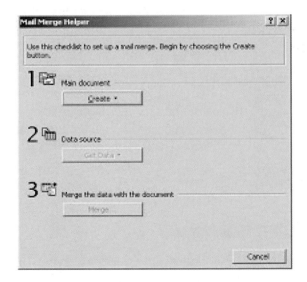

The Mail Merge Helper dialog box opens. This will guide you through the three steps of Mail Merge.

Click on Create and choose Envelopes.

Choose whether you wish to create the envelopes in the Active Window (i.e. the current window) or a new document window.

The next step of the Mail Merge is to specify a data source. Click on the Get Data button.

If no data source exists, choose Create Data Source. If the data source already exists in Excel or Access, choose Open Data Source. (You can also use an Address Book from Outlook or Schedule+).

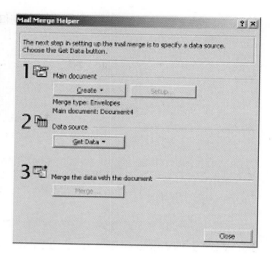

Setting up the Envelopes Once you have created or opened the data source, you will be prompted to set up the main document.

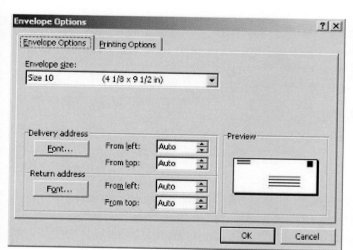

You need to choose the envelope size that you wish to print onto from the list. You can also specify the font for the delivery and return addresses (if there is one) and where the text should appear on the envelope.

Click OK.

Insert the Merge Fields at the appropriate place on the envelope.

Click OK.

A sample envelope will appear in the document window and the Mail Merge helper will open.

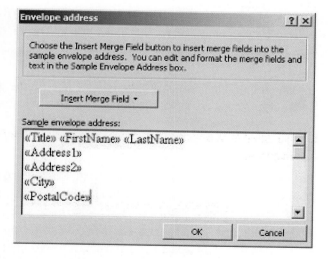

Carrying out the Merge To view how the envelope will look when merged, click the View Merged Data button.

If you discover there is an error in the envelope, click the View Merged Data button again to switch back to the unmerged envelope and make any necessary amendments.

If you discover there is an error in the data source, click the View Merged Data button again to switch back to the unmerged envelope and then press the Edit Data Source button at the end of the Mail Merge toolbar. This will open the data form. Navigate through the records and make any necessary amendments.

Once you are happy that the merge is correct, you can choose to merge the envelopes into a new document window or directly to the printer. If you wish to set any other options, click on the Start Merge button to access the Merge dialog box.

Once you have completed the merge, save the files that you may wish to use in the future.

Query Options

You can filter and/or sort records by clicking on the Query Options button in the Mail Merge helper dialog box, or the Merge dialog box.

Click on the Filter Records or Sort Records tab and set your options.

For example, you can specify that only records where the Last Name is equal to Smith should be merged.

You can sort your merged records by any field in the data source.

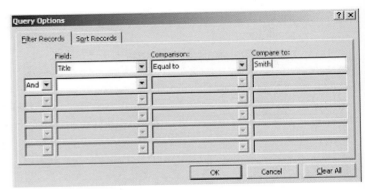

Working with the Data Source

Sometimes it is useful to be able to view the source of the data. If you wish to be able to add and delete records while viewing the data table, sort records in the table or bring in data from a database, you need to be viewing the source. Also, if you need to add, delete or amend the field headings in the data source, you need to go to Manage Fields.

Switch on the Data Form (last button on the Mail Merge toolbar). Click on View Source. The data source appears on the page as a Word table. The Database toolbar replaces the Mail Merge toolbar.

Data Form – this switches on the data form, for inputting new records.
Manage Fields – this opens the Manage Fields dialog box where you can remove fields, add new fields and rename fields.
Add New Record – this enables you to add a new record directly into the data table by adding a new row.
Delete Record – this enables you to delete a record from the data table by deleting the selected row.
Sort Ascending – you can sort the records in the data table in ascending order.
Sort Descending – you can sort the records in the data table in descending order.
Insert Database – you can insert information from a database or another data source.
Update Field – this will update the contents of the field you are sitting in. (You can also press F9 to do this).
Find Record – this opens the Find in Field dialog box so that you can search for data in a specified field.
Mail Merge Main Document – this switches you back to the main document (form letter, label or envelope).

Using an Excel Spreadsheet as a Data Source

Choose Mail Merge from the Tools menu. Click on Create and choose Form Letters, Labels or Envelopes.

Choose whether you wish to create the letter in the Active Window (i.e. the current window) or a new document window.

The next step of the Mail Merge is to specify the Excel data source. Click on the Get Data button and choose Open Data Source.

Navigate to the folder where the Excel file is stored. (You will need to change the Files of type to MS Excel Worksheets.)

Select the file and click Open.

If the spreadsheet file contains named ranges, you will be asked to specify the named range you wish to use as your data source. Alternatively, you can choose Entire Spreadsheet.

You will now be prompted to edit the Main Document.

When you press the Edit Data Source button on the Mail Merge toolbar, you will be taken to the Excel spreadsheet file.

Using an Access Database as a Data Source

You can use a table or query created in Access as the data source for a mail merge in Word.

Choose Mail Merge from the Tools menu. Click on Create and choose Form Letters, Labels or Envelopes.

Choose whether you wish to create the letter in the Active Window (i.e. the current window) or a new document window.

The next step of the Mail Merge is to specify the Access data source. Click on the Get Data button and choose Open Data Source.

Navigate to the folder where the Access database is stored. (You will need to change the Files of type to MS Access Databases.)

Select the file and click Open.

You are now prompted to choose the Table or Query in the Access database that contains the information you wish to use as the data source.

Choose the Table or Query you wish to use and click OK.

You will now be prompted to edit the Main Document.

When you press the Edit Data Source button on the Mail Merge toolbar, you will be taken to the Access database file.

Using Data from an Access Table or Query in Word Mail Merge

You can start the mail merge process from within Access. Select the table or query you want to use and choose Office Links from the Tools menu. Click on Merge It With MS Word.

The Word Mail Merge Wizard will be launched. Choose the options in the Wizard. Word will launch with the main document in the active window. Use the Insert Merge Field button to insert the required fields into the document.

TASK

Create a mail merge letter informing account card holders of an autumn sale at your shop.

Set up at least six people in the data source.

Merge the letter with the data source and print. Save the letter and data source.

Create labels to go with your letters.

Create a list of 10 people in Excel. Create a column for Title, First Name, Last Name, Address 1, Address 2, Town, Post Code. Save and close the Excel workbook.

Use this file as the data source to create another 10 letters to account card holders.

Save all files.

PRINTING LABELS

If you use any of the listed Label products, then setting up your labels to print is a very simple process.

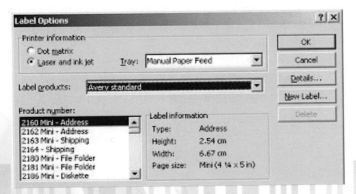

Choose the Label product from the list and then select the Product number.

If you don't use any of the listed products, try to find a label product that matches the dimensions of your labels and contains the same number of labels per page.

If you need to set up a label from scratch, click the New Label button.

Specify the top margin and side margin for the label. Specify the label height and width and the number of labels across and down the page.

Set any other options and click OK.

Labels are set to print manually. When you press the Print button, your printer will wait for the manual feed of the label sheet.

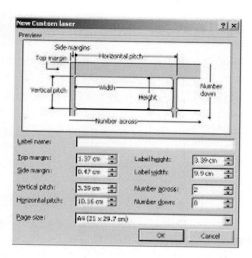

PRINTING ENVELOPES

If you use any of the listed Envelope sizes, then setting up your envelopes to print is a very simple process.

Choose the Envelope size from the list.

Specify the font for the delivery and return addresses and where you want the addresses to appear on the envelope.

Click OK.

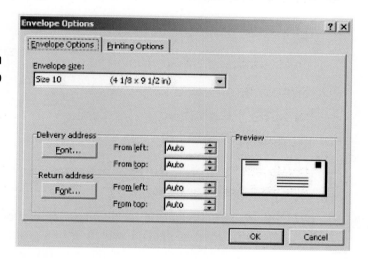

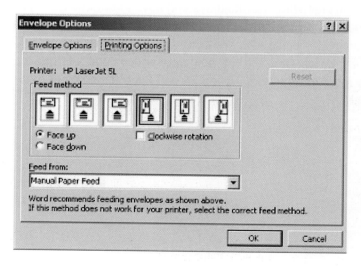

Click on the Printing Options tab and specify which way round your envelopes will be fed.

Click OK.

Envelopes are set to print manually. When you press the Print button, your printer will wait for the manual feed of the envelope.

CREATING CUSTOM PAPER SIZES

If you wish to print onto a paper size that is not a standard A4 or letter page, you can set up a custom paper size.

Choose Page Setup from the File menu and click on the Paper Size tab.

Choose Custom size from the Paper size list. Specify the width and height of your paper and the orientation.

Click OK.

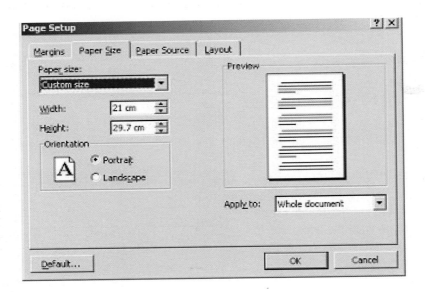

TASK

Type the following passage:

If you are responsible for planning travel then you can tackle this either in an amateurish, just-do-what-is-needed way or with a professional, well-organised approach. The difference lies in the detail. Anyone can ring a travel agent but a good PA will check the fine print, make sure the trip doesn't coincide with local holidays and have information to hand on climate, local customs and medical precautions. The good PA will also be capable of coping with group bookings, liaising with those who are away and keeping the office well organised in their absence. Finally, by knowing the full range of services and alternatives available and who to contact for more information, a good PA will keep the costs of business travel within or below budget.

Set the document to print onto A5 paper size.

Set up and print an envelope to:

Mr John Sykes
Ingleside
43 West Street
BEDFORD
MK42 8JA

WORKING WITH WORD AND EXCEL

Using an Excel Spreadsheet in a Word Document

You can create an 'embedded' object or a 'linked' object in Word.

To create an embedded object, open the Excel workbook and select the range that you wish to use in Word. Choose Copy from the Edit menu or press the Copy button.

Switch to Word, open the document you wish to use the Excel spreadsheet in and navigate to the location where you wish to insert the data. Choose Paste Special from the Edit menu.

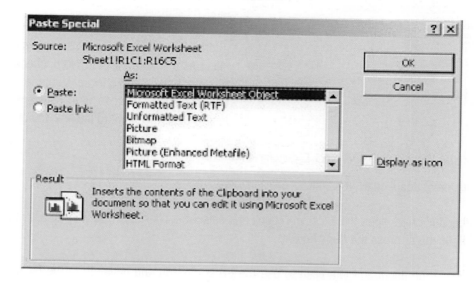

Make sure the Paste button is selected and Microsoft Excel Worksheet Object is selected in the As list.

Click OK.

To update the embedded object, double-click on it to activate the Excel worksheet.

Alternatively, if you want to use an entire Excel worksheet as an embedded object in Word, choose Object from the Insert menu and choose Create from File. Browse to the file you wish to use, select it and click Insert. Click OK.

281

To create a linked object, open the Excel workbook and select the range that you wish to use in Word. Choose Copy from the Edit menu or press the Copy button.

Switch to Word, open the document you wish to use the Excel spreadsheet in and navigate to the location where you wish to insert the data. Choose Paste Special from the Edit menu.

Make sure the Paste link button is selected and Microsoft Excel Worksheet Object is selected in the As list.

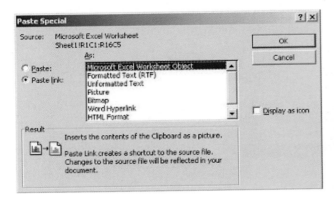

Click OK.

To update the linked object, double-click on it to launch Excel.

Alternatively, if you want to use an entire Excel worksheet as a linked object in Word, choose Object from the Insert menu and choose Create from File. Browse to the file you wish to use, select it and click on Insert. Check the Link to file box and click OK.

Using an Excel Chart in a Word Document

You can create an 'embedded' chart or a 'linked' chart in Word.

To create an embedded chart, open the Excel workbook and select the chart that you wish to use in Word. Choose Copy from the Edit menu or press the Copy button.

Switch to Word, open the document you wish to use the Excel chart in and navigate to the location where you wish to insert the chart. Choose Paste Special from the Edit menu.

Make sure the Paste button is selected and Microsoft Excel Chart Object is selected in the As list.

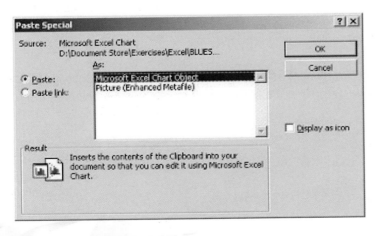

Click OK.

To update the embedded chart, double-click on it to activate the Excel chart sheet.

Alternatively, if you want to use an Excel chart sheet as an embedded object in Word, choose Object from the Insert menu and choose Create from File. Browse to the file you wish to use, select it and click on Insert. Click OK. (N.B. The chart sheet must be the first sheet in the workbook).

To create a linked chart, open the Excel workbook and select the chart that you wish to use in Word. Choose Copy from the Edit menu or press the Copy button.

Switch to Word, open the document you wish to use the Excel chart in and navigate to the location where you wish to insert the chart. Choose Paste Special from the Edit menu.

Make sure the Paste link button is selected and Microsoft Excel Chart Object is selected in the As list.

Click OK.

To update the linked chart, double-click on it to launch Excel.

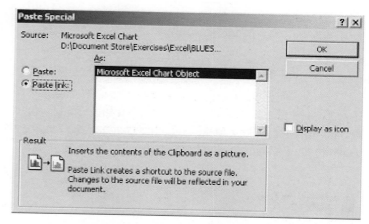

Alternatively, if you want to use an Excel chart sheet as a linked object in Word, choose Object from the Insert menu and choose Create from File. Browse to the file you wish to use, select it and click Insert. Check the Link to file box and click OK. (N.B. The chart sheet must be the first sheet in the workbook).

WORKING WITH ACCESS AND WORD

Inserting Information from a Database into a Word document

Switch on the Database toolbar (View menu, Toolbars) and click on the Insert Database button.

Click on Get Data.

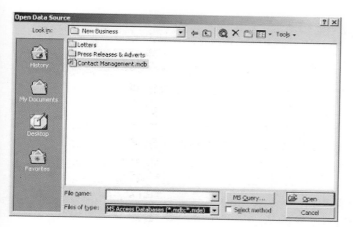

Browse to where the database file is located. (You will need to change Files of type to MS Access Databases).

Select the file and click Open.

Select the Table or Query that you wish to use information from and click OK.

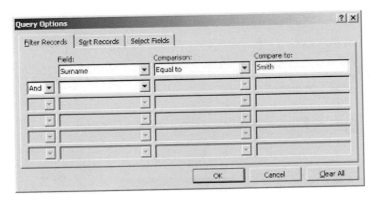

Click on Query Options and choose any Filter, Sort or Select Fields options you require.

Click on OK to return to the Database dialog box.

If you wish to customize the table, click on Table AutoFormat and choose a Format from the gallery. Make any other changes you require and click OK to return to the Database dialog box.

Click on Insert Data and choose whether you want to Insert all the records or a subset of the records. If you want to be able to update the data in Word when the information in the database changes, check the Insert data as field box. Click OK.

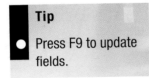

Tip

Press F9 to update fields.

The data is inserted into a Word table. The data is linked to the database file. To update fields in the Word table, click in the table and click the Update Field button on the Database toolbar.

WORKING WITH EXCEL AND ACCESS

Inserting Charts into a Database Report

You can insert a chart that you have already created in Excel into a report in Access. You can embed the chart in the Access report, or link it.

In Access, open the Report that you wish to insert the chart into in Design view.

Click on the Unbound Object Frame tool in the toolbox and then click on the report where you want to put the chart.

Choose Create From File in the Insert Object dialog box and then browse to the file that contains the chart.

If you want to link the chart, check the Link box. Click OK.

Using Excel Spreadsheet Data in an Access Database

Open the Access table that you wish to bring Excel data into and choose Get External Data from the File menu. Click on Import and browse to the Excel file that contains the data you wish to import. (You will need to change the Files of type to MS Excel). Select the file and click Import. The Import Spreadsheet Wizard will launch.

Follow the steps of the Import Spreadsheet Wizard through to import the data into an Access table.

You can import the data into a new table or an existing table. If you wish to import the data into an existing Access table, each field in the Excel table must have the same data type as its corresponding field in the Access table.

When you click on Finish, the Excel file will be imported into the Access table.

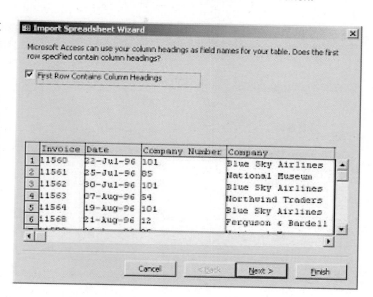

Click OK and then open the table in Access in the normal way.

Converting an Excel Spreadsheet into an Access Database

Alternatively, you can convert a list in Excel to Microsoft Access.

Click in your Excel list and choose Convert to MS Access from the Data menu in Excel. (If this command is not available, choose Add-Ins from the Tools menu and check the Access Links box.)

Choose whether you wish to create a new Access database or whether you wish to add the list to an existing Access database.

Click OK.

This will launch the Import Spreadsheet Wizard. Follow the steps of the Import Spreadsheet Wizard through to convert the data to an Access table.

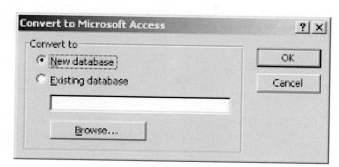

Once you have converted the data, a message will appear on the Excel spreadsheet stating that the list has been converted to Access.

Using Database Records in an Excel Spreadsheet

It is very easy to use database records in an Excel worksheet by simply copying them from the table in Access into Excel.

Open the table or query that contains the records you want to copy into Excel in Datasheet View. Select the records that you wish to copy and choose Copy from the Edit menu (or click the Copy button). Switch into Excel, click in the first cell that you wish to copy into and choose Paste from the Edit menu (or click the Paste button).

You may need to adjust column widths and row heights to accommodate the pasted data.

TASK

Type the following data into an Excel spreadsheet:

Staff Holidays

	Jan	Feb	Mar
Bob	5	4	12
Helen	3	10	5
Trevor	12	2	8
Anne	8	9	16

Start a new document in Word and embed the Excel spreadsheet into this document.

Create a chart in Excel based on the data on the worksheet. Link the chart as an object in the Word document.

Save both files.

TASK

Create a new Access database and start a new table. Use the above spreadsheet data in the table. Create a report in Access. Link the chart on the worksheet as an object in the Access report.

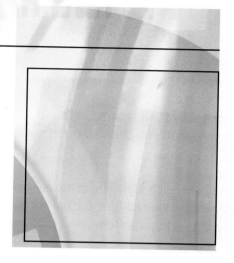

e-Quals
UNIT 030 MULTIMEDIA

WHAT IS MULTIMEDIA?

Multimedia is the presentation of integrated text, movies and sound to educate, advertise or inform. Multimedia is delivered as a co-ordinated system of computer files 'compiled' upon a recording medium suitable for play-back on microcomputer equipment. Physically, this recording medium almost always takes the form of an optical disk: a CD-ROM or for certain high-capacity applications, a DVD.

The basic character of multimedia, and the character of its programming arrangements, is very like that of websites. Hypertexts, hyperlinks and still images are all well-represented in typical multimedia productions. But movie (video) and sound (audio) components are both very demanding of 'bandwidth', much more so than text or even still pictures. Therefore, it is impracticable to provide moving pictures and audio as Web page components unless your surfer is willing and able to wait minutes for the material to load. Even then, there may be frequent annoying delays as the 'live' action stops in mid-flow for the next chunk of audio-visual data to download. On the other hand it is practicable to install audio-visual material on CD-ROM disks which operate on a purely local basis, using only the computer's internal high-speed digital bus circuitry.

Even so, a simple two-minute film comprising 12bit-color frames with sound, may occupy approximately 243Mb in an uncompressed state, whilst ordinary CD-ROMs are limited to 165Mb total capacity. Therefore, audio-visual files will need to be compressed using special CODEC (Compressor-Decompressor software) before they can be packaged in multimedia disks.

THE PURPOSE AND EFFECTIVENESS OF PRESENTATIONS

Presentations are designed to sell, to persuade, to inform or to educate. In all such cases, they should be clear, as brief as practicable, free of irrelevancies and annoying features of tone or style.

Because of the mixed manner of multimedia presentations, special care must be taken not to overload too much *simultaneous* information into a given time-frame. For example, in a disk about The Age of Sail, a jerky sepia movie is shown of frantic reefing and pumping aboard a storm-lashed wind-jammer's deck. The old movie is captivatingly interesting in its own right so you do not attempt to explain the finer points of guano economics *as it is*

287

playing. Instead you play it in silence. When the clip stops explanatory text appears on screen, preferably whilst the last frame is still displayed. That text and its accompanying still image waits on screen till the reader wishes to replay or move on.

INTERACTIVITY

Despite CGI scripts and JavaScript bolt-ons, the ability of a user to carry on a dialogue with Web material is very restricted and generally limited to click responses or to very short text answers.

With disk-based multimedia there is much more scope for positive interaction, a fact that is particularly useful in educational and training contexts. In principle it is possible to integrate user response with graphical outcomes to simulate all manner of real-life processes.

For example, in elementary geometry a student can be invited to choose between a variety of compass and straight-edge settings and positions to attempt various constructions, and witness the real-time outcome of his efforts in the form of an animated GIF drawing, which may be edited or played back from hard disk.

This interaction challenges the learner, makes him or her 'lean forward', gain control and become cognitively-engaged with the learning process.

THE UK COPYRIGHT, DESIGNS AND PATENTS ACT, 1988

The Copyright, Designs and Patents Act 1988 attempts to consolidate and modernise the law of intellectual property as it relates to British jurisdictions, including (explicitly) British shipping, aircraft and hovercraft.

The sections on Copyright and Design alone run to some 191 A4 pages and we will only be able to make brief mention of highlights relevant to multimedia producers, for the Act makes specific recognition of computational electronic media, as well as conventional analogue sound and video.

In particular, computer programs and databases are 'literary works' whilst a photograph is an 'artistic work'. Other multimedia entities include 'sound recordings' and 'films'. The combined arrangement constitutes a 'published edition'.

In the case of a sound recording or film, the 'author' is the person who 'makes the necessary arrangements' for making the recording or image; or for a typographical arrangement, the publisher.

The Act acknowledges that 'works of joint authorship' exist, severalising the ownership of copyright. It also presumes the inherence of copyright in the employer, where a literary or musical work is made in the course of employment.

Copyright is confirmed as expiring at the fiftieth anniversary of the author's death, though in the case of joint authorship it expires with the fiftieth anniversary of the death of the last surviving joint author. For a sound recording or film it is fifty years from the end of the calendar year in which it was 'released'.

The copyright owner in the United Kingdom enjoys exclusive rights to copy the work, to issue copies to the public, to show the work in public, to broadcast the work, to adapt the work, and to undertake 'acts restricted by the copyright'.

Copyright is infringed by a second party who performs these acts, or causes such acts to be performed, without the licence of the copyright owner. Infringement applies to a whole or a "substantial" part of the work (considered to be more than 1%). Copying is defined as reproducing any literary, musical or artistic work in *material* form, including electronic storage. Copying includes rendering a 2D image as a 3D one; or a 3D image or sculpture as a 2D representation.

- Possession, reception, sale or hire are all infringements of copyright by virtue of 'secondary infringement' if the handled material is itself infringing copyright. (I.e. trading in "pirated" copy is infringement of copyright.)

- Knowingly supplying apparatus for the enjoyment of infringing material is infringement. (E.g. you cannot give or sell a multimedia browser to someone you think will use it to infringe copyright or view infringing copy.)

- Imported materials whose production in the UK would have infringed UK copyright law automatically infringes UK law.

Fair dealing for scientific, scholarly or critical purposes is confirmed and safeguarded. Librarians may provide bona-fide students (broadly defined) with single copies of up to 1% of a work in any calendar quarter, or alternatively a "short passage" or "short passages", but unlicensed mechanical reprography by whatever technology of multiple copies for classroom or other use is an infringement unless explicitly licensed (e.g. you must not mount multiple copies of a multimedia CD-ROM or put it on a network server unless you have a consensual arrangement with the author).

It is not clear, however, to what extent these provisions apply to electronic multimedia as opposed to printed media. For example, is a 2cm by 3cm 17Kb JPEG picture more than 1% of a 100Kb text file which would print out as twenty closely-typed pages of A4?

THE COMPONENTS OF MULTIMEDIA

Multimedia contains the following typical website components:

Text This can be presented in a number of different fonts (styles), sizes, colours and layouts.

Still Pictures These include photographs and diagrams, whether as GIFs or JPEGs. Much higher resolutions are feasible with disk multimedia than is the case on the Web, and more space-demanding formats, such as bitmaps, can be included if necessary, e.g. for user-editable pictures. Simple GIF animations such as mobile logotypes and marquees are practicable in both media.

Hyperlinks The all-important 'trapdoors' for linking between pages of material. As on the Web, hyperlinks can be ordinary blue-text clickables, or pictures or mapped graphics zones.

In addition to this, disk-based multimedia contains:

Video Clips Brief bursts of moving photographs (with or without a soundtrack) which may be used for:

- Talking-head Intros

- Promotional Clips (e.g. car handling)

- Time-Lapse Demonstrations (e.g. plant growth)

- Slow Motion Demonstrations (e.g. muscle co-ordination)

- Historic Footage (perhaps in 4-bit monochrome)

Animations Moving diagrams which may include:

- Cartoons

- Machine Drawing Explosions or Moving Isometrics

- Process Illustrations (e.g. machine part actions, fluid or electrical flows)

- Procedural Schematics (e.g. the sequence of delineations in bisecting an angle)

Audio Sequences Sound episodes which may or may not accompany visuals and could include:

- Partially-sighted User Assistance

- Intros

- Noodling (background or 'mood' music)

- Quotations from Experts, Historical Figures or Literature

- Supplementary Guidance and Software Help Descriptions

- Diagnostic Sound (e.g. bird song, machine tunes, pulmono-cardiac rhythms)

BASIC HARDWARE NEEDED FOR MULTIMEDIA PRODUCTION

This is a typical lower middle-range machinery configuration for the production of multimedia compilations:

- **CPU** A central processor unit equipped with an Intel Pentium iii or AMD Athlon microprocessor operating at a nominal 2GHz clock speed and having 256Mb of RAM

- **Monitor** A good-quality (e.g. Mitsubishi Diamond Pro 730) colour monitor supported by an adequate video controller to at least 1024×726 pixels with 2^{24} colour depth

- **Keyboard and Mouse** Good-quality (e.g. Microsoft) keyboard and scroll mouse

- **Sound System** A good quadraphonic sound system (four tweeters and a woofer: e.g. Cambridge Soundworks) supported by an adequate sound card

- **Optical Disk Drives** One reliable CD-RW burner drive (e.g. TEAC CD-W58E) with also one reliable CD-R drive (e.g. Pioneer DVD-ROM DVD-116)

- **Magnetic Disk Drives** One excellent 40Gb (e.g. Seagate, Western Digital, Quantum) hard drive and one standard 1.44Mb Sony-pattern floppy drive

- **Scanner** A good-quality flat-bed A4 scanner to at least 600×1200 pixels per inch (e.g. Epson Perfection 1240U) for inputting bromide photographs (prints) or other paper documents. Adaptors or dedicated scanners can be purchased for 35mm bromide negatives

- **Printer** A good-quality photographic ink-jet printer (e.g. Epson Stylus Photo 875DC)

  Colour laser printers are far faster and cheaper to run but lack colour fidelity and are unlikely to be able to handle photographic calibre papers, when necessary.

- **Webcam** An up-to-date webcam equipped with integral microphone (e.g. Phillips Toucam PCVC740K Professional) for capturing 'talking-heads' video clips indoors

The total cost of this hardware is about £1600 (September 2002).

In addition, students or other novice producers may consider a good amateur digital camera for outdoors direct capture of still and brief video clip images. Such cameras should record on standard CD-R ROM disks. Sony Mavica CD series or high-end Nikon amateur digital cameras are worth looking at. Expect to pay £600–£2000.

THE TARGET AUDIENCE

With all media communications great care needs to be given to the needs and aspirations of the users, whether they are television viewers, newspaper readers or multimedia users.

Marketers often make a distinction between passive 'lean-back' media like television and magazines which are viewed, listened-to or read and active 'lean-forward' participatory media such as the Internet, games and multimedia. All media production is highly-speculative and the production of participatory media especially so, since the exact character of the potential buyer and his abilities and preferences matter. A further complication with books or multimedia is that sufficient customer motivation must exist or be created for him or her to make a journey, take a look and certainly to spend some cash.

To write for the love of writing or make films for the sake of art is very laudable and should be encouraged. But any commercial creativity needs careful study of its feasibility in terms of the number and wealth of potential customers.

The target audience needs to be identified in terms of:

- **Population**
  The numbers of potential multimedia CD-ROM purchasers for a learner-driver's theory and practical aid will differ from the number of potential purchasers for a CD-ROM about the secular iconography of The Arnolfini Wedding.

- **Income**
  A multimedia disk is always a luxury, even for a student to whom it is a 'recommended course requirement'. Inevitably, as the size of the potential market diminishes, the unit price of a disk must increase, whatever the degree of sophistication (or lack thereof) in its production values.

  If your net production and marketing costs are £10,000 and your readership contains 500 purchasers then you must charge £20 per disk to break even. If you have 5000 buyers you can theoretically break even with a £2 disk. But there will be a marked non-linearity as a bargain price attracts the less motivated buyers.

- **Demography**
  Population and income come together in demography. Demography is the statistical profile of a large group of people in terms of age bands, numbers, educational levels and economic classes. The demography of your potential customers is crucial to the viability of your product.

  The age, education and class profiles of people who will buy a multimedia video disk are different to the statistical groupings who purchase GameBoy modules. And the age and economic status of iconographers differs (on the whole) from the age and economic status of people who want to learn how to drive.

STRUCTURE PLANNING

Terms of Reference

Terms of reference encapsulate the limitations and opportunities that characterise a particular production and marketing product cycle before the other stages of planning are attempted.

The terms of reference are a guideline agreement with the client about the scope and character of the deliverable and address these points:

- **Budget**
  How much can be spent upon production and marketing?
  How much, if any, of the initial finance may be assigned to profit or to contingencies?

- **Projected Return**
  What is the amount, broken down by time-period, of the profit accruable?

- **Resourcing**
  How much time and resources, especially labour, may be applied to each stage of the multimedia production project and to the promotion, distribution and support of the disk in the market?

- **Content**
  What is the information content of the multimedia project and how is that content to be assembled and structured?

- ## Technology

  What hardware and software resources are needed for production, distribution and support of the product? Can these technical resources be developed or acquired using the time and financing available for development?

  This is not an exhaustive list of points but it is ordered in the commercial importance of the various headings from the point of view of the multimedia developer, and can be expanded into a programme of activity for the Project Feasibility Study.

Navigational Considerations

The linkage of multimedia pages is subject to the same sorts of typological (layout pattern) considerations as is the linkage of Web pages.

Basically there are three multimedia navigational topologies:

Linear In a linear layout, one page follows another in a simple sequential chain and therefore this basic format is comparable to the 'broken ring' cycloid context in Web planning.

The linear layout lends itself to these situations (amongst others):

- Developing or explaining a logical argument, including a mathematical derivation or scientific theory

- Recounting a story narrative

- Tracing a chain of events, such as the proximal causes of World War I

Hierarchical The hierarchy is a 'family tree' structure of linkages: the taxonomy of Web pages. The hierarchy is a development of the linear paradigm in the sense that there are things at the 'top' and at the 'bottom', but it also implies relationship and category.

Among the possible applications for a hierarchic topology are:

- Showing biologically-grouped articles or pictures about plants or animals

- Classifications of rock, chemicals or chemical elements

- Explaining the government of a nation, army or corporation

- Implementing branching 'decision trees': useful in many kinds of interactive diagnostic or educational multi-media

- Exploring the consequences of choices

Non-Linear The non-linear scheme of multimedia page and resource layout relates directly to the reticular network scheme that is used in planning Web page linkages.

It implies a multilateral association of objects in a conceptual 'space'.

Possible applications include:

(a) Collections of pages or pictures about objects contingent in actual space, e.g. rooms or buildings in an architectural disquisition

(b) Pages relating the interaction of people, or groups or states in 'anthropological space'

(c) The relation of articulated functional parts, as for example in media describing the interaction of components in a self-regulating mechanical system.

Your choice of hyperlinkage topology will reflect not only the technical limitations and possibilities of your multimedia design system, but also the aspects of the real-world object-system you wish to emphasise, and the needs and capabilities of your audience.

The Style Sheet

A style sheet is an HTML or other programming language code sequence which determines the format and layout of displayed objects on a Web or multimedia page. Style sheets can be cascaded, that is to say nested within each other so that you can for example include a style sheet which controls indented picture titles and GIF images within one which controls paragraph layout, both within a third which determines page margins.

The purpose of style sheets is to speed the generation of documents, to assist clarity and accuracy of presentations, mitigate drafting costs and to maintain uniformity of look, feel and tone.

Style sheets are made up of style rules, which can be defined in three places:

● With or within the particular HTML tags to which they apply

● Grouped together in the page HEAD

● Placed in associated style sheets (i.e. in separate free-standing computer files)

Style sheets are used in association with the DIV tag, to apply to defined document divisions, or the SPAN tag, to apply to chosen bits of paragraphs.

A Scheme for style implementation in HTML Style is not a feature of standard HTML and a number of implementation conventions exist. One early proposal outlines this syntax: you may place style sheet content in free-standing data files (Cascading Style Sheets) with the extension .css.

For example, our text style sheet is in the pre-existing file textfile.css.

This style material can then be invoked from within a page HEAD using:

<LINK REL=stylesheet HREF="textfiles.css">

The REL parameter signifies that the link is to a style sheet, whilst HREF contains the URL.

Another syntax for the local and specific definition of text style is:

```
<STYLE TYPE="text/css">

    p { font-size: 12 pt }

</STYLE>
```

The details will always depend upon the source of the style data; the extent of its implementation in the present page; and the medium to be styled, e.g. screen or print presentations.

The ideal style sheet

The ideal style sheet supports these features:

- **Flexible placement of style information** Style information should be local or global, with local taking precedence in implementation. Global styling may be applied by invoking external files or defining style in the HEAD. Local style may be applied around or even within BODY tags.

- **Language independence** Although many users will want to apply CSS (Cascading Style Sheets) language, implementations of HTML should contain the facility for any style sheet language to be invoked.

- **Cascade** Cascading style sheets should be able to be used to simplify global and particular style application to different categories of corporate documentation.

- **Media dependency** Whilst HTML itself is designed to be independent of particular display devices and technologies, style expressions ought to be definable for different communications modes (print, screen, speech, Braille, etc.) and differing hardwares.

- **Alternative styles** Styles should be author-switchable, and be capable of being suspended altogether in a particular documentation job.

The Storyboard

The storyboard is a sequence of pages (paper or electronic) containing structured forms which you fill in to define the format and content of each successive scene.

Storyboards originated in the film industry where they are used to plan each coherent sequence of frames (scene or 'shot') in terms of visual and sound content, and production settings such as lighting, camera angles, foreshortening and so on. Traditionally, part of the storyboard pro forma consists of artist sketches of shots as they are proposed by the director, with the dialogue beneath so that the plan can be used to guide actors and technicians during the actual film making. The concept is very easily extended to the planning of Web or multimedia pages.

In the multimedia context you should apply two distinct sorts of storyboard plans:

- **Topological structure diagrams**
  At the strategic level you should sketch out a topological diagram to show the planned page linkages between named pages, according to your rationally-chosen layout scheme, whether linear, non-linear or hierarchical. A

numerically-based faceted unique code scheme should be used to label each page's position in the structure, and the page label should tally with that entered on the page storyboard sheet.

- **Page storyboard sheets**
  Use a simple storyboard with picture and text layout cartouches to plan each page, placing freehand sketches of named graphics files where you intend pictures or videos to appear. Rough out by hand the format and content of text areas, noting typographic characteristics (font, size, colour, justification) as well as background motifs and colours. Do not forget to include details of audio sources, fades and durations.

The Merits of Different Layout Styles

It is wise to prepare several different printed storyboard pro formas, each guiding different types of page structure in terms of the amounts, styles and layouts of the several media components. Some projects will have occasional pictures, others no pictures or formal picture galleries, either hyperlinked or integral with a text page.

Other projects will include differing amounts of sound or video and may or may not require animations. Voice-over speech may or may not enhance a particular presentation for a defined market whilst 'talking heads' (or worse still 'talking bodies') will surely alienate otherwise promising prospects, especially if the bodies are speaking in foreign, elite or vulgar accents.

Examples of Outline Style Planning

1 You are preparing a 45-minute CD-ROM about the role of 16th century Venetian diplomacy in the control of Habsburg and Ottoman expansions.

   Video clips are unlikely to appeal: obviously there is no original footage and your public will find acted snippets superfluous and irritating. They will expect and get masses of analytic text linked to plenty of academic URLs (some on-board) and occasional integrated JPEG photographs of contemporary portraits or dioramas, and also GIFs of campaign plans.

   A simple, straight-forward production for a lone content specialist.

2 You are going to produce a 20-minute multimedia lesson entitled 'Practical Wheel Balancing on Small Cars'.

   Plenty of still, labelled JPEGs of wheel suspensions with and without wheel will be shown with sequential, pithy 'how to' text. Near the end a compressed silent or lightly voice-overed video will show a technician balancing a wheel from removal to replacement. Also an interactive mouse-swivelable isometric diagram will invite the trainee to choose, position and test virtual counterweights.

   This is a project for several experts: video and animation specialists as well as, of course, automotive operatives.

3 You are making a ten-minute presentation about pirates to be packaged with a 'Come to Devon' promotional CD.

   An attractive animated introduction of a lively 'Restoration' dockside is noodled with a jaunty shanty succeeded by a character voice-over which continues to alternate with the music on a long loop as thematic thumbnails appear, each clickable to brief acted compressed full-screen videos with narrative voice-overs on other thematic pages. A small scripted (i.e. programmed, probably in Java) 'Treasure Hunt' game completes the ensemble, with textual addresses and telephone numbers of places to visit. The emphasis is upon acting and animation artistry.

Production Constraints

In this section we touched, directly or indirectly, upon the limitations and constraints which impinge upon multimedia production. Four issues, listed in order of significance, may be emphasised:

- ### Production Length

  The attention span of a child is not, as often claimed, 20 minutes: that is the attention span of an educated adult. Any 'lecture-type' production, including a multimedia disk, must either be very brief or very varied if it is to be popular. Heavier, more specialised fare or lengthy 'how to do it' multimedia offerings will be up to 60 minutes long but include plenty of imagery, bland music and opportunities for user interaction. Advertisements, promos or children's multimedia will be short, heavily-topspun and conceptually simple, avoiding any diffusion or message ambiguity.

- ### Timescale

  The production timescale will be proportionate to the product length, but will rise more than proportionately with complexity in terms of planning, technical sophistication and the number of specialists involved. It is best to set up a multimedia facility with small, unambitious projects and expand into complex lengthy work as capital, expertise and personnel accrue.

- ### Storage

  The physical storage of the finished stock should be kept to the merest minimum unless a mass market is assured. Indeed, for specialised (let alone commissioned) work it is often enough to copy disks to order using a small float of blanks kept on the premises.

- ### User Hardware Requirements

  You will find it difficult to justify anything which cannot be condensed to a 650Mb CD-ROM or maybe a DVD.

  You may safely expect all your potential public to own, or readily lay their hands on, the requisite kit.

PRODUCTION QUALITIES AND FILE SIZES

As with many, though not all, things, when it comes to audio and picture computer files, bigger is better and better costs more.

Video files improve with greater pixel resolutions, deeper colour depths (i.e. more colours and colour brightnesses) and faster frame rates. The human eye scans at 24 frames per second. Any fewer frames and the movie will appear "jerky", except in time-lapse contexts. For slow-motion reproduction you need more than 24 frames per second. Standard video capture rates of interest to us are 15, 25 and 30 frames per second.

'Raw' video files as generated by video capture devices (i.e. digital cameras, especially 'Web' cameras) are often in uncompressed .avi, or audio-visual interleave, format. AVI files may or may not have active soundtracks, though the interleaving technology is designed for alternately intercalating video and audio information. Whichever the case AVI files are always playable using Windows Media Players. Raw video files are horrendously large compared with any other kind of microcomputer data file. In fact reasonably well-defined uncompressed AVI files of useful length are much too big to fit on a CD-ROM. A two-minute colour film of about 300×200 pixels and 15 frames per second consumes 250Mb of storage, more than a third of an ordinary CD-ROM disk.

Something must be done if we are to put this movie on a disk. We can vitiate (make worse) the picture by reducing the frame count, the pixel resolution, or colour variation. All this may have to be done, but a more promising approach is to compress the data mathematically.

'Raw' audio files may be linked into video files as sound tracks, or be free standing affairs generated by audio capture devices (i.e. microphones). A typical audio-only file format as it is saved from capture is the .wav (wave) protocol. The 'resolution' of an audio recording is a parameter known as the Sampling Rate, which relates to the statistical frequency at which the audio spectrum 'snapshot' is recorded. Sampling Rate is quoted in Hertz or cycles per second, where one KiloHertz is 1000 Hertz. 11.025 KHz is typical. The quality of digital sound definition is also a function of bit resolution – 16-bit resolution is typical.

If you need to increase the quality of a video file you therefore increase:

(a) Pixel Resolution

(b) Colour Depth

(c) Frame Rate

and to increase the quality of an audio track you increase:

(a) Sampling Rate

(b) Bit Resolution

As noted, more is bigger as well as better and accordingly more expensive in time and storage.

CODECs

We have seen that to use digital video in microcomputer multimedia some reversible multi-fold compression technology must be applied to the 'raw' capture.

A CODEC (compressor/decompressor) is a computer program that compresses the raw data and stores it in a different file with a different extension. This file will be a tiny fraction of the size of the original capture-file. When the file needs to be played back, the CODEC will reflate the content and feed it to the reproduction software.

There are many thousands of CODECs in existence, and hundreds can be pulled down off the Internet at little or no charge. Audio CODECs (e.g. RealAudio) may do little in the way of compression, confining themselves to converting the analogue sound signals into digitised sound just like a hardware modem converts analogue electric signals into digital ones.

MPEG Audio Layer-3 (MP3) is however an audio compression CODEC that can compress CD-quality audio 12-fold with little apparent quality loss.

A reasonable video CODEC will not only convert analog video to digital (where necessary) but also perform major compression.

The major CODEC standards are the MPEG (Moving Pictures Experts Group) series. MPEG1 produces a result a bit worse than TV VHS reproduction. MPEG2 is an improved standard that involves little perceptible vitiation and is used in DVD disks and digital TV broadcasts. MPEG4 is a new (September 2002) standard being introduced for streaming multimedia data over a wide range of bit rates.

SCANNING PAPER IMAGES

Modern A4 flat-bed scanners connect to microcomputer USB ports and are capable of a typical 600×1200 pixel per inch 24-bit colour scan.

To use it you lift the reflective hood, which can be detached altogether if you need to scan a bulky item such as a book.

Position the picture that you wish to scan with the edge flush, for registration.

Gently lower the scanner's hood, then you are ready to scan the image.

A number of good photographic software packages enable you to do this, and to choose whether to use their algorithms or the device-specific programs that gadget makers bundle with their products. It is usually wise to use the latter.

For the purposes of this book we will use the photographic package Microsoft PhotoDraw.

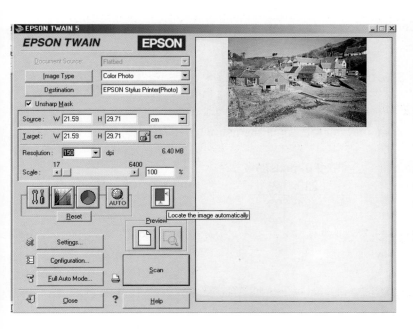

Click on the Microsoft PhotoDraw V2 icon and select **File**, **Scan Picture**. When the **Scan** window appears click the **Your Scanner Software** radio button and then Scan. If you are using the software that comes with your scanner follow the instructions within the accompanying manual.

The **EPSON TWAIN 5** window will appear as below and the scanner will perform a quick automatic pre-scan to define the working image of the photograph in the top right.

In this context, make sure that:

> **Image Type:** Color Photo
> **Resolution:** 150 dpi

Source and **Target** dimensions do not need to be altered at this time, since sizing is better performed at a later editing stage. Raw image file size will be 6.4Mb in this case, *but this includes the redundant white reflector area*.

Click the green image resize rectangle in mid-window. This generates an animated black pecked rectangle which you can mouse-drag to frame or crop the payload image. This is seen below:

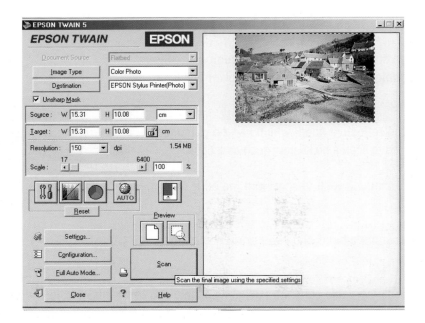

Now click **Scan** to perform a fine, slow scanning. When it completes select **File**, **Save As**. Enter the **File Name** certifying that the correct folder is in play. Now select **Save as type**: as JPEG filter and then click the **Options** button.

When the **Export Options** window appears select **Compression Level** 50 and **Export Size** 904×596 as here.

Click on OK on the Export Options window and click Save on the Save As window.

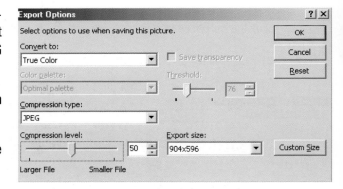

The cropped, saved scan is only 99Kb. For comparison we may tabulate some alternative saved file sizes as:

File Name	File Size (Kb)	Compression	Pixel Dimensions
CAD1	7	50	226×149
CAD2	99	50	904×596
CAD3	149	25	904×596

IMAGE MODIFICATION

Using PhotoDraw we can modify and enhance the image file in many ways. We will see how to change:

(a) Pixel or absolute picture dimensions

(b) Colour hue, saturation and brightness

(c) Image transparency

Changing Size

The most convenient juncture at which to change pixel resolution or image size is when saving: Select **File**, **Save As** in the normal way, select the appropriate destination folder, define **File name:** and **Save as type:** JPEG filter.

Now click the **Options** button. In the **Export Options** window click the **Custom Size** button at lower right and change the required data in the **Custom Size** sub-window.

The cascade of windows is shown here:

Click **OK**, **OK** and **Save**.

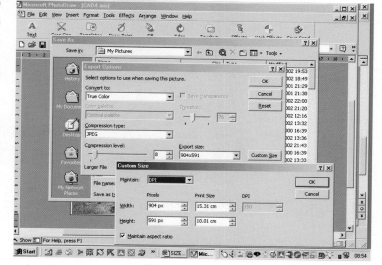

Changing Colour and Brightness

These can be modified when editing. Select **Format**, **Color**, **Hue and Saturation**. Image appearances can be changed in real-time using the slider bars in the Color window.

Changing Transparency

Select **Effects** from the main toolbar and **Transparency** from the drop-down menu. A **Transparency** window will appear at the right. Use the slider bar or the textbox to select the degree of transparency, where 0% is a solid image and 100% is a blank picture.

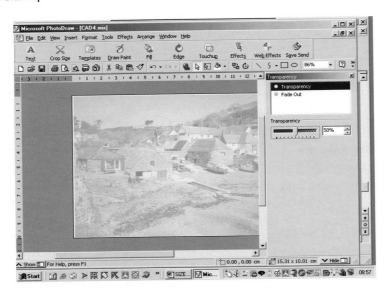

THE CAPTURE OF STILL IMAGES FOR ANIMATION

There are a number of approaches to the generation of still image frames for the compositing of animations:

1   Traditional photo-capture of progressive artwork gels

2   Photo-capture of incrementally-adjusted 'live' scenes (e.g. Aardmann-type plasticene work)

3   Computer-generated, algorithmically-adjusted vector diagrams (e.g. CAD machine action animations)

4   Scanned capture of paper compositions

We will study technique 2: photo-capture of incrementally-adjusted realities.

In this approach any photo-capture software is useable. For the purposes of this book we will use the Ulead Photo Express 2 program bundled with the Phillips Toucam Pro Web camera.

Scenario

A lamb doll is placed on the scanner hood overlooked by the Web cam.

The doll will be rotated through 360° to give the illusion of a full spin with no apparent turntable. One complete turn will take one second at play-time and comprise 25 frames for a natural scan rate. Accordingly, the doll will manually be turned through 360°/25=14.4° (say about 15° judged by eye) at each take.

We will set a 5-second timed automatic photo capture and study the first eight frames representing some 115° of turn.

Capture

Ulead Photo Express is started by icon double-click and **File** selected from the main menu bar. We then click **Acquire** and **Digital Camera** from the drop-down menus. When the **View Finder** window appears we select **Adjustments**.

The **Auto Image Capture** section is changed as shown opposite.

Browse for the desired **Filename** destination path and select **Filetype** JPEG.

Set **Interval Timer** (sec) to 5 and click both **Auto Capture** and **Incremental File Save**. Check the **Play Shutter Sound** tick-box at the bottom of the **Adjustments** window. When ready, click the **Auto Start** button on the **View Finder** window.

When you hear the 'shutter click' turn the doll through 15°; wait for the next click; then turn it another 15° until you have the full 25 frame set.

Then click on the **Auto Stop** button and check that the full series of 25 JPEGs have been saved before exiting Photo Express.

The first eight frames should appear as below:

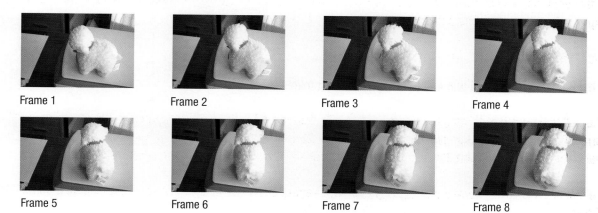

Frame 1   Frame 2   Frame 3   Frame 4

Frame 5   Frame 6   Frame 7   Frame 8

COMPILING AN ANIMATED GIF

For the purposes of this workbook we will use Jasc Animation Shop Version 3.04, the sister program of Jasc PaintShop Pro, to compile the first eight frames of doll rotation into a playable series of animation frames stored in a single GIF file.

Phase 1: Concatenation with the Wizard

When Animation Shop starts select **File, Animation Wizard**.

The **Animation Wizard** window will then appear centre-screen. Accept **Same size as the first image frame** by clicking **Next**. Then click **Next** to accept **Opaque**. Thirdly, click **Next** again to accept the **Upper left corner of the frame** and the **With the canvas colour** defaults.

The fourth frame asks how long we want each frame to be displayed in hundreds of a second. Clearly, we will change this parameter to 4 eventually. *For now, leave it at 25.* Also, accept the default indefinite looping by clicking **Next**.

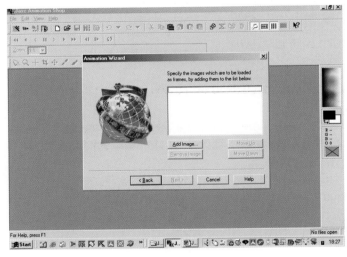

The fifth frame of the **Animation Wizard** gives us the facility to load our captured JPEGs *ad seriatim* in order to compile the animated sequence.

Click **Add Image**.

Use the succeeding **Open** window to identify the right folder and **Open** (i.e. load) the appropriate JPEG.

Click **Next** and **Finish** to compile the animation.

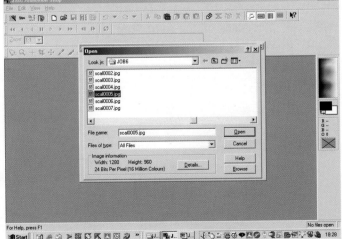

Phase 2: Review

The apparent frame size is likely to exceed the available view window, so select **View**, **Animation** and change the **Zoom** to a 1:11 zoom factor in order to inspect the first six of the eight frames as shown here.

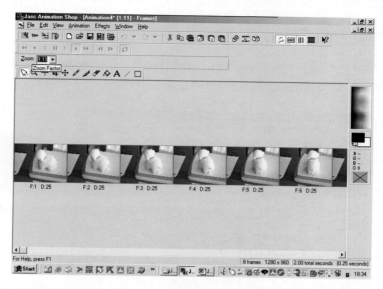

(The selection of **View**, **Zoom Out by 5** would have a similar desirable image shrinkage effect.)

To finish the job select **File**, **Save As** and use the **Save As** window to select the correct destination folder and enter the filename in the **File name:** window as LAMBANIM.gif.

Review the Settings Specification on the **Animation Quality versus Output Size** window and click **Next**.

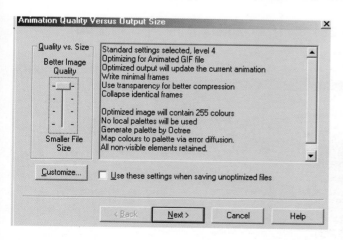

When the **Optimization Progress** is complete click **Next**.

Thirdly, again click **Next** when the **Optimization Preview** play-through appears.

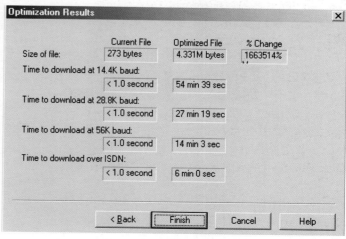

Study the **Optimization Results** window and click the **Finish** button.

Finally, click **File**, **Exit**.

VIDEO CAPTURE

Phase 1: Set Up

For the purposes of this book, video capture will be explained using a Webcam mediated by Ulead Photo Explorer and Philips VRecord camera-side software.

Load Ulead Photo Explorer, preferably by clicking its Desktop icon if available, and then click the **TWAIN Acquire** icon visible in the secondary toolbar.

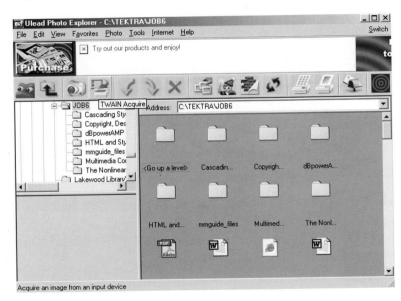

Select **Adjustments** from the **View Finder** window and then click **Camera Controls** at the top right of the **Adjustments** window.

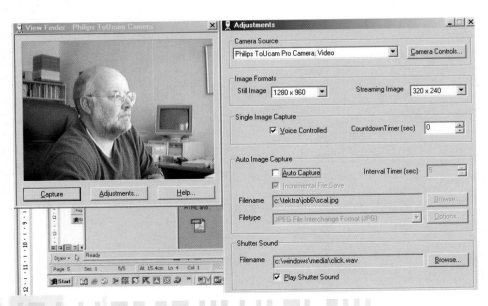

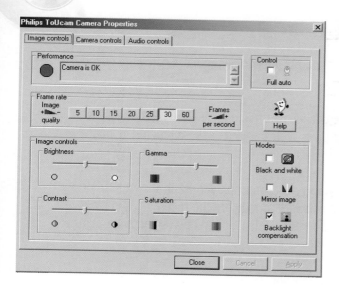

In the **Image Controls** tab, select **Frame rate** 25 (it has probably defaulted to 30) and check **Backlight compensation**.

Click the **Close** button.

Phase 2: Capture

In the **Phillips VRecord** window (or your local equivalent) select **File**, **Set Capture File**. Use the **Set Capture File** sub-window to select the right destination folder and set the filename for the captured video. Click **Open**.

The **VRecord** window **Set File Size** sub-window is set to **Capture File Size** 10Mb (*Warning: This feature is unreliable, DO NOT SWAMP YOUR DISK!*) and then OK is clicked.

Now in the **VRecord** window select **Capture**, **Start Capture**.

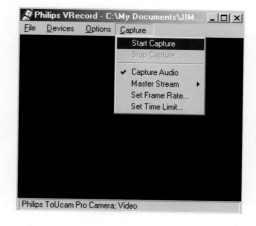

In the **Ready to Capture** sub-window click **OK** to start capturing the clip.

When you have taken the clip select **Capture**, **Stop Capture**. Select **File**, **Save Captured video As**, and use the Save window provided in the usual manner. Access **File**, **Exit** to return to your Desktop.

GENERATING AUDIO FILES

Many programs are available for recording audio files in a variety of formats, though all require a hardware sound card and all require a microphone if you are to record your own work.

The type of microphone is not vitally important. Common or garden condenser microphones are more than adequate for multimedia voice-overs and you can even use that on a Web camera (assuming that it has a microphone of course!).

For the purposes of this book we used the Via Voice microphone headset, and played back through some Cambridge quad speakers. We will use Microsoft Sound Recorder software to mediate the recording and playback of uncompressed .wav files. This data can later be reformatted for size if desired, and played back through any suitable software including Windows Media Player.

From **Start**, select **Programs**, **Accessories**, **Entertainment**, **Sound Recorder**.

A small **Sound – Sound Recorder** window will appear on your Desktop.

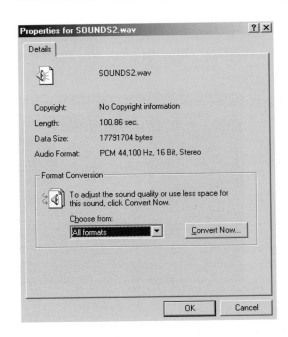

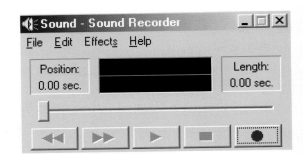

In the **Sound Recorder** window select **File**, **Properties** to obtain the **Properties for...** window (SOUNDS2.wav is the last file I was working on: ignore it, it won't appear on your machine).

Select All formats from the **Choose from** drop-down menu and click the adjacent **Convert Now...** button.

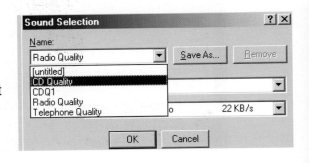

In the **Sound Selection** window click the **Name:** drop-down and select CD-Quality.

Click OK and then OK on the underlying Properties for... window.

Now back at the **Sound – Sound Recorder** window choose **File**, **New** and click on the red dot button when you are ready to record.

Click the black square button when you wish to stop (it is possible to record more than 60 seconds).

Save your recording by selecting **File**, **Save As** on the **Sound Recorder** when you will be offered a separate **Save As** window which you address in the usual manner, after checking that **Save as type:** registers *.wav and noting that we have a Sampling Rate of 22.05 KHz and an 8-bit mono Bit Resolution.

To play back, select **File**, **Open** on the **Sound Recorder**, select the appropriate file from the **Open** window, click the **Open** button and click the black triangle **Play** button.

To cease play-back click the **Sound Recorder** black square **Stop** button.

MULTIMEDIA OBJECT PROGRAM COMPILATION

When you are ready to publish your multimedia presentation you will need to compile all of the disparate file components into a unified executable machine-code binary file called an object program. In fact all the programs which computers run are compiled object programs.

There are numerous advantages to distributing the copy on object form. Some of the chief are:

(a) Software is immediately runnable on any suitable hardware with only minimal operating system mediation.

(b) The software system is optimised.

(c) Binary code is difficult to read and virtually impossible to fraudulently doctor.

(d) Different presentation features are integrated into a 'one-stop-shop' user file.

In Microsoft terms, an object program has the extension .exe and when recorded on a disk needs the user explicitly to command its execution via MS-DOS or Windows Run procedures; otherwise you can place ancillary programs on the delivery disk to automatically instigate a Startup process whenever the CD-ROM is physically mounted.

To help multimedia compilation tools to compile this .exe file it is sensible of you to assemble all the needful HTML pages, audio, video and graphics files in one folder just as you would if you were about to load a website.

Sometimes the recorded multimedia compilation is called an ebook. A number of packages can be purchased for the compilation of ebooks. They vary enormously in price and sophistication.

HyperMaker HTML 2002.14 provides an extended dialect of HTML for writing multimedia pages and managing associated audio-visual file media.

HyperMaker will take the contents of your designated folder, including your pre-selected home page and convert it into a single, encrypted, compressed file. It will manage GIF, JPEG, .bmp and .png graphics, .avi movies, TrueType fonts, and .wav and .mid sound files. A royalty-free view-time system is provided to read the resulting compilation.

HyperMaker provides additional HTML tags to mediate the audio-visual elements, and to provide other features. These tags are best illustrated by the extended HTML Home Page called demo.htm which houses play links to the following files:

Animated gif	lambanim.gif
Video file	jimdesk4.avi
Audio file	sounds3.wav
Still photograph	cad4.jpg

Here is the HTML:

<HTML>

<HEAD>

<TITLE>A Multimedia Demonstration</TITLE>

<!--The .wav file will play once after load-up -->

<BGSOUND>SRC="sounds3.wav"

</HEAD>

<BODY BGCOLOR=WHITE TEXT=BLACK LINK=BLUE VLINK=MAGENTA>

<FONT FACE="Arial" SIZE=12>

<DIV ALIGN=CENTER>

A Multimedia Demonstration Home Page

For Use with A HyperMaker HTML 2002.14 Demonstration

</DIV>

<DIV ALIGN=LEFT>

<!--Show the Still Picture -->

<IMG SRC="cad4.jpg" WIDTH=400 BORDER=1>

<!--Click to Play the Audio -->

<A HREF="sounds3.wav">Click to Play the Audio File Again</A>

<!--Click to Play the .avi file -->

<A HREF="jimdesk4.avi" 400 500 CLOSE>Click to Play the Video Clip</A>

<!--Click to Play the Animated .gif>

<A HREF="lambanim.htm">Go to Animated .gif Page</A>

<!--The sub-page lambanim.htm contains IMG SRC="lambanim.gif" -->

</DIV>

</FONT>

</BODY>

</HTML>

A second, ancillary page lambanim.htm is written to house the playable GIF.

All six files are placed in a directory (folder) which we will call MMDEMO:

demo.htm   HOME PAGE
lambanim.htm
lambanim.gif
jimdesk4.avi
sounds3.wav
cad4.jpg

And HyperMaker is called into play, preferably using a desktop icon such as:

HyperMaker
2002.14

First click the **New Publication** blank sheet icon:

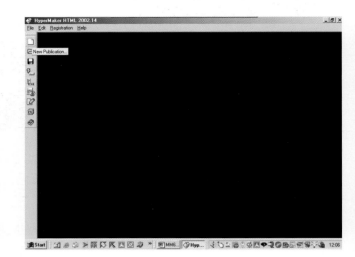

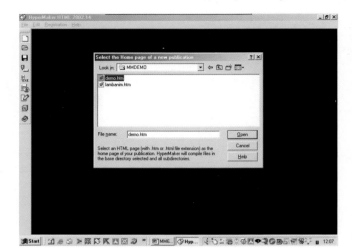

Then browse for the Home Page file that you wish to nominate.

Confirm the title using the **Publication Title** window.

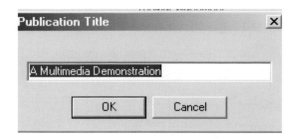

And then choose the **Files** tab and **Add** the requisite directory. All its sub-folders (none in this case) will also be included in the compilation.

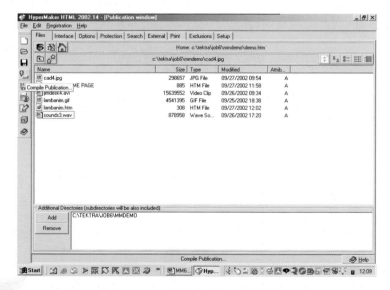

Finally, click the **Create Publication** icon to generate the compilation mmdemo.exe.

UNIT 208

WEB SITE DESIGN

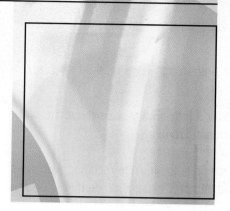

WEB PAGE DEVELOPMENT

Web pages can be drafted using two basic instrumental approaches:

- ● Programming

You can draft pages by writing actual program code yourself. The computer will follow your instructions one-by-one to achieve the desired results.

The usual Web programming language is HTML (HyperText Markup Language). HTML is being superseded by XML (Extended Markup Language) and D-HTML (Dynamic HyperText Markup Language) for more sophisticated developments.

- ● WYSIWYG Editors

WYSIWYG means 'what you see is what you get' so Web pages created using these editors appear at design time the same as they will appear on the published page.

This is not true of markup program coding which appears as a list of text instructions in modified English, just like any other computer program.

If you want to view the presented effect of your code you must 'run' the markup language program in a browser or in a browser emulator, for example the preview function of a design editor.

Browsers

Browsers are programs designed to present Web pages in the way the writer intends them to be seen complete with required colours, text layouts and pictures.

Ultimately, browsers use a markup program, whether written by hand or using a Web page editor.

You are unlikely to develop a browser for yourself. The usual browser commonly employed (2002) is Microsoft Internet Explorer 5 (IE5) for actual Internet access work, or the very similar Microsoft Windows Explorer, which is intended for operations involving local disk files. You always develop Web pages offline, using your local hard disk, in the interests of speed, economy and reliability.

Good browsers are also supplied by other companies, but in the PC realm, only Netscape Navigator has a significant market presence.

Browsers offer the following basic functions:

- **Page Address** The pathname and filename of the page to display can be entered in an Address Bar. In the InterNet context this address will be the URL (Universal Resource Locator).

- **WYSIWYG Display** The browser will display the summoned page exactly as it will be seen by the Internet surfer after it has been uploaded to the website.

- **Source Access** The list of program code commands in HTML or some other high-level markup language is called the source program.

  This source program may have been written by hand, wholly or in part; or it may wholly or partly be the product of a proprietary Web page editor program like DreamWeaver or Microsoft FrontPage.

Whatever the origins, a developmental browser must let you edit this source code to alter the resulting Web page presentation. A related text editor program, such as NotePad, may be called into play to help you do this.

A browser will also provide the following standard edit software functions:

File Load This is another avenue for bringing pages from disk to display, but it can also be used to load and display certain types of animations and other graphics files.

File Save This is essential to record modified pages back to disk and is therefore the key to progressive development.

String Finder This is an editing tool that locates a given text pattern within a source program, and if required deletes it or replaces it with alternative command material.

PICTURE CREATION

The colour picture on a computer screen is created from thousands of tiny dots of coloured light. Each dot is called a pixel (picture cell). The maximum number of pixels is ultimately determined by the hardware (machinery and circuits) but software (programs) can choose a number of pixels up to this maximum to project a given picture.

Resolution is the fineness of detail shown in the picture. Low resolution pictures are blurry or blocky. High resolution pictures are difficult to discriminate from live scenes. The more pixels there are in a given area of screen, the higher the resolution. Today (2002) the 'lowest common denominator' standard for pixel resolution is 800×600: i.e. 800 pixels across the screen by 600 down the screen making 480,000 displayed dots of light on the screen.

Sophisticated hardware can give 1024×768 or even 1600×1200 resolutions, but you should not assume everyone will be using these standards when you present a website.

Colour depth (US programs and manuals will of course write of "color depth") is the variety of colours which each pixel can assume. The number of colours is always a power of two: for example a black-and-white screen has $2^1=2$ colours; a choice between red, green, blue and nothing ("black") is $2^2=4$ colours. That would make for a very garish, unrealistic colour scheme. The usual basic standard for today's colour depth is $2^8=256$ colours and we should assume such colour definition when planning Web graphics. Bear in mind, however, that your video hardware is likely to be configured to represent up to $2^{24}=16,777,216$ different shades. You could of course alter this if you want to gain an impression of how things look on more primitive equipment.

The greater the colour depth the more realistic a photograph will look.

GRAPHICS FORMATS

Web pages are composited of both text and graphics: a text only page is certainly possible but very dull except in the most skilful hands.

Graphics can take several forms:

(a) Full-colour photographs (including pictures of paintings)

(b) Black-and-white photographs

(c) Colour or black-and-white diagrams (including statistical graphs and company logos)

(d) Animations

(e) Typographical ornaments (for example, text separator bars)

Your choice of graphics format depends upon what you wish to depict and upon the resolution and colour depth you need. You also need to take into account the limitation of telephonic data transmission and in particular the slow speed of data download times over narrowband connections.

There are three main classes of graphics files.

Vector Graphics

These are drawn from lines whose lengths, orientations and positions are compiled using the laws of analytic geometry. Data storage and transmission is economised because only a few short numbers called parameters need be stored for each line or other regular figure. Vector graphics enable complex, scalable diagrams to be drafted using a little, economically-stored data, and are thus ideal for engineering drawing and manufacturing systems.

But browsers lack the mathematical programming needed to handle vector graphics files, so vector graphics are of limited Web interest. Having said that, high-end Web editor programs like DreamWeaver contain systems to vectorise animations.

Bitmapped Graphics

Bitmap graphics files represent each pixel in terms of its position and colour. With significant colour depths and high resolutions this can lead to each file occupying several megabytes of storage, which in turn can lead to

picture download times of many minutes or hours over a 56Kbps narrowband modem, and the possible swamping of CM allocations leading to system hang-ups.

Therefore, only the lowest-definition monochrome bitmaps are suited to Internet graphics programming.

Raster Graphics

In raster graphics each picture is built up of horizontal 'scanning lines' like those which build a TV picture. Most pictures contain a good deal of visual redundancy in the form of large areas of constant shade and colour along raster lines (e.g. blue sky on photographs), or of repeated patterns (e.g. distant sea waves in a light breeze). The tracts of constant colour along raster lines are especially susceptible to abbreviation by various "packing" schemes which are used to optimise (make the best use of) graphics file storage.

It is these several packing schemes that compress graphics storage without diminishing picture quality too much which enable Web graphics, even photographs, to be downloaded across slow telephone lines.

MAJOR GRAPHICS CONVENTIONS

There are two key graphics compression standards used for Web pictures:

JPEG (Joint Photographic Experts Group)

Named for the committee which adopted it, the JPEG data compression standard is versatile enough to offer a continuous gradation of compression strengths, and allows dramatic 16- or 32-fold compressions to be applied to many pictures before a person with normal eyesight and a standard 800×600 screen notices any crudity in unenlarged picture quality.

JPEG files are therefore very useful for transferring full-colour or tonal monochrome photographs, though decompression delays usually make JPEGs impracticable for real-time animations.

Note, however, that although a good LAN JPEG may be as big as 200Kb and offer considerable scope for editing and enlargement, the version actually uploaded to your site should not exceed 15Kb maximum if you want your readers to be able to download it. Indeed, anything larger is likely to be garbled by the cheaper server services.

GIF (Graphics Interchange Format)

GIF files do not offer user-defined compression but provide good detail resolution at limited colour depths and are therefore useful for transmitting colour diagrams including drawings, maps, charts, graphs and logos as well as complex typographical features such as mathematical equations and coloured ornaments (e.g. toned separator bars).

GIFs are even more size-economical than highly-compressed JPEGs and are therefore preferred to JPEGs except when photographic resolutions is needed. It is also practicable to create stand-alone Web animation files as GIFs. These GIFs can automatically be loaded and played by ordinary Web pages coded in HTML.

HTML (HYPERTEXT MARKUP LANGUAGE)

The traditional, ordinary Web programming language is called HyperText Markup Language or HTML for short. HTML is highly non-technical and is very easily mastered. Some people call it "hotmetal", phonetically it is pronounced "Haich Tee Em Ell" as HotMetal has been assumed by proprietary site editor software and confusion could now result.

HTML offers a limited range of basic design tools the most important of which is the hyperlink, a programmatic 'trapdoor' that enables you to access other Web pages when you click on the designated picture or text string.

Other devices include ways to choose the style, size and colour of text fonts (within system limitations); ways of laying-out the text including basic bulleting and tabulation tools; and ways of locating pre-existing filed pictures and partitioning them for linkage purposes.

HTML lacks intrinsic typographical and pictorial creation and editing and any dynamic programmatic action in terms of decision or iteration. The lack of dynamic features is very limiting, even implying that an HTML page cannot show today's date without a special embedded program written in another computer language.

Whilst JavaScript and Java applets can be 'bolted-on' to enhance HTML action, modern dynamic markup languages offer a more powerful, integrated solution to reactive Web page design.

COPYRIGHT AND THE INTERNET

Traditional English copyright law is designed to prevent the trading advantage of information owners being damaged by others unfairly using the copy they have authored or purchased.

Legally-speaking, Web pages are 'unpublished' but nevertheless copyright is assumed to reside singly or severally in the originators who have contributed text or pictures to a Web site. Whilst in textual work copyright attaches to the form of words rather than the information content, in graphical work it attaches to the whole picture and any photographically or electronically modified rendition of it.

A work does not have to bear the © symbol or any other distinguishing mark or words to be copyright.

You may assume anything written after 1952 in any jurisdiction, including virtually all software and Web productions, is copyright. You may collate and re-express information from a variety of sources in your own work, but not reproduce pictures or whole verbatim tranches without permission of the copyright holder. The exception is that you may quote 'reasonable amounts' of attributed copy for scholarly or critical purposes.

Where you take information from Net or printed resources for your own site it is both courteous and useful to provide a links page or links section on your site. Here you can provide hotlinks to other writers' pages with brief factual descriptions of their content. Where hotlinks are not practicable, as for instance with traditional books and papers, provide full bibliographical details. It is these referential hotlinks that make the Web truly a 'net' and reinforce its immense power.

THE FUNCTIONS OF WEB SITES

The function of all Web sites was intended to be the public presentation of information, and especially the swift but accurate exchange of scientific research. This purpose arose naturally from the ethos of scientists who developed it as a forum for informal research sharing.

To a great extent this short tradition of openness has been preserved and is often helped rather than hindered by the purposes of the governmental and commercial organisations who have taken a Net presence.

Educational websites are often presented by English or German-speaking academic institutions, usually with the domain designations .edu or ac.uk. They may be used either for the actual presentation of distance-learning provision (in which case public access will often be restricted) or for the display of general prospectus information.

Governmental sites include military information websites that may be more or less successfully restricted; fiscal information including secure taxation facilities; or more general press or public briefing sites about e.g. environmental issues.

Commercial sites include briefing and reporting resources for salesmen and other remote employees, or for stakeholders such as shareholders; publicly-available catalogues with secure ordering facilities; chamber directories (restricted or public); agency catalogues and presentations, with or without client-response facilities; and vast numbers of general publicity vehicles for tourist boards and the like.

Still important in volume and diversity are sites provided by scholars and amateurs. These vary enormously both in the professionalism of their presentation and in the reliability of their content but the best present information which is either difficult or expensive to access in print, or which is simply unavailable elsewhere. Besides specialised mathematical and scientific work, we may mention such things as Web art galleries that enable the contents of great museums to be studied without the purchase of very expensive monographs or international travel to the cities involved.

TARGET AUDIENCE AND HOUSE STYLE

The "target audience" is the average standard of education and intellectual maturity for which a particular Web site is designed.

Some target groups, for example children, may be presented with simple vocabulary and sentence structures and direct, colourful images, though care may be taken with photographs and other images of potential situational ambiguity. Other readers, such as students, may deliberately be presented with challenging language or concepts in addition to the actual topic content. Otherwise care may also be exercised with very diverse adult audiences (e.g. self-employed tax returners) amongst whom standards of personal literacy are highly variable.

At the opposite extreme are university-trained scientists and scholars who recognise and employ unusual technical vocabularies and a generally "higher language" syntax, who value complex diagrams and typeset equations, but who may put up with mediocre or amateurish presentations as long as the content is timely, useful and reliable.

In between, the vast majority of us need sites which are tasteful, legible, free of irrelevancies and rich with links, contact details and even secure online form structures to assist the ordering of goods, services or printed literature.

The nature of the target audience will therefore lead you to design your site with regard to:

(a) Vocabulary

(b) Sentence lengths and structures

(c) Number, content and colour of photographs and art work

(d) Taxonomic site structure (the pattern and complexity of internal page links)

(e) Bibliographic resources including hotlinks

(f) Form upload facilities and other interactive resources

(g) Content suitability

Because of the very public character of the Internet special care should be taken to avoid unnecessary and unintended distress to surfers and others. Sensitivity should be exercised where religious, racial or political matters are addressed or where news exchange may aggravate existing suffering (e.g. in publicity or other help lent to political prisoners).

House style is your complete textual and graphical presentational response to your intended audience. It will embody attractive and clear standards of visual and perhaps audio presentation with content desirability, and seek to show you and your organisation in a light that encourages return visits and good reports.

SETTING PAGE COLOURS

Tthe background and text font colours can be set using either 'raw HTML' or a proprietary Web page editor program.

The editor program we will use will be Microsoft FrontPage.

As noted above, 256 colours are usual on modern monitors and many installations can represent many more shades, though the physiological and electrotechnical reality of these fine colour gradations is often debatable.

Using RGB colour definition syntax we can access $16^2 = 256$ shades each of red, green and blue and blend them to a precise hue, but standard HTML offers us only eight $= 2^3$ nameable colours: Black, White, Yellow, Cyan, Magenta, Red, Blue, Green. (Note: Netscape calls Cyan 'Aqua' and Magenta 'Fuchsia').

In the interests of clarity and reproducibility it is often wise to stick to these eight basic colours when defining page text and background hues.

Except in the case of black text on a white background, which is always a safe choice, it is best to arrange light text on a dark field. One bright possibility is 'Royal Swedish' (yellow text on a blue background) and another 'Reverse Terracotta' (red-orange on a black background). Since red-orange is not a standard HTML colour it would need to be blended using the RGB code "FF8F00".

A basic HTML program has this structure:

<HTML>

<HEAD>

<TITLE>My Little HTML Web Page</TITLE>

</HEAD>

<BODY BGCOLOR=WHITE TEXT=BLACK LINK=BLUE VLINK=MAGENTA>

<FONT NAME="Arial" SIZE=6 ALIGN=LEFT>

This is my text in lower case with an initial capital

THIS IS MY TEXT IN UPPER CASE (CAPITAL LETTERS)

</FONT>

</BODY>

</HTML>

The screen below shows the source code and realisation of this program in Internet Explorer:

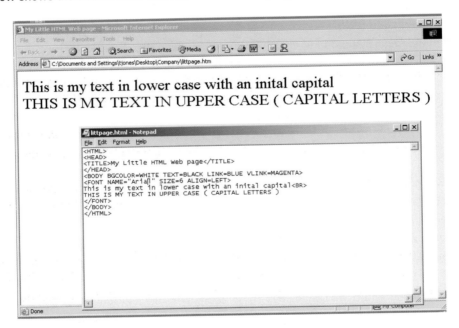

Because we are running offline, we have placed this file on the local path C:\Documents and Settings\tjones\Desktop\Company\littpage.htm, where littpage.htm is the actual program file name.

The program commands in the <...> marks are called tags. When you want to end a command, you use the formula </...>.

The <BR> tag does not have a closing tag. It indicates a line break, equivalent to a line feed.

All HTML programs must be introduced with the HTML tag because other markup language possibilities exist and the browser does not know which you are going to use before you tell it.

HTML programs are interpreted by the browser as Web pages. Each program has HEAD and BODY regions. The HEAD specifies identification and bibliographic information, including keywords to help search engines. Our HEAD only specifies the Page Title, which appears in the blue bar at the top of the page window. The BODY region contains all the page content specifications, including format and layout commands, and the actual words and pictures themselves. Some kinds of free-standing audio and video files can be embedded in the BODY, as of course are the all-important hyperlinks to other pages.

Of special interest at this time are the BODY parameters BGCOLOR, TEXT, LINK and VLINK.

BGCOLOR specifies the background colour. It is enough to type e.g. BLUE or "BLUE" if you are using a basic nameable colour. Alternatively, use the syntax BGCOLOR="FFFF00" for RGB color hues (in this case a greeny-gold colour).

TEXT specifies the TEXT colour which applies until we later perhaps countermand it with a:

<FONT COLOR=RED>

command.

LINK specifies the colour of the underlined textual hyperlinks not yet clicked by the surfer.

VLINK is the colour that hyperlink phrases assume when your surfer clicks them to access the underlying page. Call this Magenta. If you are worried about possible Netscape problems use VLINK="FF00FF".

If you are a confident programmer you will probably want to save time and trouble with such simple scripts by writing your own raw HTML as we have done with our 'My Little HTML Web Page' source code.

You can enter your code in any basic text editor or word processor, save it to disk and load it straight into a browser. You can even use an FTP (File Transfer Protocol) utility to upload it straight onto the Internet, if you have purchased Web space.

As we have just seen, we can change the colour of a text presentation using the COLOR parameter in the FONT tab, and it is in the FONT tab that it is possible to name the font style. Arial and Times New Roman are safe choices; fancier fonts, including Symbol for mathematicians' Greek letters may not be supported by some of your readers' computers.

It is wise explicitly to define the font SIZE using a small integer number as shown, and to experiment to see how big and how clearly this actually shows the type. We cannot confidently translate these figures into points or other typographic size measures. Some programmers use the <Hn>...</Hn> size definition tag system, but better control is usually possible with the SIZE parameter; though old, primitive browsers may baulk at it.

Finally in the FONT tag, the ALIGN parameter allows us to specify an initial text justification. Justification is the way in which the type is ordered with regard to the margins. LEFT justification gives the text body a flush alignment on the left margin, ragged on the right. RIGHT justification is flush on the right and ragged on the left like

Arabic script. JUSTIFY gives fully-justified text which is proportionately-spaced to give flush alignments on both left and right, like professional typesetting.

ALIGN formattings will be conserved under client window resizing (i.e. the surfer squeezing or broadening his screen page).

PARAGRAPH TABS

HTML offers limited typographical page formatting, and paragraph indent conventions are notoriously difficult to program in this language.

However, block paragraphs separated by single blank lines in the manner of this workbook are easy to set up, and these will maintain their formatting integrity under window adjustments. The appropriate syntax is:

<P ALIGN=JUSTIFY>

Here is my standard block paragraph which is fully-justified adaptably to client window re-sizing and which is followed by a single blank line of height adjusted to the FONT SIZE of this paragraph.

</P>

SETTING FORMATS WITHIN FRONTPAGE

To invoke the Web page editor program FrontPage click on the blue Desktop icon with the scroll and the arrow.

Microsoft FrontPage

FrontPage may then ask you whether you want it to be your default browser. Click the **No** button.

Now you should see a blank white screen with a **Normal** tab at the bottom. There is also a tabbed **HTML** source display screen which at the moment contains HEAD and BODY tags with some basic META descriptors in the HEAD. Thirdly, beneath these is a **Preview** screen to give *an impression* of what the Web surfer would see if your current development was posted without further ado.

Right-click your mouse and select **Page Properties**.

Click on the **Background** tab of the **Page Properties** window to view this.

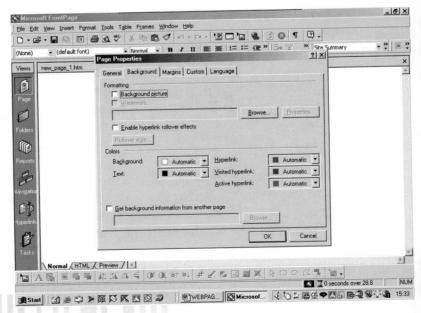

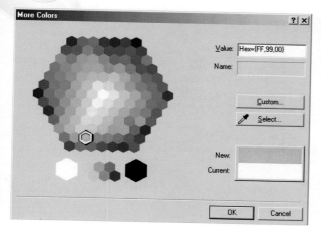

To set up a Terracotta page showing a big "MY TERRACOTTA TEXT" caption, first of all click the **Background** menu down arrow. Select **More Colors** from the palette and then select the orangey honeycomb palette cell indicated in the **More Colors** window.

Click **OK**.

You will be returned to the **Background** tab on the **Page Properties** window. Text will probably be set to black automatically. We, however, will positively select black text. Click on the **Text** menu down arrow.

Select the basic black as shown here.

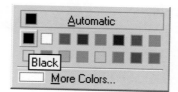

You will now be returned to the FrontPage Normal designing screen which has changed to terracotta orange.

Use the toolbar menus to select Copperplate Gothic Bold at size 6 (24pt nominal).

Now type MY TERRACOTTA TEXT. This gives the **Normal** screen seen here.

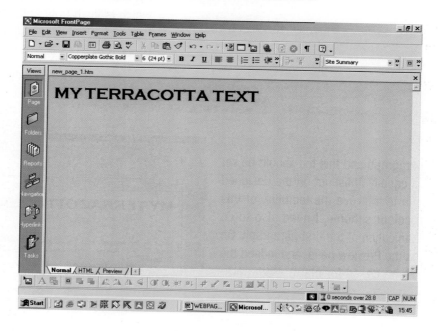

Check the generated HTML source code program by clicking the **HTML** tab.

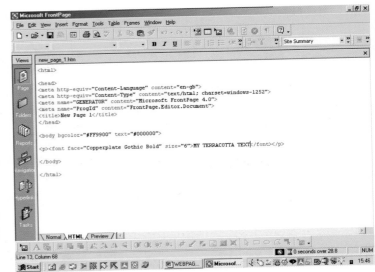

In this example the **Preview** screen appearance should be identical to the **Normal** screen.

Change the font to Arial 3 (12 pt) and enter two lines with the Return key.

Now select **Format** on the main toolbar, followed by **Paragraph**, **Indents and Spacing**, **Alignment** and select **Justify** from the drop-down menu as shown below:

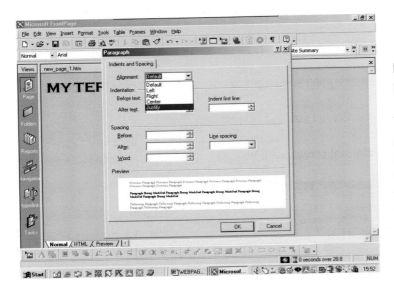

Now press **OK** and type the following two paragraphs:

This is the first paragraph which I hope to see prepared through FrontPage as a hypertext fully-justified test paragraph which is flush right and flush left and is in front of the second paragraph which should be a single blank line below it.

This is the second paragraph and this too should be set in 12 pt Arial and be equally indistinct on the designed Web page. I will have to improve the legibility of this font size, style and colour scheme. I need also to do more work on the justification of the first paragraph. Oh no, silly me! If I check the Preview page, and indeed the source code, there is no cause for alarm: Both paragraphs are correctly justified.

The **Preview** page now shows this correctly-formatted page draft.

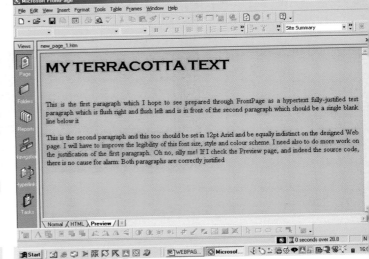

PLACING IMAGES

HTML allows us to insert images into pages by loading graphics files from specified locations.

In practical terms, the display of a picture with light edges (e.g. a photograph with clouds in a light blue sky) on a white or light page can cause a confused visual field. Therefore, a narrow and dark border is often programmed to frame Web pictures. This should be subtle enough not to be noticed by the casual viewer.

The general syntax involves the IMG SRC (Image Source) tag:

<IMG SRC="C:/MyDirectory/SubDirectory/MyPicture.gif" ALIGN=MIDDLE BORDER=2>

The argument of the SRC parameter is the pathname to the graphic to be displayed. If your graphic file is in the same directory as the Web page program file then "MyPicture.gif" is sufficient.

ALIGN sets the position of the picture on the Web page. Alternatives include LEFT, MIDDLE and RIGHT.

Finally, BORDER specifies the width of the fringe in pixels.

IMAGE FORMATION

Much of the effort in Web image formation is invested in the electronic enhancement photographic images, followed by optimisation of the image file size for Web transfer purposes. It is this latter problem that we will briefly focus upon.

First of all we will use Microsoft PhotoDraw to prepare a GIF file containing a page head logo. I hope to get this logo size down to about 5Kb. It has been pre-prepared using MicroGrafx Simply 3D 3, a cheap but useful 3D Graphic Design package. The logo graphic will involve a fancy rendition of the phrase "Wild Goats". The source GIF is about 65Kb, undesirably large for use as a Web header.

Secondly, we will use Microsoft PhotoDraw to re-create a pre-enhanced scanned bromide picture of a baby goat as a reasonably-clear JPEG, target size 15Kb.

Thirdly, we will attach both pictures to a very basic Web page.

If these resources are not available, create suitable trial pictures.

Many photographic enhancement programs such as Adobe PhotoShop can be used rather than PhotoDraw.

The Logo

Enter PhotoDraw by clicking the appropriate shortcut icon or by running the program from the **Start** menu.

Load the GIF file wildgoat.gif created via MicroGrafx.

Choose **File** from the main toolbar, followed by **Save As** and select the right directory and sub-directory by browsing or other direct path entry.

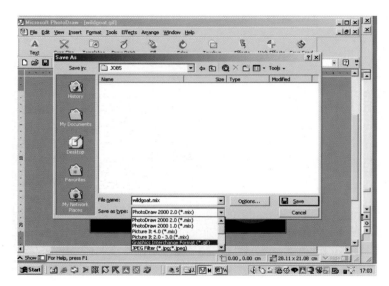

Select **Save As type:** and choose the **Graphics Interchange Format (*.gif)** option from the drop down menu.

Click the **Options** button.

Click off **Save Transparency** and quarter the apparent file size by halving **Width** on the **Custom Size Screen** (i.e. reduce 1660 px to 840 px).

Click **OK**, **OK**, **Save** and **Yes** in response to the safety overwrite warning.

The file wildgoat.gif is now 37Kb (it was not cut by 75% because of file overheads).
Reload the file into the PhotoEdit viewer window to check the image quality and cautiously repeat the process until the file size is within the right quality–size parameters.

The 37Kb file will not produce a noticeably different image to the original. Will the 15Kb version be any worse?

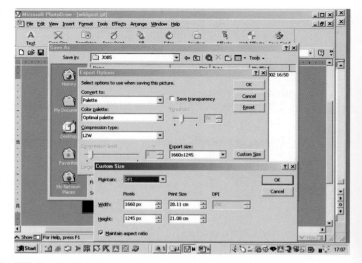

The Photograph

The JPEG picture, scanned from an ordinary Kodak 4"×6" bromide print, has been pre-treated to be a 50Kb file called GOATS.jpg and is now in our directory.

We will first "blow it up" electronically in PhotoDraw to see if definition falls off too much, and if necessary we may improve the brightness or contrast along the way.

We will then try to render it as a 15Kb JPEG saved as goats1.jpg, using a slightly different approach to the one which we tried with the gif.

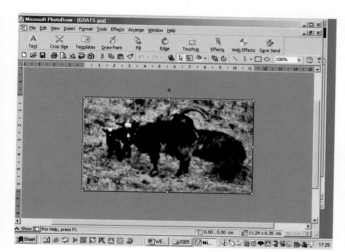

Loaded into the enhancer, GOATS.jpg looks like this.

Enlarged and slightly enhanced for sharpness, brightness and contrast, this delightful family looks like this.

Now click **File**, **Save for Use In...** and thus enter the **Save for Use In** Wizard.

Checking that the **On the Web** radio button is selected click **Next**.

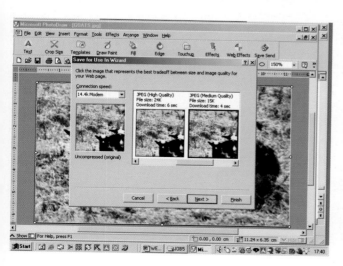

Check **As a Picture** and click **Next**.

Now click the **JPEG (Medium Quality) File Size 15K** option (a black border marks your selection) and click **Next**.

We are now told that we have 70-fold True Color compression for a 420×240 pixel picture. Click **Save**.

Edit GOATS to goats1 in the **File Name:** text bar and click **Save**.

When you go through this process with your own pictures can you see any difference when you cut a JPEG's size by 68%?

Using FrontPage to Put the Logo and the Goats on a Web Page

To finish the job we will put the goats' images on a page. First, call upon FrontPage in the usual manner. If you do not have the goats' images you can of course follow the general pattern to set up your own graphics within a HTML Web page file. Indeed, you can use DreamWeaver or of course 'roll your own' program code.

Click **File**, **Picture**, **From File**.

Locate the right path and use the **Select File** screen to choose wildgoat.gif:

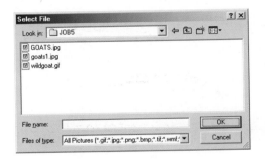

Then Click **OK**.

The gif image will swamp the whole screen. Click on the HTML tab, locate the **width** and **height** parameters in the IMG tab and divide each by four.

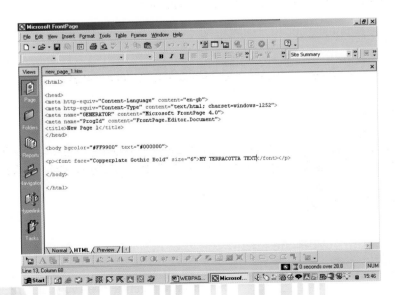

We now have the much more reasonably-sized image seen in the **Preview** below:

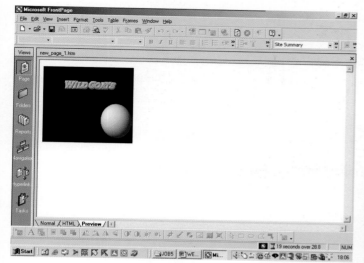

After going through a similar routine with goats1.jpg, the goat family picture appears below the introductory logo as here.

This needs a lot more work but it is a start!

CREATING HYPERLINKS

Hyperlinks are the important "trapdoors" that your Web page user clicks to access other pages on your site, or other sites on the Internet.

Hyperlinks are thus the links in the chain of pages worldwide.

A textual hyperlink shows on your page as a blue underlined phrase as in:

Click here to read about goats. Cheviot sheep can be seen on this site...

The phrases are linked to pathnames, filenames or URLs with this 'anchor' syntax:

<A HREF="PathName">Link</A>

For example, the bit about goats is in the same local directory (or eventual website) as our Web page containing the "Click here" sentence, and is itself a page called "goats.htm". The appropriate hyperlink is:

<A HREF="goats.htm">Click here</A>

On the other hand the "Cheviot sheep" information is on someone else's website at http://www.cheviots. co.uk/csheep/. The access link is:

<A HREF=http://www.cheviots.co.uk/csheep>Cheviot sheep</A>

You can also install hyperlinks behind pictures so that when a surfer clicks on a drawing or photograph he 'falls through' to another page of relevant information.

Remember our photo of the goat family in goats1.jpg?

If the surfer clicks on it he or she accesses a page about the circumstances in which I took the picture. This page is called galloway.htm.

The required HTML syntax is:

<A HREF="TargetPage"><IMG SRC="PictureFile" ALT="DefaultCaption"></A>

where "DefaultCaption" is explanatory text that appears if the picture fails to load on the reader's computer.

In this example the appropriate link is:

<A HREF="galloway.htm"><IMG SRC="goats1.jpg" ALT="A family of wild goats"></A>

It is possible to create HTML hyperlinks that invoke a ready-addressed browser email form to simplify a surfer's sending of a message to you.

The general syntax is:

<A HREF=mailto:EmailAddress>Link</A>

For example the phrase:

I too like goats and want to tell Jim Warren

renders to HTML as:

I too like goats and want to

<A HREF=mailto:capricious@www.capric.com>

tell Jim Warren

</A>

where capricious@www.capric.com is a (fictitious) email address and   is a special separator-space coercion code to prevent the formation of the word "totell".

Lastly, it is also feasible to enable your readers to download whole programs or other files from your website by using FTP (the File Transfer Protocol) embedded in a hyperlink anchor.

For example, you have a small program that displays a map showing the strengths and locations of known wild goat clans throughout The British Isles. The user can alter the map via entries in a table. The downloadable program is in your site's root directory and is called clans.exe

You give this option on your home page:

Download Wild Goat Herds Map Program (150Kb)

The general syntax is:

<A HREF="ftp://DomainPath">Link</A>

where DomainPath is the pathname to the file minus the "www" qualifier.
The program is in the root directory of www.capric.com so the special syntax is:

<A HREF="ftp://capric.com/clans.exe">Download Wild Goats Herds Map Program (150Kb)</A>

It is courteous to include the file size in the link so that your reader can estimate the download time on his or her system. It could freeze up his computer resources for many minutes.

STRUCTURES OF PAGE LINKS

The mathematical pattern in which things are linked is called a topology. Topology is also the name of the science of linkage patterns.

It must be stressed at the outset that a topology is about linkage relationships and may or may not reflect the actual position or order of items in physical space, or in time.

Three basic topologies interest us in planning a set of Web pages:

(1) The Taxonomy or 'Tree Structure'

(2) The Cycloid or 'Ring Structure'

(3) The Reticulation or Network

All three basic patterns have sub-categories.

The Taxonomy

The taxonomy is a 'family tree' of hierarchical relationships. Philosophically-speaking, a taxonomy always implies *logical inclusion,* whatever the exact scientific details that relate the members of the tree-structure.

For example, you want to set up a website about interesting animals and realise that your readers will probably find your site clearer and easier to get around if you classify the animals into orders and genera.

So you decide to go for an initial seven-page structure with a Home Page (which you must call index.html). The home page contains links to sub-pages called reptiles.htm, birds.htm and mammals.htm. Also mammals.htm has a sub-page called apes.htm, which in turn holds links to the chimps.htm and humans.htm pages.

The total linkage system looks like this:

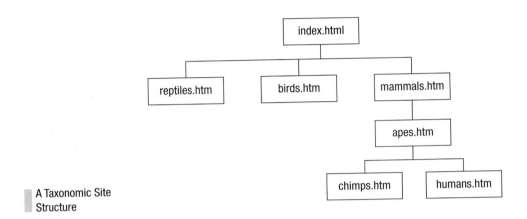

A Taxonomic Site
Structure

Each link is bidirectional, meaning you should reciprocate the Calling hyperlink from the page "above" with a Returning hyperlink from the sub-page.

Taxonomies are easy and clear to navigate *if you know how things are ordered* but are rigid and difficult to adapt.

The Cycloid

The cycloid is a real or imaginary ring or wheel layout. You may or may not choose to position your home page at the hub of the wheel.

Cycloids imply *logical continuity*.

For example, you want to set up a site about animals to look out for in Winter, Spring, Summer and Autumn. You want your reader to be able to choose any of the four seasons from your home page index.html, but also be able to follow the links from one season to another. The season pages are called winter.htm, spring.htm, summer.htm and autumn.htm.

The linkage layout of the first five pages looks like this:

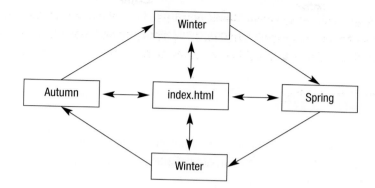

A Cyclical Topology

Links to the hub are bidirectional. Season links are unidirectional clockwise, because you have decided that whilst we can pass forward from Autumn to Winter, we do not need to be able to pass back from Winter to Autumn.

Cycloids are good for systems that contain chronological successions, because they can easily be made discontinuous to represent recipes, instructional programs or other sequential systems, but are poor for showing or using intrinsic entity features.

The Reticulation

The reticulation is a network linkage in which "nearby" pages are linked in a multilateral way to many or all of their neighbours.

A reticulation implies *logical association* measured by a propinquity metric. This propinquity metric is a scale for measuring the strength of community of the networked objects and could be, but is not necessarily, related to the physical distance that they stand apart.

For example, you wish to design a set of pages about different countries related to each other in 'social space'. In this scheme, America has 'more to do' with Britain than with Mexico, and Britain is 'more like' America than Belgium, but Belgium is 'closely related to France'.

A possible reticule (literally "little net") is:

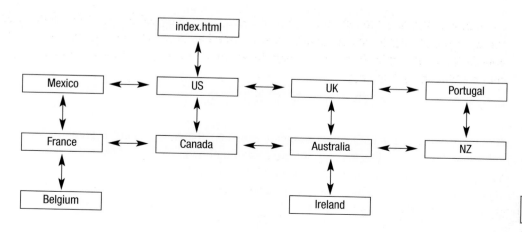

A Reticule (Reticular Topology)

All linkages are bilateral. More complex multilateral linkages are feasible.

Reticulations tend to evolve organically despite any planning attempts, but can be useful structures where conceptual affinities, and especially 'space' relationships, are agreed to exist. They are more robust than cycloids or taxonomies when links are broken or eliminated and this lends great strength and permanence to any network structure.

THE STORYBOARD

The storyboard is a project planning device borrowed from the movie industry. It enables images, sound and text to be assembled into scenes; the scenes timed, lit, angled and furnished; and then the packaged scenes ordered into a continuous succession in time.

In the Web page planning context you will use two main storyboard plans:

- The topological plan
  This shows the overall linkage pattern for each of the pages on your site, and shares some features with a traditional programmer's flow diagram.

- Page plans
  Page plans are written for each page and will typically include your design intentions for:

  (a) Title
  (b) Font Styles, Sizes and Colours
  (c) Background Colours and Images
  (d) Links
  (e) Picture Content
  (f) Text Content

Fortunately, HTML is much more forgiving than other computer languages but we still cannot over-emphasise the importance of patient prior planning of all programs unless we want to suffer a lot of frustration, expense and wasted time.

There is little reason why a storyboard should not take the form of rough freehand sketches and handwritten jottings on a printed pro forma designed to cover the major points and serve as a memory aid. After all, in a well-planned Web design project, each storyboard page will advance through several versions, even if designed by a single individual.

ASSEMBLING OUR FACTS

When our storyboard is in the early stages of evolution, it is time to start researching the content which we intend to include. Many think this is risky, and we should gather all our facts before we start work, but you can bet your bottom dollar that the facts really are out there if only they can be found, and when they are found they will inevitably colour and condition the way in which they are presented.

There are four main sources of site content:

Experiential Knowledge

In any writing there is no substitute for accumulated background expertise about your subject or your life. But it helps to write that knowledge down, and more of it than you actually need to display, so that gaps in cover can be identified, ordered and clarified. You may have stocks of previous writings and of drawings and photographs which you can marshal and modify if they are relevant to the new production.

Do not attempt to write about the life history of the beaver if you are a specialist in differential equations: it will show.

Do not be afraid to boldly invent new concepts, or even new words, if nothing well-known seems to fit the ideas you want to publish. But if you do that take care to explain everything novel in plain language.

Internet Research

The Internet itself is by far the world's largest resource of factual text and images and is cheap, quick and easy to access, as the enormous amount of plagiarised copy on the Web indicates.

Amongst the repetition and the triviality is a certain amount of deliberate and accidental factual error, because no learned editors vet the contributions, except for the occasional conscientious institutional webmaster.

But in experienced hands, the Internet is a golden research resource, and will yield up hundreds of links and citations that you can follow to learn more facts and techniques. These citations will include plenty of bibliographic details about printed books and papers.

Library Research

This includes all study of printed hard copy, including unpublished treatises and manuscripts. This printed material may take the form of books, journals and reports, or legal or cartographical documentation, whether in actual libraries or other repositories.

Printed copy has almost always been checked over by editors, often assisted by specialist referees, and is therefore guaranteed to reflect the wisdom of the day.

Printed information in learned journals is more reliable than in trade magazines or newspapers; and that in books is more reliable than that in journals because the compositing and production of books takes time.

Original Research

Last but not least.

This is the most costly form of research in time and money, but the most exalted and from your viewpoint the most trustworthy.

It includes classical laboratory scientific research and mathematical derivations, but also more mundane activities like going out and photographing animals in their natural habitats, or conducting interviews with people. It also

includes whole categories of data acquisition activities and statistical post-processing, everything from traffic-counting to questionnaire campaigns.

Proper Attributions

Never transfer portions of text to your own page, unless you wish to acclaim or disparage the actual form of words. Not only is such cheap work unethical and possibly illegal, but it also cramps your own style. Assemble, order and edit facts from several sources, allowing your own thoughts to form and mature.

It is best to set up a special bibliographic sub-page on your site for academic citation references. Part of this page, or better still a dedicated second page, will marshal hotlinks to relevant sites you have consulted, with very brief factual descriptions of each. If, however, you consider a site to be well-illustrated or simply excellent you can afford to say so.

Besides being very useful to other serious students, a choice but adequate list of publications and sites that you recommend lends immense authority to your own production, and rightly or wrongly will mark you out as a powerful force in the topic area, as well as defusing any potential jealousies, acrimonious exchanges of correspondence or even legal action that may result from the careless oversight of information sources.

TABLES

HTML allows us to incorporate simple but versatile row-and-column tables into Web pages. Each table drawn is included between <TABLE>...</TABLE> tags.

Each row is introduced by a <TR> tab and terminated by </TR>. Each piece of data in a row, which contributes to the building of a column, is enclosed within <TD>...</TD> tags.

The general syntax of the <TABLE> tag is:

<TABLE BORDER=pixels CELLSPACING=pixels CELLPADDING=pixels>

where all the parameters, which control the internal appearance, are optional. If you just use <TABLE> the tabulation has no visible internal rulings.

For example, I want to present this table about goat populations in national parks on a Web page:

	1990	2000
Galloway	2789	4867
Snowdonia	326	687
Lake District	155	212

The row and column headings are in bold and the actual head counts in feint. (The figures are left justified above but we expect them by default to be left justified in the Web page table: this can be altered if required).

Use the <DIV>...</DIV> tag to centre the table on the page. Note that <DIV>...</DIV> can be used to format any block of Web output, not just tables.

Here is the table coding:

```
<DIV ALIGN=CENTER>
<TABLE>
   <TR>
      <TD></TD>
      <TD><B>1990</B></TD>
      <TD><B>2000</B></TD>
   </TR>
   <TR>
      <TD><B>Galloway</B></TD>
      <TD>2789</TD>
      <TD>4867</TD>
   </TR>
   <TR>
      <TD><B>Snowdonia</B></TD>
      <TD>326</TD>
      <TD>687</TD>
   </TR>
   <TR>
      <TD><B>Lake District</B></TD>
      <TD>155</TD>
      <TD>212</TD>
   </TR>
</TABLE>
</DIV>
```

Note two other interesting features about this code. Firstly, this is one of those instances where it is sensible to indent program code to reflect design structure. The computer does not care how we lay out our programs, but clear indentations help us humans to understand what is going on when we initially write the programming, and when we come back to alter or correct it.

The other more minor point is our use of the enclosing <B>...</B> tag to embolden textual content. If we had used <I>...</I> it would have italicised the text. Because HTML is not a computational language it will treat any numbers in your table as text.

LAYOUTS AND TEMPLATES

The content of computer source code programs, especially those written in languages like COBOL and HTML, is both stereotyped and wordy, as the tabulation example demonstrates.

For certain, all HTML programs have HEAD and BODY sections and any worth their salt will also have TITLES and (as we shall see later) META statements.

A simple but useful page layout scheme is this:

PAGE HEADING

REGISTERED ADDRESS AND VAT NUMBER
(companies)

PHOTO1   PHOTO2   PHOTO3

PHOTO4   PHOTO5   PHOTO6

VERSION NUMBER
DATE OF CREATION
DATE OR REVISION

Not all elements of this basic structure will appear in every page we create, and some elements will be repeated more often, but this could be the fundamental layout for many hundreds of pages and it would pay to use it as the basis for a storyboard form; as a general *aide memoire*, and as re-usable code skeleton called a template.

Now standard HTML will not accept data arguments at run-time, unlike virtually every other computer language. So we will have to edit-in the variant content by hand. Therefore we will use the character sequence XX- as a prefix of all the data elements we wish to replace with content for a particular page:

So a useful HTML template will look like this:

```
<HTML>
<HEAD>
<TITLE>XX-TITLE</TITLE>
</HEAD>
<BODY BGCOLOR=WHITE TEXT=BLACK LINK=BLUE VLINK=MAGENTA>
<BR><BR>
<FONT SIZE=4>
<A HREF="XX-CALLINGPAGE">Click to Return to the Calling Page</A>
</FONT>
<BR><BR>
<DIV ALIGN=CENTER>
    <FONT FACE="Times New Roman" SIZE=7 COLOR=MAGENTA>
    XX-PAGEHEADING
    </FONT>
    <FONT SIZE=4 COLOR=BLACK>
    <BR>
    XX-ADDRESS
    </FONT>
    <BR><BR>
</DIV>
<DIV ALIGN=LEFT>
    <FONT FACE="Times New Roman" SIZE=3>
    <P ALIGN=JUSTIFY>
    XX-INTRODUCTORYTEXT
```

```
    <P>

    </FONT>

</DIV>

<DIV ALIGN=LEFT>

    <FONT FACE="Arial" SIZE=3>

    <B>

    XX-RUNNINGHEAD1

    </B>

    </FONT>

    <FONT FACE="Times New Roman" SIZE=3>

    <P ALIGN=JUSTIFY>

    XX-PARAGRAPH1

    </P>

    <FONT FACE="Arial" SIZE=3>

    <B>

    XX-RUNNINGHEAD2

    </B>

    </FONT>

    <FONT FACE="Times New Roman" SIZE=3>

    <P ALIGN=JUSTIFY>

    XX-PARAGRAPH2

    </P>

    <FONT FACE="Arial" SIZE=3>

    <B>

    XX-PHOTOGALLERYTITLE

    </B>

    <BR><BR>

    </FONT>

</DIV>

<DIV ALIGN=CENTER>

    <TABLE CELLSPACING=20>
```

```
        <TR>

            <TD><IMG SRC="XX-PHOTO1.jpg" HEIGHT=128 WIDTH=192
                    BORDER=1></TD>

            <TD><IMG SRC="XX-PHOTO2.jpg" HEIGHT=128 WIDTH=192
                    BORDER=1></TD>

            <TD><IMG SRC="XX-PHOTO3.jpg" HEIGHT=128 WIDTH=192
                    BORDER=1></TD>

        </TR>

        <TR>

            <TD><DIV ALIGN=CENTER>XX-PHOTOCAPTION1</DIV></TD>

            <TD><DIV ALIGN=CENTER>XX-PHOTOCAPTION2</DIV></TD>

            <TD><DIV ALIGN=CENTER>XX-PHOTOCAPTION3</DIV></TD>

        </TR>

        <TR>

            <TD><IMG SRC="XX-PHOTO4.jpg" HEIGHT=128 WIDTH=192
                    BORDER=1></TD>

            <TD><IMG SRC="XX-PHOTO5.jpg" HEIGHT=128 WIDTH=192
                    BORDER=1></TD>

            <TD><IMG SRC="XX-PHOTO6.jpg" HEIGHT=128 WIDTH=192
                    BORDER=1></TD>

        </TR>

        <TR>

            <TD><DIV ALIGN=CENTER>XX-PHOTOCAPTION4</DIV></TD>

            <TD><DIV ALIGN=CENTER>XX-PHOTOCAPTION5</DIV></TD>

            <TD><DIV ALIGN=CENTER>XX-PHOTOCAPTION6</DIV></TD>

        </TR>

    </TABLE>

</DIV>

<FONT SIZE=3>

<DIV ALIGN=LEFT>

    <BR><BR>

    <B>XX-LINKS</B>

    <BR><BR>
```

```
   <A HREF=mailto:capricious@www.capric.com>Send an Email</A>

   <BR><BR>

</DIV>

<DIV ALIGN=CENTER>

   XX-HITCOUNTERHERE

   <BR><BR>

</DIV>

</FONT>

<DIV ALIGN=LEFT>

   <FONT SIZE=3>

   Version: XX-VERSION<BR>

   Date of Creation: XX-DATEOFCREATION<BR>

   Data of Revision: XX-DATEOFREVISION<BR>

   </FONT>

   <BR><BR>

   <FONT SIZE=4>

   <A HREF="XX-NEXTPAGE">Click for the Next Page</A>

   </FONT>

</DIV>

</BODY>

</HTML>
```

I think that you will agree that with all this formatting and repetition it will be a great saving of time, money and sheer boredom if we only write this code template once and then use it as the basis of many Web pages.

Even with this template, the static character of HTML implies that we will have to do an awful lot of cutting and pasting work to adapt the outline to a particular job. It is best to pre-prepare the text to be cut and pasted in some text or word processor file, and that has the additional advantage of simplifying spellchecking and other editorial work.

Another use of templates is that they help you to maintain and project a uniform and consistent house style which presents your readers or customers with your characteristic corporate 'look and feel'. This helps to build customer confidence in the integrity of your firm. It also clarifies and simplifies the user's different dealings with it.

HOW TO ESTIMATE MINIMUM GRAPHICS FILE SIZES

Computer files are made up of two kinds of data: stored information about the relevant real-world application, and carrier data, which defines the internal character and structure of the data file.

This latter structural data includes header information about the file's name, description, type, author and generation date as well as more technical material; and secondly delimitation data that defines the extent or limits of the internal data compartments such as fields and records, and the entire file itself.

It is very difficult for us to estimate this structural data, or how many kilobytes of memory it occupies, unless we are privy to the file design, or have conducted appropriate experiments.

But we can estimate the amount of payload data, which probably accounts for 90 or 95% of the total filesize demand.

Graphics file sizes increase with resolution (i.e. pixels per picture) and are thus proportional to the product of the horizontal and vertical pixel counts; and increase exponentially (to the base 2) with colour depth.

In the case of compressed graphics files, notably JPEGs, the extent of compression also, of course, influences the file size: the more compression, the smaller the size.

Vector graphics files summarise instructions for re-creating shapes on screen with a few short numbers and so will be smaller than raster structures that summarise all parts of the screen. Raster types like GIFs and JPEGs are in turn smaller than bitmapped image files that characterise the exact colour, brightness and position of every individual pixel.

A useful formula for estimating the *minimum* file size due to payload data is:

$$S = \frac{xy}{c} 2^d$$

where S is the file size in bits, x is the horizontal image pixel count, y is the vertical image pixel count, d is the colour depth (4 for sixteen colours or shades of gray; 8 for 256 colours of variable brightness), and c is the compression factor.

For example, we have a 256-colour JPEG creation with 400 vertical pixels and 600 horizontal pixel positions. Its compression factor is 70-fold. What is its apparent size S in bits?

$$S = \frac{400 \times 600}{70} \times 2^8$$

$$= \frac{240000}{70} \times 256$$

$$= 877714 \text{ bits}$$

To reduce this to kilobytes we have to divide S by 8 bits per byte × 1024 bytes per kilobyte, which means we divide by 8192. This gives us a minimum file size due to content of 107.14Kb.

We can of course re-arrange the equation to compute suitable dimensions and colour depths for given size limits.

ICONS, THUMBNAILS AND BACKGROUNDS

Icons are very small stylised pictures used to denote programs, files or operations in GUI (Graphical User Interface) screens. It is possible to generate icons from any appropriate artwork and adopt them as markers and effectively as clickable hyperlinks. Because of their small pixel dimensions, limited colours and need for rapid deployment, icons are often bitmapped graphics files.

Thumbnails are very small diagrams or pictures placed on Web pages to give hyperlink access to descriptive pages or enlarged images. They are usually appropriate GIFs or JPEGs, but download times and storage are minimised by their restricted pixel dimensions.

Suitably-designed graphics files, often GIFs, can be used as the motifs of feint, repeating background 'wallpaper' patterns on Web pages. This repeating pattern, technically known as a tessellation, is used for decoration or corporate identification. Because the background is a repeating structure, storage and processing overheads are little greater than those of the motif image.

Good graphics software, including photo-enhancement software such as PhotoEdit, provides facilities for the creation of icons, thumbnails and backgrounds from your pre-existing artwork files.

TRANSPARENCY

It is possible to alter the screen presentation of GIF, JPEG and certain other graphics files so that any background colour, text or artwork will 'show through' the overlying picture.

Good software allows you to adjust this transparency effect continuously between 0% (the overlying image we are working with totally hides any image over which it is superimposed) to 100% (the overlying subject image will appear invisible against the background).

This is of use in the production of backgrounds, overlays including those for 'fade-away' machine drawing, and for 'then and now' photographic images of e.g. industrial landscapes.

THE WEB SAFE COLOUR PALETTE

The Web-safe colour palette, sometimes called the browser-safe colour palette, is a set of 216 colours common to most computer systems. You can convert colour GIF images to use the Web-safe palette using any good artwork or photo-enhancement software. The examples below are composed for PhotoDraw, but PhotoDraw offers several different avenues for implementing Web-safe in a GIF.

Use of the Web-safe palette helps to ensure against computer systems that are foreign to your development system distorting the colour scheme presentation of your GIF.

Load the GIF to be treated into PhotoDraw.

Using the paint-pour (area fill) drop-down menu found on the tertiary toolbar select **More Colors**.

When the **More Colors** window appears choose **Web-Safe** and click **OK**

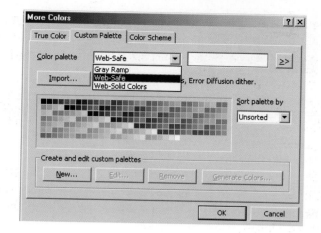

IMAGE MAPS

Using a Cartesian co-ordinate system (a set of numbers that determine the location of a point in space by its distance from two fixed lines) it is possible to split an image into two-dimensional geometric zones, each clickable zone connected via a hyperlink to its own Web page or programmatic process. The 'polygonal' zones can also be programmed to be rectangles or circles.

Tip

Remember that in HTML images the origin of the coordinates is at **TOP Left**; not at bottom left as in normal mathematical analysis.

Clearly, clickable image zones could be employed on maps, where you might click on England or Wales to see a relevant page. They could also be used with certain engineering diagrams and whole classes of two-dimension schematics.

The following illustration uses a very stylised coloured GIF view of typical categories of interest in the landscape of the Gower Peninsula, an area of outstanding natural beauty near Swansea, and a centre of concentrated scientific and antiquarian interest.

Amongst the primary areas of interest in Gower are hills, sea, beaches, cliffs, churches, castles and prehistoric sites. The seven are respectively explained by the site's sub-pages hills.htm, sea.htm, beaches.htm, cliffs.htm, churches.htm, castles.htm, and sites.htm.

gowervew.gif is the image file to be loaded to a homepage and partitioned into nine clickable polygons which call the seven sites, plus two non-clickable areas coloured as sky and land.

Think of the resulting 'map' as a 200×150 pixel sheet of graph paper with the category symbols drawn on the grid and each vertex assigned to an x,y coordinate pair.

Here is the schematic:

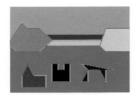

You can measure the co-ordinate pairs, n+1 of them for each n-vertexed polygon, and list them within the defining COORDS parameters of the shapes' respective AREA tags as illustrated by the following HTML code:

```
<! Associate Internet HTML Map with GIF File>
<IMG SRC="gowervew.gif" USEMAP="#gowerview"
<! Define the Map of the Schematic View>
<MAP NAME="gowerview">

<! Invoke Churches Page>
<AREA SHAPE="polygon" COORDS="30,100,40,120,60,120,60,140,20,140,20,120,30,100"
    HREF="churches.htm">

<! Invoke Castles Page>
<AREA SHAPE="polygon" COORDS="70,100,80,100,80,110,90,110,90,100,100,100,100,130,70,130,70,100"
    HREF="castles.htm">

<! Invoke Prehistoric Sites Page (by Clicking any Dolmen Component)>
<AREA SHAPE="polygon" COORDS="120,100,170,110,130,110,120,100" HREF="sites.htm">
<AREA SHAPE="polygon" COORDS="130,110,130,130,120,130,130,110" HREF="sites.htm">
<AREA SHAPE="polygon" COORDS="160,110,160,130,150,110,160,110" HREF="sites.htm">

<! Invoke Hills Page>
<AREA SHAPE="polygon" COORDS="20,30,30,40,50,40,70,60,50,80,10,80,0,70,0,60,20,30"
    HREF="hills.htm">

<! Invoke Sea Page>
<AREA SHAPE="polygon" COORDS="60,50,157,50,153,60,70,60,60,50"
    HREF="sea.htm">

<! Invoke Beaches Page>
<AREA SHAPE="polygon" COORDS="70,60,153,60,150,70,60,70,70,60"
    HREF="beaches.htm">
```

```
<! Invoke Cliffs Page>

<AREA SHAPE="polygon" COORDS="160,40,200,40,200,80,160,80,150,70,160,40"

    HREF="cliffs.htm">


<! Do No Action if Land or Sky are Clicked>

<AREA SHAPE="default" NOHREF>


</MAP>
```

MAKING JPEG FILES FOR THE WEB

We will prepare the JPEG photograph oxchurcb.jpg from the pre-existing file OXCHURB.mix.

OXCHURB.mix was scanned from a KODAK 4"×6" bromide print using an Epson Perfection 1240U 600×1200 scanner.

The mediating photo-enhancement software was Microsoft PhotoDraw (hence the .mix format) but you could use any high-quality photo-package, including any Adobe or any Kodak product. As a general rule, however, it is sensible to allow your scanner to mediate its uploads to your enhancer using the manufacturer's bundled scanner-specific software. The Epson program was used to transfer these pictures.

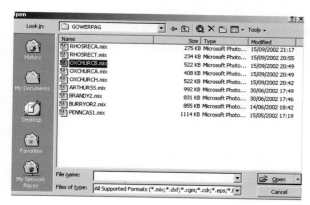

During this process we will take good care to make sure that the resulting JPEG is not much bigger than 15Kb, and preferably smaller, so as not to stall our readers' computers, or waste their download time.

Call up PhotoDraw using the Desktop icon and click **File** and **Open** to reach this screen.

Now click on **OXCHURCB.mix** and **Open.**

If your picture is already a JPEG due to your differing program defaults, then format conversion is not necessary.

Select **File**, **Save for Use In...**

and then follow through the **Save for Use in** wizard:

On the Web
As a Picture
Fill them with the background color

347

Click **Next** to accept white as the transparent areas fill color.

Select **56k modem** from the **Connection speed**: drop down menu.

Select the **JPEG(Low Quality) File Size: 20K Download time: 5 sec** frame, and click **Next**.

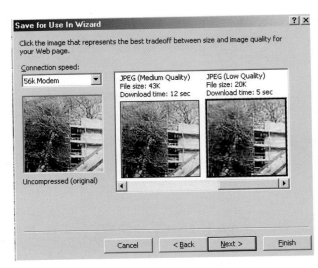

This gives a True Color JPEG with 90-fold compression and 579×380 pixels. It is admittedly rather big but at least has the virtue of some reader enlargeability without immediate pixelation.

When you generate your own JPEGs with this wizard some files will require you to opt for Medium Quality to preserve useful resolutions. Do not worry about this. If it later transpires that the sizes are causing annoyance, it is a simple matter to reduce the JPEG sizes even further.

Click **Save**.

And confirm the Save by clicking **Save** on the succeeding **Save As** window *taking care to save the file to the right directory.*

PUTTING IT ALL TOGETHER

We have seen how we can format text and process images for the Web. We have also seen how we can erect hyperlinks and tables using raw HTML and touched upon the possibilities afforded by proprietary Web design programs like FrontPage.

We have also seen how an HTML program template can lend structure and discipline to our programming efforts, speed our work and help reduce errors and omissions.

Any template is only a guide and in a meaningful job there are parts of it we will suppress and other parts we will repeat or embellish.

We will now integrate these principles in the design of a Web page called 'Haunted Gower'. We will set the page heading 'Haunted Gower' in Old English Black Letter just to set the spooky scene and suppress the company name part of the template code. When we save the new page we will have to call it something sensible like gowerpag.htm, taking care not to overwrite our template!

Conveniently, the six template photograph nests are just right, but we will have to repeat the two template running head paragraph structures to make six.

Furthermore, we will have to research and prepare the links to other websites.

Below is reproduced the entire HTML markup program, followed by the browse-time page image so that you can see precisely how each feature is implemented and how it all comes together.

The HTML Markup Program for 'Haunted Gower'

```
<HTML>

<HEAD>

<TITLE>Haunted Gower</TITLE>

</HEAD>

<BODY BGCOLOR=WHITE TEXT=BLACK LINK=BLUE VLINK=MAGENTA>

<BR><BR>

<FONT SIZE=4>

<A HREF="XX-CALLINGPAGE">Click to Return to the Calling Page</A>

</FONT>

<BR><BR>

<DIV ALIGN=CENTER>

    <FONT FACE="OLD ENGLISH TEXT MT" SIZE=10 COLOR=BLACK>

    Haunted Gower

    </FONT>

    <FONT SIZE=4 COLOR=BLACK>

    <BR>

    <!-- XX-ADDRESS could go here -->

    </FONT>

    <BR><BR>

</DIV>

<DIV ALIGN=LEFT>

    <FONT FACE="Times New Roman" SIZE=3>

    <P ALIGN=JUSTIFY>
```

Europe is a colourful counterpane of quilted states distinguished by language and history. Always at the fluid borders of these great nations, fossilised in everlasting debate, have lain wide frontier lands of empty, mournful beauty celebrated in countless strange stories of the supernatural, of chivalry, and other honours better and baser.

```
    </P>

    <P ALIGN=JUSTIFY>
```

Tiny as it is, the "English" Gower Peninsula in South Wales is one of these haunted hinterlands.

```
    </P>
```

349

<P ALIGN=JUSTIFY>

By a deserted sandy bay, my wife, Jana, and I slept in a caravan, sheltered in the South by a steep oak-clad slope. This thickly-wooded acclivity was guarded by a single owl. One Sunday night there was a force-nine gale that roared and whistled through the bare trees, while the owl maintained a constant hooting of admonition to the careless storm. The succeeding nights were calm and silent until three busloads of ladies opened the neighbouring hotel with a raucous hen-night disco. Our friend the owl hooted his complaints and congratulations until they left, when he too retired.

</P>

<p ALIGN=JUSTIFY>

The nearest neighbour on the other side of the hotel was a bashful centaur. If he had gate-crashed the party, surely he would have stolen the limelight from the male strippers?

</P>

</FONT>

</DIV>

<DIV ALIGN=LEFT>

<FONT FACE="Arial" SIZE=3>

<B>

Oxwich Church

</B>

</FONT>

<FONT FACE="Times New Roman" SIZE=3>

<P ALIGN=JUSTIFY>

Numerous ghosts loiter their churchyard keeping the builders company as they restore St Illtyd's tiny Norman tower. But the real hero is a centaur who lives in the thick woods above the tiny fane, descending at midnight for a quick dip in the bay below. He does not like to bathe in the daytime, for lack of a swimming costume.

</P>

<FONT FACE="Arial" SIZE=3>

<B>

Arthur's Stone

</B>

</FONT>

<FONT FACE="Times New Roman" SIZE=3>

<P ALIGN=JUSTIFY>

A Neolithic dolmen with dramatic views from Gower's hogback summit Cefn Bryn. King Arthur and his army made a long detour to this spot to worship before marching East to defeat invaders.

</P>

<FONT FACE="Arial" SIZE=3>

<B>

Pennard Castle

</B>

</FONT>

<FONT FACE="Times New Roman" SIZE=3>

<P ALIGN=JUSTIFY>

Cursed by a 13th Century witch, Pennard was overwhelmed by migrating sand-dunes from the sea, and has been deserted ever since. It is said that ghostly custodians supervise modern-day visitors, who must never stay in hours of darkness.

</P>

<FONT FACE="Arial" SIZE=3>

<B>

Rhosilli Old Rectory

</B>

</FONT>

<FONT FACE="Times New Roman" SIZE=3>

<P ALIGN=JUSTIFY>

The 1887 wreck of the sailing ship <I>Helvetia</I> dominates this view of the distant white vicarage isolated behind the breath-taking sweep of Rhosilli Sands.

</P>

<P ALIGN=JUSTIFY>

The Rhosilli Old Rectory is the Welsh answer to Borley Rectory, with revenants crowding every corner. Like Borley, it burnt down, but Rhosilli was restored by The National Trust as a holiday cottage. Archaeologists have found the remains of old Rhosilli and its Dark Ages graveyard around and beneath the Victorian building. On stormy nights a horrific shadowy entity emerges from the foam briefly to view the exterior. He (She? It?) may be acting for the late Dylan Thomas, who considered purchasing the house in 1946.

</P>

<FONT FACE="Arial" SIZE=3>

<B>

The Brandy Cove

</B>

</FONT>

<FONT FACE="Times New Roman" SIZE=3>

<P ALIGN=JUSTIFY>

During much of the Twentieth Century, visitors and locals returned from the cove with lurid tales of blood-curdling female screams. These sounds ceased when in 1962 the murdered remains of Maisie Stuart were located in a disused lead mine at the cove, and buried in Bishopston Churchyard.

</P>

<P ALIGN=JUSTIFY>

The Brandy Cove is one of two or three wild places where I have sensed some cold, malign ambiance in bright sunlight. I did of course hear and see nothing.

</P>

<FONT FACE="Arial" SIZE=3>

<B>

Burry Holm Oratory

</B>

</FONT>

<FONT FACE="Times New Roman" SIZE=3>

<P ALIGN=JUSTIFY>

This tiny prayer-cell is almost the last vestige of St Cenydd's (Kenneth's) monastery. Cenydd was born out of wedlock to a princess of Carmarthen and consigned aboard a wicker basket by the king to the waves of The Loughor Estuary.

<P ALIGN=JUSTIFY>

Thirty seagulls rescued the babe and raised him to Christian manhood on their little island, Burry Holm, from which the saint strode forth to convert Glamorgan.

</P>

<FONT FACE="Arial" SIZE=3>

<B>

The Haunted Gower Photograph Gallery

</B>

</FONT>

```
</DIV>

<DIV ALIGN=CENTER>

  <TABLE CELLSPACING=20>

    <TR>

      <TD><IMG SRC="oxchurcb.jpg" HEIGHT=128 WIDTH=192
          BORDER=1></TD>

      <TD><IMG SRC="arthurss.jpg" HEIGHT=128 WIDTH=192
          BORDER=1></TD>

      <TD><IMG SRC="penncas1.jpg" HEIGHT=128 WIDTH=192
          BORDER=1></TD>

    </TR>

    <TR>

      <TD><DIV ALIGN=CENTER>Oxwich Church</DIV></TD>

      <TD><DIV ALIGN=CENTER>Arthur's Stone</DIV></TD>

      <TD><DIV ALIGN=CENTER>Pennard Castle</DIV></TD>

    </TR>

    <TR>

      <TD><IMG SRC="rhosreca.jpg" HEIGHT=128 WIDTH=192
          BORDER=1></TD>

      <TD><IMG SRC="brandy2.jpg" HEIGHT=128 WIDTH=192
          BORDER=1></TD>

      <TD><IMG SRC="burryor2.jpg" HEIGHT=128 WIDTH=192
          BORDER=1></TD>

    </TR>

    <TR>

      <TD><DIV ALIGN=CENTER>Rhossilli Old Rectory</DIV></TD>

      <TD><DIV ALIGN=CENTER>The Brandy Cove</DIV></TD>

      <TD><DIV ALIGN=CENTER>Burry Holm Oratory</DIV></TD>

    </TR>

  </TABLE>

</DIV>

<FONT SIZE=3>

<DIV ALIGN=LEFT>
```

<B>LINKS</B>

"Gower Story and Structure" by Ted Nield

Scholarly but accessible geological reports, maps and field itineraries provided by the Geological Society of London.

<A HREF="http://geolsoc.org.uk/template.cfm?name=Gower1test">

http://geolsoc.org.uk/template.cfm?name=Gower1test

</A>

Wonderful writing and lavish photographs provided on a professionally-presented site by a lover of Gower.

Natural history, history, pre-history, villages, churches, beaches and folklore.

<A HREF="http://www.explore-gower.co.uk/">

http://www.explore-gower.co.uk/

</A>

A selection of places to stay with other Gower facts.

<A HREF="http://business.virgin.net/t.lyne/index.htm">

http://business.virgin.net/t.lyne/index.htm

</A>

<A HREF="mailto:capricious@www.capric.com">Send an Email</A>

</DIV>

<DIV ALIGN=CENTER>

XX-HITCOUNTERHERE

```
        <BR><BR>

    </DIV>

    </FONT>

    <DIV ALIGN=LEFT>

        <FONT SIZE=3>

        Version: 1.0<BR>

        Date of Creation: 16 September 2002<BR>

        Data of Revision: 16 September 2002<BR>

        </FONT>

        <BR><BR>

        <FONT SIZE=4>

        <A HREF="XX-NEXTPAGE">Click for the Next Page</A>

        </FONT>

    </DIV>

    </BODY>

    </HTML>
```

The Web Page Realisation for 'Haunted Gower'

Click to Return to the Calling Page

Haunted Gower

Europe is a colourful counterpane of quilted states distinguished by language and history. Always at the fluid borders of these great nations, fossilised in everlasting debate, have lain wide frontier lands of empty, mournful beauty celebrated in countless strange stories of the supernatural, of chivalry, and other honours better and baser.

Tiny as it is, the "English" Gower Peninsula in South Wales is one of these haunted hinterlands.

By a deserted sandy bay, my wife, Jana, and I slept in a caravan, sheltered in the South by a steep oak-clad slope. This thickly-wooded acclivity was guarded by a single owl. One Sunday night there was a force-nine gale that roared and whistled through the bare trees, while the owl maintained a constant hooting of admonition to the careless storm. The succeeding nights were calm and silent until three bus-loads of ladies opened the neighbouring hotel with a raucous hen-night disco. Our friend the owl hooted his complaints and congratulations until they left, when he too retired.

The nearest neighbour on the other side of the hotel was a bashful centaur. If he had gate-crashed the party, surely he would have stolen the limelight from the male strippers?

Oxwich Church

Numerous ghosts loiter their churchyard keeping the builders company as they restore St Illtyd's tiny Norman tower. But the real hero is a centaur who lives in the thick woods above the tiny fane, descending at midnight for a quick dip in the bay below. He does not like to bathe in the daytime, for lack of a swimming costume.

Arthur's Stone

A Neolithic dolmen with dramatic views from Gower's hogback summit Cefn Bryn. King Arthur and his army made a long detour to this spot to worship before marching East to defeat invaders.

Pennard Castle

Cursed by a 13th Century witch, Pennard was overwhelmed by migrating sand-dunes from the sea, and has been deserted ever since. It is said that ghostly custodians supervise modern-day visitors, who must never stay in hours of darkness.

Rhosilli Old Rectory

The 1887 wreck of the sailing ship *Helvetia* dominates this view of the distant white vicarage isolated behind the breath-taking sweep of Rhosilli Sands.

The Rhosilli Old Rectory is the Welsh answer to Borley Rectory, with revenants crowding every corner. Like Borley, it burnt down, but Rhosilli was restored by The National Trust as a holiday cottage. Archaeologists have found the remains of old Rhosilli and its Dark Ages graveyard around and beneath the Victorian building. On stormy nights a horrific shadowy entity emerges from the foam briefly to view the exterior. He (She? It?) may be acting for the late Dylan Thomas, who considered purchasing the house in 1946.

The Brandy Cove

During much of the Twentieth Century, visitors and locals returned from the cove with lurid tales of blood-curdling female screams. These sounds ceased when in 1962 the murdered remains of Maisie Stuart were located in a disused lead mine at the cove, and buried in Bishopston Churchyard.

The Brandy Cove is one of two or three wild places where I have sensed some cold, malign ambiance in bright sunlight. I did of course hear and see nothing.

Burry Holm Oratory

This tiny prayer-cell is almost the last vestige of St Cenydd's (Kenneth's) monastery. Cenydd was born out of wedlock to a princess of Carmarthen and consigned aboard a wicker basket by the king to the waves of The Loughor Estuary.

Thirty seagulls rescued the babe and raised him to Christian manhood on their little island, Burry Holm, from which the saint strode forth to convert Glamorgan.

The Haunted Gower Photograph Gallery

Oxwich Church

Arthur's Stone

Pennard Castle

Rhossilli Old Rectory

The Brandy Cove

Burry Holm Oratory

LINKS

"Gower Story and Structure" by Ted Nield

Scholarly but accessible geological reports, maps and field itineraries provided by the Geological Society of London.

http://geolsoc.org.uk/template.cfm?name=Gower1test

Wonderful writing and lavish photographs provided on a professionally-presented site by a lover of Gower.

Natural history, history, pre-history, villages, churches, beaches and folklore.

http://www.explore-gower.co.uk/

A selection of places to stay with other Gower facts.

http://business.virgin.net/t.lyne/index.htm

Send an Email

XX-HITCOUNTERHERE

Version: 1.0

Date of Creation: 16 September 2002

Data of Revision: 16 September 2002

Click for the Next Page

META TAGS

Meta statements are page descriptive information placed in the HEAD of a HTML page. Many different kinds of information can be inserted in META statements, and proprietary software generates a lot, but we will concentrate only upon information that assists search engines in finding our site.

So our information will be based upon relevant keywords descriptive of, or associated with, the page content. We can also use a formal short page description of the kind pithy enough to be printed out in search listings as a mini-abstract, this will guide the human searcher as to whether he really wants to load up our page or not.

Keywords should be guided by the following considerations:

1. Use of American English words and spellings

2. Use of place names supplemented by name of state, province or prefecture

3. Use of other proper names

4. Non-trivial words, i.e. not 'the','of','and', etc.

5. Avoid ambiguities (but a goods road vehicle is a 'truck' not a 'lorry')

6. Suppress hyphenations

7. Retain spaces only in natural multinomials e.g. Tyrannosaurus▼Rex

Suitable keywords for the 'Haunted Gower' topic may be:

hauntings,ghosts,Gower,Peninsula,Wales,Glamorgan,United Kingdom,folklore,Rhossilli,Pennard,Oxwich,Arthurs Stone,Brandy,Cove,Maisie Stuart,superstition,paranormal

This list is 161 characters long including the commas. Some search engines prefer spaces as word separators. Standard HTML presumes comma separators without flanking spaces and no other punctuation, e.g. possessive apostrophes. **The total keyword content string must be less than 256 characters**.

Secondly we need the mini-abstract Page Description. This should not exceed 30 words of coherent English and, as for the keyword list, **must be less than 256 characters**.

For the 'Haunted Gower' page we might use:

Brief tales of ghosts and other apparitions in Britain's beautiful Gower Peninsula are illustrated with six color photographs and links provided to scientific, antiquarian and commercial sites

This is 27 words and 192 characters.

Thirdly, there is provision for an "Author" META tag and we should place our name as its Content.

The general syntax of the META tag is:

<META NAME="Type of Information" CONTENT="Content">

and the resulting META statement scheme for 'Haunted Gower' is:

<HTML>

<HEAD>

<TITLE>Haunted Gower</TITLE>

<META NAME="AUTHOR" CONTENT="James R Warren">

<META NAME="DESCRIPTION" CONTENT="Brief tales of ghosts and other apparitions in Britain's beautiful Gower Peninsula are illustrated with six color photographs and links provided to scientific, antiquarian and commercial sites">

<META NAME="KEYWORDS" CONTENT="hauntings,ghosts,Gower,Peninsula,Wales,Glamorgan,United Kingdom,folklore,Rhossilli,Pennard,Oxwich,Arthurs Stone,Brandy,Cove,Maisie Stuart,superstition,paranormal">

</HEAD>

META statements are very useful to the human programmer, let alone automatic search systems and should always be included. Having said that, the bad news is that some engines ignore them entirely.

OBTAINING A DOMAIN NAME REGISTRATION AND A HOSTING SERVICE

Your Web site URL address, which has the pattern www.stargazer.com or www.cloudgrasper.co.uk, can be hired for 1, 2, 5 or 10 years at a time for a highly-variable fee of between $10 and $25 per annum.

The actual server storage of your Web site content is called a hosting. Hosting can be bought separately at the even more variable fee of between $15 and $2500 per annum. This drastic variation depends upon the space that you want, in megabytes; your intended use for the site; the number of email ports it supports (if any); CGI-bin and other management provisions; and a host of other technical considerations.

Many hosting service companies will sell you a bundled package of domain name registration and hosting for your chosen URL. It is your responsibility to check beforehand that the name you fancy has not already been spoken for.

The following sequence shows how we can book Web hosting provision with the British agent Compila Limited. It exemplifies the online process we would use with almost any provider.

We will choose an inexpensive but adequate provision of 60Mb site space, enhanced for FrontPage support. The total charge for an international .com domain in that space will come to just over £30 sterling (2002).

Navigate to http://www.compila.com and choose Domain Registration from their home page:

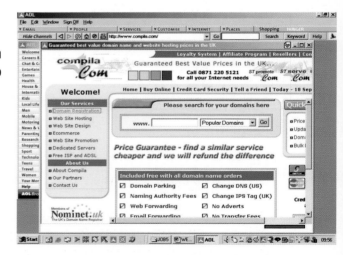

Use the search tool provided to test if your preferred domain name is available. If it is you will get the following invitation to purchase **which you do not act upon:**

We will buy the name as a package, but for the meantime we will trawl for other interesting names by clicking on **Click here** and using the successor screen presented below:

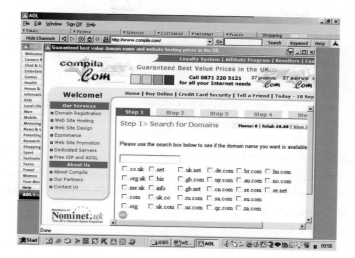

When we have confirmed the availability of the name we want we go back to the Compila home screen using the browser's **Back** button and click **Web Site Hosting** to access this screen:

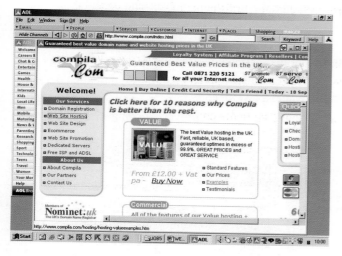

Select the US Domains Bargain service and add it to your cart:

Check over the following details and add your chosen domain name to the package. I selected www.stargrasper.com for the site on which I intend to install 'Haunted Gower'.

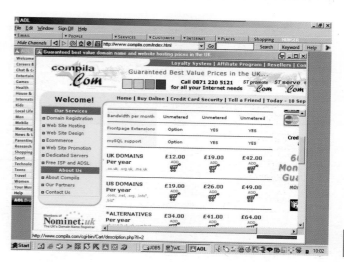

Select **New** registration for **1** year and **Yes** to FrontPage support, followed by **Add This Item To My Cart**. Select **Check Out Now >>>** when you get the purchases tally screen:

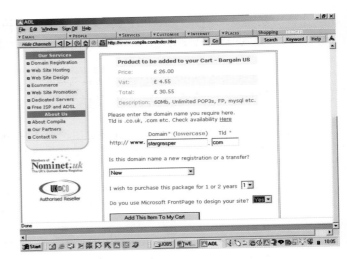

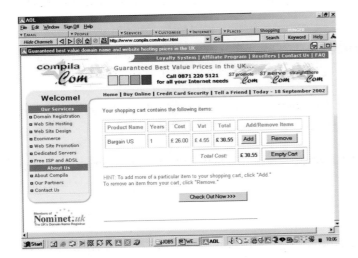

An order confirmation screen will appear after you have passed through several screens concerning identity, home and delivery street addresses, and your credit card details.

It has got your Vendor's and Money Transfer Agent's transaction serial numbers on it.

Both Compila and the transfer agent will send you confirmatory emails within a few minutes.

The Order Confirmation Screen is illustrated below:

Tip

Print the Order Confirmation Screen and the confirmatory emails.

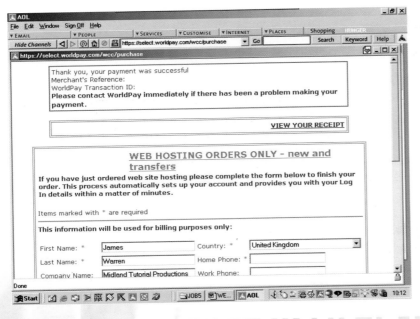

It will take Compila between 24 and 48 hours to mount your new site. In the meantime browsers will fail to locate a domain. When your site space is ready a blue page placeholder form, prominently displaying your domain name at the top, will be accessible through normal URL address procedures. *Print this fourth document too*.

We are now ready to upload our pre-prepared Web page, or system of pages, to the website.

USING FTP SOFTWARE TO UPLOAD PAGES TO WEBSITES

We upload Web pages and all their ancillary files, such as any GIFs or JPEGs they will need, using File Transfer Protocol (FTP) mediation programs.

Such programs can be located on the Internet itself and downloaded to your local client machine for permanent residence on your hard disk. An inexpensive but entirely effective option is the program WS-FTP95 LE.

If you are an educator or student you can use WS-FTP95 LE for free, as long as you use it for non-profit purposes. If you will use it for profit, or if you are a commercial user, you must pay a small licence fee.

At the time of writing in September 2002 the tucows download service is withdrawn but a convenient alternative source is accessible at www.ipswitch.com.

Installing WS-FTP95 LE

After you have downloaded WS-FTP95 LE, the program will ask you for your intended use. If you are a non-profit personal user, educator, or student you select **Other**, **From Home** and **For personal use**.

You will be invited to install it to your chosen directory, but if WS-FTP95 LE suggests you place it in a sensible location, such as its own sub-directory of the Programs folder, accept this.

A **Session Properties** Window will appear; select the **General** tab and complete it in this pattern:

Profile Name:	(HostsRecommendationOrListChoice)
Host Name/Address:	ftp.(HostURL)
Host Type:	Automatic detect
User ID:	(YourUserID)
Password:	(YourPassword)
Account:	

for example:

Profile Name:	Compila
Host Name/Address:	ftp.www.compila.com
Host Type:	Automatic detect
User ID:	JudySpiers
Password:	Twinkleshears
Account:	

Click **OK**.

Now select the **Startup** tab, and delete all the information in its textbox fields.

Click **OK**.

The major File Transfer Window with the probable title **WS_FTP95 LE ftp.www.compila.com** will now appear but we do not wish to complete the upload yet. So click **Exit**.

COMPLETING THE UPLOAD

Check the availability of your new Web site by logging-on to your Internet browser.

Assemble the HTML pages and graphics files that you wish to upload into a specially-created Upload folder and make a note of its exact pathname. I put my 'Haunted Gower' files into C:\SITES\STARGRAS\STARG-UP\.

Change the upload home page name to index.html; e.g. but only in GOWERPAG.htm becomes index.html STARG-UP.

In the case of my 'Haunted Gower' example I log on to AOL and enter the booked URL, www.stargrasper.com, into the Address Bar.

On this occasion I see the following white placeholder page:

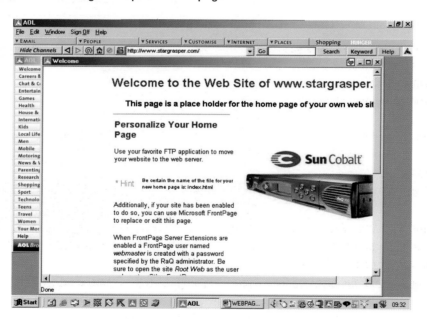

Tip

Stay logged-on until you have completed the upload.

The WS-FTP95 LE download procedure may automatically have installed a WS-FTP95 LE shortcut icon on your Desktop. If it has not you can soon add one using the normal Windows procedures. This icon will look like this:

Click on this icon.

When you get the **Session Properties** window click the **Startup** tab and certify that all the text boxes there are empty.

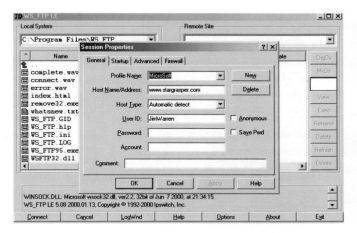

Return to the **General** tab, enter Microsoft profile and *your* site name as the **Host** and Automatic Detect for **Host Type**. Enter the **User Name** and **Password** arranged with your hosting service.

Check **Save Pwd**.

Click **Apply** and **OK**.

The **Session Properties** window above will now be super-seded by the **WS_FTP LE www.stargrasper.com** window below:

Check that the **Binary** radio button is selected.

Browse the **Local System** to access your uploads local directory (double-click the green crook arrow at the top left hand corner of the current directory listing).

Select all files with shift-click.

Select the **->** transfer button to map the files to **Remote Site**.

Copying of the files to your Web site will take some minutes, the graphics files taking an especially long time. At completion there will be a speaker warble and the selected files' names will appear in the **Remote Site** listing.

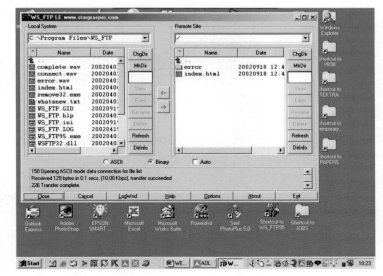

Click **Close** and when the Close button changes to **Connect** click it again.

Click **Exit.**

It will take some hours for your upload to propagate through the server net and for your composited page to be accessible to the surfing public.

SUBMITTING YOUR SITE TO SEARCH ENGINES

Many agencies will submit your site (which you have hopefully already META-tagged) to up to a thousand search engines, and charge you a handsome fee.

But only a handful of international search engines really count: HotBot, Google, GoTo, Lycos, and AltaVista top the bill, together with one or two Microsoft proprietary engines.

It is much better to place your site with these engines individually for nothing, or even to use the free multi-site placement service offered by co-operatives and other programmers' service sites such as the HTML help site www.hypergurl.com whose site submission service can be located direct at www.hypergurl.com/submit.html

When you summon www.hypergurl.com you see this screen which offers many helpful features to HTML programmers:

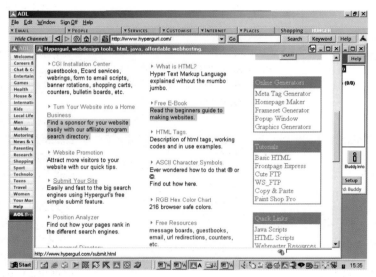

Click **Submit Your Site** to obtain this:

and insert your relevant particulars.

After completing the details in this screen, scroll down slightly and click the **Submit your Site!** button just below.

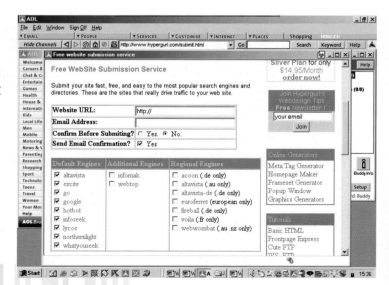

e-Quals
Index